W9-CRT-616

The Casablanca Connection

William A. Hoisington, Jr.

The Casablanca Connection

French Colonial Policy, 1936–1943

The University of North Carolina Press

Chapel Hill and London

© 1984 The University of North Carolina Press

All rights reserved

Manufactured in the United States of America

Library of Congress Cataloging in Publication Data

Hoisington, William A., Jr., 1941–

The Casablanca connection.

Bibliography: p.

Includes index.

1. Morocco—History—20th century.   1. Title.

DT324.H54   1984   964'.04   83-5902

ISBN 0-8078-1574-8

Frontispiece: General Charles Noguès,
resident general of France in Morocco,
1936–1943. *Courtesy Verthamon Collection, Paris*

To my parents

Contents

	Preface	xiii
ONE	The Lyautey Touch	3
TWO	The Revolt of the Cities	29
THREE	The Economics of Pacification	74
FOUR	The Colonial Question	104
FIVE	Three Tangled Zones	136
SIX	The Fall of France and the Vichy Change	159
SEVEN	The American Road to Morocco	194
EIGHT	Casablanca and Beyond	224
NINE	The Lyautey Legacy	245
	Notes	249
	Bibliography	293
	Index	309

Illustrations

General Charles Noguès, resident general of France in Morocco, 1936–1943 / *frontispiece*

Map of Morocco, 1936–1943 / *x–xi*

The Lyautey statue on Place Lyautey / *4*

The Residency at Rabat / *41*

Sidi Mohammed ben Youssef, sultan of Morocco / *46*

Noguès and Mohammed el-Mokri / *57*

Noguès, Moulay Hassan, and Jean Morize / *58*

Thami el Glaoui, Paul Ramadier, and Noguès / *66*

Walking the Medina at Fez / *70*

Walking the Medina at Fez / *71*

Pasha Hassan / *87*

Camp Marchand, September 1941 / *88*

Tahar Souk, May 1942 / *89*

Tissa, September 1942 / *90*

Azemmour, 1942 / *91*

Meknès, June 1942 / *121*

Meknès, October 1942 / *122*

Meknès, October 1942 / *123*

Moulay Hassan, Noguès, and Moulay Abdallah / *160*

Moulay Hassan, Sidi Mohammed ben Youssef, and Moulay Abdallah / *161*

General Maxime Weygand / *185*

Weygand, the sultan, and Noguès / *205*

Admiral François Darlan / *215*

General Henri Giraud / *238*

General George S. Patton, Jr. / *240*

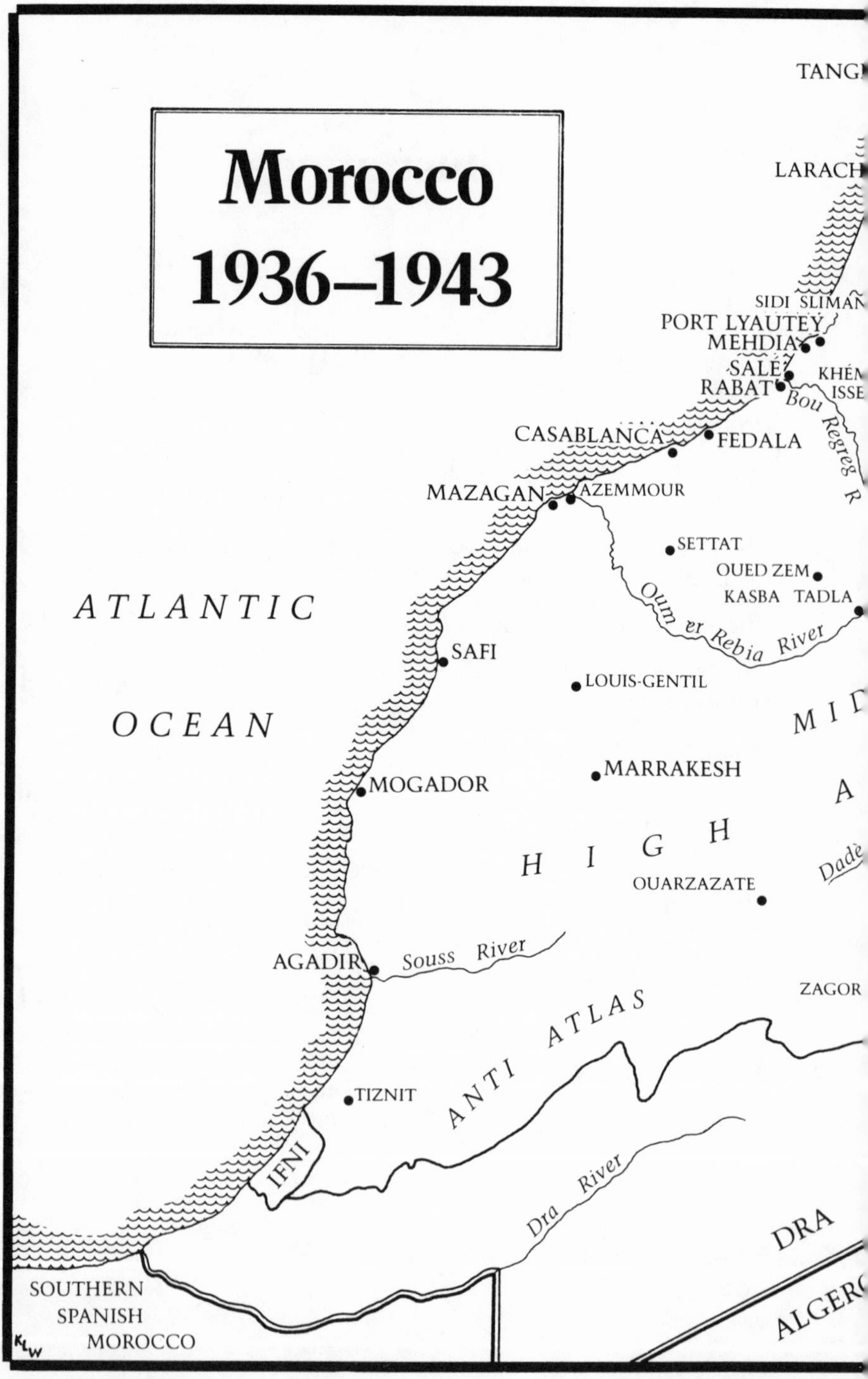

Morocco 1936–1943

TANG

LARACH

SIDI SLIMAN

PORT LYAUTEY
MEHDIA
SALÉ   KHÉM
RABAT   ISSE
Bou Regreg R.

CASABLANCA   FEDALA

MAZAGAN   AZEMMOUR

SETTAT
OUED ZEM
KASBA TADLA

Oum er Rebia River

ATLANTIC

OCEAN

SAFI

LOUIS-GENTIL

MID

MARRAKESH

MOGADOR

A

H I G H

OUARZAZATE

Dadè

AGADIR   Souss River

ZAGOR

ANTI ATLAS

TIZNIT

IFNI

Dra River

DRA

SOUTHERN
SPANISH
MOROCCO

ALGER

K L W

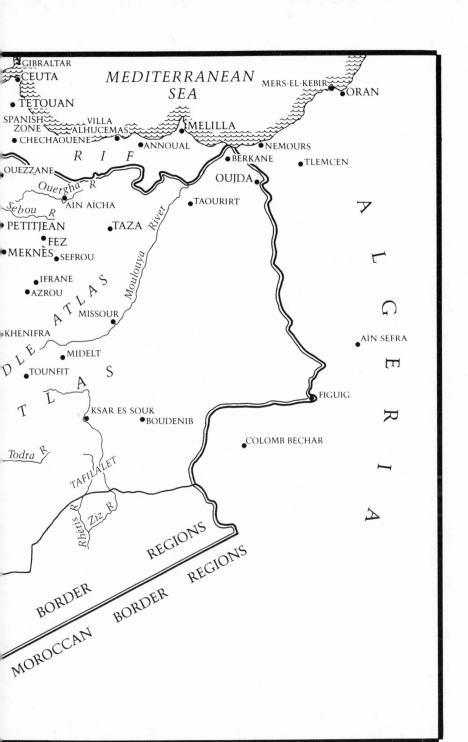

GIBRALTAR
CEUTA
MEDITERRANEAN
SEA
MERS-EL-KEBIR
ORAN
TETOUAN
SPANISH
ZONE
VILLA
ALHUCEMAS
MELILLA
CHECHAOUENE
ANNOUAL
NEMOURS
R I F
BERKANE
TLEMCEN
OUEZZANE
OUJDA
Ouergha R.
AÏN AÏCHA
TAOURIRT
Sebou R.
PETITJEAN
TAZA
A
FEZ
MEKNÈS
SEFROU
L
IFRANE
AZROU
G
A T L A S
MISSOUR
E
KHÉNIFRA
AÏN SEFRA
R
MIDELT
Moulouya River
I
TOUNFIT
T L A S
FIGUIG
A
DLE
KSAR ES SOUK
BOUDENIB
Todra R.
COLOMB BECHAR
TAFILALET
Rhèris R.
Ziz R.
REGIONS
BORDER
REGIONS
BORDER
BORDER
MOROCCAN

Preface

The subject of this book is General Charles Noguès and French colonial policy in Morocco from the Popular Front to the end of the Vichy regime in North Africa. Noguès was France's sixth resident general at Rabat, the prize pupil of Marshal Hubert Lyautey (1854–1934), the "creator" of the modern Moroccan state whose maxims on colonial rule filled the notebooks of overseas administrators and foreign admirers and who is still revered by Frenchmen as a symbol of what was finest in their empire-building experience.[1] Noguès had ideas of his own, but his real ambition was to emulate Lyautey, to work the marshal's magic and breathe new life into the French protectorate over the sharifian empire at a moment of economic hardship, political disorder, and social crisis. Intelligent, disciplined, and sensitive, he was committed to creating bonds of interest and affection between Frenchmen and Moroccans that he hoped would be of ultimate benefit to France. "I believe with all my heart, all my soul, and all my experience," Lyautey said, "that the best way of serving France in this country, of ensuring the solidity of its presence, is to win over the soul and heart of this people."[2] This was the task that Noguès wanted to pursue.

Noguès was also charged with protecting Morocco from the dislocations of the worldwide economic depression and shielding it from the disruptions of the Spanish civil war and World War II. Both jeopardized French control and made the contract with the sultan hard to fulfill. According to the 1912 Treaty of Fez, France had entered Morocco to establish "a stable government based on internal order and security," to allow "the introduction of reforms," and to

1. For a summary of Lyautey's career and a good bibliography, see Scham, *Lyautey in Morocco*. Also see Le Révérend, *Lyautey écrivain*. Opinion has always been divided on Lyautey's methods and accomplishments. For a recent irreverent evaluation, see Porch, *The Conquest of Morocco*.

2. Lyautey, "Aux personnalités venues pour l'inauguration du grand port de Casablanca et du premier tronçon de chemin de fer à voie normale de Rabat à Fès," 4 April 1923, in Lyautey, *Paroles d'action*, p. 395. Unless otherwise indicated, all translations of quotations from manuscript or published sources in French are mine.

ensure "the economic development of the country." The "new regime" permitted France to occupy the land and to rule in the sultan's name through the French resident general (*commissaire résident général*), the "holder (*dépositaire*) of all the powers of the Republic in Morocco." In return France pledged to safeguard "the religious position [and] the traditional respect and prestige of the sultan"; to support him "against all dangers which may threaten his person or throne or which may compromise the tranquillity of his states"; to sustain his central government, the Makhzen; and to protect the exercise of the "Muslim religion" throughout his empire.[3] To Noguès fell the responsibility for keeping these promises.

During his tenure in Morocco, Noguès felt the reverberations of the erosion of French power and influence in Europe and the world. When the collapse came in 1940, North Africa was the one spot on the map where resistance to Germany might have continued. Instead, Noguès led the African empire into the Vichy fold. Geography, politics, and the colonial facts of life determined his course, which two years later led to an unhappy military collision with the Allies. The successor to Lyautey ended his career in exile and disgrace.

I am glad to acknowledge the grants from the American Council of Learned Societies, the American Philosophical Society, and the University of Illinois at Chicago. The French Colonial Historical Society fellowship at the Hoover Institution on War, Revolution, and Peace made possible the writing of "Cities in Revolt: The Berber Dahir (1930) and France's Urban Strategy in Morocco," *Journal of Contemporary History* 13, no. 3 (July 1978): 433–48, which has been incorporated into chapter 2.

I owe an unrepayable debt to Colonel Guy and Odile de Verthamon, who permitted me unrestricted access to the papers of General Noguès. Agnes F. Peterson of the Hoover Institution also deserves special mention. I wish to record as well my appreciation to the family of Paul and Jeanette Binachon, who welcomed me to France twenty years ago, and to Gordon Wright, who introduced me to France's history. Finally, I am grateful to Sharon, Anne, Sarah, and Kate, who shared every step of this project with me.

3. The Treaty of Fez (30 March 1912) is printed in Halstead, *Rebirth of a Nation*, pp. 273–74.

The Casablanca Connection

ONE

The Lyautey Touch

In November 1938, when France was enjoying what Léon Blum called a "cowardly sigh of relief" that a European war had been averted over the Czechoslovakian crisis, an article appeared in *La Revue hebdo-madaire* honoring Marshal Lyautey and his role in the creation of France's overseas empire. The purpose was not only to celebrate Lyautey at a time when French heroes were scarce but to underscore the importance of Morocco to metropolitan France and to familiar-ize Frenchmen with the accomplishments of its current resident general, General Charles Noguès, Lyautey's "spiritual" heir, who had been posted to Rabat in 1936. Written anonymously by Noguès's press secretary, it mixed public relations puff with an official view of what was happening in the western corner of North Africa. Lest Frenchmen forget the empire while their eyes were riveted on the Rhine, the author warned: "The time is past when [Lyautey] could say that Morocco's fate depended upon what happened in Lorraine; today the fate of Lorraine, as well as that of our entire country, de-pends upon Morocco and the whole of our colonial domain. An im-perial policy boldly undertaken and energetically supported by every group in the population is more than ever necessary to ensure the safety and independence of our country."[1]

The empire coming to the aid of the homeland was a familiar tune. The French had heard it played during World War I. What was surprising, however, was that Morocco, which had been the scene of much social and political disturbance since 1934, was presented as an element of French strength rather than weakness. For this turn-about, Noguès was given full credit, especially in the important realm of native policy. The author insisted that Noguès, one of Lyau-tey's collaborators "from the beginning," had faithfully taken up where the marshal had left off, reviving his precepts and his manner. With firmness and generosity, he had staved off the colonial collapse that the urban riots of 1936 and 1937 seemed to forecast and reestab-lished the protectorate on secure economic and political founda-tions. This was only part promotion. Fourteen years earlier, Lyautey had snugly wrapped the young colonel in his mantle. "You know the

The Lyautey statue on Place Lyautey.
Casablanca, November 1938.
Photo Jacques Belin

country, you are imbued with 'my method,' you are extra-intelligent and quick, and you radiate enthusiasm." On claiming the Residency, Noguès pulled the cloak tighter; he confessed that he had "no other ambition" than to walk in the footsteps of "the illustrious marshal, his chief and venerated mentor."[2]

The protectorate concept was popularized by Lyautey. He thought of it as a means by which a non-European state could survive and progress in the modern world, retaining its own institutions and administering itself under the "simple guidance" of a European power,

which represented it abroad, oversaw the administration of its army
and finances, and directed its economic development. "What gives
this concept its special character," Lyautey explained, "is the notion
of *guidance* (*contrôle*) rather than *direct rule* (*administration di-
recte*)."[3] For Lyautey the protectorate was the political manifestation
of "associationism," which held that the empire should link diverse
peoples with France, preserving as much as possible their cultural
forms and structure of government while providing the benefits of
Western civilization and French governance. This was in contrast to
"assimilationism," which aimed at turning Africans, Asians, and
South Sea Islanders into cultural Frenchmen and for whom direct
rule by France was seen as a logical and liberating necessity. In both
cases the goal was the same, the expansion of French influence. But
with a protectorate it could be achieved by working with, not against,
the "former ruling groups" who would help to pacify the country "at
less expense and with greater success than with all our military col-
umns." There was no question who would be in charge. France intended to "hold the reins." Harnessing this "great social force" was
to serve French purposes. It was the core of the entire protectorate
philosophy.[4]

Lyautey put indirect rule to work in Morocco, wooing the "most
important personalities" wherever possible and "an infinite number
of petty notables" everywhere else.[5] Always the effort was to cooperate with the established order. "You know how careful I have been
. . . to see that rank and hierarchy are respected," he told the sultan's
ministers, the tribal chieftains, and the city governors, "that everyone and everything remain in its traditional place, that the natural
leaders lead and are obeyed."[6] Given the hierarchical divisions in traditional society and the leadership responsibilities of a governing
elite, he argued that this was the secret of his success, for in Morocco these things mattered most.

To be consistent, Lyautey warned against the creation of a large
and cumbersome French bureaucracy overseas that would duplicate
the "semi-autonomous" native network. To hold down costs and to
permit indirect rule to work as it was supposed to, he wanted the
bare minimum of military personnel, control officers, and administrators—*peu de gendarmes*—but he felt that strong direction had
to come from the top. Each colonial governor or resident general
needed to be a proconsul endowed with the moral and political authority that the term implied and, above all, supplied with energy. "I
conceive of command as a direct and personal expression of faith and

enthusiasm for the task at hand by being present on the spot, through countless tours of inspection, through speeches, persuasion, and visual and verbal communication."[7]

Lyautey's personality shaped his philosophy of command and colonial rule. He needed people, admiration, and affection. He got them all in large doses in Morocco. He magnetized the junior officers who served with him, making them lifelong disciples who recalled with pride the precise moment when he asked them to drop the ceremonious "Monsieur le Maréchal" for the less formal "mon Général" and were "admitted to the honors" of familiar speech (the *tutoiement*), the sign by which he indicated his approval and confidence.[8] His doctrine of personal fulfillment through responsible social endeavor permeated the ranks of his civil and military subordinates. Acting, building, creating were the starting words of an alphabet of accomplishment. Serving him, passing through his "school," belonging to his Moroccan "team," were indelible experiences, unforgettable memories for a generation of young officers.

Among the native population, Lyautey had a similar impact. His paternal care for the Moroccan people was in its time taken for what it was, a deep, genuine emotional attachment, not a condescending concern bred of noblesse oblige. This, added to his energy and goodwill, his courage and flair for showmanship, his intelligence and respect for Islam, won him the admiration of Morocco's elite and made him a heroic, mythic figure among the common people. The English journalist Walter Burton Harris captured the moment after the defeat of the Beni M'guild and Zaian tribes. "I was with him on the next day when the submitted tribesmen with their women and children came down from the higher mountains to look at 'Lyautey.' The women, decked in their best, and weighed down with their silver jewellery, offered him the traditional bowls of milk, and he walked about amongst them, gazed at wonderingly by the small children who pressed round to touch or kiss his hand. It was the magic of his name, the magic of his personality. He had the greatest gift of all the qualities of colonial administration—sympathy."[9]

Lyautey explained this prestige, charisma, *baraka*, or "magic" matter-of-factly. It resulted from his high regard for the Muslim identity. The inviolability of the native persona was the "one principle" that had to remain "sacrosanct" in Morocco. By respecting religion and tradition, Lyautey reasoned that he had sheltered the individual, the family, and the community from the uprooting effects of contact with the West. This was why support for the sultan, the spiritual commander of the faithful, was so important. "When the Muslims realized that their sultan, restored to his authority and sovereign prerogatives, [could] carry out the solemn rites ordered by the Prophet in complete independence without any interference from us, [they] recognized our resolve to respect scrupulously [their] religion and customs." There was the political purpose as well. Lyautey hoped that by sustaining him "who is the living symbol of tradition" the concerns over France's presence would be permanently dispelled.[10]

The marshal celebrated the political payoff. He never missed an opportunity to display publicly the confidence that existed between him and the sultan or between the administrators of the protectorate and the officials of the sultan's government, the Makhzen. What he accomplished in thirteen years—the pacification of the tribes, modernization of the state, and development of the economy—he credited to his native policy. It was a wager on the past to manage the future. The building up of sharifian political power, the maintenance of the great feudal institutions, the perpetuation of social and communal organizations, the unification of the sultan's empire: these were the essential reasons that Lyautey believed accounted for Morocco's international reputation as a success story.[11]

Despite the words and deeds that brought Lyautey fame as a colonial soldier and administrator, he more than anyone else was conscious of his failures. Troubled by the revolutionary implications of the notions of self-determination and colonial emancipation in 1920, he admitted that he was disappointed with the protectorate. It had not evolved fast enough to keep pace with the expectations of those thousands of Moroccans who had fought for France in Europe and, having returned home, were now ready to play a more important role in their own society. "Now is the time," he felt compelled to write, "to give a new direction (*un sérieux coup de barre*) to our native policy and to the participation of Muslims in public affairs." Eight years of protectorate rule had done little to make the Moroccans true partners of the French. Although all legislative acts, *dahirs*, were promulgated in the sultan's name and signed by him, Lyautey acknowledged that he had no "real power" and that his advice was asked for only as "a matter of form." "He is isolated, closed-up in his palace, outside of the mainstream of public life, taking no initiative, going to see nothing by himself, despite the certain desire that he must have and the very real interest that he takes in everything, but he holds himself back, waiting to be asked—and no one asks him. . . . And if [I] did not see the sultan from time to time . . . ," Lyautey confessed, "he would live in total seclusion." Thus described, Sultan Moulay Youssef came close to being an exquisite French marionette brought out for command performances.

With the Makhzen, the situation was no different. At one time the department heads of the French administrative services had come in turn to the weekly meetings of the sultan's ministers, the Conseil des Vizirs, to report and answer questions. This was no longer the case. "For years," Lyautey lamented, "no director or service chief has gone to the Conseil." As a result, the grand vizier and the other ministers participated in no discussions on matters of substance, all of which were handled "exclusively" by the French services. In short, there was no communication between the department heads and the sultan's ministers. The Makhzen was slipping into a "sweet drowsiness."

Everywhere else the involvement of Moroccans in public affairs was virtually nonexistent. Fez was the one exception: the elected native municipal council, the Medjlis, really did administer the city. But in other municipalities, even if the city councils or commissions had native members and were presided over by the pasha, decisions were made by the French members and the French city manager. Other native institutions were dormant or dying. Native chambers of commerce and agriculture were only paper creations and the native craft corporations or guilds, which had been "in the past so solidly organized," had disappeared except at Fez and Marrakesh.

The conclusion was obvious. Morocco was edging "closer and closer to direct rule," contrary to the course Lyautey had intended to steer, and this posed serious dangers to the protectorate. "It would be an illusion to imagine that the Moroccans do not realize that they are being left outside of the administration of public affairs and that they are treated as 'minors.' They are aware of it and they suffer because of it." It was only a small step from consciousness of their exclusion to outright hostility. Lyautey was particularly troubled by the plight of Morocco's educated youth. Because of the few low-level administrative posts allotted them, he feared that they might organize and take matters into their own hands. "[O]ne of these days all this could take shape and explode if we do not concern ourselves with it right away and begin to guide these young people."[12]

Oddly enough, Lyautey complained bitterly about a situation over which he had much control. Yet his room for movement was not always as wide as one might expect. He was constantly pressed by colonists and pro-empire politicians in Paris to junk the protectorate and adopt more efficient Algerian methods. The talk of indirect rule and shared responsibilities with the native elite conjured up visions of a colonial sellout to those who saw Morocco as a permanent French acquisition. Moreover, Lyautey himself was a prisoner of what he called the "practical difficulties" of Franco-Moroccan cooperation: he had direct rule in his bones—as did all the bureaucrats coming from France and all the officers coming from Algeria—and was impatient and authoritarian by nature. To build a good working relationship with the native population was often a "thankless task" and "wearing" because of the difference in "mentalities" and "work habits." Too many Frenchmen tended to regard the native people as "an inferior race, as a negligible quantity."[13] Ironically the insurmountable object to Franco-Moroccan collaboration may have been the protectorate itself since its very existence implied that the Moroccans were incapable of managing the sort of government that the twentieth century required. Even Lyautey seemed to draw "a fairly sharp line of distinction" between Moroccans and Frenchmen in almost every sphere of activity.[14] It is tempting to conclude with Charles-André Julien that the protectorate was a "fiction," indirect rule a charade.[15]

In fairness to Lyautey it is important to point out that he was seriously troubled by this dilemma. He established the Direction des Affaires Chérifiennes (Department of Sharifian Affairs) in 1920 to begin again the "education" of the sultan, his ministers, and the Makhzen personnel; it was to be a "constant link" between the Moroccan government and the French services. The directors and service chiefs were ordered to initiate meetings with the sultan and to come before the Conseil des Vizirs to describe their responsibilities, methods of operation, and current projects. In particular, Lyautey desired that the grand vizier be "involved more and more with the general administration" of the protectorate and to that end required that he be invited to attend all meetings where administrative reports were presented as well as to the monthly Conseil du Gouvernement, which advised the resident on budget and economic matters. "His presence among us will be the first and best affirmation of the practices of the protectorate." Two and a half years later, Lyautey enlarged the Conseil du Gouvernement (until then composed exclusively of Frenchmen) to include Moroccan members. It may have been too little too late, but it signaled the direction in which he wished to go: to keep the sultan and his Makhzen "up-to-date on everything which affects the government and administration of the empire and thus to encourage them to get involved, to participate."[16]

To head off the crisis among Moroccan youth, Lyautey reasserted his determination to train a "young governmental personnel" by ordering his service directors to seek out and employ young Moroccans in "honorable and rewarding posts." "The protectorate ideal would be served by seeing the *djellabas* of young Moroccans mixed among our coats and ties throughout our offices. In this way we would be forming a second team capable of progressively replacing Frenchmen in many jobs, thus solving our staffing needs." He knew this would not happen overnight, that there would be "resistance and inertia to conquer." He recalled that his 1916 request to establish training programs for young Moroccans had remained a "dead letter." But he believed it important to try again, if not to revive the protectorate spirit, then because of the fear he harbored that, should France fail to prepare for the future, the Moroccan elite would "evolve without us, succumbing to foreign influences or revolutionary suggestions."[17]

All of what he proposed fell into the category of education and information, an important first step. But to be more than window dressing it had to be followed by the delegation of real authority and decision-making power to Moroccan leaders. This step Lyautey refused to take. It may be that this was the natural impulse of a proconsul, for he fought the political pretensions of French colonists as well. But the colonists, even though they called themselves *Marocains*, were the real strangers in the land, whereas, as Lyautey pointed out many times, the native elite was the "living substance" of the protectorate. By holding back, he permitted a gulf to form between Moroccans and Frenchmen at the highest levels where collaboration should have been tightest. It set an example that would be followed elsewhere.

Despite its limitations and contradictions, Lyautey was convinced that the protectorate would ultimately satisfy the moral and material needs of the Moroccan people and in so doing serve France and Frenchmen. His role was to build Moroccan "confidence" in France, a sturdier foundation for cooperation than French bayonets. Cooperation was the essence of the protectorate, a goal to which he was "passionately dedicated by patriotism as well as by personal conviction. For the good of my country, I hope that my successors are as committed to it as I have been."[18]

Lyautey's successors were a mixed bag. To mark the end of the Lyautey era with éclat and some brutality, the marshal's replacement was his antithesis, a civilian politico who was then governor general of Algeria. Théodore Steeg was a convivial parliamentarian and a good administrator whose tenure in Algeria had made him one of the reigning experts on overseas matters in the governing Radical Socialist party. However, his appointment must have been a bitter pill for Lyautey since it was medicine from those who had chafed under his personal rule—Hubert the First he was sometimes styled —and the martial tone of the protectorate, resented his disdain for the world of politics, and begrudged his haughty disregard for things Algerian. Still, while resident general, Steeg remained on good terms with Lyautey, publicly praised his Moroccan endeavor, and worked as harmoniously as possible with the team Lyautey had assembled, even though, as expected, he shaped the protectorate along Algerian lines by increasing settler participation in government, encouraging colonization, and expanding the bureaucracy. Steeg was not cut out to be a *vieux Marocain* and when forced to decide whether to give up a seat in the French senate and remain in Morocco or to give up Morocco and return to France, he easily chose the latter.

Steeg was succeeded in 1929 by Lucien Saint, a senior public administrator who had been France's resident general in Tunisia for the previous nine years. Nearing retirement, he was shifted to Rabat to top off his career, an accolade for years of distinguished service. He was suited for the job; in fact, Lyautey had wanted him as his immediate successor. In civil and administrative matters, Saint relied on his own expertise and that of his collaborators brought from Tunisia. For native affairs and military questions, he turned to Lyautey men. Diligent and experienced, Saint was a model of the professional high civil servant who carried on the business of government with efficiency and dispatch. Surprisingly, things did not turn out well for him and in retrospect it is a credit to his talent for survival that he lasted until his first pension check in 1933. It was he who sponsored the judicial reform, known to history as the Berber *dahir*, that touched off a summer of urban rioting in 1930. Rather than admit to a serious mistake, Saint kept the law in place (although later it was modified) and rode out the storm, the first violent public manifestation of offended Moroccan opinion that Lyautey had warned against. Planned as a period of quiet administrative articulation and reform, Saint's tenure worked out otherwise. For all his good intentions and solid accomplishments on the structure of the protectorate, he was remembered with bitterness by Moroccans.

Saint's immediate successors, Henri Ponsot, the French high commissioner in Syria and Lebanon from 1926 to 1933, and Marcel Peyrouton, who came to Morocco as Saint had from the Residency at Tunis, were also technicians whose major dealings were with the staff of the protectorate and the French community rather than with the sultan and the protectorate's people. Ponsot, for example, devoted an inordinate amount of time to working out the proper equivalencies in rank, salary, and function between overseas administrators and those of the Metropole, a thorny issue of considerable importance to Morocco's bureaucrats but irrelevant to Moroccans. Peyrouton, on the other hand, was transferred to Morocco to help the protectorate sandbag itself against the consequences of the worldwide economic depression. Neither Ponsot nor Peyrouton was particularly interested in or adept at matters of native policy even though Lyautey considered it the rock on which the protectorate had been built.

When General Charles Noguès was appointed resident general in September 1936, the Lyautey line was reestablished. He had been taught by the marshal and sought to follow his tracks. What began as youthful ambition, fired by hero worship, became a life work: to succeed Lyautey, to continue his work in Morocco, to be transformed from the loyal lieutenant—"from the first you were one of my best collaborators, one of the most active and always faithful"—to the continuator of his thought and action.[19] Lyautey was both inspiration and guide. In retirement Noguès wrote: "It was Marshal Lyautey who taught me to love Morocco and if I accomplished something during my administration of this country, it was due to him. I tried in my way to continue the Lyautey tradition and to assemble a 'team' of my own motivated by that same faith and love for Morocco."[20]

The selection of Noguès was the apotheosis of the continuity principle. It was no secret that Lyautey believed that he had achieved so much only because he had stayed so long. Noguès stayed close to seven years, second to Lyautey in tenure of France's fourteen residents general. His positive impact was everywhere apparent to his contemporaries. For Lyautey's private secretary and the chief assistant to all the residents from Steeg to Noguès, there was never any doubt of Noguès's place: "After Lyautey," wrote Georges Hutin, "Noguès was France's greatest resident general in Morocco." General Augustin Guillaume, soldier, *vieux Marocain*, and resident general in his own right, repeated the tribute: "I believe with all my heart and soul that next to Marshal Lyautey, General Noguès was France's greatest resident in Morocco." Partisan voices to be sure, but they expressed sentiments that tallied with public opinion. In a poll taken by the Casablanca weekly journal *Paris* in October 1947 (four years after Noguès's resignation), 68 percent of those asked which of Lyautey's successors had "best served the interests of France and Morocco" answered "Noguès."[21]

Born in 1876 in the mountain village of Monléon-Magnoac in the High Pyrenees—Foch country, his biographers were fond of calling it—Noguès grew up in nearby Garaison, where his parents kept the local hotel. He attended Notre-Dame de Garaison for nine years; then, to better his chances for admission to one of the competitive *grandes écoles*, he was sent to Caousou, the Jesuit secondary school at Toulouse, and from there he went to Sainte Geneviève, the preparatory school at Versailles. Admitted to the prestigious École Polytechnique, Noguès was graduated in 1897, having chosen the army as his career, the artillery as his specialty. After two years of training at the École d'Application de l'Artillerie at Fontainebleau, he was assigned to the Twelfth Artillery Regiment at Vincennes. Then the promotions stopped. Within three years he was posted to far-off Fort Tournoux, which he described as "the worst garrison in the Alps," a casualty of the Third Republic's discrimination against those officers who were practicing Catholics. Once he realized that his career was to be blocked at home, he vowed to pursue it overseas. He confessed that this was the origin of his "African vocation."[22]

While at Fort Tournoux he studied geography with the army's geographic division and law by correspondence through the University of Aix-en-Provence, where he passed the exams and submitted the thesis for the *doctorat en droit*. He resented his forced exile, but at the same time he admitted that his former life at Vincennes seemed "narrow and without interest" compared to the wilderness existence he now experienced. This too changed his life. Although he was eventually returned to his unit at Vincennes, he requested reassignment overseas with the Service Géographique. After six months training in Algeria and Tunisia, he was sent in 1909 to the southern Algero-Moroccan border regions under Lyautey's command.[23]

Noguès's introduction to Morocco was as a mapmaker of areas still not under French control. Here he engaged an enemy in combat for the first time and here he made his first command decisions. Along the way he won the confidence of Lyautey, who recommended him for the Legion of Honor and who began to have a decisive influence on his life.[24] "I will never forget that it was in the Algero-Moroccan border regions where the marshal set down the principles of his native policy and where he taught a team of enthusiastic collaborators to know and to love Morocco and the Moroccan people."[25] Promoted to captain, he joined the expeditionary force against the

Beni Snassen in 1910. He prided himself on his good relations with native leaders, becoming adept in the political action that Lyautey felt indispensable to the success of every military undertaking. "Already having a good deal of understanding and sympathy for the native population and moving about the countryside in a small detachment escorted by spahis, native infantrymen or legionnaires, I began to make friends. When I was camped at the confluence of the Za and Moulouya rivers—a very important spot—one of them saved me from an armed attack. It came from the Spanish zone and had the enemy tribesmen been able to cross the ford in the river, it would have succeeded."[26]

Noguès returned south in 1911 at a time when French policy aimed at keeping a steady pressure on several points in the sharifian empire (Casablanca and Oujda had been in French hands since 1907) while awaiting the events that would produce the go-ahead for complete intervention. The appearance of the German gunboat *Panther* off Agadir in July, ostensibly to protect German civilians from native outrages, staked out the Reich's claim in Morocco and began the diplomatic haggling. By November, Germany had agreed to give France a free hand in Morocco in exchange for territory in French Equatorial Africa. Now only the formalities with the Moroccans remained. The Treaty of Fez, signed in March 1912, established the protectorate, and the following month Lyautey was named France's first resident general. Noguès was appointed to the general staff of the occupation troops of western Morocco and in 1914 he joined Lyautey at Rabat.

The European war pulled Noguès back to France like a magnet, for he was eager to fight on the western front. The call of the country in danger, the settling of scores with the persistent continental antagonist, the test of skill and training against a European adversary, the rapid promotion of the battlefield—these were the reasons why. Lyautey too felt the tug of the Great War, but he had not been offered a metropolitan command. At moments of pessimism, he imagined that he was purposely being kept out of the war by his enemies to destroy his "strength and authority for the future."[27] At the same time, he fretted about the war's impact on Morocco. Fearing that the dissolution of the protectorate would come with the scattering of his team, he released his subordinates reluctantly. His time was spent trying to patch things together. He was a good tailor. When ordered to send thirty-five battalions to France and to withdraw his remaining forces from the interior to the coast, he volunteered to send more men than the government had requested if he could hold on to every meter of "pacified" soil. Surprisingly, at war's end he controlled more territory than he had at the war's beginning.

Alone in Morocco, Lyautey concentrated on his pet projects of road building and public works. Like many a big-city mayor, he believed these were the most important signs of government activity because they were the most visible. Among his wartime initiatives was the mounting of elaborate trade fairs to emphasize the tranquillity of the protectorate and its economic contribution to the war effort. Throughout Morocco the message was that despite the fighting in Europe, things would continue as before or get better, a French twist on the English "business as usual." In all this the "magician" in Lyautey was apparent. Regardless of his personal despair, he put on a happy face and turned it into protectorate policy—*la politique du sourire*—raising morale, fostering confidence, and cementing solidarity with France.

In Europe, Noguès got the fight he wanted. In 1915 he commanded an artillery battery and in 1916 an artillery group (four batteries). When Lyautey was unexpectedly offered and accepted appointment as France's minister of war, Noguès was transferred to his staff in Paris as a liaison officer between the war ministry, the armaments ministry, and the headquarters staff of the commander-in-chief. Brief and disastrous, Lyautey's ministerial career ended forever any secret thought he may have hidden about high government office. He could not adjust to the procedures of parliamentary government and was angered at civilian "interference" in military matters. Worse, he had a poor working relationship with the premier, Aristide Briand, and the commander-in-chief, General Robert Nivelle. Worn out and shaken after three months (January to March 1917), he asked for and got Morocco back.

With Lyautey gone, Noguès returned to the field, earning citations for his "technical competence" and the "excellent military spirit" of his command, for the precision of his artillery batteries and their contribution to the success of infantry operations. His Seventeenth Artillery Regiment was singled out as a "first-class instrument of war" under the command of a "bright and energetic" leader.[28]

After the armistice, Noguès was named *chef de cabinet* to Alexandre Millerand, France's *commissaire général* in Alsace-Lorraine. An authoritarian with a social conscience, Millerand was a Lyautey admirer and the marshal had a hand in securing Noguès's peacetime post. Here Noguès got his first taste of administration, for his main responsibility was to oversee the adaptation of German legislation (in force for almost five decades in the "lost provinces") to the French legal system.[29] When Millerand was elected president of the Republic in 1920, Noguès followed him to the Élysée as a member of his military staff. In addition to his regular duties, he became a lobbyist for the protectorate, often channeling Lyautey's requests directly to Millerand or to Premier Raymond Poincaré and advising the marshal on the best strategy to employ to broach a troublesome topic with the government.[30] Although Millerand needed no prodding to defend and expand French imperial interests, Noguès tightened the knot between Paris and Rabat.

To show his gratitude for Millerand's steady political support, Lyautey persuaded the president to visit Morocco in 1922 on the protectorate's tenth anniversary. Arranged by Noguès, the trip was supposed to call attention to the unfinished business in North Africa. In fact it was more tourism than anything else. Anxious and agitated Europe took precedence. When French troops occupied the Ruhr in January 1923, the empire was forgotten. Lyautey was haunted by the fear that Morocco and the colonial mission had lost their power to stimulate and enchant. The specter had some substance. The dismaying postwar world of inflation and tax increases, of the reparation tangle and financial crisis without end, had altered the priorities of the Metropole. Although the empire was not abandoned, it would never again receive the attention of balmier days.

At the Élysée, Noguès was introduced to the political world so foreign to the marshal. His marriage in 1921 to Suzanne Delcassé, the daughter of France's most distinguished diplomatist, ensured his professional advance. He was welcomed into the salons and country homes of France's political elite, who had once stalled his military career. Given the chance, he rallied to the Republic. With his father-in-law there was no need of an accommodation, for Noguès already admired Delcassé, the champion of the protectorate, the architect of the Entente Cordiale. Honored as an empire builder who had outfitted France with the diplomatic armor necessary for victory in the Great War, Delcassé had been as formidable at the Quai d'Orsay as Lyautey had been in the field. Whatever one thought of Delcassé's sentiments—his imperialism, his implacable anti-Germanism, and his tendency to see in the maneuvers of almost every foreign power calculated thrusts against French interests—there was genuine affection for the man and universal agreement on his preeminence among France's modern foreign ministers. It was apparent from the start that Noguès had married the father as well as the daughter.

Like her husband, Suzanne Delcassé-Noguès was determined, tireless, and ambitious. Her special interests became the promotion of Morocco's arts and crafts and the patronage of the protectorate's museums, hospitals, and charities. Their union lasted until the general's death in 1971, perhaps made stronger by the death of their only child, Jacques, from leukemia at the age of thirteen and the decade of exile in Portugal.

It is difficult to measure the political impact of a marriage or of friendships made at the Élysée. Before 1920 Noguès was already well on his way to a promising career by dint of his own effort, talent, and Lyautey's push. But after the years in Paris, it is clear that he had attracted the attention and could count on the support of Maurice Sarraut, éminence grise of the Radical Socialist party (whose political base, Toulouse, was just a few kilometers from Noguès's hometown), and his brother Albert, Millerand's minister of colonies, a former governor general of Indochina, and the acknowledged leader of the interwar colonialist movement. Both men exerted considerable pressure on Noguès's behalf in 1936 to win his appointment to Morocco. Having friends at home was important to every overseas administrator, especially at budget time, for when the troops and the money stopped coming, a colonial governor was either forced to resign or watch the withering of his patrimony, with the resultant native and settler discontent and the defections from his own staff. It was no accident that Lyautey's troubles in Morocco, which ended with his humiliation and replacement during the Rif war, began in 1924 when the Center Left won control of parliament and Millerand resigned to avoid a constitutional crisis. Unlike Lyautey, Noguès was as comfortable in Paris as in Rabat.

When Millerand gave up the presidency, Noguès was momentarily without a job. But Lyautey took him back "with enthusiasm." "I will give you Chambrun's place, that is, command of the Fez territory, with the special title of Governor of the City of Fez, which should be sufficiently prestigious to suit your wife."[31] General Aldebert de Chambrun was to be promoted to head up the Fez region, and, as Lyautey described it, Noguès would be Chambrun's assistant. Generous and agreeable, Chambrun was in total accord. He needed an assistant because of the "incredible amount of work" that had fallen on his shoulders after a serious battle injury had put the previous regional commander in the hospital, and he was particularly pleased at the "quality" of the one he was being offered. He warned, however, that Fez was the "most complicated prefecture in the world." In France there was "nothing like it." It was a political and military command to be handled with the utmost delicacy, sensitivity, and caution.[32]

Even if Lyautey could not come through with the promised title in the end, Noguès accepted what was offered. Lyautey explained that to squeeze him into the existing structure of command, it would have been necessary to name him the "military governor" of Fez, a rank that "exists nowhere" in Morocco "and that might cause people to believe that there was an abnormal military situation at Fez and alarm the natives." In sum, a "useless precedent" and perhaps dangerous as well. But he assured Noguès that "the command of all the troops stationed in the Fez territory—infantry, cavalry, artillery, and the military corps of engineers—is so clearly spelled out (in truth a brigade command) that I am willing to be hanged if anyone can find the least ambiguity on the matter of who is in charge of the troops."[33]

Noguès returned to Morocco at a moment when the Rif tribes of the northeast were in revolt against Spain, France's partner in the protectorate. With each passing day, the threat to French security increased. Under the inspired leadership of Mohamed Abd el-Krim, once called the "Vercingetorix of the Rif," the mountaineers had inflicted such severe defeats on Spanish forces (the most humiliating at Annoual in 1921) that Spain's military dictator, General Miguel Primo de Rivera, declared for the semiabandonment of Spanish Morocco and pulled back to a fortified line south of Tetouan, leaving a good four-fifths of the zone in rebel hands. Although the Riffians avoided any quarrel with the French because they feared the results of a joint Franco-Spanish military expedition against them, the French were unavoidably drawn closer to the conflict as the rebellion spread. In the first place, Spanish Morocco was the "political child" of the French-controlled sultanate.[34] Although the Spaniards spoke of their *protectorado* over Morocco, legally there was only one protectorate, the one given to the French by the Treaty of Fez. It was divided into three zones: the French zone, the Spanish zone (retroceded to Spain by France), and an international zone, Tangier. Since the sultan was sovereign everywhere—at Rabat, Tetouan, and Tangier—a Rif state would of necessity be carved out of the sultan's patrimony that the French had sworn to protect. Second, the zones had not been drawn along tribal lines so some tribes straddled the border. The French were particularly uneasy about the important Beni Zeroual; although technically in the Spanish zone, they were administered by the French. Victory for the rebels would surely disturb this group and perhaps undo throughout Morocco what years of hard fighting and patient negotiating had accomplished. "Nothing would be so bad for our regime," Lyautey concluded in December 1924, "as the installation near Fez of an independent Muslim state, modernized and supported by the most warlike tribes, with a spirit exalted by success against Spain . . . in short, the most serious kind of menace, which should be dealt with at the earliest possible moment."[35]

Lyautey hoped to keep the frontier quiet by using the vigorous political action that he preferred and even bargaining with Abd el-Krim to secure his submission. Neither tactic worked. In the end, the war ministry in Paris ordered the occupation of the territory north of the Ouergha River, part of the French zone but never staked out until now. The French advance, led by Chambrun, forced the Rif army to retreat; and in its wake the French constructed a series of fortified outposts. Lyautey still wished to stay clear of the Rif, which he called a "hornet's nest," and to avoid a major military operation that might encourage pro-Rif sentiment among the tribes in the French zone. He surely wanted nothing to do with a combined Franco-Spanish military venture.[36] But he was ready to fight, if need be.

The French presence was taken as a provocation and it probably was unavoidable that it should have been. Abd el-Krim still insisted that war with France was the farthest thing from his mind, "inconceivable" unless he was attacked.[37] However, the French moves had ousted him from a region that he considered to be within his domain and that supplied his army with much-needed grain and had cut him off from a people that he counted as an ally. As a counter, he tried to negotiate, but since the French were now unwilling to parlay on any issue, he switched to war making. He planned a move against Taza to cut French communications, then a strike toward Fez to demonstrate his power and to force the French to the bargaining table.

The attack began on 13 April 1925. The Riffians easily penetrated French lines and within a few days stood twenty miles north of Fez. If this was a response the French had deliberately provoked, they had badly underestimated the fighting capabilities of the rebel soldiers, having credited their past victories to the poor shape of the Spanish army. The secret satisfaction of seeing the Spaniards whipped by rebel bands disappeared with the April offensive. After the initial shock of the breakthrough, Lyautey called for reinforcements, braced for further thrusts, and prepared his countermeasures. At first, however, the best Lyautey could do was to hold back the rebel tide. Weeks after the attack, he reported that the situation was as serious as it could be and continued to appeal for more men and equipment from France and Algeria. Without speedy action, he wrote to the minister of foreign affairs, "I can tell you squarely that we risk losing Morocco."[38] The extent of the French setback was withheld from the public, and, like Napoleon returning from Moscow, Lyautey issued communiqués to Paris that masked the truth, so much so that Noguès wrote from the front asking if he really understood the depth of the crisis and the urgent needs of the army. Horrified that his own officers had been taken in by the public relations game, Lyautey assured Noguès that he knew what was going on and was doing his best to secure what was needed. "The slogan that I used in one of my telegrams is: 'Send me as much as possible as soon as possible.'" The delays, he said, were neither his fault nor the fault of the government—"Painlevé and Debeney, Briand and Berthelot understand completely the gravity of the situation and are doing everything they can to get us out of it"—but the result of the "disorganization of our army" and the eighteen-month military service law, which had made it hard to find enough combat-ready units.[39] What troops there were had been assigned to the Rhineland, the Ruhr, and the Levant; even though the Ruhr forces were slated to be evacuated by late summer, there was no public sentiment to get involved in yet another thorny military situation. Lyautey was left to deal with the crisis as best he could.

Chambrun commanded the entire northern front with headquarters south of the Ouergha in Aïn Aïcha; each of his immediate subordinates, Generals Paul Colombat, Henri Freydenberg, and Albert Cambay, was charged with a portion of its defense. After "eminent services" as Chambrun's second, Noguès was attached to the Colombat group on the west and participated in the rescue and stabilization operations along the Ouergha and into the heart of Beni Zeroual country, including the battles over Bibane, the largest French outpost north of the Ouergha, which was bitterly contested throughout May. Many of the advance posts had been overrun by the Riffians in cruel hand-to-hand struggles, with the survivors killed and mutilated. Others were holding out, desperately awaiting relief. Saving them was Noguès's "agonizing preoccupation." Modern materiel of every sort was needed, he told Lyautey: heavy artillery, armored cars, aircraft, even gas (morally outlawed after its use in the Great War). Lyautey agreed with all this, and although he admitted that using gas would be difficult, he ordered its preparation. But "this must remain absolutely secret, *don't talk about it*, because there must always remain some doubt among the natives and international opinion until the very moment when we use it." Although gas bombs were never exploded, the suggestion was proof that the grim fate of the outposts was pushing the exhausted field commanders to consider desperate measures. Lyautey understood this and recognized its ill effects. Once the posts were freed, he wanted them aban-

doned since they were diverting the attention and energy of his officers from the overall objectives of the campaign and had cost too
many lives. He wanted Noguès liberated from his field responsibilities: "It is your brain and your vision of the operation as a whole, as
well as your freedom of movement to handle the political strings,
that we need the most."[40]

The deteriorating military situation prevented Noguès's release.
Chambrun was replaced at the end of May by General Albert Daugan,
commander of the Marrakesh region, who in 1918 had led the famous Moroccan Division to a series of victories on the western front
in France. His objective remained Chambrun's, to create a stable defensive line as a prelude to offensive operations, but he fared no
better than his predecessor. Distracted by the continuous raids on
the outposts, Daugan could do no more than hold his own and parry
the rebel strikes. In June and July, he girded for renewed rebel advances on Taza and Fez since Abd el-Krim had boasted that Fez
would fall at the beginning of July. With the defection of the Tsoul
and Branes tribes to the rebels, his goal seemed in reach. Taza was
now on the edge of the dissidence, and the tribes north of Fez, the
Cheraya and Hayaina, were thrown into disarray, flooding Fez with
terrified refugees. Unsure whether the attack would come at Taza,
Fez, or some point in between, and with his forces stretched uncomfortably thin, Daugan reluctantly talked of a withdrawal in the east
toward the Moulouya River and Algeria and in the west toward an
area north of Meknès, abandoning Taza for certain and perhaps Fez
as well.[41]

Noguès counseled defending the cities. "Even though the threat is
serious, we are still holding our own everywhere. We must fight to
stabilize the situation. Nothing is lost yet." Sent to Taza for a first-
hand look, he returned convinced that it was better to stand than to
run. This was Lyautey's inclination as well: "To abandon a city of
Franco-Moroccan population without a fight would place us in such
a situation before the world, the Muslims, Morocco, and our enemy
that I would prefer to run any risk rather than to resort to such a
measure." To desert Fez, the capital of the north, the intellectual
center of the empire, was to surrender the protectorate. Lyautey
took for granted that its survival had to remain the "essential objective from both the military and political point of view." His orders
were to contain the Rif advance "at whatever cost" and to counterattack wherever possible. That same day (5 July) General Gaston Billotte surprised a Rif column headed toward Fez and "literally tore it
to pieces," while to the southeast Colonel Henri Giraud engaged

rebel forces moving toward Taza, "broke their ranks and threw them into disorder." The next day Lyautey signaled a general counterattack that those close to him called "an immense success."[42] Like a screenplay for a colonial epic, the rebels were routed and the protectorate's cities saved.

Shielding Fez had a psychological as well as a political and military importance. Because of his part in Fez's defense, Noguès believed that its citizens singled him out for their special gratitude. He was not wrong. It created a "fund of affectionate confidence" on which he later drew to tackle some of the hardest tasks of his residency in the city he gently called "so magnetic and yet so difficult."[43] When he left Fez at the end of 1926 with his wife and infant son (born at Fez in December 1925), the members of the Medjlis wrote: "During your stay among us, you have been a model of frankness and sincerity. With a limitless kindness you have helped all those who needed your aid. We are very grateful to you and your memory will remain engraved on our hearts forever." They noted in a letter to Resident General Steeg that Noguès was the sort of man who had "made France loved" by the population. "The men you choose to head up our large cities and regions are really the most important policy decisions that you can make."[44] It had always been obvious to Lyautey.

The fighting was not finished, although the worst was over, and Lyautey began to map offensive operations. Unfortunately, his "system" had suffered: he had become a warrior in spite of himself. He had been forced to engage the enemy in battle, call for modern equipment, and even recommend military cooperation with Spain and England, all that he earlier had argued against. The only bright spot was that the tribes of the north had remained loyal.

In July, Marshal Philippe Pétain, inspector general of the French army and vice-president of the Supreme War Council (Conseil Supérieur de la Guerre), toured the northern front. He appreciated neither Lyautey nor his method and was constantly vexed at hearing "Lyauteyisms." At the reference to a combat zone as a "good field for political action," he allegedly retorted: "In war the only fields I know about are battlefields." He lectured members of Lyautey's staff on the error of giving priority to political aims that had no "durable and decisive value." "You people are making political decisions, I make strategic ones."[45]

Crudely put, this was the basic difference between the Lyautey and Pétain approach to war. Lyautey held that the task of the colonial soldier was more political than military. Pageant, prowess, and promises played the major role. Force was necessary: "The Muslim, the Moroccan understands and respects only force," Lyautey told France's premier in 1925. But it was to be used sparingly and only as a last resort.[46] The objective was to secure the land and to "win over" its people, enriching both for the profit of the sharifian state and ultimately for the benefit of France. Until the April attack, Lyautey had concentrated exclusively on the Beni Zeroual, hoping to rally them and the tribes lost to the rebels with a massive show of force. If successful, Abd el-Krim's power would be slowly whittled away without the bloody battles that marked the "Spanish style" in the north. "It is a question of defeating rebels, and rebels only," Lyautey explained to newcomers. "When we have enough battalions, the dissidence will weaken, and then disappear. . . . Kill as few people as possible, send reinforcements where they need to be, and all will be well."[47]

For Pétain all of this was nonsense. The aim of war was victory in the shortest possible time. It was won by inflicting heavy casualties on the enemy while husbanding your own troops: the modern machines of war were to be employed to their fullest. Working with the Beni Zeroual was a silly diversion. Pétain wanted direct contact with the rebels on their own turf in the Rif so he could defeat them once and for all, and he was committed to cooperating with Spain to get the job done.[48] He got what he wanted. Within a month of his return to Paris, he was handed full direction of the Moroccan campaign.

Throughout the summer and fall, Noguès served the two marshals working north of Fez on both sides of the Ouergha clearing the areas near the posts of Aïn Maatouf, Kelaa-des-Sless, and Aïn Aïcha of rebel forces. In August he helped to pacify the Tsoul tribe, "one of the first striking successes of the 1925 campaign."[49] Raised to the rank of commander of the Legion of Honor, he sentimentally asked that Lyautey decorate him before the marshal left for France, their final meeting on Moroccan soil.[50] To be sure, Noguès grieved at Lyautey's shabby treatment and shared the marshal's resentment. Privately he kept him informed of the progress of the military operations, reversing the liaison of the Millerand days. "You are the *only* soldier from whom I like to hear the news from Morocco," Lyautey confided. "As for Pétain and his crew, I have burned my bridges with them as well as with everyone at the Rue St.-Dominique [the ministry of war] and the Boulevard des Invalides [the Supreme War Council], except for Foch and Weygand who are the only two I can talk with and still want to."[51]

Noguès had little contact with Pétain. As promised, the marshal reshaped the command to his liking and pursued the conduct of the campaign in his own way, remaining in Morocco just long enough to ensure victory. The final submission of Abd el-Krim, achieved through Franco-Spanish military cooperation, came in May 1926, and Noguès shared the laurels. Resident General Steeg made a point of pressing for his promotion to the rank of general even though Noguès's superior, General Edmond Boichut, a Pétain man, thought him too young for the jump. Steeg argued that in the post-Rif period of military contraction Morocco needed soldiers who could double as political leaders of "talent." Of the officers currently working in Morocco, Steeg said he knew of no one "who could better handle the complex functions of a regional command, who had more Moroccan experience, more knowledge of how things worked and more persuasive authority than Colonel Noguès." Denied promotion and thus command of a region, Noguès resigned his territorial command, the Territoire de Fès-Nord, to accept the directorship of the École d'Application de l'Artillerie at Fontainebleau, the artillery's alma mater. Steeg approved the leave-taking since it seemed the right move to advance his career. "But I must tell you," he wrote the minister of war, "that it is not without some regret that I let him go. He is a superior officer who by his courage, strength, intelligence, and knowledge of and feeling for the native population has rendered so many remarkable services during the critical hours of summer 1925, through the winter of 1925–26, and during the recent Franco-Spanish conference at Paris. He has been a valiant soldier, an informed administrator, a skillful negotiator." In pushing a second time for Noguès's promotion, which finally came in June 1927, Steeg called him "a model of the compleat colonial officer, as good a soldier as a politician." And it was Steeg who put into typescript for the first time the fact that Noguès had "saved" Fez in 1925.[52]

In April 1929 Noguès was recalled to Morocco to exercise the dual responsibility of *directeur général des affaires indigènes* (director of native affairs) and *chef de cabinet militaire* to Resident General Lucien Saint. It was another Lyautey initiative. Saint had asked the marshal for a recommendation. He answered: "Take Noguès!"[53] The double post was to enable Noguès to link "as closely as possible" political action with the employment of military methods, the classic Lyautey formula. Problems of insecurity and unsubmissiveness continued to plague the protectorate. Saint targeted "the particularly aggressive dissidence" of the central High Atlas, which threatened the colonization of the Tadla and the safety of the "constantly troubled" Algero-Moroccan border regions. Noguès reorganized the command structure in the danger spots, creating an autonomous Tadla territory and a single command for the border regions, adapting his military plans to the "political situation of the moment" in order "to wear down" the resistance of the native bands and avoid violent reactions to the steady French penetration. Saint credited him with spectacular success: in the High Atlas, the opening of the High Moulouya corridor, the occupation of Tounfit, the penetration of the Dra, Dadès, and Todra; in the border regions, the conquest of the Tafilalet oasis and its connection with the Marrakesh region. All of this, which Saint had been told on his arrival in Morocco would take oceans of men and money, had been accomplished at small cost with the "minimum loss of life." It was a method of penetration characterized by careful political preparation and the widespread and intensive use of local partisans. "His authority and prestige with the tribes on the frontier and the vigorous impetus that he gave the Service des Affaires Indigènes," Saint wrote of Noguès, "enabled him to coordinate in perfect agreement with the military command the technique of advances along wide fronts in which regular forces were only employed to back up the auxiliary troops and to equip a region once it had been occupied."[54] In short, it was colonial warfare in the Lyautey manner.

Less spectacular was Noguès's involvement in the Berber *dahir* crisis (examined in chapter 2), which made the summer of 1930 difficult to forget. The cities exploded in anti-French violence reminiscent of the 1912 riots in Fez that had greeted the announcement of the protectorate. Others might have paid dearly for the lack of foresight and preparedness, but he managed to put the episode behind him, first because his strategy to restore urban order worked, and second because he left Morocco to take command of the Tenth Infantry Division in Paris.

When he returned to North Africa in 1933, it was as commanding general of the Nineteenth Army Corps at Algiers. Glad for the shift to Paris and Algiers, he remembered this as a "happy period of soldiering when I had only military responsibilities. I was able to devote myself completely to these top-notch units."[55] This was only partly true, for if he delighted in the training, organization, and troop maneuvers—and was justifiably proud that he had set up the mobilization plan used in 1939—he was of necessity constantly embroiled in native affairs (including the 1935 anti-Jewish riot at Sétif, which called into question the loyalty of native troops). After all, native affairs were one of his specialties.[56] His tenure at Algiers proved that he was still an expert.

During the six years that Noguès was absent from Morocco, the protectorate was seriously affected by the world economic crisis, which reversed the prosperity of the past. The concerns of European farmers and businessmen, never uppermost in Lyautey's mind, now moved to center stage, shoved there by the collapse of farm prices, the quotas placed by France on the import of colonial commodities, and the protectionism of Morocco's foreign customers. The 1906 Act of Algeciras, which guaranteed an open door to the commerce of all nations and forbade the French to tamper with Morocco's tariffs, now made the empire a dumping ground for cheap goods. Ponsot bravely tried to shore up the protectorate's finances by slashing expenses, reducing the salaries of government personnel—hitting hard the large number of low-level civil servants—and cutting aid to commerce and industry. This was precisely what the colonists did not want. In the resulting tug-of-war, they exerted enough pull to have him recalled.[57]

On the other hand, Marcel Peyrouton, Ponsot's successor, spoke the colonists' language and initiated belt-tightening administrative reforms and created confidence-building economic defense committees. He was ousted by the leftist Popular Front because of his rightist past, his strong-arm reputation, and his antisocialist prejudices; while at the Residency in Tunis, he openly accused French socialists of being in league with France's enemies—the young Tunisian nationalists. The fear was that Peyrouton, embraced by the colons, would be impregnable in Morocco at a time when the government contemplated reforms. So he was fired unceremoniously after a meeting of the Conférence Impériale in Paris, told he could not even return to Morocco to pack his bags, and shipped off to Buenos Aires as France's ambassador to Argentina, given, he recalled, "no explanation" of what he was supposed to do there. No one took his leaving with good grace. There were demonstrations in Casablanca and petitions sent to Paris demanding his reinstatement. Even the sultan was distressed. He had earlier broken with protocol to write directly to the president of the Republic, protesting the anti-Peyrouton campaign in the metropolitan press and pointing out what the resident had already accomplished in his first month on the job. What Peyrouton needed, said the sultan, was "time." "We must not forget that the work of Marshal Lyautey (to which everyone renders just tribute) took him fourteen years and that his successors, regardless of their competence, have only been able to outline programs which they have never had the time to put into operation."[58]

Two months before Peyrouton knew he was slated to be replaced, the Residency was offered to Noguès. (In March 1936 the general had been given membership on the Supreme War Council, promoted to the rank of *général d'armée*; in June he was appointed inspector general of the troops in North Africa.) Minister of War Édouard Daladier telegraphed him at Algiers in July to ask if he would accept the nomination. Noguès refused "outright," explaining that he feared being obliged by a government committed to far-reaching colonial reform to carry out policies in Morocco that he considered "disastrous." He worried that the native structure of command would be destroyed by abrupt change and in consequence "set a large part of the population against us." The complete pacification of the country had been achieved less than two years before and "to launch experiments and upset our old friends who had helped us to accomplish this with so much devotion" seemed a risky business. At the same time, he wanted no part in the ouster of Peyrouton, with whom he had "very friendly relations" when Peyrouton was secretary general to the government in Algeria.[59]

At the beginning of August, Noguès was invited to Paris so that Premier Blum could press him to reconsider. "He was evidently rather surprised by my attitude," Noguès decided, "for I told him straight out my thinking on many issues and that far from being a support to the government, I might even become an embarrassment, for if I were asked to impose a measure which I considered contrary to the interests of France and Morocco, I would ask to be relieved of my post." To avoid such a dilemma, Noguès asked Blum to guarantee him that on Moroccan matters his judgment would be given priority. He later vaguely referred to this as the "indispensable" condition to his accepting the job. The meeting with Blum went well. Noguès spoke openly of having been "seduced" by the premier's "great intellect" and "breadth of vision." Still, nothing happened. A second conversation brought them no closer to agreement. Noguès was still troubled by the "Peyrouton matter." Furthermore, he told Blum what he imagined would put an end to the discussions once and for all, that while he respected "all opinions" in France, they were not items of export to the colonies: "To introduce communism to Africa would be to set the stage for a native revolt."[60] In other words, he would not be the advance man for the Popular Front.

A week later, Daladier phoned to say that Noguès's "conditions" had been accepted and that he would do his best to see that they were respected. Peyrouton's departure had been decided upon and there was no chance for a last minute reprieve; should Noguès refuse the post, it would go to someone else. Based on this and the

urgings of Gamelin, Weygand, and Pétain, a diverse group of coun-
selors, he accepted. When he saw Blum for a third time, the premier
told him with a laugh that when he had spoken to Communist party
chieftain Maurice Thorez about his apprehensions, Thorez said there
was no cause to worry since he was "totally uninterested" in Morocco. Noguès later attested that Blum and Daladier had kept their
word and "always approved" his decisions, even when it caused
them some discomfort with their colleagues on the Left.[61]

For Blum the Noguès appointment served many purposes. It rid
him of Peyrouton, replaced by an authoritarian loyal to the government, without causing the colons to revolt. This was quite an accomplishment because the anti–Popular Front fever ran high in
North Africa, creating almost a "pre–civil war atmosphere."[62] Noguès's nomination was received with surprise and suspicion—since
he came, after all, under the sign of Blum—but not hostility. As a
soldier, *vieux Marocaín*, and Lyautey man, he was a known quantity, far preferable to the leftist politician or bureaucrat that the
colons had feared would be thrust down their throats. Named both
resident general and commander of Morocco's troops, *commissaire
résident général commandant en chef*, the first since Lyautey to
combine both civil and military authority, Noguès symbolized the
government's vigilance in the face of the increasingly dangerous
Mediterranean situation brought about by the military uprising in
Spain. When the ministry of foreign affairs informed Rabat of the
change in residents, this was emphasized: "Kindly let his Majesty
know immediately of [our decision], making it clear that the events
in Spain and their possible repercussions in Morocco have led the
government, responsible for the maintenance of order and security
in the French zone of the sharifian empire, to name a general officer
to Rabat, qualified by his past to guard the tranquillity of the protectorate and at the same time to continue the work pursued by his
predecessors in the social, economic, and financial fields."[63] Foreign
danger, economic maladies, political discontent, native stirrings:
this was the Morocco that Noguès inherited, so different and yet so
much the same as the Morocco Lyautey first saw thirty years before.
Ironically, although the socialists had been among Lyautey's chief
critics, dancing at his downfall and disgrace, Blum now turned to the
marshal's most adept student in the hope that the country would respond once again to the Lyautey touch.

TWO

The Revolt of the Cities

In April 1929 Noguès resigned the directorship of the École d'Application de l'Artillerie at Fontainebleau to return to Morocco as Lucien Saint's right-hand man for native affairs and to be responsible as well for the protectorate's internal security. It was a job that ought to have kept him on the empire's edges. But fourteen months later he found himself on city streets that the French usually took for granted, putting down the first explosion of urban violence attributed to native nationalism. The summer of 1930 was only the beginning. In 1936 and 1937, his first two years as resident general, Noguès confronted street demonstrations and riots that ultimately required armed police and military intervention. The year 1930 marked the naming ceremony, the time for sorting out what was happening and why and for devising a strategy for urban pacification. It was the prologue to Noguès's residency.

When Sultan Sidi Mohammed ben Youssef sealed a *dahir* in May 1930 on the system of Berber justice, officially recognizing Berber common law and transferring criminal cases to French courts, the cities exploded in anti-French fury. The French were accused of forcing the sultan to give up his rights in the Berber lands—thereby threatening the religious and political unity of the empire—attempting to divide Berber from Arab, and stepping up evangelism among the Berbers by Christian missionaries. All were considered Machiavellian moves to strengthen French control over Morocco. The menace to Islam raised the ire of the city dwellers. Protest was at first limited to prayers and petitions but later extended to street demonstrations and clashes with the local authorities. "Your Excellency knows," wrote the protectorate's *délégué général*, Urbain Blanc, to the minister of foreign affairs, "that since its publication, the *dahir* on Berber justice has provoked some emotion in our large cities. Certain inhabitants of Salé, Rabat, and Fez in particular have seen this *dahir* as an instrument of combat against their religion. Agitators of bad faith have denounced it as destined to prepare for the 'de-islamization' of the Berber world and its eventual conversion [to Christianity]."[1]

Through it all the French maintained that the *dahir* had been purposely misunderstood and exploited by a group of young nationalists, an educated bourgeois elite, bent on denigrating the protectorate and enlisting the Muslim population in a movement of national renewal and reform. They had not intended to muzzle the power of the sultan nor to meddle in the religious affairs of Morocco. The law had been written to firm up the system of Berber justice in order to protect the rights of those engaged in property transactions and litigation in Berber territory and to ensure the swift punishment of crimes. In other words, it was designed to benefit men of affairs and colonists, who frankly would have preferred the wholesale importation of French justice rather than the patch-up job of protectorate officials. Regardless of intent, it did limit the sultan's prerogatives, and General Henri Simon, assigned by the Residency to write a retrospective analysis of the crisis, called it "a real coup d'état."[2] Moreover, by putting the use of customary law on a solid legal footing, the *dahir* created an obstacle to the continued progress among the Berbers of the "revealed" or Koranic law, the basis of Muslim civilization. This appeared to reverse the policy of Lyautey, who had encouraged the red-robed Muslim jurists to administer their law in the areas controlled by the French armies.

From the beginning, Resident General Saint admitted (and here he was seconded by Noguès) that it was inevitable that the *dahir* would be considered an attack on religious orthodoxy.[3] But the interests of property prevailed. No one could have predicted the intensity of the reaction. Even Urbain Blanc, whose "profound knowledge of North Africa and Islam" had made him Lyautey's "most informed and sure adviser" was taken aback.[4] Here the Lyautey precedents were not much help. Those in favor of the law argued that it merely continued the "Berber policy" begun in the *dahirs* of 1914 and 1924, which decreed that the Berber tribes should be administered "according to their own laws and customs" and gave legal powers to Berber councils. Lyautey had adamantly refused to touch tribal institutions if they answered the needs of the population and did not outrage French sensibilities. In addition, the early *dahirs* were used as bait to make it easier for unconquered Berber tribes, fearful of losing traditional practices, to submit to the French.

At the same time, the existence of a Berber system outside sharifian authority permitted the French to act as champions, first of the Arabs, then of the Berbers, playing one off against the other. To perpetuate this division for political reasons was the undisguised grand plan of many French officials. At times it seduced Lyautey as well.

One purpose of the protectorate's Berber schools, he admitted, was "to maintain discreetly but as firmly as possible the linguistic, religious and social differences that exist between the Islamized and Arabized countryside under Makhzen control and the Berbers of the mountains, who are religious but pagan and do not speak Arabic."[5] Saint was also taken with the idea. "We must not be in any hurry to reap the political and social benefits of the [Berber] *dahir*," he reported to Paris. "They will follow naturally from the state of equilibrium judiciously maintained between two races, one of which, the Berber, must remain of great importance to our firm establishment in this country."[6]

It may have been this that convinced the soldiers and administrators in the field to accept the *dahir*. Lyautey had pinned his hopes for the future of the protectorate on the young Arab bourgeoisie, but his successors were far less enthusiastic. Eminent French teachers and Arabists, such as Robert Montagne and Roger Le Tourneau, found Moroccan youth lacking in "moral qualities." They were intelligent but vain, venal, and physically and sexually dissipated, without perseverence, discipline, or the will to work. Those few Moroccans who had finished the first complete course of studies designed to prepare them for Makhzen jobs were dismissed as worthless. Their angry attack against France and the protectorate was attributed to their frustration at not being able to achieve and succeed according to European standards.[7] This was hardly the clay from which to mold giants.

Therefore, the French were not innocent of political ulterior motives. Saint might reject out of hand the concern of devout Muslims over French proselytizing for Christ as something "easy to combat" since "French policy in Islamic countries has never . . . given cause for any suspicion of intolerance." But a political purpose was hard to deny. The so-called Berber regionalism was a crucial element in the French attempt to prevent the spread of "nationalist tendencies" among the Moroccan population.[8] In any event, denials did not stop the spread of the anti-French feeling.

Throughout June and July, prayers were said in the mosques of Salé, Rabat, and Fez, invoking God's protection, and the *latif*, recited in times of disaster, was adapted to the political crisis at hand: "O Savior (*Ya Latif*), protect us from ill treatment by fate and allow nothing to divide us from our brothers, the Berbers." Since the nationalists stressed the religious impact of the *dahir*, the mosques provided a forum for their protest as well as a sanctuary from the reprisals of the authorities. It was also a clever way of using religion and religious symbols in order to mobilize support within the Muslim community.[9] Street demonstrations, however, were another matter. In mid-July, Mohammed Hassan el-Ouazzani, a student at the École des Sciences Politiques in Paris and secretary general of the Association des Étudiants Nord-Africains, led a street march in front of the pasha's residence in Fez. The demonstrators were directed to disperse and to return the next day to present their grievances in a proper manner. When they reappeared, Pasha Mohammed el-Baghdadi had them arrested, flogged, and imprisoned. Stunned by the duplicity and the harsh punishment, young Moroccans gathered at the Karaouiyne Mosque the following day, where speechmakers encouraged them to continue their protest. The pasha ordered the arrest of nineteen of the leaders and, as a precautionary measure, put three companies of regular troops on alert.

Public support for the arrested youths surprised the French. Not only family and friends but "notables and even the *oulema* [religious scholars]" intervened to obtain their release, which was granted immediately on the promise that there would be no further attempt to disturb the public order. At Rabat and Salé "no repression was necessary," but at Salé a young bookseller, Mohamed Chemao, was sentenced to forty-five days in prison for having insulted and threatened a *cadi*, a judge in a Muslim religious court. In Marrakesh, Abdellatif Sbihi of Salé, identified by the French as "a notorious nationalist and recognized leader of all the young agitators of Morocco," who had helped mastermind the adaptation of the *latif* to political purposes, was arrested and convicted in Marrakesh of having publicly "incited the citizens to revolt." Noguès's services noted that the agitation had been confined to the "religious elements among the city populations" and listed the cities in order of virulence: Salé, Rabat, Fez, and Marrakesh. Only at Fez had there been any difficulty: "a small demonstration, rapidly repressed by the local Makhzen authorities."[10] At no time, however, had the public order been seriously disturbed.

Once the religious nature of the protest became apparent, the French resolved not to intervene directly. "It is evident," wrote Blanc, "that any repression coming from us would have been a mistake. We did not make it." The sultan would take the next step. A letter from him was read in the mosques on 11 August. An accompanying note from the grand vizier ordered the pashas and khalifs (the pashas' deputies) to have it delivered "clearly and in a strong voice so that all who are in attendance will understand its seriousness and comply with the instructions it contains." The sultan described the *dahir* as simply an administrative measure. He condemned the young people who, "devoid of any sort of judgment, heedless of the consequences of their reprehensible actions," had "misled the crowd" and transformed the recitation of the prayers into a "political demonstration"; and he forbade the use of the mosques as political meeting places. Yet, in a statement startling in its phraseology, he made a dramatic concession: "To show that no ulterior motive has guided Our action We have decided that any Berber tribe which expresses the desire to submit to the jurisdiction of the Chrâa [Muslim religious law] will immediately get a *cadi* for the regulation of its transactions. This proves Our concern for the protection of their religion and for the maintenance of Islam among them." The letter closed with a command "to observe order and tranquillity."[11]

Blanc hoped that "Muslims of good faith" would submit immediately to the sultan's orders, but with the nationalists it was impossible to be too optimistic. Should the commotion persist, however, the sultan was prepared to act. "[If] disobeyed, the sultan will be justified in using his sovereign prerogatives to force obedience. No one, here or anywhere, can challenge this right. What we have to look forward to is a sharifian repression through the legal channel of the pashas or *caïds* [city governors]." France's attitude would be to hold to the obligations of the treaty of protectorate: "Our authority must support and aid that of the sharifian government. It must guide its actions, bringing them back—should they stray—to the path of a sound, moderate, and comprehensive justice." The danger might come if the agitation persisted. "It is thus essential that the Makhzen stand firm and make its authority respected." The sultan's letter was counted on to create a "détente," but if it did not, "a limited and firm repressive action would remind these restless ones of the need to respect our authority and that of the Makhzen."[12]

The sultan's words had some effect but did not put an end to the troubles. Of the nationalists at Fez, the majority agreed to stop the recitation of the *latif*, as their sovereign demanded, but determined to send a delegation to discuss the crisis with him. Four days later, however, the *latif* was recited in Casablanca, previously untouched by the turbulence, at the instigation of leaders from Rabat and Fez. The leaders and twenty-three of their Casablanca followers were arrested and sentenced to a month in prison. Among them was Mohammed el-Ouazzani, now considered "one of the most dangerous" nationalists. Simultaneous with the Casablanca action, the nationalists began organizing delegations in cities throughout the country to transmit their grievances to the Makhzen.[13]

The sultan received the Fez delegation on 27 August, but the audi-

ence was not easy. He reportedly wept with emotion when Mohammed ben Abdesselem el-Halou, a former president of the Fez Chamber of Commerce, presented the group's plea that he revoke the
dahir. Still, although he promised to consider their petition, the sultan sent them home without a response. Disappointed, the nationalists began the preparations for a demonstration on 1 September. On
orders from the Makhzen, however, the pasha of Fez arrested eight
"notorious agitators," including el-Halou, whom the French called
the "real leader" of the Fez movement and who had declared that he
was acting against the French "in full agreement" with the Makhzen
and with the "tacit support" of foreign governments.[14] Despite the
preventive action, a group of 150 to 200 youths began the recitation
of the *latif* at the Karaouiyne Mosque and tried to march outside it.
About sixty arrests were made, mostly of young people between fifteen and twenty years of age, including an Italian subject and five
British *protégés*. El-Halou was sent to forced residence at Missour,
seven of the leaders were sentenced to three months in prison, and
the rest were sentenced to one month. "This rapid and justified repression," Blanc told the minister of foreign affairs, "has manifestly
reinforced the prestige of sharifian authority. We have not at any moment been called upon to intervene in any manner whatsoever.
What is more, these events have had the advantage of clearing the air
and unmasking the leaders of this agitation."[15]

The number of foreign nationals and *protégés* among the protesters troubled the French. Moroccans employed as secretaries or interpreters by foreign legations and consular services or hired as agents
or brokers (*censaux*) by Europeans engaged in the import-export
trade were "protected" from prosecution in sharifian courts as the
result of nineteenth century capitulation treaties negotiated with
the sultanate. It was not really surprising, therefore, to find them involved in actions that might land other Moroccans in jail. Nevertheless, their presence conjured up visions of foreign intrigue and ran-
kled the French. Three Italian subjects were arrested for participating
in demonstrations at Casablanca and Fez. At Tangier, Marrakesh,
and Fez, British *protégés* were known to have played an "important
part" in encouraging disobedience to the sultan's commands and
urging recitation of the *latif*.[16]

British and Italian authorities cooperated wholeheartedly with the
French to end the sedition. The British consul sent to Fez a representative who gathered the *protégés* together and threatened them with
loss of their *cartes de protection* should they continue their involvement in the agitation. The Italian government was equally quick to

warn its subjects and *protégés* to stay clear of antigovernment political activities. Still, despite the words and deeds, the French suspected that the British, Italian, and Spanish governments were not unduly distressed at France's predicament. British money and moral support were allegedly behind the violently anti-French actions by the Syro-Palestino-Maghreb Committee of the pan-Islamic guru Chekib Arslan, whose delegate in the French zone was Omar Hadjoui, a British *protégé* residing at Fez. French reports from Tangier and Fez indicated that Muslims under Italian jurisdiction were engaged in subversive activities with the "secret but certain encouragement" of Italian diplomatic agents. Finally, the Spanish, always credited with enjoying the difficulties of their protectorate partners, were accused of not taking strong enough measures to prevent the spread of the anti-French disturbances. The recitation of the *latif* in the Spanish zone, the Arab boycott of French products, and the reception of Arslan in Tetouan were all laid at the doorstep of Spanish officials. To the French, Spanish policy was both "lax" and "shortsighted." Spain and the other European powers had not recognized that the turmoil in Morocco was not only anti-French but anti-European as well.[17]

The scope and violence of Muslim agitation seemed to confirm French concerns. The press of the Middle East conducted a vigorous anti-French drive, playing on themes that had already become familiar. The *dahir* was portrayed as a decisive step in a French plan to extinguish Islam in Morocco and as a lever for French political control. "Regardless of the cost, [the French] must divide-to-rule. Just as in the Middle East, [where] they opposed Lebanon to Syria, they are trying to separate the Berbers and the Arabs."[18] Orchestrated by Arab leaders in Paris and Cairo and by Chekib Arslan in Geneva (where he headed an unofficial delegation to the League of Nations), the campaign made Morocco a front line of pan-Islamic action. The French were convinced that the initial objective was "to involve Morocco in the nationalist and pan-Islamic movement which has been disturbing the Middle East for several years." But in the long run, Morocco was seen only as a pretext for the more important goal of vilifying and weakening France. The protectorate responded to the attacks with public statements in the press and private explanations to French authorities in Algeria, Tunisia, Syria, and Egypt. All the same, the resident was under no illusions. He had little faith that this would still the frenzy of the Muslim world.[19]

Following the "incidents" at Fez, there remained a predictable restlessness among the nationalist youth who continued to find sympathy and financial support from "the most discreet elements" of the urban bourgeoisie. The French attributed the sustained bourgeois backing of the nationalists to more than religious fervor. They saw economic concerns at the heart of the matter. Fez merchants, engaged in commerce with the Berber tribes, were not at all anxious to fall under the jurisdiction of the customary courts. But the unease went deeper than that. At Salé the city economy was at a standstill, partly because of three consecutive years of drought, partly because of strong competition from Japanese imports that pushed Slaoui goods off the market; Slaouis remembered 1930 as the "Year of Japan." It was the beginning of a crisis that would force about one-fourth of Salé's merchants out of business and reduce small merchants and artisans to a subsistence level.[20]

Understandably, this nourished the protest movement. Blanc concluded correctly that the wave of worldwide economic discontent had finally begun to wash over Morocco and that the nationalists and foreign propagandists were riding it against the protectorate. At the same time, he admitted "with regret" that the religious issue, which the French usually dismissed as a "convenient pretext," was not inconsequential. "Influential Muslims could sincerely believe that the government of the protectorate looked without disfavor upon the projects to Christianize the Berbers," given "the imprudent campaign emanating from certain Catholic circles," in particular the "maladroit writings" and "thoughtless actions" of the apostolic vicar of Morocco, Monsignor Henri Vielle. On the religious question, he was forced to conclude that neither the explanations of the sultan nor of the Residency had been entirely convincing. Quiet had returned to the protectorate's cities, but Blanc, no friend of reform from the streets, sounded a somber note: "A new phase of Moroccan history seems to be opening. . . . We know that from now on we shall have to deal with a movement that misrepresents itself as national in scope and feeling. . . . This will require on the part of the government of the protectorate a vigilant attention to all aspects of the administrative and political life of the country."[21]

Because of this experience, the French modified their views on the cities and adopted measures that, when taken together, might be called a strategy for urban pacification. It was conceived and executed by Noguès. At its base was the reluctance to become directly involved in confrontations with city protesters; in consequence, the French delegated to sharifian authorities the tasks of both explaining the *dahir* and restoring order. By lowering their profile and shifting responsibility to the sultan, they hoped to avoid direct attacks on the protectorate and to realize in less happy form the Lyautey commitment to indirect rule through native elites.

Before and after the Fez incidents, the French counted on the "game of patient diplomacy," in which the sultan and the Makhzen would be given "complete authority" to do the trick. But as circumstances proved, the sultan required more than moral influence. He needed force. This the French were willing to permit, in effect turning over the control of the cities to him in a way that military operations elsewhere would never have been. To be sure, the French remained masters of the situation from the barracks and caserns on the sidelines to sustain, aid, and oversee the actions of the sharifian government. But sharifian authorities had some room for movement and decision making in a way that almost surprised the French. The "energy" of the old pasha of Fez and his "rapid" extinction of the agitation delighted them. "We can be sure," the resident reported to Paris, "that Fez will remain calm under his vigilant surveillance." For Abderrahman Bargach, pasha of Rabat, in whose city "the public order had never been disturbed," there was similar praise; the French admired his "firm yet benevolent" stance. The Makhzen's sanctions were a combination of "firmness and moderation," and had the "happy effect" of showing that it could act severely when necessary without losing control or perspective; the resident described the Makhzen as "a government conscious of its force and authority," many steps from the "sweet drowsiness" of Lyautey's day. Surely the glowing report on the results of what the resident called this "enlightened and loyal collaboration of His Majesty the Sultan and his Makhzen" was written with the satisfaction and relief of having navigated difficult waters successfully.[22] It could not be forgotten, however, that the sultan had been moved to tears by the appeal of the Fez delegation, that the Makhzen had at first shown some reluctance in approving the *dahir*, and that the pashas had fired new resentments with their punishments. Nevertheless, it captured the essence of the contribution of the sharifian authorities in the pacification of the cities and the enthusiasm of the French over their accomplishments.

The divide-and-rule concept, so often considered at the core of the "Berber policy," would now be applied to the cities, first to split apart the various groups of urban discontents, who were moved by a variety of religious, economic, political, or family concerns, then to adopt in good Lyautey fashion "a political action appropriate to each" in order to reduce them "one by one." Here the need for information was crucial, and protectorate authorities, always so sure of their knowledge of the Muslim world, were understandably embarrassed at the outbreak and persistence of the unrest and the paucity of their information on the nationalists. After the emergencies of July and August had passed, Noguès requested the commanders of the civil and military regions to "follow very closely" the activities of the opposition groups, gathering information on their origins, organization, and evolution. The protectorate needed to know "in a very precise manner" who the active members and their followers were and the kind and degree of support provided by the rest of the population and by foreign nationals and *protégés*. There could be no better indication of the protectorate's lack of preparedness and the distance that had grown between governors and governed than these directives.[23]

The policy was implemented by combining the penalties of sharifian authorities with the public and private mediations of French officials. Sharifian discipline against the "very small number of individual agitators" had on the whole "a favorable impact" on the city populations because by demonstrating the will and force of the sultan's government, it both frightened and reassured. "The calm which reigns at present in the cities proves that these judicious and moderate sanctions have been completely effective. The sound elements which constitute—and we must not forget it—the immense majority of the population are now totally in control. They regret the thoughtless acts of certain young leaders overexcited by the misguided enthusiasm which swept through the cities." "At no time," Saint added in a later report, "did the action of the Makhzen take the form of a brutal or systematic repression." The resident and Noguès toured the cities with the necessary explanations, reassurances, and promises, and were pleased with the results. "The spontaneity of the welcome given by the Fassis to General Noguès during his recent visit and the cordiality of the conversations he had with the *chorfa* [patrilineal descendants of the Prophet Mohammed], the *oulema*, and the notables of this great Muslim city of the north are characteristic." Nevertheless, Saint detected a continued resistance and "uneasiness" and he was forced to hedge a bit: his appeal to "reasonable men" for confidence in French institutions "was not without success," a positive statement put in a negative way. He was probably right not to put too much stock in the response of the city fathers. Although the Fassis answered with "flowery expressions of gratitude," Le Tourneau believed that they remained what they had been for centuries: "discontents and *frondeurs*." As a final gesture, an amnesty was proclaimed. The agitators were released from prison and those held in forced residence permitted to return home. With regard to the *dahir* itself, the resident assured the minister of foreign affairs that it would be applied with "the most prudent discretion."[24]

A final aspect of the urban strategy dealt with the rural populations, Arab as well as Berber. Throughout the crisis, protectorate officials had reported that the agitation was exclusively an urban phenomenon, "strictly limited to some large Moroccan cities." It had not "penetrated the countryside" nor the Berber lands. Berber tribes appeared "satisfied" with the *dahir* and had expressed their gratitude to the sultan; they remained "faithful subjects of the Makhzen and good Muslims, but [were] happy to keep their local customs." The resident general confirmed that there had been "propaganda attempts" made in the countryside, specifically in the Berber areas, but that they had "come up against a general indifference" and had "no success" whatsoever. Nevertheless, the *délégué général* warned that in the future "our most constant concern must be to prevent the diffusion of the ferment of insubordination throughout the countryside." Had the urban agitation continued unabated, there was always the danger that the mass of ordinary people would sense that "sharifian authority [was] discredited"; should the French appear indifferent to this, anarchy would be the result.[25] Here new stereotypes emerged: the cities were the hotbeds of sedition and revolt, the countryside was the bucolic *bon bled* of trustworthy farmers. This altered the French perceptions of the cleavages in Moroccan society. Now the line of division seemed to be urban-rural rather than Arab-Berber, and although the phrase "Berber policy" never disappeared from the policy maker's lexicon, a new expression entered it—"native rural policy" (*politique indigène rurale*)—which lumped together the Berber and Arabic-speaking tribes for the first time.[26]

What of the validity of the protest and the future of French policy toward the nationalists and their demands for reform? At the time, the nationalists were dismissed as troublemakers, malcontents, or foreign agents, and their protest was blamed on youthful exuberance, subversive propaganda, or economic distress. Few Frenchmen recognized the legitimacy of their concerns or that the very presence of France created an intolerable situation for educated Moroccans; most preferred to explain the outburst over the *dahir* in terms of a "convenient pretext" for revolt. Regardless of how it was explained, no one forgot it. It made a deep impression on Noguès. When he returned to Morocco in 1936, he was still convinced that the nationalists were responsible for the Berber *dahir* incidents and that their ultimate aim was to oust France. He did not believe their professions of loyalty nor that all they wanted was reform. But he had come to see Moroccan nationalism as something inevitable and in that way natural and legitimate, and was willing to try to channel it down paths beneficial to France and the protectorate.

During Noguès's absence, the nationalists built an organization called the National Action bloc (Comité d'Action Marocaine), established a program, and concentrated on winning friends among French political groups in the Metropole. Their principal pursuit was the writing of the celebrated 1934 Plan of Reforms, which Noguès believed was put together "to avoid the criticism that had been leveled against them of engaging in subversive activities and to interest influential elements in French public opinion in their cause." It did create an interest in native Moroccan nationalism that street marches had been unable to do. The plan envisioned the creation of a liberal constitutional monarchy, the establishment of a national council elected by universal suffrage in two stages, and the institution of civil rights and obligatory education. Unstated but clearly implied, according to Noguès, was that the protectorate was merely a mandate, "essentially provisional and revocable." It was rejected by protectorate authorities as "too theoretical to be applied to a hierarchical, traditional Muslim state on the eastern model," that is, incompatible with the French-supported sultanate, but Noguès insisted that it had been "attentively examined" and had served as the inspiration for reforms that had been considered "possible and reasonable."[27] To the nationalist leader Allal el-Fassi, the message was clear: the French would never turn over their obligation as reformers to those for whom the reforms were intended.[28]

Temporarily stalled by the closed doors of the Residency and the ministry of foreign affairs, the nationalists soon regained their spirit and energy because of the dramatic changes in the Mediterranean world. The civil war between Arabs and Jews in Palestine resounded throughout North Africa, renewing fears about the intentions of European imperialists in Islamic countries. At the same time, the Popular Front in France and the military revolt in Spain brought to power political groups pledged to sweeping changes in colonial relations.[29] This was more than enough to buoy the nationalists and intensify their pressure on the protectorate.

The French in Morocco watched with dismay the progress of the nationalists in the schools, their outreach to other social groups, the sympathetic support they received from political organizations in France, and the impact that events in the Spanish zone were having on the population in the protectorate. Koranic schools were tagged the national movement's "kindergartens," where the teachers were

The Residency at Rabat.
Courtesy Verthamon Collection, Paris

"carefully chosen" to implant the nationalist message in the hearts
of their pupils. French schools, even the Muslim Karaouiyne University at Fez, counted many nationalists among their alumni and were
good fishing grounds to hook young activists; their student associations were transparent political groups. Under the leadership of
el-Fassi and el-Ouazzani, and with the aid and advice of European
"extremists," the nationalists had begun to work the artisans and laborers of the cities, who were stung by the economic crisis. "The
French administration," Noguès told Delbos, "is held responsible for
all the problems of the working population." Promising to protect
them and their rights, the nationalists organized collective complaints and demonstrations, protest marches, shop closings, discussion groups, and meetings encouraging a "spirit of hostile opposition
and even of rebellion." As if that were not enough, nationalists
speaking by radio from Tetouan and Seville encouraged their brethren of the French zone to seek the satisfaction of their grievances,
contrasting their "freedom" under Franco with French "oppression,"
fascist strength with French weakness.[30]

In such an atmosphere of "uneasiness and excitement," Noguès
returned to Morocco as resident general. Quite naturally his appoint-

ment occasioned an exchange of letters between the representatives of the National Action bloc, Under Secretary of State for Foreign Affairs Pierre Viénot, and Noguès himself. This was an opportunity for the nationalists to explain themselves once again, to recall their understanding of the commitments made in the past, and perhaps to gain the government's pledge to act in the ways that they wanted. Omar Abdeljalil and Mohammed el-Ouazzani reminded Viénot that shortly after the Popular Front had taken office in May he had spoken warmly and enthusiastically of the reforms planned for Morocco and promised that as soon as the Syrian problem was solved he would turn to Morocco. Syria had now been granted independence, which was guaranteed by a treaty of alliance and friendship with France. In addition, Morocco had been given a resident general named by the Popular Front, thereby ensuring that whatever decisions were made in Paris would not be blocked in Rabat. "The time has come, *Monsieur le Ministre,* for the Popular Front government to take the necessary steps to implement our Plan of Reforms, which was sponsored by persons supporting the Popular Front, some of whom belong to the present cabinet . . . and to respond to our immediate grievances." First, they asked for the appointment of a committee composed of representatives of the French administration and the National Action bloc to study the Plan of Reforms and any counterproposals of the French government. Second, they requested the government to authorize all the democratic freedoms, including freedom of the press and of education. In this regard, el-Ouazzani and Abdeljalil pointed out that in the Spanish zone, even under a military regime and in wartime, freedom of speech, freedom of the press, and the right to assemble were respected and that Spanish authorities seemed resolved to grant autonomy to their part of the protectorate. "It is truly regrettable that we are reduced to such a level of inferiority in comparison to other protectorates and colonies that we envy the situation of our brothers of the Rif under a military dictatorship in time of war." Recalling the words of Léon Blum on his faith in democratic liberties and their own "indescribable joy" at the political victory of the Popular Front, which was "for us the equivalent of the Great French Revolution in which we all believe and of which we all hope to be the beneficiaries," the authors asked for a "decisive answer" to their requests.[31]

Viénot responded politely but evasively. To be sure, there was much that was justified in their demands and he was always ready to hear the legitimate requests of the Moroccan people. But the French government would never impose a reform plan on the sharifian state that had been drawn up as a political action proposal by a study group or even discuss it officially with those who wrote it. Rephrasing a Popular Front line that had by then become apology, he wrote: "No political group, whether in Morocco or France, can pretend to act for the Nation as a whole." It was for the resident general, together with the Makhzen, to prepare such reform programs: this was in fact the raison d'être of the protectorate. "Take up your concerns with Noguès," Viénot told them, "you will be certain to find him a most attentive listener."[32]

The message was interpreted to mean, perhaps unfairly, that France's policy in Morocco would continue as before with changes in style but not in substance. Boldly, Abdeljalil and el-Ouazzani challenged Viénot's closing remark. "You are undoubtedly aware, *Monsieur le Ministre*, that the Popular Front's representative is no stranger to the Moroccan people. To put it plainly, as *directeur général des 'affaires indigènes,'* General Noguès became acquainted with those of us involved in the events of 1930–1931 over the protectorate's 'Berber' policy. We mention this without bitterness, only to document our old ties with the resident general."[33] There was apprehension at the Popular Front's choice of Noguès. Had he been chosen to keep the colonists at bay while the business of colonial emancipation was carried out, or did his selection mean the abandonment of reform? The two Moroccans told Viénot that they had written Noguès and received the following: "For almost a quarter of a century I have been very closely associated with the material and moral protection that France has afforded the sharifian empire and am willing under every circumstance to study in good faith the possibilities of the practical realization of your suggestions in light of the general requirements of the evolution of the country." It was noncommittal but encouraging. Its impact was "somewhat diminished," they said, by Noguès's public statements to follow the lead of his predecessors, his comments to the press about the plight of the "impoverished European" in Morocco, and his speech at Fez in which he referred to the nationalists as "youngsters" and "rowdy children" whose parents ought to keep them in tow until they were better behaved.[34] It had to be admitted that there was a striking discordance between Noguès's public and private words that only increased the nationalists' fears about the future.

The representatives returned to Morocco emptyhanded and discouraged. While Noguès was still in Paris, they began a public campaign at home, convinced that all their efforts for the past year and a half had been "in vain."[35] Mass meetings in Fez and Salé in Novem-

ber attracted people from "all classes in the population and every artisan corporation." At Casablanca a gathering was planned for 14 November to which European journalists and political personalities
had been invited. No doubt this was to be a showcase affair to demonstrate that the nationalists were serious about reform, to dissipate
the rumors circulating through the European community about
their violent designs, and to prove that they had support within the
Moroccan populace.[36]

On the morning of the fourteenth, the word was passed that the
sultan, who was in Casablanca at the time, approved of the meeting
and would send a message to those present. Alerted by the municipal authorities, Délégué Général René Thierry visited the sultan for
explanations. Knowing nothing about the meeting and angry at the
use of his name, Sidi Mohammed decided "spontaneously" to forbid
it. In consequence, the entrance to the meeting hall on Boulevard
Victor Hugo was blocked and the crowd ordered to disperse.[37] The
Europeans left the scene. But amid shouts of "Long live the sultan"
and "Long live Islam," the "noisy and threatening" group moved off
the boulevard toward the south gate of the palace. One of the meeting's organizers, Mohammed el-Ouazzani, was heard to call out
"obey the police," but he was drowned out by yells of "Long live the
people."

After chants before the palace, the demonstrators (numbering
close to one thousand) marched down Rue de Langemark toward
Parc Murdoch in the French city with el-Ouazzani, Allal el-Fassi,
and Mohamed Lyazidi vainly trying to convince them to stop and go
home. Unable to make themselves heard, they directed the cortege
back toward Boulevard Victor Hugo by way of Rue du Général Hum-
bert. At the intersection of the two streets, several unarmed *gardiens de la paix* blocked the way. The nationalist leaders turned the
column to avoid contact with the police and halted the march at
a vacant lot between the New Mosque (later the Moulay Youssef
Mosque) and the boulevard, where again the leaders asked the people to disband, aware that the *gardiens* were being reinforced by
armed gendarmes. After a half hour of animated discussion under
the eyes of the police, the group broke up "without causing the
slightest incident." El-Ouazzani was arrested on the spot at the instruction of the sultan, and orders were issued for the arrest of el-
Fassi, Lyazidi, and Mohamed Chemao. Lyazidi surrendered, el-Fassi
was apprehended the next morning, but Chemao was not found.[38]

The nationalists were as surprised and distressed at the turn of
events as the authorities were. The crowd's angry mood was fash-

ioned by circumstances and was not of their making, although they
surely must have anticipated the sultan's reaction and the effect of
the meeting's cancellation on those present. Their lack of foresight
and their helplessness to control events were hardly proof of their
leadership ability. The showcase meeting had been turned into a
shambles, confirming fears rather than dispelling them. Still, although el-Ouazzani was no hero, he was no scoundrel either—to his
credit he had succeeded in avoiding violence—and his arrest along
with the arrests of his comrades, although understandable, grated.
The nationalists felt that they were being struck with "arbitrary"
measures and could not believe that General Noguès was aware of
what was happening. As for the sultan, they were certain that he had
been "misled" by the French.[39]

The next evening the sultan called Thierry to his residence and
told him "with a remarkable firmness and precision" that he blamed
the French for the Casablanca incidents; they were the logical consequence of the series of meetings held by the nationalists, meetings
that "had provoked no reaction from the authorities." Thus encouraged, young Moroccans had thought the way clear to organize demonstrations with ever increasing boldness, drawing larger crowds
and attracting those previously uninvolved in protest. This time
they had even used his name and authority, pretending that he had
encouraged their activities. "I could not tolerate it," the sultan exploded. "I let my subjects know that they have been misled and I
forbade any demonstration. What is more, I ordered the arrest of the
principal organizers." He then posed the question to the startled
delegate, who reproduced the sultan's phrases exactly for the ministry of foreign affairs: "Now I want to know what you plan to do. I am
ready to punish those who not only are agitators but have outraged
their sovereign. The evil must be destroyed while there is time; if
not," and here the delegate underscored for emphasis, "*Morocco is
lost*." The sultan remarked angrily that the nationalists had taken it
upon themselves to speak in the name of the Moroccan people.
"They are usurpers. Have they received their authority from the sultan, from the protector state? Or even from a fraction of the Moroccan people? Are they *oulema*? For my part, I think it is necessary to
deal severely. But if, for reasons unknown to us, the French government should feel otherwise, I will not insist, but I must tell you that
in such a case"—and again Thierry underlined the sultan's words—
"*I will not be responsible for what happens, for things can only get
worse*." The sultan was convinced that this was "a turning point"
and wanted the French government and General Noguès to be fully

Sidi Mohammed ben Youssef,
sultan of Morocco, 1927–1957; king of Morocco, 1957–1961.
Photo Jacques Belin

informed of his feelings. As for the penalties for those arrested and
who were at present being held under the pasha's watchful care, he
suggested banishment from the cities.[40]

Without doubt grieved at the nationalists' insult and at what he
judged the lack of French support, the sultan sought to use the moment both to express his displeasure and to firm up France's commitment to himself and the sharifian state. He too wondered what
changes the Popular Front had in store for Morocco and what impact
the nationalists were having on socialist circles in Paris. Since his
political authority was in large part the result of French bayonets
and since the entire structure of native government worked in sym-

biosis with the protectorate administration, challenges to this system, regardless if they were couched in professions of loyalty to the sultan, inevitably threatened sharifian authority and control. Despite his sensitivity to the pleas of nationalist groups and his intervention at times on their behalf (as he did when the French considered exiling the authors of the Plan of Reforms), he realized that a Morocco molded in the image of the Plan of Reforms would be a state wherein his power would be severely curtailed. Certainly the French were aware of all this. Three years earlier, Ponsot had described as a "dangerous game" the sultan's desire for the support of France but refusal to break completely with the nationalists. Some even thought that the sultan wanted the French to move strongly against the nationalists so that he could later emerge as their shield.[41]

Thierry answered as carefully as he could. He thought that the sultan ought not to overreact to what were, after all, only "the deeds of young people who were far from having the masses behind them." Still, they had committed a "serious injury" to his person and for that he felt the proposed punishment was merited. He also assured the sultan that the French government and General Noguès would do whatever had to be done to safeguard his prestige. In his telegram to Paris, Thierry stressed the importance of the conversation. "We have very good relations with him and it is essential that he remains well disposed toward us." He summarized the sultan's concern about the nationalists and over his loss of authority and prestige, and then, perhaps to prod Paris to take the sort of action he felt warranted, he concluded: "For the moment [the sultan] depends on us, but if he perceives some hesitation on our part, he will quickly lose confidence [in us] and completely change his position." This was certainly the message that the sultan wanted to get across and Thierry endorsed it.[42]

Viénot answered by charting the course that the Popular Front hoped to follow in Moroccan affairs. He was glad to see the sultan take such a clear stand against the "separatist" nationalists who had "always wanted to use him in the action against the protectorate," and he considered it an "absolute necessity" to preserve his authority. Yét the government had no intention of letting itself become boxed in by "the dilemma that so many powers have encountered in their colonial policy: either to tolerate abuses or to grant independence." The government rejected the notion that the protectorate could maintain itself solely by forgoing "its essential duty" to institute reforms. It was thus "impossible" to imagine that France would ever permit the restoration of an "arbitrary" central authority freed from France's tutelage, if that was what the sultan expected, even if that power bound itself heart and soul to France. It was important to remember that a good many of the nationalists' demands, "inspired moreover by [the Popular Front's] own program," were "justified" and would have to be taken into consideration if France wanted to avoid violent confrontations in the streets. The government's plan was to detach the "separatist extremists" from the majority of Morocco's youth, who still needed France's guidance, and to work with the latter to shape the future of the protectorate. Collaboration with the Moroccan people would thus be extended far beyond the confines of the "old Makhzen," and since France wanted to do this "in full agreement with the sultan," he would have "to prepare himself to go forward with us." In the future, therefore, punishments of the sort meted out to the nationalists at Casablanca would be "very inopportune," for they would push them into the arms of those who wanted a Morocco without France or the sultan. For the time being, Viénot concluded, this policy ought not to be presented to the sultan because it might "frighten" him. "You can give him the assurance that, faithful to the letter and spirit of the treaty of protectorate, we will undertake to safeguard the 'traditional prestige' of the sovereign [and] pursue in confident collaboration with him the work of reform and in so doing triumph over moral dissidence, as we have in the past over armed dissidence, through action." Thierry was also told to point out to the sultan that stiff penalties for those who had not disrupted the public order risked making martyrs of them and stirring up other malcontents, which would only make matters worse.[43]

This was precisely what happened. After the midday prayers at the Djemaa Chleuh Mosque in Casablanca on 17 November, two hundred demonstrators marched through the Place de France and onto the Boulevard de la Gare headed for the sultan's palace. At Place Nicolas-Paquet a *contrôleur civil* and twenty *gardiens de la paix* blocked their path, but the marchers shoved him aside and attacked the police line with empty bottles taken from a parked wine van. One officer was thrown to the ground and manhandled "rather severely." The group was broken up in short order. Six of the demonstrators, judged "the most aggressive and the most incorrect," were arrested. As they were being hustled into the police wagon, one of the prisoners turned and slapped the *contrôleur* in the face. Here was a story worth retelling. Director of Municipal Services Jean Courtin believed it was "extremely serious from the point of view of our authority and our prestige. It is the first time that we have seen in incidents of this type demonstrators not only resist French authority but also strike one of its representatives."[44]

Those who had escaped the police at Nicolas-Paquet reformed their procession closer to the sultan's palace and with new recruits emerged on the palace square three hundred strong. Four men at the head of the column were immediately arrested and the police scattered the others while being bombarded with stones. Later that evening, the police were called out once again, this time to clear the area around the Dar el-Makhzen, where two or three hundred young Moroccans had gathered to protest the sixteen arrests made during the day.[45]

The Casablanca events were duplicated in Rabat, where an attempted march was disrupted and five marchers arrested, and at Salé, where demonstrators left the mosques after prayers carrying banners demanding freedom of the press. In Fez the troubles were probably the worst. After the prayers at the Karaouiyne Mosque, a train of five hundred persons wound its way through the medina, halting at two other mosques to pick up sympathizers. At the last stop, the pasha's *mokhazenis* (native policemen), who had barricaded the route, were pelted with rocks. Troops of the Fez garrison were alerted, but in the end order was restored without their intervention. One hundred and forty demonstrators were arrested.[46] "Odious insults, assault and battery, nothing was spared by the police, the *assès* [the pasha's guards], and even certain khalifs of the pasha of Fez," the nationalists recounted. "Half-dead men were led to prison on the backs of donkeys in Fez; others were dragged in the mud like assassins."[47] Not surprisingly, all of the demonstrations on the seventeenth followed an identical pattern: they occurred at the same hour and had been preceded by speeches and "specially chosen prayers" in the mosques. In this "concerted action" French authorities saw the hands of the nationalists at work on a plan "carefully prepared in advance by what amounts to local subcommittees in various cities of Morocco." Noguès later noted that it was "the first time that such a command [had been] followed so fully and earnestly."[48]

Assessing the disturbances, Thierry concluded that their impact was more striking among Europeans than Moroccans. The press sounded an "alarmist note" reflecting the concern over the increasing anti-French propaganda that had begun to make inroads among the artisans. "We must stop those who would sow the wind for we will reap the whirlwind. And the whirlwind is blind and savage, sparing nothing and no one." The Casablanca Municipal Council sent an urgent message to Noguès demanding that "the most ener-

getic measures be taken immediately to put an end to the unfortu-
nate and dangerous agitation." Outside the major cities (in Settat, for
example, south of Casablanca), the unrest was known to only a "few
notables" and then imperfectly. But as the European press rightly
understood from its reporters in the streets, the arrests on the fourteenth had made a "strong impression" on the Muslim inhabitants
of the city. (In point of fact, the 17 November demonstration was
the first in which the artisans took an active part.) French authorities agreed. Contrôleur Civil Émile Orthlieb, head of the Chaouïa
region, wrote of the Casablanca events: "They constitute a particularly important stage in the evolution of the Moroccan nationalist
movement."[49]

The working out of French policy was never without its difficulties. Thierry reported to Viénot that he had met with the sultan and
explained the government's concern about harsh penalties against
the Casablanca demonstrators and the need to distinguish between
the reasonable requests of educated young people and the outra-
geous demands of separatist agitators. Surely the most powerful argument was that what Viénot had predicted had come true. "Without going too deeply into the matter in our conversation, the sultan
seemed favorable to these principles and I think that he is prepared
for the future conversations that he will have with General Noguès
on this subject." The sultan had agreed to await Noguès's return before deciding what to do about those arrested. Thierry nevertheless
backed up the sultan's independent action at Casablanca. He was
sure that the sovereign was not trying to wiggle free from French tutelage. "But his person was involved and it was impossible for him to
remain indifferent to this attack. From our side, we could not, by virtue of the treaty of protectorate, object to the measures that he
wanted to apply since 'the respect and the traditional prestige' of the
sultan was at stake. This is what the Casablanca authorities understood immediately and I approved their action entirely when they
consulted me."

Viénot had already expressed his disapproval of the course they
had taken. To make matters worse, Thierry revealed that the sharifian authorities had given those arrested in the Casablanca, Rabat,
and Fez disorders of 17 November prison sentences ranging from fifteen days to one year. In addition, after renewed violence at the Karaouiyne Mosque on 20 November, which resulted in thirty arrests,
the Fez authorities handed out prison terms of from three to six
months; for certain second-time offenders, the terms were as long as
two years. Viénot was furious. The sentences were "excessively re-

pressive" and had made his task more difficult. Since the government had no intention of inflicting harsh punishments on the leaders of the National Action bloc, as Viénot had thought he had made clear, how could their followers be treated differently? In the second place, such repression compromised the implementation of "desirable reforms and risks putting us in contradiction with ourselves."[50] Viénot, who proudly called himself one of Lyautey's disciples because he had served on Lyautey's civil staff in Morocco from 1921 to 1923, needed no introduction to the realities of Morocco. But despite goodwill and the best of intentions, events and decisions made on the spot had narrowed his ability to shape Morocco's relations with France.

On Noguès's return to Rabat, he analyzed the situation, then sided with Thierry, convinced that the "energetic measures" taken in his absence had "avoided an aggravation of the disorders and calmed the uneasiness of the European and even the Moroccan population." He was certain that the nationalists had taken advantage of his trip to France to create a "state of agitation," and he accepted the sentences imposed on the demonstrators by the sharifian authorities. His meeting with the sultan, who expressed himself "with great firmness," resembled Thierry's conference with him at the height of the crisis. "I found before me," Noguès wrote, "a man determined not to have his prerogatives challenged and disturbed at the pattern of these demonstrations, particularly those outside the palace, which he did not hesitate to call 'revolts' and 'revolutions.'" The sultan could not accept the notion that these men, who had raised the cry for a "holy war," had good intentions. Only "a firm attitude" could spare Morocco from further disorders, and he called on France "to fulfill the obligations that we have contracted by the treaty of protectorate." "I do not see any possibility of getting around this request so clearly expressed by the sultan," Noguès reported to Viénot. "The risk would not only be to lose the benefit of the sultan's loyalty in the present circumstances, but even the principle of the protectorate would be called into question." He recommended the continuation of "the policy of firmness . . . imposed on us by the conjuncture of events," a plan that he hoped would lead to a "calmed atmosphere" in which to begin the work of reform.[51]

Fez had been the scene of the worst disturbances and it was there that he started. In his published remarks, there was much of the parent-child dialogue that had so exasperated the nationalists in the past, but notwithstanding the tone, Noguès conducted serious business with the pasha and the native leaders on the morning of 28 November and with the *oulema*, members of the Medjlis, the chambers of commerce and agriculture, the native welfare society, and representatives of all the corporations of Fez in the afternoon. These personal contacts, treasured by Lyautey as an essential part of a successful colonial policy but uncomfortable for his successors, were revived by Noguès as the prime element in his relations with the Moroccan elite. He promised new schools and clinics and, perhaps most important, the abolition of certain "vexing" taxes on housing, rented space, and merchandising. For the artisans, whose receptivity to the agitation bothered him, he pledged something akin to a cooperative for purchases and sales with the resources to advance credit and make loans to its members. He believed this had achieved a "détente" with the Fassis. To buck up Viénot, understandably discouraged at the Moroccan happenings, Noguès added in his report: "I had the satisfaction besides of verifying the perfectly loyal attitude of the members of the Association des Anciens Élèves du Collège Musulman de Fès who spontaneously told me of their devotion to France. They represent an excellent social group on which our policy toward the young people can easily be based." [52]

In Fez, Noguès conferred with Contrôleur Civil Rosario Pisani, on whose suggestions he had relied for the reforms he announced. Pisani recommended the authorization of private meetings and asked the resident to consider freeing the press, but Noguès was unwilling to commit himself to more than he had already. On matters of politics, Pisani reported that the pasha was a man of "fine qualities" and loyal to France but that he ought to act with "more adeptness toward certain old Makhzen families. . . . [If] well advised, the pasha would be loved and [could] render signal services to the sultan and the protectorate." On the distressing side was the information Pisani had on the foreign sources of the funds of the National Action bloc and the action of foreign *protégés* in the Fez disturbances. He revealed that large sums of money had been promised the nationalists by the German and Italian consulates at Tetouan (fifteen thousand francs from each). Of the *protégés*, three under English protection and one under the protection of the United States were of greatest concern. The latter, Abdelkadar el-Leujd, an enthusiast of direct action, had all the rug merchants "in hand" and was often seen at the head of their group in demonstrations. The brothers Hassan and Ahmed Bouayed worked among the corporations, recruiting demonstrators and speaking against France, while Omar Hadjoui supplied money and advice. In his message to Paris, Noguès added the names of Ahmed Mekouar and Abdelkadar Berrada to the list of enemies of France under the foreign umbrella. Viénot responded by telling Noguès that he should do what he deemed necessary to end the foreign influence and protection of the nationalists, but only after he had conclusive proof. "Several times of late I have had the opportunity to mention to London the activities of certain powers in the vicinity of the protectorate (Balearic Islands, Canary Islands, Spanish zone), pointing out that they not only compromise the security of our establishment in North Africa but also British communications. If we have proof that Tetouan is distributing subsidies to foment trouble in the French zone, our case would be strengthened."[53]

Noguès's visit to Fez ended without mention of those imprisoned as a result of the demonstrations. He was also silent on the fate of the three arrested in Casablanca still awaiting sentencing by the Haut Tribunal Chérifien (a secular high court of appeals for Muslims). He had already obtained the sultan's halfhearted consent for some measures of clemency with which the French, in the manner of Lyautey, always liked to sweeten the process of reconciliation, but it was not firm enough to act on. What he wanted, as a fitting conclusion to the "moderating action" he had begun at Fez, was for the sultan to liberate the majority of the offenders and to reduce the penalties of the rest. In the end the sultan agreed, but only after Noguès had arranged for a delegation of notables and artisans from Fez to come to Rabat and humbly petition their sovereign for the acts of grace. They did more than that, explaining the outburst as an expression of "national feeling" and a desire for social reform and insisting that it was neither directed against France nor supported by foreign governments. "This audience took on more importance because His Majesty, who received the delegation alone (although I had thought that at least the grand vizier and Si Mammeri would be present), was very touched by this gesture. Firm at the beginning, he then promised, in agreement with me, that extensive measures of clemency would be considered if calm was maintained."[54] At the same time, the sultan had a letter prepared to be read in the mosques, affirming (as he had done before but to no avail) their essentially religious character and forbidding any political meeting within their walls.

The problem of the "Casablanca Three" was more delicate. Noguès was certain that if the Haut Tribunal, which began hearing the case on 7 December, decided on prison terms, Fez would explode. In a French court he felt sure the offenders would be acquitted. After gathering as much information as he could in private conversations with native leaders, including a secret meeting with the nationalist

Ahmed Mekouar, he informed Viénot that he would urge the sultan to use his right of *nafi* to exile the three from the major cities for a while, an appropriate punishment and one acceptable to public opinion. Should he fail, he would try "to influence" the Haut Tribunal to get it to render a similar sentence. "It seems to me essential to maintain calm at Fez. New incidents would inevitably produce new sanctions, delaying the moment when the sultan could take the desired measures of clemency, and would aggravate even more the present misunderstanding." Even so, despite the seriousness of the situation at Fez that Noguès forthrightly admitted he still did not have completely "under control," the sultan's meeting with the Fez delegation had complicated matters further. Rumor had it that the promised clemency would be close to a complete amnesty, which had had the effect of forcing the French to consider even broader measures than they thought justified and which risked "being seen as a sign of weakness and a blow against the authority of the pashas." After a period of détente, "given the intensification of foreign propaganda at Fez, there is reason to fear that we will experience new and equally serious difficulties."[55] The interplay of events, interpretations, rumors, misunderstandings, and distortions unavoidably conditioned the appropriate responses at any given moment.

In summarizing the "regrettable incidents" that had so inauspiciously launched Noguès's residency, French authorities returned to the patterns of the Berber *dahir* crisis. First there were the nationalists and the urban nature of the unrest. "The National Action bloc [seemed] determined to move to direct action after having minutely prepared in advance the program of its propaganda meetings like a European political party. . . . Outside of Casablanca, Rabat, Salé, Fez, and Oujda, the movement did not affect any other urban center and the rural populations remained totally indifferent." Then there was the nationalists' use of the mosques to assemble their followers out of the reach of the authorities, "to inflame them with recitations from verses in the Koran hostile to infidels and with violent speeches," and to spread propaganda among groups in the population hard hit by the economic crisis, in this case city merchants and artisans. Finally, there were spiritual, financial, and physical links to the international scene: pan-Arabism, money from abroad, and foreign *protégés*.[56]

Once again, the French had remained in the wings, aiding, advising, overseeing. The actors had been the Moroccans. But strangely absent in the reports was the list of achievements of the sharifian authorities, the praise for their resolution, determination, and loyalty that had earlier dotted the papers on the Berber *dahir*. There was a good reason. Paris did not want to be reminded of the initiatives of the sultan and his government. Although it was good politics for the nationalists to portray the sultan as the unwilling instrument of the French—the *machine à dahir*—and much later for the partisans of the monarchy to accept that version of history, it did not correspond with the facts. In reality the sultan emerged as a resolute and willful monarch, much changed from the weeping sovereign of the Berber *dahir* although still sensitive to the pleas of his subjects, jealous of his prerogatives, eager to rule, and prepared to use the French to gain his own ends, which were, at that moment, contrary to those of the nationalists.

Once calm had been restored to the streets of Morocco's cities, Viénot outlined his plans and concerns for Morocco to Noguès in a long letter, typed for security reasons by "an absolutely reliable person." His main worry was the renewal of German influence as a result of the political changes in the Spanish zone. For the first six months of 1937, France would be crossing a "terribly dangerous zone" when Germany's military strength would be relatively greater than that of Britain and France combined. Although the German high command seemed reluctant to risk war, Hitler and the National Socialist party were impressed with the results of brinkmanship, so recently demonstrated by the French backdown in the Rhineland crisis of March 1936, and "influential German circles" were once again "taken with the illusion of the short war." Morocco was a natural spot for German intervention and a convenient casus belli, regardless of the outcome of the Spanish war, for either the victorious republicans would abandon the zone, opening it to German penetration, or the triumphant nationalists would invite the Germans to use it "as a sort of *place d'armes* from which to threaten our North Africa either through propaganda or military means." In either case, France would have to act. But once determined for action, at what precise moment would the government choose to intervene? The burden of timing would be on France, and the prospect weighed heavily on Viénot, who would be called upon for advice in this crucial matter. "And, if we waited too long," he thought out loud to Noguès, "wouldn't it be impossible to act militarily to occupy the Spanish zone, should we decide on it?" The sudden intrusion of foreign policy and military matters to perplex the Paris policymakers further complicated the Popular Front's Moroccan policy.

Given the dangers he had explained, Viénot told Noguès that Morocco had "*to 'hold together' during the coming year*," which meant "a new orientation [in policy] to cut the ground from under the feet of nationalism." Everything, he ordered, was to be "subordinated to this necessity." *"For the moment the Frenchmen in Morocco do not count.* Their petty commercial interests [in parentheses Viénot wrote, then crossed out, that he had almost put *intérêts d'exploiteurs* instead of *intérêts d'exploitants*] are nothing compared to the larger French interest which is at stake. Morocco must be governed *for* the Moroccans (which is the way to assure its loyalty) and some decisive measures must prove it. Native policy presently is more important—much more—than all the rest." It was a strong, almost hysterical statement of policy, in conformity with his previously expressed reform priorities but now made urgently and desperately clear because of the foreign menace. Returning for a moment to military and political questions, Viénot concluded: "Finally we must be militarily prepared for every eventuality . . . and do not hesitate . . . to ask for what you need. Morocco has become one of the critical points in the world on the international and French scene and from the standpoint of our military and political force. You can count on me to make that understood. We must see things as they are: the life of our country depends on it."[57]

This was an important switch. Noguès's appointment had been seen as a sign of firmness and reconciliation, a sword that would tolerate no nonsense from excitable nationalists or foreign meddlers and an olive branch that reassured colonists who feared a flood of social reforms. Reform was to be postponed (not abandoned) until the Popular Front felt secure at home and abroad. But despite four months of a deteriorating internal and external situation, government policy had been changed. Now, having witnessed the nationalists' bitter and violent reaction to its plans, Paris argued that reforms alone would keep Morocco together and safe from foreign predators.

Following instructions, the resident immediately authorized the freedom of the press that had been at the top of the nationalists' list of demands. This, coupled with the sultan's amnesty, was interpreted by the nationalists as a signal victory for their cause. They announced the transformation of the National Action bloc into the National Action party and began a membership drive to build a mass organization, precisely the course that Viénot had hoped they would not take. The French saw the construction of a political organization on the totalitarian pattern in the blueprints for a disciplined, centralized party with recruitment centers in every major city, whose members swore a secret oath "incontestably contrary to the sovereignty of the sultan and the traditional principles of Islam." Even

Noguès and Grand Vizier Mohammed el-Mokri. Rabat, 1937.
Courtesy Verthamon Collection, Paris

though it had been illegal, the existence of the National Action bloc
had been tolerated; the party would not be. With regret Noguès ordered the party dissolved by vizierial decree (18 March 1937), a decision he justified privately because the nationalist influence was now
penetrating the tribes. The fears of six years before were now coming
to pass. Délégué Général Jean Morize, who replaced Thierry, made
the danger crystal clear to Foreign Minister Delbos: "To permit the

Noguès and Moulay Hassan (Hassan II), the sultan's elder son.
Seated on Noguès's right: Délégué Général Jean Morize. Rabat, 1937.
Courtesy Verthamon Collection, Paris

contamination of the *bled* is without any exaggeration to place our
establishment in Morocco in peril."[58] Reform had made matters
worse, which to some may have seemed paradoxical. But the French,
brought up on the history of the Great Revolution, ought to have remembered that concessions made at a moment of weakness only encouraged new demands.

The outlawed party was secretly reconstituted in April as the
National Party for the Realization of the Plan of Reforms (*el-Hizb el-
Ouatani li Tahqiq el-Matalib*) under the presidency of Allal el-Fassi.
Through its policies and leaders, the underground group continued
the action of its above-ground predecessor with one important exception. El-Ouazzani resigned as secretary general and with other
defectors formed a rival party. The French imagined that the rift indicated serious doctrinal differences and disputes about money; and
later commentators have seen disagreements over strategy as the
main bone of contention between the two. Halstead concluded, as

the French ultimately did, that "the chief factor was temperamental incompatiblity," an inability of the men to get along amicably.[59] Whatever the reason for the split, the French were glad for it, even though the aim of the two groups was identical—the emancipation of Morocco—and their methods differed but slightly.

For a time the nationalists remained quiet. Then, at the end of July, the sultan received a flurry of deferential telegrams from cities all over the empire signed by the former local representatives of the National Action bloc on behalf of a *section locale* of the new Moroccan national party, all of which were published in the nationalist press. Most of them mentioned the sons of the sultan and one referred to the elder as "the heir apparent," which, "given the present laws of succession in Morocco, constituted almost an innovation and a shrewd move toward Sidi Mohammed." The purpose was to demonstrate that the nationalists were still alive and loyal to their sovereign, and to test the Residency's tolerance. The French were aware that the nationalists were on the move, particularly in Fez and Marrakesh, where their offices had discreetly been reopened and their presence had been noted in street incidents. Reluctant to begin the process of arrests, seizures, and closings again, Morize informed el-Fassi through the head of the Fez region that he was flirting with danger and ought to shut down his political operations. While admitting that he had been imprudent, el-Fassi claimed that he had the right to set up a political party on the European democratic style rather than of the association type that had so troubled the authorities. Morize made it clear that this would not be tolerated, and, should the nationalists ignore his warnings, they would suffer the consequences. The sultan agreed. Morize reported that despite the telegrams of loyalty, the sovereign "took the illegal opening of the Fez office as a personal affront and earnestly desired measures to be taken against Allal el-Fassi and his lieutenants at the slightest infraction of the law."[60]

At the same time, Morize confirmed that what the French most feared with the authorization of the nationalist press was happening. "I am shocked," he confided to Noguès, "at the more and more aggressive tone of the nationalist press." The nationalists had not kept their promise to use discretion in their journalism and to refrain from personal attacks against the representatives of the Makhzen. The ties of authority in the towns and villages were being undone. "The mentality of our protégés is such that they cannot conceive of their leaders being attacked in such a manner without these campaigns having the support or approval of either the Makhzen or the

protectorate. It is reasonable to fear that in a short time the authority of the *caïds* and pashas will be compromised and the population
will believe that the true representatives of the Makhzen are the nationalist agents." More serious was the progress of the nationalists
in the countryside, and here Morize summarized the correspondence of the regional heads (*chefs de région*) and the impressions
from his last inspection tour in the Central Atlas and Tafilalet. Nationalist emissaries were being sent out from the cities to inquire
among the tribes about individual grievances. Tribesmen with real
or imagined complaints (most often about market taxes), fretful
minor officials, or troubled merchants were directed to the local
nationalist-in-residence, who took their cases to the appropriate
officer at the *cercle, territoire,* or *région* level. As redressors-of-
grievances and interceders-in-high-places, the nationalists sought
to break the traditional chain of control, substituting their authority
for that of tribal leaders and the *contrôleurs* and officers of native
affairs. "By so doing," Noguès wrote to Delbos, "the nationalist
movement demonstrates that its first objective is to destroy the
structure of native leadership which permits France to govern this
country."[61]

The nationalists were meeting with success. French reports indicated that they had found adherents in the Beni Yazrha, Cheraya,
Marmoucha, and Tsoul tribes and in the Beni Ouarain, Hayaina,
Zaër, and Zemmour confederations. Among the Beni Yazrha, both
the khalif and *caïd* had been personally assaulted, the latter "gravely
wounded." A subsequent investigation revealed that "a good part of
the population had been urged to revolt by violent diatribes from agitators taking orders from Fez." According to the head of the Taza territory, there was a definite anti-Makhzen prejudice among the tribes
in his area and an almost mystical attraction to Allal el-Fassi as a
leader figure. He reported that nationalist followers were usually
younger adults of modest social standing—*chorfa,* former *goumiers*
(native soldiers), and those who had attended Koranic schools—but
few notables and recruits (in marked contrast to the situation at the
time of the Berber *dahir*) were coming exclusively from the Berber
tribes; the Arabic-speaking tribes were "far less contaminated." Nationalist propaganda, which played on economic difficulties, religious feeling, xenophobia, or simply the longing for independence
and adventure, was creating in the tribes "a most dangerous spirit of
dissidence."[62] Morize warned rural officials to be on their guard, ordering them to oust nationalist agents foreign to their area and to
refuse to hear cases presented by persons who were not members of

the tribe. "We must put up barricades," explained Colonel Albert Mellier, the assistant *directeur général des affaires politiques*, "to protect our tribes from any propaganda and any action which tends to increase nationalist activity."[63]

At Fez, Morize complained that French leadership was confused and that General Blanc was not acting quickly enough to close down nationalist operations. The general had spoken with el-Fassi and el-Ouazzani on 21 August and received their promise, given "without any hesitation," to stop organizing tribal protests, but he had done nothing about the illegally constituted party. Noguès, who was in France, thought the matter urgent enough to send Morize to Fez. "I had it in mind to go but I hesitated," Morize wrote in reply. "For I know your particular solicitude for this city and I feared it might displease you if I got myself directly involved in this matter. I am glad that you asked me to go." After his conversations at Fez, he remained "disturbed" about the situation. "Just as you wrote me, there is no leadership in this city. General Blanc does not yet have a sure footing. He seems like a cat walking on hot bricks. . . . At bottom there is no doctrine nor team spirit at Fez. It is indispensable that this change. . . . [W]hat we need for the general, who has his strong points, but lacks fire, is a *contrôleur civil* who is both brilliant and an Arabist."[64] Morize's diagnosis was probably correct because he was known for his hardheaded and thorough analyses, but unfortunately the tension could not be eased before violence erupted again.

The beginnings of tribal unrest did not take the pressure off the cities, which were in a "state of tension" almost unknown since the beginning of the protectorate. Instead of awaiting events or being swept along by them, the nationalist party was now strong and disciplined enough to pick the time and place of its next protest. After a summer of drought, with the northern cities crowded with refugees fleeing the the famine of the south, Meknès—unaffected by serious disorders since the Berber *dahir*—became the site of the worst city fighting of the decade. Admittedly the cause was tailor-made for an agent provocateur: the cry had gone up that water from the Boufekrane River, destined for the people of Meknès, was being diverted for the use of European colonists. Residents of Djebabra, a native community near Meknès, complained that they lacked water for their market gardens, and the citizens of Meknès, who had experienced water stops in certain mosques during the summer, joined to protest the ongoing public works river project, which they claimed was robbing them of precious water. Although it was true that a water redistribution plan had been put into effect in November 1936 on a trial basis and did supply water to European farms, the amount diverted was small. The water shortages were probably due to the low level of the river and to a break in the water line, not because the water was being siphoned off. Noguès explained that the main purpose of the project was less redistribution than "the recovery of important quantities of water lost as a result of the decayed condition of many of the water mains." Nevertheless, water questions were always explosive and there was real concern among the notables of Meknès that their present and future interests were in jeopardy because of the population pressure and the continued expansion of cultivated fields needing irrigation. Even the director of municipal services concluded that redistribution was at that moment unwise and decided to oppose it. To put minds at rest, municipal authorities agreed to turn the matter over to a study committee and in the meantime ordered Djebabra to receive more water than it had in years past.[65]

The nationalists refused to let the issue evaporate. In the press and in petitions to the sultan and city officials, they hammered away at the government for handing over "the last of our riches" to the colonists and demanded that all the water of the Boufekrane should go to Meknès as one of its "natural and sacred rights." The campaign was even given a religious twist because historically all the rights to the waters of the Boufekrane belonged to the Service des Habous (Department of Religious Property) and had been transferred to the Service des Travaux Publics (Department of Public Works) in January 1936. The nationalists argued that this violated religious law. In the stormy sessions of the study committee, they disputed every statement and countered every claim of the authorities. Here time worked for the nationalists, because as the meetings dragged on, the native population became exasperated. The colonial rule of thumb to act quickly in native affairs was disregarded in an effort to grant due process, and technical considerations were given precedence over political ones, a fatal reversal of priorities. During a meeting held on 1 September to finalize an agreement between the French administration and the delegates from Djebabra and Meknès, a crowd of four to five hundred persons gathered outside the municipal building chanting "They have taken our water," "Not a drop of water for the colons." The demonstrators had converged on the building from several points and had taken the police by surprise. It was an uncontrolled, noisy affair, insulting to both native and French authorities, and not ended without some difficulty. In the afternoon all the shops in the native quarter closed and the protesters filed into the mosques, where nationalist litanies were recited and verses from the Koran read. "The efforts of the pasha and certain notables to calm things down," Noguès informed Paris, "were ineffective."[66]

The nationalists had instigated the demonstration and succeeded in exciting "the notables and the mass of the townspeople of Meknès" by spreading false information about the river project. The French were sure that the purpose was to demonstrate the power and organizing ability of the national party in a traditionally quiet agricultural center outside the mainstream of the nationalist movement. Morize thought that it was time to be "firm." "I think, like the old Jacobin that I am, that some humiliating setbacks would do [the nationalists] a lot of good." To restore the balance on the following morning, the pasha ordered the arrest of the ringleaders and sentenced each of them to three months in prison.[67]

News of the arrests brought groups of young nationalists into the streets, calling for the closing of all shops and announcing a meeting in the Grand Mosque. After the meeting, the crowd moved to the Place el-Hédime in an attempt to invade the pasha's *mahakma* (courthouse) and free the prisoners. Police barricades, also manned by spahis and legionnaires, blocked the way and for two hours three to four hundred demonstrators tried to break through the resolute human barriers. Twice the spahis tried to sweep the area, but they were unhorsed, disarmed, and stoned. When they retreated, the rioters advanced, became bolder, and sought hand-to-hand combat. Their hail of stones, mixed with intermittent pistol shots, nearly forced the soldiers off the square. The legionnaires and *tirailleurs* (native infantrymen called in as additional reinforcements) then intervened in earnest, firing first above the crowd, then into it. The fight was soon finished. Thirteen demonstrators were killed, fifty wounded, and sixty arrested. Among the police, spahis, legionnaires, and *tirailleurs*, fifty-two were wounded.[68]

Noguès was in France when the riot occurred, but he was kept informed by Morize's telegrams to the ministry of foreign affairs. Morize had telephoned the Meknès commander, General Henri Caillault, that he wanted no massacre, that the troops were to hold their fire until the "last possible moment" and to shoot only on the word of their officers. At day's end, when he learned of the number of deaths, he was horrified. How to explain it? The troops had been "very patient" and Caillault had taken all the right measures. Morize was convinced that the rioters had been set on provoking a fight: "The coup was prepared. Supplies of stones had been stockpiled. . . . They wanted to overwhelm us." He regretted the embarrassment that these events were causing Noguès. But he insisted ("whatever it may cost me") that he was determined to remain firm, "for if we show the slightest sign of weakness, the trouble will only get worse. . . . Have no fear that I am exaggerating. That is not part of my nature. But I believe that it is my duty to give the nationalists an impression of our strength." Morize's version of events was disputed by one of the officers on the scene, who saw no evidence of prior planning or stockpiling of ammunition by the demonstrators; but he found this even more disconcerting. In less than an hour, a few bands of young people had managed to whip the normally loyal and good-natured Meknès population into a white rage. Everyone, he said, had been taken by surprise.[69]

After he had returned to Morocco and assessed the situation for himself, Noguès concluded with some bitterness that whether prepared or unprepared—and he sided with Morize—the events were the "logical result of the insidious and false campaigns by the nationalist press" in the matter of the Boufekrane and of the "tenacious propaganda of the nationalist leaders to glorify violence and persuade their followers that the hour of sacrifice is come."[70] His reports to Paris, always distrustful of nationalist motives and ends, now took on a harder, more severe tone. He felt personally betrayed. As in the past, the nationalists had struck while he was out of the country, when his presence and counsel might have prevented bloodshed; and this time they had attacked a place where neither the local authorities nor the security forces had expected a disturbance or experienced street violence. It was an absurd drama. He was being pushed by the nationalists toward a policy of repression that both he and Viénot had earlier determined would not work. Still, something had to be done. "The government must decide," wrote the editorialist for *La Vigie marocaine*, "either to quell the agitation before real trouble occurs or to resign itself to using force and spilling blood once the trouble gets out of hand."[71] Even the pro-French Moroccan leadership was confused: "First you let some young troublemakers stir things up and look the other way. Next you permit the problem to become serious, but refuse to get involved. Then one fine day you fire into a crowd without warning and people are killed. We do not understand."[72] Viénot had not remained at the Quai d'Orsay long enough to see his plans sour, but his successor, François de Tessan, another warm friend of reform in Morocco, tasted the cup and poured it out. Regardless of who held office in Paris, the reform plans of the Popular Front, intended to steel Morocco for days of international crisis, would not be implemented.

There was an ambiguous aftermath to Meknès. On the one hand, the citizens seemed relieved to have order restored, and, once the authorities explained what was being done about the water shortages, there was a clear easing of tension. (When the Boufekrane project was completed, it substantially increased the water flow to Meknès—and cost 2 million francs.)[73] After shops reopened, Contrôleur Civil Raymond Bouyssi, head of the Meknès territory, and Director of Municipal Services René Brunel walked through the medina without escort in a display of what the French aptly called "guts" and were applauded. The notables quietly admitted that nationalist propaganda had provoked the trouble. On the other hand, nationalist rumors continued to plague the native city. Talk of a flour shortage caused the townspeople to stockpile large quantities of wheat and semolina, cleaning out stores and skyrocketing prices. The distress and confusion even led to an unsuccessful attempt at a food riot on 9 September.[74] Meknès was still, but the nationalists had made their point. No city was secure from their touch, despite the explanations and repression of the authorities.

Throughout Morocco the nationalist press condemned the crimes of the assassins and praised the heroism of the martyrs at Meknès. To avoid the turbulence that had followed the Casablanca arrests, the resident forbade the publication of nationalist newspapers and withdrew permission for the meeting of the Association des Étudiants Musulmans Nord-Africains en France scheduled to open in Rabat in mid-September. A proclaimed day of national mourning for the Meknès victims (7 September), essentially a day of prayer and shop closings, passed with only minor street trouble.[75]

Marrakesh was the next target of the nationalists and here there was a double purpose: not only to stimulate nationalism in a city like Meknès that had been quiet since the Berber *dahir* but also to confront an important representative of France with the nationalist presence. The occasion was the visit of Paul Ramadier, under secretary of state for public works, who was accompanied on his tour of the city by General Noguès. On the afternoon of 24 September, nationalists ran through the souks urging the population to scream out against France as the official party passed. Few calls were heard in the markets, but at the Medersa Ben Youssef there were hostile shouts and "some pushing and shoving" that resulted in arrests. Later three hundred demonstrators swarmed onto the Place Djemaa el-Fna, tried without success to interest the crowd already assembled in marching on police headquarters, pelted European cars with stones, and then turned toward the Jewish quarter, perhaps to sack

Left, Thami el-Glaoui, pasha of Marrakesh;
center, Paul Ramadier, under secretary of state for public works;
right, Noguès. Marrakesh, November 1937.
Courtesy Verthamon Collection, Paris

it. At this point, the police intervened and made another fifty arrests. In all likelihood, Ramadier was unaware of the turmoil around
him (although the soldiers who formed the honor guard were terrified of snipers on the walk through the canyonlike streets of the
native city), and the deeds themselves were insignificant, but the
aim had been a public show of disrespect for French authority. That,
Noguès believed, was "serious."[76]

After the events of Meknès and the incident at Marrakesh, Noguès
revealed his disappointment with the way things had gone and told
Delbos of the new course that he had taken. "If the real intentions of
the leaders of the Moroccan national movement have escaped us
for the past several years and prompted us to follow a liberal policy,
these last events should leave no doubt as to their bad faith and the
anti-French nature of their activity." This tenacious and two-faced
"minority of young bourgeois town dwellers" would do or say anything to achieve their "real and unstated objective," which was "the
abolition of the protectorate and the formation of a nationalist government which would strip the sultan if not of all, then at least a

large part of his prerogatives and authority." There would be no clemency for those arrested in the recent demonstrations, and he promised to "deal severely with any new attempt at agitation." He had begun the reorganization of the protectorate's press and propaganda services to combat the "insidious propaganda" of France's domestic and foreign enemies, and he had issued precise instructions to put an end to the agitation in the countryside. Overall, his approach was to strengthen the authority of the native leaders responsible for order and security; he admitted that in the past French officers of control had often taken this authority as their own. Sharifian authorities were to receive instructions and the means to implement them, together with "firm and discreet" French guidance to guard against abuses of power and to ensure an absolute loyalty to France.[77] This was pure Lyautey as well as a return to the days of the Berber *dahir*, when native action had been encouraged while the French advised and cheered from the sidelines. Since that time, the pattern had broken down, first with the too independent stance of the sultan at Casablanca and then with direct French intervention at Meknès. Noguès wanted to breathe life into the urban pacification strategy that had worked before.

France's presence was to be reserved for creating the environment in which the native leaders could operate most freely and effectively. The regional heads were to increase their contacts with the native population to restore confidence and to counter subversive propaganda. The resident would do his part as well, appealing directly to "the healthy elements in the population for their collaboration and confidence" and stamping out unhealthy influences. He would continue to prohibit the publication of Arabic-language newspapers that "flaunt the counsel to restraint that they have been given. . . . At the first organized demonstration I will not hesitate to imprison or banish the leaders. These measures are in fact desired by the native leaders whose authority is constantly challenged and who presently show a real uneasiness about the situation which seems to be deteriorating each day. They will result in depriving the movement of its principal leader, Allal el-Fassi—that great ball of fire—and of some of his most influential satellites." Noguès hoped that this would have a salutary effect on the nationalist party, causing some of its members to reflect soberly on the future, and lead to an area of understanding from which to begin "a profitable collaboration in the interests of all concerned." But he was also aware that the arrest of nationalist leaders could provoke "very strong reactions" in the cities, particularly at Fez. "We no longer have any choice. Vigorous measures against the leaders of the movement are necessary, if they continue to pit the people against the Makhzen and against France, regardless of the consequences. They are the only way of ensuring the future of French Morocco and of creating a new climate to permit us to follow our civilizing mission." So as not to end on a bleak note, Noguès told Delbos that once the "bad shepherds" had been chased away as stewards of the flock, "it will be possible to continue the liberal and generous policy which has been and must remain France's policy in Morocco." But he added sternly: "Such a task can only be handled successfully if the government gives its complete confidence to those who must carry it out and if the necessary measures are taken to prevent certain French extremists from aiding the nationalists in their work of systematic opposition to French authority in Morocco."[78] These guarantees Delbos was willing to give.

During October the nationalist agitation continued unabated in the city streets and the tribal marketplaces. The weekly *el-Atlas*, the first Arabic-language newspaper authorized in the protectorate, called for "rebellion" in the pages of its 16 October issue and was suspended. At Ouezzane the local nationalist leaders were arrested and charged with spreading false and libelous information among the tribes. At Khémisset four young students from Karaouiyne University at Fez disturbed the afternoon prayers and incited three hundred persons to march on the offices of the *contrôleur civil* to demand "the return of the religious law of the Chrâa." The *caïd*, Allal ben Achir, pleaded for calm, but he was pushed aside. Order was only restored with the aid of Zemmour tribesmen. Four demonstrators were wounded, seven among the police; one officer had been stabbed several times with a dagger. Seventy arrests were made. At Fez the chiefs of the national party reiterated the need for discipline and dedication and called for acts of heroism and sacrifice of the sort that marked the liberation movements in Syria, Egypt, and Palestine. Convinced that they were preparing "to unleash a real rebellion" throughout the sharifian empire, Noguès ordered the dissolution of the national party in accord with the sultan and had its leaders arrested. Allal el-Fassi, Ahmed Mekouar, Omar Abdeljalil, and Mohamed Lyazidi were taken into custody on 25 October.[79]

Despite Noguès's public warning that new disturbances would be "severely repressed" by protectorate authorities "determined to maintain order," demonstrations occurred in some of the major cities—not Meknès or Marrakesh, however—and were most dramatic in Fez, where regular troops invested the medina, street by street, and in Port Lyautey, where two protesters were killed. At Fez security measures were initiated on the day of the arrest of the nationalist leaders. The following morning the nationalists ordered the medina shops closed. For the moment they were the undisputed "masters of the medina." At the noon prayers at Karaouiyne, the *latif* was recited, followed by inflammatory speeches and a call for a march across the medina. But a heavy rain washed the streets clean of demonstrators.

General Amédée Blanc, military commander of the Fez region, and the pasha appealed for calm, and the sultan issued an edict against speechmaking in the mosques that would be enforced by the use of arms. The words and warnings fell on deaf ears. More prayers and speeches on the twenty-seventh triggered a government display of force: a battalion tramped the medina, military aircraft buzzed the city, and the police began making arrests. News of the Port Lyautey deaths filtered into a city beginning to feel the hunger pangs brought on by the closed marketplaces. Fez was gripped by a nervous fear that some said bordered on terror.

To act before events forced his hand, Blanc decided to occupy the medina. Although intended as a preventive measure and carried out with great skill, it could not help but be seen as a provocation because this was the first time since 1912 that regular troops had entered the old city in strength. When later asked about the wisdom of such a move, Blanc, a veteran of city fighting in Damascus, allegedly answered: "I regretted it, but I had to make up my mind to do it. So much the worse for tradition."[80] Earlier he had confided to Noguès: "Using the precedents of the Middle East as a guide, I believe that the serious danger lies in the medina, and especially in the intellectual centers: Karaouiyne, the Muslim schools, the free *medersas* [boarding schools]."[81] Ironically, although he was right, he had targeted as enemies the very groups that France needed as friends if the protectorate was to survive. By midafternoon on 28 October, all but the very heart of the medina—the Karaouiyne, Moulay Idriss, and Rsif Mosques—had been secured. The maneuver was not without incident. A group of twenty legionnaires, sent to the Rsif Mosque to prevent its use as a rallying point, encountered a hostile crowd of several hundred demonstrators. Unable to cut an escape path with their rifle butts, they threw two hand grenades, wounding six people. But surprisingly, given the temper of the population and the number of soldiers about, this was the only reported confrontation.

The occupation of the entire medina was completed by 29 October. The noonday speechmakers at Karaouiyne were more violent than usual, demanding the release of all political prisoners and the

Walking the Medina. Fez, October 1937.
Courtesy Verthamon Collection, Paris

Walking the Medina. Fez, October 1937.
Courtesy Verthamon Collection, Paris.

ouster of the French. Blanc sealed all the exits of the building save one, and while the nationalists recited the *latif*, the pasha's *mokha-zenis* entered the mosque and drove them into the street, where they were met by legionnaires and *goumiers* armed with truncheons. A "serious scuffle" took place and over three hundred arrests were made. By evening the city was quiet. The "revolt," as Le Tourneau called it, had been broken. On the thirty-first, Noguès inspected the medina and met with members of the corporations and city notables, promising to help the "hard-working, orderly people," but damning the others. Although he was criticized in the metropolitan press for the indelicate, uncharacteristic outburst, *L'Afrique fran-çaise* came to his defense: "The resident general knew to whom he was speaking and what to say to be understood. He was understood and that is the important point."[82]

The troops remained in the medina for ten days and there were no further difficulties. Following Noguès's lead, Blanc in turn made contact with native leaders, explaining that the occupation was only the enforcement of public order in the interest of the city, not an act of hostility against its inhabitants. Whether he believed it or not, Blanc had no illusions about the future: he ordered one post in the medina garrisoned permanently and two more constructed at strategic points to be occupied whenever the need should arise. Publicly the operation was hailed as a great success for combined political-military action. Without the loss of one life, the turbulent city had been brought to heel. Privately there was great regret that the military had had to be used at all, and for that Blanc, a sensitive warrior but perhaps still out of his depth at Fez, was held responsible.[83]

The Port Lyautey deaths, which had unsettled the Fez population, occurred on 27 October. Submerged in a flash flood of demonstrators, the police fired into the crowd to free themselves and then called for reinforcements of regular troops to restore order. When the fight was over, two demonstrators were dead, ten wounded, and seven police officers were wounded. Fifty arrests were made. Disorders at Oujda on 28 October and Rabat on 29 October were also put down by police supported by soldiers. On the last day of October, Noguès made official the strategy of repression approved by the government in Paris, a strategy already put into practice. To end the threat of rebellion, force would be employed wherever and whenever necessary. It was a question of "public safety." "We have already used force and we will continue to do so."[84]

The exile—forced and voluntary—of the nationalist leaders (el-Fassi to Gabon; el-Ouazzani, Lyazidi, and Mekouar to the Sahara; Abdeljalil to the Spanish zone) did not put an end to nationalist activities altogether, but it did end the turmoil in the cities. No street demonstrations of the sort that had plagued the protectorate since 1930 would occur until the end of World War II. Stern repression, coupled with well-publicized statements to begin anew the calm, orderly process of social and economic reform, had had its effect. Noguès boasted to the foreign minister in 1938: "Through a vigilant political action I have maintained calm and won back the affection and loyalty of the native population to our country."[85] But it had taken the army and the banishment of the nationalist leaders to accomplish the task. To many the revolt in the cities recalled the rebellion in the Rif, a traditional, xenophobic *jihad* whose leaders preached the return to old ways, blamed current ills on the colonial protectors, and promised a more independent, adventurous existence. It was something that Noguès thought about all the time, for the Rif war had brought about Lyautey's downfall and exposed the fragility of the Pax Gallia in Morocco. If the parallels were disconcerting, the contrasts were downright terrifying. The Rif war had begun in a poverty pocket of the Spanish zone among a fierce mountain people on the reaches of the sharifian empire, but the turbulence that now confronted the French started in the empire's heartland, in the protectorate's richest cities, among the best educated of France's protégés.

What is more, the urban pacification strategy had proven to be a disappointment. Politics and promises had not short-circuited the nationalists' electric appeal, nor had they unplugged the nationalists themselves. Regardless of what the French said or did—and they were discreet, patient, and long suffering—the nationalists were determined to provoke a fight, playing on circumstances or actually plotting them. Here the Lyautey touch was no use at all. The sultan and the native authorities had not been able to maintain order unaided, which compelled the French to resort to military force, unmasking the brute in the French presence—precisely what the nationalists wanted to show. Who could blame them? Judging by the preferences of French policymakers, in particular the shift from reliance on the cities to dependence on the countryside, the urban bourgeoisie of a nationalist stripe was destined to be sidelined, excluded from the protectorate's future, and replaced by new friends of France. The trouble, of course, had not been confined to the cities. The Berber tribes, so solid for the French in 1930, were now defecting to the nationalists. What of the sultan? Now he seemed content to sit under the French umbrella, but how long would he stay if the nationalists continued to make marks on the protectorate's walls?

All of this boded evil for the future. It was said that peaceful reform had run its course in Morocco and that now only repression could preserve what Lyautey had created. Noguès did not believe it. Despite his rocky beginning, he was convinced that he could recapture the initiative for France and, with the economic and political support of Paris, build the partnership on which the survival of the protectorate depended.

THREE

The Economics of Pacification

By the terms of the Treaty of Fez, the French accepted the task of the economic betterment of Morocco, and there is no doubt that they took the charge seriously. It was not only a question of pacifying an area so that the tax collector could operate in security, although that was important, but of making a positive imprint on the lives of tribesmen and townspeople. Here the effort was to introduce modern methods in place of ancient routines, to instruct, persuade, and pressure on matters of trading and plowing, tractors and bookkeeping. Next to bringing peace to Morocco, this was the greatest benefit given by France to the native population and was the source of intense personal satisfaction and pride to scores of *officiers des affaires indigènes* in the military regions and their civilian counterparts, the *contrôleurs civils*, in the pacified districts. Quiet accomplishments, they added up: one English observer, reviewing the establishment of permanent rural marketplaces in what had been open, empty countryside, called it the beginning of a real "economic revolution."[1]

Lyautey planned on a Napoleonic scale. The writing on his tomb in Les Invalides, only steps away from Bonaparte's, paraphrases the words he first used in 1896 to describe his own hopes for achievement: "To be one of those in whom men believe, in whose eyes thousands seek command, with whose voice roads are opened, countries populated, and cities built."[2] Morocco was to be his monument, the Moroccan people his beneficiaries. He never doubted for a moment that the prosperity of the native populace was France's ultimate goal (even though along the way Frenchmen of all sorts would benefit as well) or that it was attainable. Many, however, scoffed at his bold vision of triumph over the seemingly eternal powers of poverty, environment, ignorance, and war. It was just so much "Jules Verne-ism." How could one combat the chief evildoer—unpredictable, uncontrollable weather? In Morocco Steeg pronounced, "Gouverner, c'est pleuvoir," wittily adapting the French aphorism to the situation. There was a drop of truth in this. Climate and the economic fate it meted out counted for much in the lives of Morocco's inhabitants; drought dominated the south, rain ruled the central plains, and everywhere water commanded the cities. It was not strange that on his first visit to France in 1931 Sidi Mohammed ben Youssef was as impressed by the physical attributes of the land as with Paris and the gold ingots in the Bank of France: it was an "immense garden" with animals of a size and quality unknown at home and with rivers and streams whose waters did not have to be carefully and jealously apportioned.[3] Lyautey had come to free the Moroccan people from this bondage. With Noguès the battle that he had begun was rejoined, the mission that he had undertaken was proclaimed once more. For Noguès not only believed in Lyautey's commitment but was convinced, as his mentor had been, that whatever future France had in Morocco depended upon the prosperity of the Moroccan people.

These two concerns, Morocco's prosperity and France's future, were interconnected in Noguès's thought and action, forged together as much by sentiment as by memory of the rebellion in the Rif and the revolt over the Berber *dahir*, where economics played a significant part. The steady progress of nationalism in 1936, a year of dryness and famine, brought home the point. He believed that the economic distress had been cleverly exploited by the nationalists. "Our familiarity with the things and the people of Morocco," Noguès told the Conseil du Gouvernement, "lets us say unequivocally that poverty brings with it political illness as well as diseases of the body."[4] Predictably, his cares tallied precisely with the priorities and sympathies of the Popular Front government. Noguès's charge was to concentrate on the welfare of the native population; Blum stated it clearly in 1936, Viénot repeated it in early 1937, and Delbos confirmed it in midyear. Improvement of native life was of paramount importance, first, because it was an urgent necessity, given the economic catastrophe; second, because Europeans had profited enough from Morocco's development. The need was to redress the balance, to create an equilibrium that alone, in Delbos's words, "can ensure the survival of our work in this country in harmony with the spirit of the protectorate."[5] Third, improvement was crucial because it was counted on to ease the political situation, halt the nationalist increase, and win friends for France.

Noguès's plan was deceptively plain—and expensive. To deal with the immediate crisis, he employed massive state aid: the free distribution of food and seed, coupled with the expansion of credit to the native farmer and artisan. To implement this program of handouts and loans he relied on the Sociétés Indigènes de Prévoyance (SIP, the

farmer aid organizations) in the rural areas and the artisan corporations in the cities; both were traditional institutions renovated for
their new assignments. For the future, he vowed far-reaching tax reform and the accelerated economic development of the countryside.

Noguès described his design for Morocco's people as soon as he
was named resident general, and, although his words were almost
drowned out by a chorus of European complaints, he made certain
that they were understood. From the first, he said that the only solution to the problems plaguing Morocco was a policy that gave preference to economic and social progress. Although he pledged himself
to protect European interests and praised Peyrouton, who had recognized the needs and apprehensions of the colonists, it was clear that
they were of secondary importance. On this point Moroccan nationalists misread Noguès, believing that he would continue to place
Europeans above Moroccans. Or, more likely, they deliberately dis-
torted his thought, fearing that an energetic socioeconomic program
would steal their thunder. His thesis, stated cautiously but soon argued with force, was simply that the economic troubles of Europeans would only diminish by improving the conditions of native
life, a proposition that was at the moment more politically wise than
economically sound. "In a country where everyone's interests are so
closely linked," he told listeners at Taza, "anything that can be done
for the fellahs and shepherds will have a happy effect on every group
in the population." And he challenged the Conseil du Gouvernement: "No one can deny that the prosperity of the native rural class
is a factor in the general prosperity of Morocco."[6]

This was the message that he carried across the land. The task of
bringing back the days of plenty would not be easy and would take a
long time, but he was convinced that if anyone could begin a revival,
he could. "I cannot work miracles. No one can. But my good faith,
my dedication, and my energy will all be put in the service of the
material, moral, and social requirements of the country." The result,
he hoped, would be a "New Morocco." But he warned the Europeans
of Meknès that the all too often "inflated expectations" of the past
would have to give way to a "less splendid" existence, yet one that
would surely be healthier and more solid, a better guarantee of a
bright future. It was a gentle reminder that the time of promises, illusions, and lavishness was over. The period of "methodical reform"
had begun.[7]

In his meetings with Europeans and Moroccans, he accented his
Moroccan past. Lyautey would "always" inspire his words and deeds.
He pointed out that he had returned to Morocco on the cruiser *Du-*

pleix, which a year earlier had brought Lyautey's ashes to their resting place in a mausoleum on the grounds of the Residency.[8] Physically and—through Noguès—spiritually, Lyautey was present once more on Morocco's soil. Noguès claimed "no other ambition" than to follow the trail blazed by his predecessor, "the illustrious marshal, his chief and venerated mentor." In Rabat the "former *r'bati*" recalled his years of service at the protectorate's capital. In Fez the "*vieux Fassi*" remembered aloud the "somber hours" of the Rif war and the successful struggle to keep the mountain rebels from the city's gates.[9] Now, as then, he was ready to chase the wolves away from their doors.

Across Morocco the harvests had been bad, far worse than the mediocre yields of the two previous years. Too little rain had destroyed the crops of the south while too much had ruined the plantings of the north and east. Hungry people fleeing the drought found only typhus and famine in impoverished northern cities. To make matters worse, a lack of seed for fall sowing seemed to cut off the hope of relief, however distant. Compounding the distress of the cities was the dramatic increase in their population. Between 1931 and 1936 the total Moroccan population in the eighteen largest municipalities rose from 636,839 to 821,628, a 29 percent jump in five years. Casablanca became the empire's largest urban center with a population of 184,668 (a startling increase over the 105,127 of 1931), edging out Marrakesh, which had a slight decline from 186,334 to 183,465. Fez, Meknès, and Rabat registered equally impressive gains; Fez climbed from 98,205 to 134,801, Meknès from 44,211 to 62,392, and Rabat from 32,204 to 57,123.[10] In the overall pattern the statistics revealed, the French detected three discernible movements—from country to city, from south to north, and from the interior to the coast—all traditional, all expected, and all speeded up by the effects of drought and famine.

Wherever Noguès went, he announced the distribution of food and seed. With the gifts came the promise, made at Fez, Meknès, and Marrakesh, that the cities would see better days. He spoke of the need to stimulate the artisan corporations, which had fallen on hard times and which, when properly mended, could preserve the "purest traditions" of Muslim art and enable craftsmen to earn a decent living. There was more. Noguès pledged protection against crop, livestock, and property losses, the development of institutions of credit and insurance, and the elaboration of a comprehensive "land policy." At Marrakesh he endorsed water projects that would irrigate the Souss region and the southern territories (*territoires du sud*), which were constantly plagued by drought. Although water might aid colonist and native alike, Noguès made plain his preference. He told the Conseil du Gouvernement that he favored small, short-term projects in tribal territory rather than those that flooded large areas of uncultivated land, usually to the profit of colonial agriculture; it would be a "modest, but effective" program. The point was to do something quickly with an "immediate return" that would make "a solid improvement" in the native way of life. The ultimate aim was not only to feed the local population but to put a permanent end to the annual northward trek produced by poverty. For the unemployed, whether native or European, the public projects would provide immediate and desperately needed jobs.[11]

In all of this the antinationalist thrust was evident, for the French wanted to isolate the urban bourgeoisie with its seemingly irrepressible urge for quick political action by ministering to the material needs of its potential followers. Political reform was not neglected, yet in remarks to the sultan, Noguès stressed the "methodical" and "evolutionary" nature of the changes he had in mind. At Fez he told the nationalists that he understood their "aspirations" but could only satisfy them "progressively" because it was vital to take the "country as a whole" into account. He promised that he would do all that had to be done as soon as it was possible. For the moment he asked for patience and the "active and confident cooperation" of all groups in the populace. He would close no doors, build no barricades, cut himself off from no one. No "watertight compartment" would seal off the leader of the protectorate from its people. "I have begun a policy of direct contact. And I will pursue it, especially when it involves the fate of the most humble among us, be they Europeans or natives."[12]

Trust and collaboration, understanding and love—the sinews of the Lyautey litany and part of the marshal's contribution to the protectorate mystique—were words with less power to sway than in the past. Nationalist meetings, marches, and violence proved the point. Certain that the nationalists were out to embarrass and undercut him, Noguès threatened the lawbreakers with severe punishments. Yet it was clear that he wanted to avoid a policy of repression. To counter nationalist propaganda that the French cared not a bit for the hardships of the people, he moved from vague phrases to precise measures in the matter of taxes, abolishing those on rented space (the *taxe locative*) and market transactions (the *droits de marché*), and exempting almost all of the native inhabitants of the cities from the housing tax (the *taxe d'habitation*).[13] This was a powerful play even though his hand had been forced.

By far the most unpopular tax with townsmen was the housing tax, which raised 6 million francs a year for the protectorate but caused more "public disaffection" than it was worth. Each year it required a storm of inquiries and investigations, a flood of orders-to-pay and seizures. With a stroke of the pen, the burden was eliminated. The market taxes were longstanding grievances of the rural population and actually discouraged commerce. For years the Residency had sought their abolition, but the 30 to 40 million francs in annual revenue they produced usually counted for more than the voices of their opponents. Now politics took part in the debate. "The suppression of the rural market taxes will bring such relief to the native economy and such joy to the mass of native farmers," wrote an officer of the Direction des Affaires Politiques, "that I do not hesitate to say that it will be a more resounding success than any other government measure since the installation of the protectorate." "Market day," he concluded, "would become, as it once was in the past, a holiday." These considerations were decisive. Interpreting the initial reaction of native leaders in Fez, Noguès wrote confidently to Paris: "I feel that I have achieved a serious détente, especially among the artisans who have been worked up so dangerously during these past days by a very clever propaganda."[14]

There was no applause for the measures from Europeans because they were coupled with the announcement of increased consumption taxes on a long list of essentials, including sugar, candles, matches, and vegetable oils. To be sure, these taxes hit both communities. But in fact there was a conscious effort not only to redistribute the tax burden but also to shift part of it to Europeans. The revenue lost from the housing tax was to be regained by the increase in sugar, and monies needed to fill the market tax void were specifically designed not to affect the same groups in the population and to tax Europeans as well.[15]

The November outbursts at Casablanca and Fez sped the execution of Noguès's program. Paris, which placed a high price on peace in the protectorate, was willing to absorb much of its cost. In fact, without France there would have been no program at all. The protectorate's coffers were empty. The production of wheat, the principal source of Morocco's wealth, had dropped from 8 million quintals in 1935 to 3 million in 1936, slashing the government's revenues. Noguès calculated the budget deficit for 1937 at 152 million francs, and even after severe cuts in administrative expenses and an anticipated increased yield in customs duties (because of the French currency devaluation in September), a balance in receipts and payments was impossible without "understanding and help" from the government of the Republic.[16]

Some of what the Popular Front agreed to do was customary. France exempted the protectorate from paying for the troops in Morocco, which served as the empire's defense force, and advanced sums to cover the losses incurred by the railway system. This amounted to 63 million francs. The major extraordinary credit came from the budget of the Metropole's 1937 Public Works Plan to Fight Unemployment. Sixty million francs were assigned to Morocco to be used to better the conditions of native life. Half of this amount was earmarked for education, public aid, and medical assistance; the other half could be employed as the protectorate saw fit. Here the French government picked up the lion's share of the tab for abolishing the market taxes, at least until permanent adjustments to the tax system could be made. The shorthand version of France's part in Morocco's budget was that the aid in 1937 was double what it had been in 1936. For the balance of the deficit, between 25 and 30 million francs, Noguès planned to juggle the taxes already on the books rather than create new ones. In particular, he ruled out a personal income tax, a mainstay of the French tax system and the one tax that the Left considered potentially the most productive if rate scales were properly set. Noguès believed that the tax would cost more to collect than it would produce and that it made little sense in a land where private wealth was so unstable and where so many of its inhabitants were in constant debt. This was true for large groups within the native population but not so for many Europeans. In fact, the colonists' chief fear was that the Popular Front would bring the income tax to Morocco. What Noguès did then was to make a trade-off. In return for European acquiescence in a program for Moroccans, he assured the colonists that no direct tax would touch their personal fortunes. All of this he had explained to Blum before taking on the Residency and the premier had approved.[17]

The commitment to native welfare was greater than the balancing of the budget suggests. Noguès revealed that he and his negotiating team, joined by Under Secretary of State Viénot, had argued successfully to have the "profits" from the revalorization of the Banque d'État du Maroc's gold reserves (another result of the French currency devaluation) put at the protectorate's disposal rather than credited to government accounts in Paris. In addition, the French government was willing to renounce that portion of the monies (ten-sixteenths) that, according to metropolitan statute, was to be applied to the Exchange Stabilization Fund. In short, Noguès thought he would receive another 30 million francs, which he planned to split between those Europeans and Moroccans in the most difficult economic straits through direct aid via regional *banques populaires* or the native SIP. In the end, Noguès received only slightly more than half of what he wanted from the revalorization, 16½ million francs, to which he added 10 million francs from the Office Chérifien des Phosphates, the state phosphate monopoly. The resulting 26½ million francs was placed entirely at the service of the native community in direct relief to the poor, aid and credit to artisans, and contributions to the SIP.[18]

The French were good record keepers, so their effort to support the native economy in times of crisis should be easy to document. This was not always the case. Any society that defines *fonds secrets* as funds that are used at the discretion of government administrators does not intend to leave history a rigorous accounting of its financial operations.[19] Frankly, modern administrators must have a bit of the sorcerer about them. While responding to a routine request from Paris in 1937, Morize at one point was even prepared to lie about monies that had not been used up, but his Calvinist conscience (or the fear that he might have been found out) got the better of him.[20] But in less serious matters and in the constant flood of reports demanded by Paris or in the endless statements on the government's accomplishments made by Noguès, the numbers became jumbled: credits appropriated might appear as money actually spent; grain purchased might be tallied as foodstuffs already handed out to the populace. This was less outright deception than honest error, resulting from attempts to squeeze the protectorate's needs into the fundable categories specified by the Metropole or to simplify the complex to audiences uninterested in technical detail. Lyautey had seen the bureaucratic side as just so much red tape and paper work; he concentrated on getting things done and left the cleanup to the clerks. Noguès was of another sort: he respected and mastered the figures and spent a good portion of each year in Paris personally presenting Morocco's case before the Republic's financial inquisitors. Still, perhaps because he became fluent in the language used in the capital, it is hard to know down to the last centime how much was spent on any given budget item and from which stocking the money was drawn. But the account books all agree on one point: recovery did not come cheaply. Whether considered a penance justified by previous sins of omission or a burden accepted in hopes of future reward, France paid a good price to revive the patrimony of the Alaouite saints.[21]

Where to put the money to get the best return was a matter of judgment. In general Noguès preferred to use familiar channels, expanding the scope and competence of existing institutions rather than creating new ones. An example of this was his reliance on the SIP (Sociétés Indigènes de Prévoyance), the farmer aid organizations created by Lyautey in 1917 as sort of rural "friendly societies" teaching thrift, community self-help, and progressive innovations. More readily recognized by its initials than its name, the SIP made loans, established cooperatives, and financed agricultural improvements such as tree nurseries and breeding stations. Their credit function, however, was of special importance because money for hire at reasonable rates had been heretofore unknown in a society where usury was notorious. In addition, credit built a relationship where none had existed before: just as farming rooted the tribesman to the soil, so credit attached him to the protectorate. Structured into sections on the tribal level, administered by councils of notables, and guided by the local *officier des affaires indigènes*, the SIP grouped about one-fifth of the native population (in 1936–37 over 1.4 million Moroccans were members), a somewhat deceptive figure since all Moroccans who paid the agricultural tax (the *tertib*) were automatically members. Since funds for the SIP came from a surtax on the *tertib*, which was the single most productive direct tax in Morocco, the *centimes additionnels* it produced provided the SIP with a steady income. By supporting the work of the SIP, Noguès ensured the continuation and expansion of rural credit and encouraged the formation of farmer cooperatives.[22]

The activity of the SIP during the Noguès tenure surpassed anything that had been done before. In 1936–37 and 1937–38, the SIP loaned over 120 million francs (50 million francs in cash and 70 million in kind) and disbursed another 23 million francs in nonrecoverable aid. Not until after the bad postwar harvest of 1945 would credit be made so abundantly available and on a scale that had been as yet unrealized in European states. Criticized because of the tight control from the top and because the loan repayment plans tended to embroil farmers in additional debts, the SIP were nevertheless important instruments of rural recovery and growth. Morize could report triumphantly in August 1938 that the loans had "borne fruit." "This year the fellahs will not only be able to reimburse the loans made to them, but to stockpile a reserve."[23] In short, a good harvest. Perhaps as gratifying to European minds were the habits of saving and storing that had begun to seep into the life and work patterns of Moroccan farmers.

The economic crisis persisted through 1937, the year that Robert Montagne named *l'année terrible*. The budget credits approved by France covered immediate emergency needs, but Noguès worried about tomorrow, knowing that there was little chance of major improvement until the 1938 harvest. The area most severely afflicted was the vast interior semicircle from the southern reaches of the Oujda region, south and east along the Algero-Moroccan border in the Tafilalet territory and the Dra border region, and eastward into the Marrakesh region. Noguès was not exaggerating when he told the Conseil du Gouvernement in June that most of his time over the last months had been spent in combat with famine, sickness, and death. He requested that Paris dispatch a team to document Morocco's distress, a team preferably headed by someone who would "champion" Morocco's cause.[24] Happily, Théodore Steeg, sympathetic to Noguès and Morocco, was chosen for the mission.

It was not a particularly auspicious moment to come hat in hand to the French government. France was consumed by its own apprehensions about the future owing to the spreading Spanish conflagration and the mounting German threat across the Rhine. As always, money was a large part of the problem, for despite the Popular Front's olive-branch gestures, the moneymen of Paris still persisted in withholding their capital, advice, and confidence—a sort of bankers' sit-down strike—in order to force the government to alter its financial practices. In late June, Blum resigned as premier and with him went Viénot, who five months earlier had told Noguès to ask for anything that he wanted. Now the government took on a decidedly conservative cast as Blum's successors scrambled to reassure their fellow countrymen of their "orthodox" (if not downright old-fashioned) economic intentions. The change meant little to Noguès. Those who now took the helm, the Radical Socialists, were his closest political friends. Although there would be cuts in the budget, there was always money to be had somewhere. Getting it meant stressing matters of national and imperial defense over questions of native welfare. This was not trumping up a danger where none existed, for even Blum was convinced that twice during his tenure as prime minister war might have come in the Mediterranean.[25] Nor was it abandoning previous priorities. Noguès believed that Morocco's security was only as good as the protectorate's native policy. Money from France would still underwrite the same lines in Morocco's budget, but the reasons why would be different.

When completed, Steeg's report did full justice to Morocco's calamity. Never had famine reached such proportions: in the south and east, the entire grain crop (hard wheat and barley) had been wiped out. Never had it affected so large a group in the population. Steeg calculated that 1.4 million people (nearly one-quarter of the native population) would need assistance in one form or another between June 1937 and July 1938, and of that number five hundred thousand would be totally destitute. Surprisingly, he argued that the human consequences of the famine were made more anguishing than in the past because of the French presence. France's accomplishment in health, for example, had resulted in a high survival rate among infants and children, helping to increase the population by more than 2 million in the previous fifteen years; in numerical terms, this meant more suffering, not less. Also, the work among the tribes had encouraged a dim hope in the future over the dismal fatalism of the past, so the current crisis, Steeg said, was resented—perhaps for the first time—by a rural people led to expect a better lot. Finally, the pacification of the south, undertaken for reasons of security in 1933–34, had brought thousands of new and impoverished protégés to the protectorate with now counterfeit pledges ringing in their ears. A failure to act quickly and decisively, Steeg warned, would weaken French prestige and Moroccan defenses to the profit of the "adversaries of French authority."

Steeg's indictment of peace and prosperity was clearly off base, but his conclusions were correct. What is more, he wove his economic, political, and moral arguments into a compelling tapestry of ironic and bitter truths, of commitments and interests that few of the lawmakers (even the most penny-pinching) could afford to ignore. He revealed that the protectorate's resources were "exhausted" from the previous ten-month campaign, which had cost 80 million francs outside of normal budget expenditures, and recommended a subsidy from the Metropole to the tune of 160 million francs, the smaller portion to be an outright grant-in-aid, the larger slice an advance—a low-interest loan, for example, made through the Caisse Nationale de Crédit Agricole—targeted for seed programs and small public works projects.[26] The subsidy was duly approved near the end of the year, although it had been reduced to 120 million francs. In the meantime, however, other funds from France for native welfare had become available, some of which could be used to advance the plans that Noguès saw as most urgent.[27] As necessary as the rain, money from France continued to water Morocco's fields and nourish its people.

By early 1937 the economic blueprints drawn up during the winter produced scaffolding to support the recovery effort. The guiding principle was that of state-directed cooperation. With the aid of the government, the aim was to pool and organize resources, to control and regulate production and marketing, and to finance improvements and expansion. In Morocco the government had always been a partner of Europeans. What was new was the invitation to the native community to join hands as well. This was the inspiration for the Office Chérifien Interprofessionnel du Blé, modeled on the Popular Front's wheat office in France. The goal was to ensure all wheat farmers "a fair profit for their labor" by protecting them against speculation and guaranteeing them a fixed price throughout the year for their grain crop.[28] As with all controls on the market, it was bitterly opposed by grain dealers and agribusinessmen as a block to profits. The Casablanca Chamber of Agriculture protested what it called the "intervention of the public authorities in the arena of economic forces."[29] European farmers were also unenthusiastic, fearing that it was a Marxist scheme to tax and harass the middle class, that, if handled deftly, could be used as a lever to redistribute Morocco's wealth. A social revolution was not what Noguès had in mind. All he wanted was to supply the cities and the stricken regions with food through massive, organized acquisitions of grain at "just prices" and to help suffering small farmers at the same time.

At first the dozen Coopératives Indigènes de Blés set up in 1937 and 1938 did little more than work with the stocks of foreign wheat purchased by the government.[30] What homegrown grain there was either had been snapped up by merchants and shipped to France (according to the terms of quota agreements) for higher prices than could be obtained in Morocco or had been hoarded by native farmers for their own use or for sale on the open market at 17 percent or more over the government price, which was legal provided the grain was for family consumption. Morize confided that he was greatly concerned for the food supply of Fez and Marrakesh because there was so little wheat available and such small quantities of other grains on hand. The lack of hard wheat was especially troublesome since it was preferred by the "comfortable bourgeoisie," who Morize knew would not give it up without a fuss. "It is dangerous to upset the ways of the bourgeoisie, particularly the Fassis. They have the gift of gab and what influence!" This was a backhanded compliment to Morocco's urban magnates.[31] The government jumped into the breach in time with imported grain but at far greater expense than it had anticipated.

By 1938 the positive effect of the wheat cooperatives had begun to be felt by native growers, and they were rightly considered the flagship fleet of rural cooperative associations. In 1938–39 they bought one-half million quintals of wheat; in 1942–43 they were buying triple that amount. Later they experimented with barley purchases and even dabbled in "futures" advances to native growers, loans based on estimated crop yields. In 1943 they were renamed the Coopératives Indigènes Agricoles and given the authority to deal with a wider variety of agricultural products.[32]

Commenting on their accomplishment, Noguès told the Moroccan section of the Conseil du Gouvernement that this was the "first time" that "the fellah has sold his crops under the same conditions as European producers, because the native cooperative, represented at all the souks, was able to counter rapidly the unjustified drops in prices which always occur right at the moment of the harvest."[33] This was surely the case with the Doukkala in the Mazagan territory, whose chief crop was soft wheat. Their cooperative saw them through the poor harvest of 1937 and brought them substantial profit from the good yield of 1938. Winegrowers of the region, witnessing their neighbors' prosperity, clamored for a cooperative of their own. In addition, the political effect was "considerable": French authority was the prime beneficiary. Nevertheless, there were detractors. Some native producers found the cooperatives inquisitorial, staffed with too many government officials, and unsatisfactory as purchasing agents.[34] During World War II, friendly persuasion gave way to rude pressure as protectorate authorities tried to make up shortages at home and in France. The *directeur des affaires politiques* admitted that cooperatives were being run "less to respond to the desire of the cooperators themselves than as an active contribution to the needs of supplying food" to the country as a whole.[35] The economic survival of the protectorate and the needs of France now took precedence. In the end, the cooperatives represented only a temporary success for the economics and spirit of cooperation: of the forty-three agricultural cooperatives created between 1938 and 1943 (excluding wheat cooperatives), less than half were still in operation in 1950.[36]

A rural project of a different sort, which also required a close partnership with the French and a cooperative mood, was the irrigation scheme for the tribal lands of the south and the west. Noguès re-

Pasha Hassan. Khénifra, January 1942.
Photo Jacques Belin

ported to the Conseil du Gouvernement in December 1937 that the
work of repairing and extending existing irrigation channels, constructing small dams, and installing water pumps was under way in
the distant valleys of the Rhir and Ziz rivers. As a result, in the Tafilalet territory, French engineers, agricultural experts, and native
workers had quintupled the land under cultivation (from five thousand to twenty-five thousand hectares) after only one year of work.
These were small symptoms of the immense change that Noguès
wanted in a country where water—not oil or gold—was the principal source of wealth, and he believed that capturing it and bringing it
to the people could alone solve the problem of poverty and root the
rural populations to the soil.[37]

In the crisis of the moment, limited efforts were all that the government could afford, and yet Noguès had designs on development

Camp Marchand, September 1941.
Photo Jacques Belin

that showed the zeal and vision of a Lyautey. He looked to a future
where the Moroccan population would quadruple within less than a
century. To feed a nation of 20 to 25 million was the "central problem," whose solution would summon up all the forces of France's
intellect and will. According to all predictions, Morocco would remain "essentially an agricultural land." To prepare it for its people,
to make it fruitful, Noguès saw "two ways . . . and only two." The
first was to increase production by better farming techniques and
the introduction of more profitable crops, a task long under way

Tahar Souk, May 1942. *Photo Jacques Belin*

through the combined efforts of the agricultural and educational services, the civil and military authorities, and the SIP, with the support of colonial farming in the role of "guide and model." The second
was the "complete and rational use" of Morocco's water resources to
transform vast stretches of wasteland into fertile fields. Blessed with
the Atlantic coast and high mountain ranges, which provided frequent and abundant rains, Morocco nevertheless had failed to exploit its "relatively privileged" geographical position to full advantage. Residency studies indicated that over time a grand plan of large
and small public projects could increase by more than sixfold the
quantity of water available for irrigation. "I have resolved to undertake this great task," Noguès declared to the Conseil du Gouvernement. "To do it right will mean long years of effort. And we will
never live to see its completion. But we will have served Morocco
and France well, if, in tens of years to come, not a drop of water from
the rivers of the Rif or the Atlas is lost to the sea or the desert sands."
This was indeed an enterprise on the Lyautey scale, phrased in his
language. It was a call for collaboration between Frenchmen and Mo-

Tissa, September 1942. *Photo Jacques Belin*

Azemmour, 1942. *Photo Jacques Belin*

roccans of unprecedented scope and duration, demanding goodwill, determination, energy, and sacrifice. "Will not such a project kindle a mystique and light fires of action? Is this not a noble aim to propose to succeeding generations?—to make hundreds of thousands of hectares of unfertile soil blossom and by so doing to ensure the survival or better the existence of millions of our protégés; in short, to make prosperity a reality, thus guaranteeing Morocco's political and social tranquillity."[38]

As a first step, Noguès presented a five-year plan to begin in 1940 and to cost about 250 million francs or one-twentieth of his estimate of the total price tag. Financing was to come from the normal resources of the state (including, appropriately enough, the water-use tax), supplemented by credit, private participation, and loans. The two most significant items in the plan were a diversion canal from the Moulouya River to irrigate 30,000 hectares of the Triffas Plain (north of Oujda) and a dam on the Oum er Rebia to water 120,000 hectares on the Abda-Doukkala Plain (from Mazagan to south of Safi). Neither was what one could term a "small" water project of the sort that Noguès said he favored in 1936, although on balance the package he described was a "mixed program" of major and minor undertakings. The emphasis on major new construction, however, was the result of the improved economic climate at the end of 1938, the greater feeling of security and confidence among the protectorate's leaders, and the fact that the beneficiaries of these projects, in the past almost exclusively Europeans, would be Moroccans. In truth, only projects of oversized proportions could do the job that Noguès wanted done. They alone could supply the "new water" to agriculture and produce the change from sand to soil, from desert to garden.[39]

The creation of the Beni Amir perimeter at Tadla provides clues to some of the notions of French policymakers and to the obstacles they encountered in the realization of their grand goals. Noguès believed that it was proof of what could be done for the native population and the promise of what the future held once water began to work its magic. Berque called it the "greatest technical achievement in Morocco." The irrigated perimeter had originally been staked out as an area for "official colonization": the land had been purchased from the Beni Amir confederation and was slated to be developed by the Residency, which intended to auction it off to European settlers. But as the plans became known, land speculators began buying up "an important portion" of the remaining Beni Amir collective lands. In 1932, to stop what was becoming a crude land grab rapidly dispossessing the tribes, the Residency reversed itself, abandoned the colonization scheme, and decided instead to concentrate on ways of consolidating and irrigating the lands that it and the Beni Amir still controlled.[40] The irrigated perimeter concept, then, grew from this commitment, which was born out of a sense of frustration and guilt for the unintentional spoliation of tribal territory.

The first step was the assessment and registration of Beni Amir lands, which proceeded simultaneously with government efforts to end sales to European buyers. Between 1933 and 1936 (a period that coincided with a downturn in colonists' fortunes), property values and ownership among the Beni Amir remained stable as the Residency quietly moved ahead with its irrigation program. So that as many members of the confederation as possible would benefit, equal shares were distributed in a fifty-hectare experimental plot, the result of complicated purchases, expropriations, and land swaps. (In a sense, the economic experiment was to go hand-in-hand with a small social revolution.) Success with the first venture brought a second experiment on two thousand hectares. But in 1936 there was a renewed surge of land buying, which posed a "real social danger" because it threatened to impoverish the native farmer on the eve of his giant step toward prosperity. By now the Residency saw the perimeter as a political as well as a socioeconomic undertaking, a positive indication of France's good intentions at a time when the nationalists were arguing that France was unconcerned with the fate of Morocco's people. Noguès labeled it a priority project and pledged the government to irrigating up to seventy thousand hectares. He accompanied his statements with a *dahir* in mid-1938 that forbade the sale or cession of rights in the perimeter to anyone not of the Beni Amir.[41]

There was no happy ending. The land speculation had embittered native leaders, already suspicious of the perimeter plan. Even with the Residency's promise that nothing would be done without their "unanimous consent" and after two years of patient explanations and negotiations, there was unexpected resistance. In October 1937 one of the tribes, riled up by nationalist agitators who told them that their lands would surely end up in the hip pockets of European colonists, asked to withdraw, stalling the entire project. When attempts at persuasion failed to get them to reconsider, the French reluctantly removed the tribal chieftains, replacing them with men they could count on. The work resumed but with understandably less enthusiasm and confidence. The nationalists had scored a victory, forcing the French to go back on their word, increasing fears and resentments. For their part, the French were disappointed at the native response. The perimeter was, as Berque said, a technical success (the return on one hectare of irrigated perimeter land was 2,550 francs in 1937 compared with a "several hundred" franc profit on the same soil in the best years of the past), but it was not a human one. The French drew from the experience the lesson that their leadership was still as vital as ever, if Morocco was to progress.[42] Given the temper of the times, they learned the wrong lesson.

The plans for the revival of the urban artisan corporations and the rebuilding of the cities were as ambitious as the rural recovery and development program. Working with the artisans might have seemed an exercise in nostalgia and romance, a fit enterprise for preservationists who bemoaned the passing of old Morocco and resented the coming of the new. It is in fact somewhat ironic that Noguès chose to reinflate a group that was in economic decline and that some considered destined to be pushed to the edges of society. But prevailing opinion held that the artisans still had a vital social and political role to fulfill in pacifying the cities, and this undoubtedly recommended them to Noguès and encouraged him to lay a wager on their survival. In any event, judging by the Algerian example, the collapse of the corporations might have transformed modest, proud, and orderly artisans into rowdy, desperate, and hungry street proletarians, ready for revolt. Like so much else Algerian, Noguès wanted none of this.[43]

Without doubt, Noguès was sensitive to the human problem, to the plight of the independent craftsman faced with foreign competition, mechanization, and the loss of traditional markets. In addition, he wanted to channel artisan demands by using the revived corporations as substitutes for the labor unions he had reluctantly granted the European workers at the end of 1936. Perhaps most important, he sought to reverse the progress of anti-French nationalism among the craftsmen who had started to blame France for the economic setbacks that they were experiencing.[44] In sum, it appeared at first to be no more than a simple exercise in division and containment: to slice the artisans from the rebellious bourgeoisie, to reinforce their own social identity and separateness, and to fill their special needs. But Noguès was also troubled by the changing politics of the city. Lyautey had governed through the bourgeois notables—the merchants, the scholars, the religious leaders—yet the sons of those who had once received so much of his affection and attention had now begun to speak and strike out against his successors. As a counterweight to these young nationalists, Noguès turned to the artisans, in part out of desperation, to make of these "little people" the partners of the future. There was a strategic shift in what he proposed but in truth no repudiation of Lyautey's practice of reliance on the native elite. Recognizing contemporary dangers and realities, Noguès had broadened and redefined the elite to fit the circumstances.

Fez was the laboratory chosen for the experiment on the corporations. Despite the changes made in the city during the protectorate, Jacques Berque, one of the local architects of the corporation policy, believed that throughout the interwar years one could still speak of a "traditional" city life where the "old order of things" survived, where the corporations were numerous and influential.[45] The effort was coordinated by General Amédée Blanc and combined the talents of municipal officers, local promoters of native arts and crafts, the Office Chérifien d'Exportation, the chamber of commerce, and the Comité de la Foire. Financing came from the Caisse Régionale d'Épargne et de Crédit Indigènes de Fès-Taza, set up in May 1937. Berque, assigned the responsibility of overseeing day-to-day operations, explained that the "central notion" of the corporative policy was that of credit, putting money into the hands of the artisans as quickly and easily as possible but in the form of loans rather than outright grants, thereby binding the artisan to his trade and to the government just as advances to the fellah had done. Ties of money encouraged stability, and perhaps loyalty, which Noguès and his economic advisers believed would serve the protectorate in the present and the future.[46]

Municipal authorities determined the corporations that qualified for credit, ensuring that those chosen were of social and economic importance and could handle the financial responsibilities involved; and the councils of the corporations identified the individual artisans to receive the loans, making certain that their past and the collateral they pledged guaranteed repayment. In both selections the French had the last word, but wide latitude was given to the *amin*, the administrative officer of the corporation, and its governing council, thus pulling the corporation together from the inside as personal and corporative interest became intertwined. One consequence was that corporation members quickly retired their former chiefs, selecting younger, more knowledgeable men as their replacements and sometimes ones with "nationalist tendencies." The French were delighted with the hard work, efficiency, and positive results of the "new" officials. In less than two years, one-half million francs in loans had been made to seventeen corporations, with the tanners, weavers, brassworkers, and sandalmakers in the lead in terms of the amount of money borrowed. Judging by the repayment of the loans (99.7 percent, Berque claimed), the French were justified in being pleased.[47]

With emergency assistance to the artisans at Fez—in the main the distribution of grain—the French called again on the *amin* and the corporation councils to act as intermediaries, much as the SIP did in the countryside. Although this pushed the French to the background, it reduced their involvement in the unavoidable disputes over who and how much, often bitter conflicts that in the past had been deliberately stirred up by the nationalists. They were content with the exchange: no praise but no blame. The result was to strengthen the healthy hand of the corporations, turning over more and more tasks to their leaders. In this the French saw a positive social goal being realized while they achieved their economic aims.[48]

In addition to the concern for the renewal of the corporation as a social institution was the protectorate's drive to better the corporation's production and increase its markets, especially at home. This was as much a question of orientation as technique. Artisan industries supplied foreign or tourist markets to the neglect of the native market, which had all but been lost to foreign imports; in shirts, sandals, and djellabas, Fez's stock-in-trade, the native consumer often chose the cheaper foreign-made product. The French wanted to revive the commercial link between the city and its hinterland by redirecting a part of the corporation's production, reconquering terrain given up as lost. The mechanization and modernization of production, so reluctantly undertaken by the corporations, were accepted as inevitable by the French but handled with great care. Master craftsmen were designated to work with corporations in Fez, Marrakesh, and Rabat-Salé to improve techniques in tanning, shoe making, and weaving. Foreign connections were also solidified and expanded. The Comptoir Artisanal Marocain, a commercial and banking institution at Casablanca with a branch at Fez, was charged with advancing credit to corporations filling orders from abroad. And the Office Chérifien d'Exportation, long a protectorate display case to the world, stepped up its merchandising of artisan crafts. The artisan fairs at Fez in 1938 and 1939, traditional since the days of Lyautey, took on new significance: the economic vigor of the corporations was on display along with the products of its artisans.[49]

The success of the artisan policy depends upon the measure. The explosive "events" of Fez came in November 1937, a full year after Noguès had begun a policy of direct and close contact with corporation leaders, twelve months after the abolition of the nagging urban taxes and the distribution of thousands of quintals of grain, and five months after the artisan credit legislation had gone into effect. In spite of these changes, the events occurred, ironically preceded by corporation protest marches in August and September, which Morize, dumbfounded, described as a new nationalist tactic: "Each corporation in turn—with a day or two of interval—is sending delegations to the authorities to demand the abolition of taxes and the granting of aid."[50] In the light of this report, the artisan policy seems to have whetted rather than satisfied appetites.

It may have been that what Noguès proposed had not happened fast enough or in the proper sequence, or had been interpreted as concessions made out of weakness. Perhaps his program went too far, was too ambitious, and touched individuals and groups too deeply, sounding what Berque called the secret preserves of their social and moral instincts. It was an audacious and dangerous enterprise, especially at Fez, where the civic spirit was so "singularly bitter and unsettled." Although the immediate aim was to ditch the nationalists, its ultimate consequence would have been to replace the "old decorative silhouettes" of the past with a new group of native leaders.[51] This shift from old friends to new allies had to be handled delicately and with tact. To alter social roles was to tamper with the urban order of things.

There were many missteps. Morize complained that some of the reforms at Fez were being botched because there was neither "team spirit" nor organization among the French command. Former partisans were being needlessly insulted and potential partners frightened away. He was even forced to journey to Fez to patch up a feud between the pasha and one of General Blanc's subordinates; the young officer in question had imprudently proclaimed "*urbi et orbi* that the new policy would oust the 'grey beards' and give younger men the spots that had long been their due." Blanc admitted the seriousness of the mistake to Noguès: the "grey beards," he said, were still "faithful" to France and necessary "supports," all of which underscored (as Blanc did in his letter) the need for "an *evolutionary, gradual, progressive,* and *discreet* effort."[52] Teapot tempests of this sort understandably compromised the future.

Then too, perhaps Frenchmen overestimated the social importance of the corporation, attributing to it a guildlike unity, identity, and power that had never existed.[53] Lyon and Fez were centuries and cultures apart. Berque, Blanc, and the others were building anew rather than renovating a broken-down house, quite a different task than the one they had set for themselves. Money might make the corporations more than they had been, but it could not turn tanners into lord mayors overnight.

Probably no protectorate reform package could have prevented the events of Fez. Some corporations were already completely penetrated with nationalist ideas. Despite significant loans to the 260 impoverished brassworkers, they were reluctantly written off as "all nationalists." Even so, Le Tourneau claimed that there were not many artisans involved in the marches in the medina and that those who were belonged to corporations that had not received much attention from the Residency, the butchers, for example. Corporations that had received loans—the weavers, tanners, copper engravers, and even "nationalist" brassworkers—were present only in token numbers. In spite of November 1937, Le Tourneau believed that a "very clear détente" had been achieved with the artisans over the course of the year.[54]

Nevertheless, it was only after the political repression had produced a calmed atmosphere that the artisan policy could have some impact in restoring prosperity and imparting confidence. At Fez brassworkers drove English wares off the market and weavers began to counter the dumping of Japanese cloth; makers of sandals and leather goods expanded their percentage of the local trade. Noguès assured Delbos that the artisans, especially at Fez, were "breaking" with the nationalists, despite efforts to keep them stirred up. Morize attributed the nationalist decrease to the increase in artisan sales (from 12 million francs in 1936 to 20 million in 1937), export orders, and credit (hurried by the opening of three new Caisses Régionales d'Épargne et de Crédit Indigènes at Casablanca, Meknès, and Marrakesh in early 1938). By March 1938 the nationalists had been all but swept from the streets into the post offices; sending petitions and telegrams to Paris and Rabat was the most activity they could muster, a long step backward to the lonely days of summer 1936. Apparently the jangle of coins in their purses had made the artisans "deaf to the calls for action."[55]

With the coming of war in 1939, some corporations did extremely well. Foreign competition was stopped abruptly and the Residency turned to the corporations to supply the army. Unhappily, past concerns over internal organization, marketing, quality, and technical improvement were forgotten in the rush to produce. For those trades dependent wholly on imported goods or foreign markets, the situation was the reverse. The dramatic price rises (up to 30 percent on commodities in some cities in October 1939), coupled with the scarcity of native necessities, caused military reports to be punctuated with somber notes on the artisans' morose mood. But on balance the economic picture was satisfactory.[56]

The armistice years gave the artisan industries a new métier, that of providing substitutes for items unobtainable or in short supply. This too brought its share of prosperity. But it was uneven and accompanied by increased direct French intervention in the marketplace. Harmony became as scarce as tea, sugar, and cotton goods in the souks, and the talk turned to the possibility of German or American protectors making good on the promises of the French.

The city slums, filled with the hungry, destitute, and unemployed, were yet another sector of the urban front on which the French were called to act. For the rural migrant and the city proletarian, the protectorate moved directly without prior consultation and without the efforts at cooperation that marked so much that was done elsewhere. In part this was because there was no "traditional" native elite in the slums, where a jumble of tribal clusters cohabited without apparent connections. In part it was because the protectorate was cold to the idea of labor unions for the native working class, seeing them as potential adversaries. On this last point, it is worth mentioning that Noguès's stance against native unions raised eyebrows in Paris among the syndicalists of the Popular Front. When pressed to justify his course, he replied that native unions were inappropriate given the "degree of evolution" of the native population, the fact that a large part of the French zone was still administered by military authorities, and the "profound differences" between the European and native working classes. The government itself brushed off persistent and often indignant inquiries, saying that it was preoccupied with "more important concerns" and that in any event it always followed the lead of the authorities in Morocco.[57] Harsh words surprisingly uttered without Blum's legendary softness.

Noguès said next to nothing about his plans for the workers to the workers. They were only a small fraction of the total labor force, had no organizations or leadership of their own, and were all but forgotten by the nationalists. One sympathetic observer described the Moroccan proletariat of 1936 as "an inorganic mass of part-time workers" lacking both institutions and consciousness of a true working class.[58] The French planned to keep it that way. According to protectorate statistics, over sixty-eight thousand native laborers were employed in the "principal industries" of the French zone in 1937, including thirteen thousand mine workers. Of this number, only "several thousand" had steady jobs and were thus fit candidates for labor groups. Fewer than that participated in them. Since Moroccans were barred from forming unions of their own and excluded from European ones (which Noguès had authorized with much hesitation in December 1936), it is hard to know the degree of union sentiment among the native population. Some Moroccans, however, did join unions despite the ban and participated in strikes as well. They provide a rough measure of militant native syndicalism. Among the more than two thousand striking workers in Casablanca on 18 and 19 June 1936—part of the strike wave that followed the Popular Front's victory in France—about fourteen hundred were Moroccans, twice the number of European strikers. In the first half of 1937, the Union des Syndicats Confédérés du Maroc boasted twelve thousand members, of which a large number, if not the majority, were "illegal" Moroccans. For the same period the following year, the government counted only sixteen hundred Moroccans among eighteen unions, in addition to the native members of the miners' union of the Office Chérifien des Phosphates (numbering between two and three thousand), who took no pains to hide their affiliation. However tabulated, this was still a tiny percentage of the entire industrial work force, about 5 percent of Moroccans employed in industry, and the lawbreakers seemed not to trouble the authorities, although Noguès was none too happy about the situation. The toleration was short-lived. Citing the fact that union rules and regulations infringed upon the Makhzen's authority (which was unquestionably true), Sidi Mohammed sealed a *dahir* in June 1938—six days after a strike at the Louis-Gentil phosphate mines had required the intervention of the Garde Mobile—that set fines and jail terms for union members.[59] This ended the native labor movement.

To tell the truth, the repression was probably unnecessary. French union organizers had mixed feelings about recruiting Moroccans (or even promoting separate native unions), fearing that Europeans would be submerged. Even the nationalists had little sensitivity to or interest in the plight or the promise of the industrial worker.[60] In fact, in their search for partners, the French may have missed a bet. Neglected by the nationalists, unionists might have found an increasingly mechanized protectorate more comfortable than did most of their countrymen. It would have been a long shot and probably would have required a proconsul of working class sympathies like Gallieni to pull it off. In any event, the facts and figures were against working-class action, however heroic the strikes of 1936 and 1937 might have appeared in retrospect. It was the golden moment of the nationalist bourgeoisie, not their proletarian brethren.

Nevertheless, the proletariat did have the power to frighten. European businessmen had been caught off guard by the summer strikes of 1936. Their overriding fear was of Moroccans and Europeans marching arm in arm in the streets and together occupying the factories. Whether worker power could have developed in such a fashion, given the widening gulf between the European and Moroccan communities, is a matter of speculation.[61] But neither the protectorate nor the *patronat* wanted to take any chances.

What the Residency planned was similar to what was being done elsewhere, namely, the organization of labor corporations and massive protectorate *oeuvres sociales*, which Gallissot termed "preventive paternalism." "When the day comes that the corporation is a job-placement bureau, a mutual aid society, and a group for the protection of worker interests rolled into one," argued Contrôleur Civil Adrien Massonnaud, "unions will have no attraction for the Moroccan laborer." Unlike the artisan corporations, however, there was more artifice about them because it was not a question of resuscitating traditional institutions but of inventing new ones. Their purposes were familiar: to achieve a measure of social stability, to divorce political grievances from professional ones, and to permit the

government to guide the labor market and thus aid economic production. "But, it is from the political point of view," emphasized
Massonnaud, "that the reorganization and obligatory nature of the
corporations seem most useful, so as to avoid in Morocco the conflicts which in other countries so often pit workers against employ-
ers." All this smacked of fascist corporatism with the workers bound
hand and foot to the state and the *patronat*. But in the end, surely
because the worker menace had abated, the labor corporations were
never set up.[62]

However, the protectorate did press ahead with other plans for the
economic betterment of the working class, this time in partnership
with the European business community, which had by then been
converted to the need for a "social policy."[63] The end, as always, was
to protect France's future in Morocco by improving the situation of
Morocco's people. The means was the rebuilding of the cities, tear-
ing down slums and constructing workers' cities in their place. A
report of October 1936 insisted that such a plan was "completely
new."[64] The shantytowns of Rabat and Casablanca were the first targets. Rabat's Douar Debbagh, described as a "vast, roadless encamp-
ment," whose population had increased from four thousand to eight
thousand in two years, was torn down. In its place went the Cité
Yacoub el-Mansour, providing inexpensive housing for three thousand Moroccans as well as schools, a medical dispensary, and permanent marketplaces. Overseen by the protectorate's Comité de l'Habitat Indigène, it was paid for by the Residency and the sharifian
Direction des Habous at a cost close to 2.5 million francs.[65]

In Casablanca the fear of a typhus epidemic, coupled with the
commitment to a "social policy," made the protectorate and the city
fathers determined to clear the slums and erect a workers' town at
Roches Noires, east of Casablanca along the shore. Casablanca's
project, more ambitious than that of Rabat, combined public and private participation in a financing pattern seen before with the Office
Chérifien des Phosphates and the Bureau de Recherches et de Participations Minières. It was a model for the sort of internal funding
practices required by the native welfare effort. With Roches Noires
there was to be an equal division of costs between the Residency and
the City of Casablanca on the one hand and businessmen (ultimately twenty-one firms) on the other; the tab was totaled at 8 million francs. But in the face of unanticipated higher building expenses
and the pressure of other pledges, the Residency was forced to reduce its portion by four-fifths (from 2.4 million to 500,000 francs),
although it promised a 250,000 franc subscription from the Chemin

de Fer du Maroc. The net effect, however, was to return the drawings to the boards. In the bargaining that followed, it was decided to settle for cheaper housing (but at higher rents) and to contract an outside loan from the Caisse de Prévoyance des Fonctionnaires (a loan of 5 million francs, amortizable in thirty years at 5 percent interest). For their part, businessmen accepted a 2.5 percent reduction on the return of their invested capital. And the Residency and the City of Casablanca agreed to forgo any dividends on their money until the loan was completely amortized and to exempt the housing corporation from all taxes as well. The settlement brought together 4 million francs from private business (including 250,000 francs from the Chemin de Fer du Maroc subscribing as a private enterprise), 750,000 francs from the protectorate (including another 250,000 francs from the railroad company, this time subscribing as a public service), 1.6 million francs from the City of Casablanca, and the 5 million franc loan for a grand total of 11,350,000 francs. Here the protectorate willingly shared the financial responsibilities, facilitated the credit operations, and lowered the economic risks to accommodate private investment.[66]

The cornerstone at Roches Noires was not placed until December 1940, but despite the date (seven months after France's defeat on European terrain), it was not a bad day: the planned sixteen hundred housing units would be completed as scheduled. Others would follow. In July 1941 Noguès discussed the plans for a second Casablancan workers' city, Ben M'Sik, and approved 20 million francs as seed money.[67] He had styled the protectorate's recovery program a "mobilization against hunger and sickness." Neither was a respecter of persons. The "material fate" of the working class, he said, was as "dear" to him as that of the intellectuals.[68] Casablanca's Roches Noires and Rabat's Cité Yacoub el-Mansour were the coastal sentinels for the protectorate's plan of slum clearance and urban renewal, model projects in the larger native recovery and welfare program.

Noguès banked on the fact that prosperity would bring peace and he was not wrong. It did help to slow the nationalist advance in the cities and the countryside. French reports were correct to credit the political quiet from 1938 to 1940 to economic well-being. Even British evaluations, so often critical of protectorate policy, corroborated the French analysis.[69] Regrettably, the plans for abundance were compromised by the unforeseen course of the war, which sealed off the protectorate from the international commerce on which it depended and bound it ever more tightly to a France now desperate to meet its own economic needs. But even where prosperity did have a surprising sticking power, it alone could not be counted on to produce partisans of the protectorate. This should not have been startling, although the French appeared to have been taken aback, because pacification and prosperity had been the preconditions for the development of the nationalist bourgeoisie. In particular, the corporations never became the protectorate's stalwart defenders or loyal intermediaries. When confronted with evidence of this, the French argued that the Moroccans were hesitant partners and unprepared for the tasks delegated them. This may well have been true. But it was equally apparent that the French considered their guidance "indispensable" and everywhere acted the part of the "good tyrants" (although they rarely admitted it), pushing the population to accept ways they deemed wise and salutary.[70] Their motives were not unworthy ones and their accomplishments were many. This was surely not benign neglect or crass exploitation but well-intentioned paternalism that was paying off. It is to Noguès's credit that he was slowly eliminating the double standard, the two weights and two measures (to borrow John Halstead's phrase) that the nationalists found so intolerable. Paternalism, however, produced resentments along with profits. In addition, there was always the sneaking suspicion that France's future counted for more than Morocco's. Resurrecting the corporations, for example, sidestepped the very groups in the population that the French said they were educating to rule. The hard truth was that despite all the hopes to the contrary on both sides, Morocco's fortune and France's future did not necessarily coincide. It was a mistake to believe that money and talent, regardless of how wisely and generously engaged, could purchase a permanent and peaceful partnership.

FOUR

The Colonial Question

Although officially Morocco was a protectorate, not a colony, the Franco-Moroccan relationship was of the colonial kind. It was no secret that Frenchmen sought exclusive and permanent possession of a land that had strategic value, primarily because of its long border with Algeria, and economic promise. There may have been sharp disagreement over the extent and method of French control but little on either the need for it (aside from the worrisome whispers of "another Mexico") or on Morocco's present and future import to France. Even when Lyautey mused about the moment when Morocco would "detach itself" from the Metropole, he presumed a continuous French involvement in Moroccan affairs.[1] The French presence in the sharifian empire, then, did not come about from an absentminded imperial quest or from false steps in the quicksands of the desert but was the result of clearheaded, tough-minded action by the tiny, influential colonial lobby in Paris, the celebrated Colonial party, which was determined to acquire valuable African territory.[2]

Origins aside, the connection with France and the colonization of Morocco by Europeans defined the colonial situation. Both were essential to Lyautey's understanding of the French role overseas. He purposely brushed the colonial enterprise with the patina of mission since he realized what many failed to grasp, that a mission brought salvation to the missionary as well as to the souls-to-be-saved. Frenchmen, he believed, needed the balm from Gilead. In fact, without an active colonial policy, Lyautey was of the "ardent conviction" that France was headed for "ultimate decadence." Viewing his country from abroad in 1897, he characterized it as "unhealthy" and "destructive of will power and confidence," a familiar critique of those who were shamed by the dreary complacency of the bourgeois Third Republic.[3]

The colonies presented an altogether different aspect. From the moment he left Marseilles, Lyautey entered a world of engineers and officers, missionaries and merchants, consuls and colonists, all drawn overseas by the opportunity to serve, to work, and to lead. Witnessing talent and vigor inspired by purpose and self-sacrifice

made him a "convinced colonialist." Colonial expansion would enlarge this "marvelous greenhouse of wills and energies," he reasoned, and, much as hardy plants revive a garden, bring new life to a
dormant France. Changing metaphors, he spoke of the colonies as a
"school for society," teaching a "social duty" that he hoped would
have a "violent impact" and shake his countrymen, like sluggish
scholars, from their inertia and drowsiness. Then, switching to industrial imagery, he depicted the strong, selfless, and farsighted co-
lonials as generators in a "continuous circuit" between the France
outside and the France inside, between France abroad and France at
home, producing a current "of physical energy, of economic activity,
of worldwide commerce, of enterprising zeal, of generous thoughts,
vast desires, and broad judgments on the world and the nations
which people it."[4] The colonies as greenhouse, school, and power
station—the farmer, the educator, the engineer—were not surprising symbols for the future proconsul of Morocco, whose vision of
the colonies and colonists went far beyond the stereotypical cap-
tains and coaling stations, merchants and trading posts, priests and
mission schools. For Lyautey the very future of France was staked to
colonialism, but colonialism with a soul.

Once in command of Morocco some fifteen years later, the early
exuberance was somewhat tempered. The energy and will remained
undaunted, but disappointments of one sort or another brought
doubt, even despair. Morocco became less and less an example, more
and more an end in itself. The First World War dispersed key members of the "team" Lyautey had assembled and death claimed others
soon after: the heavenly team "triumphant," as he liked to think of
it, was gaining on the earthbound team "militant." Given the chance
for wartime leadership in France, he failed to make a dent. The Rif
rebellion and his humiliation finished any dream of the regeneration
of the Metropole by the colonies. If anything, it clouded his native
policy as well by crowning his military and political opponents with
the laurels of victory. In the end, instead of Morocco rescuing France
with shiploads of energetic leaders, France had rescued Morocco.

What had happened? His close collaborators had lived up to his expectations, but not the French colonists for whom he once had had
such great ambitions. His early experiences in Tonkin had filled him
with respect and admiration for the individual Frenchman abroad.
Here was a valiant colonial pioneer, battling an often hostile Metropole, draconian tariffs, withering taxes, and an oppressive government bureaucracy (to say nothing of on-the-spot trailblazing tasks),
yet somehow surviving, even emerging victorious, in lands far from

home. This was a type to rival the English settler (quite a compliment, considering that Lyautey measured all things colonial by the English standard), one indication of what the French called *génie colonial*.[5] That was the positive side, the Gallic version of the American frontiersman, an image even more appropriate in Morocco, which Lyautey constantly described as France's wild West.

But Lyautey began to reevaluate the colon after seven years spent in Algeria, where he saw the dark side of colonialism up close. Here were colonists in large numbers and high concentrations (some even third generation Algerian-born) who, despite remarkable material achievements, had little sensitivity for the native people and scant regard for the heroic intangibles that Lyautey deemed so valuable. Hidebound professional soldiers and bureaucrats abounded (types that he loathed), and everywhere Europeans acted the part of the frog who wished to be king, self-important, petty people who lorded their "Europeanness" over the natives. In short, these were France's worst, not its best. Although his conclusions were overdrawn, faithfully describing only a fragment of the colonial world in Algeria, they soured him on mass immigration. What he wanted for Morocco was selective and guided colonization. He thought this could be made possible by the protectorate, pledged as it was to the perpetuation of the sharifian empire, whose land, unlike Algeria's, was not about to be handed out to any European who asked. In this case, as in others, the protectorate would serve as a shield against Algerian excesses.

Lyautey's deepest fears were never realized, but neither were his highest hopes. There was never a system of regulated immigration to Morocco. Instead of self-sufficient farmers with some money in their pockets, Morocco attracted war veterans on pensions who needed public aid to get started and state support to keep going, retired warriors in search of subsidized homes for heroes. But protectorate authorities did choose some of the sites for European farms and settlements, land set aside for "official" colonization. By 1935, 271,000 hectares of land had been sold by the government, the vast majority in plots of between two hundred and four hundred hectares. Translated, this became 1,750 farms, presumably located where the protectorate thought they would do the most good. Private acquisition of Moroccan land was uncontrolled and more than doubled the official sales: over half a million hectares were in European hands in 1935.[6] Despite the slowdowns and speedups in land purchases, which reflected immigration patterns and economic conditions, the arrows on the charts pointed ever upward.

What had disturbed Lyautey in Algeria also plagued him in Morocco, namely, the Europeans' lack of sympathy for the Moroccan people. In particular, he resented the strain of superiority epitomized by the expression *sale bicot* (dirty Arab). This epithet is "so deeply shocking and dangerous," he lectured the Lyon Chamber of Commerce, "that those to whom it is addressed cannot but understand it immediately and all the scorn and menace that it includes." "This race is not inferior to us," he told a Rabat audience in 1921, quoting his longtime companion Colonel Henri Berriau, "it is merely different." On his own, he added: "Let us learn their ways, just as they are learning ours. Let us both adapt." It was not for nothing that he targeted the conciliation of European and native interests as "perhaps the most delicate problem for colonial governments," one that was "neither easy nor pleasant, because whoever says conciliation has to make compromises and reciprocal concessions, and, consequently, dissatisfaction arises from all quarters." But how could conciliation take place in view of the persistent lopsided human relationships? Privately Lyautey confessed that the colonist had a "Kraut" mentality when it came to ideas on race, holding that "inferior races" were meant to be exploited "mercilessly." His dismal conclusion was that the pioneers who were taming the Moroccan wilderness had "neither intelligence nor a sense of humanity."[7]

Lyautey's open affection for the Moroccan people, his showy regard for Islam, and his public display of deference to the sultan were thus more than mere political calculation. He was practicing what he preached, trying to counter the racism he despised and prove that Europeans and Moroccans could respect, even love, one another. This sensitivity to the human dimensions of colonialism Lyautey willed to Noguès, who sought to inspire trust and confidence in the Moroccan people for the partnership with France. By all accounts, Noguès succeeded. His personal contacts, made solid by real friendships, gave him a standing second to none. Amid the turmoil of native nationalism, economic disruptions, and threats of war, he quoted Lyautey to Europeans: our "primary and essential duty," he said time and time again, is to promote the "cordial and sympathetic association of two races." "I hope for the sake of Morocco's future," he told the dwindling number of Frenchmen who had come to Morocco before 1917, "that this friendly cooperation will become ever wider and more fruitful." Noguès knew the statistics: in 1937 Europeans were outnumbered 7 to 1 in Algeria, 11 to 1 in Tunisia, and 24 to 1 in Morocco. But he may have been talking to the wrong group. Most accounts agree that the settlers who came after 1925 were more exclusive and less tolerant than their predecessors.[8] Yet common interests blurred the differences of years. As the power and troubles of Europe's immigrants increased, so did the gulf between the two communities.

In the years between Lyautey's departure and Noguès's arrival, the colonists' power waxed. Up until 1919 settler opinion had been expressed through "consultative chambers" as well as municipal commissions, all of whose members were handpicked by the Residency. The chambers and commissions were used to gather information and to provide advice but had no decision-making authority.[9] This was how Lyautey preferred it—he was a *démophile*, not a democrat—but the system could not last, given the colons' understandable desire for greater say in matters that would affect their future and that of the land in which they had chosen to make their homes. Lyautey put them off by protesting that France was not sovereign in Morocco, as it was in Algeria, and thus French political institutions were inappropriate, but he eventually gave way and in 1919 established the Conseil du Gouvernement. With it came the notion of dual sovereignty, shared sovereignty, or cosovereignty, which was later elegantly described by one writer as "an association of sovereignties."[10] It all came down to the same thing: a louder voice for French colonists.

Still, although the Conseil du Gouvernement could discuss and debate a wide range of issues, it did not have the power to legislate or even bring matters to a vote. Thus it could not block the Residency's plans by rejecting the budget. Perhaps Lyautey hoped the *conseil* would be just another *Schwatzbude*, a talk shop, as the old imperial German parliament was derisively called, but the *conseil*'s influence reflected the prominence of its members, the presidents and vice-presidents of the chambers of agriculture, commerce, industry and of the regional Comités d'Études Économiques (economic councils), and the delegates from the municipal commissions. Since the chambers were elective, the Conseil du Gouvernement was an elected assembly in practice, albeit partially and indirectly.[11]

This was as far as Lyautey would go. Steeg was willing to do more. After all, there were over 66,000 French citizens in Morocco when he took charge. In 1926 he permitted those among them who were hitherto unrepresented to elect delegates directly to the Conseil du Gouvernement. This was a tip of the hat in the direction of democratic reform and consistent with Steeg's procolon convictions. It was a clean break with the Lyautey past, with the marshal's political conservatism and his narrow notion of the protectorate. More generally, Steeg symbolized the reassertion of parliamentary authority over the colonies, the end of an age of military proconsuls and independent fiefdoms. As a sort of representative-on-mission, he brought what the Republic had exported since the days of the French Revolution: control, centralization, and a closer union with France. This was updated assimilationism—making the empire more like France —a repudiation of what Lyautey had come to stand for.[12]

During the Steeg and Saint years, the colonists were handled with greater care. In 1931, the third year of Saint's residency, the number of French citizens topped 115,000—a 42 percent increase in five years. Anyone with a gram of political sense could not afford to ignore that figure or the impressive European "miracles" in Morocco. In less than two decades, the face of the coast had been permanently transformed from a string of oceanside towns hugging the Atlantic shore to a bustling urban commercial cluster seeking trade ties with lands washed by the Pacific. Casablanca, a skyscraper city with a Chicago look, had no European or African counterpart; it was a metropolis of the future, a "prestigious witness to French energy and initiative."[13] French farmers, attracted by rich soil and a climate not unlike the valleys of California, had changed the central plain with equal drama, sowing fields of grain reminiscent of the Beauce flatlands, dotting the countryside with silos, granaries, and tiled-roof farmhouses, building towns where once only tents had been pitched, and raising modern cities in the shadows of centuries-old fortresses.

Among the colonists, there were many constituencies, and each resident gardened a particular plot. For Steeg it was the professionals, the middle farmers, the small businessmen and shopkeepers, and the civil servants, those who fit in nicely with his Radical Socialist background. By temper and training, Saint preferred the chamber-of-commerce types, men of established reputation and means. When divided up this way, the political landscape resembled that of France, but when it was united, as it could be on some issues, the pressure of these men and their money could be felt across the Mediterranean in Paris. For example, their collective muscle was put to the test with the unhorsing of Saint's successor, Henri Ponsot, who served an unhappy stint in Rabat and then was packed off to Ankara. Ponsot's ouster was a landmark in the emergence of settler power. It came about in the same year that Noguès was given the Residency.

Ponsot tilted with the colonists on more than one occasion before he lost the tourney. He first angered them by showing concern for the rights of the native population and sympathy for the nationalists. But however it may have appeared, Ponsot's purpose in early

1934 was only to block an incipient "reconciliation" between the sultan and the nationalists, which he rightly saw as having dire consequences for France. He explained to Paris that popular resentment of the Makhzen's role in the Berber *dahir* affair had frightened the sultan and his ministers and provoked a reevaluation of Makhzen policy. As the first step in the Makhzen's new course, the word was spread that the sultan had been "deceived" by the French. The effect was to bring the sultan and the nationalists—never completely at odds—closer together in a slow and careful rapprochement. This was made dramatic in May by the sultan's tumultuous reception in Fez, where he was greeted with shouts of "Long live the sultan!" and "Down with France!" All this was making collaboration between the Residency and the Makhzen "difficult, if not impossible," and Ponsot predicted a certain "impasse" in relations. The way out, Ponsot reasoned, was to move quickly toward the nationalists to grant some of what they wanted and, in the process, to undercut the sultan, who wished to pose as their protector. If the maneuver worked, Ponsot then planned to turn back to the sultan and the Makhzen and offer a guarantee of their authority (as in the past) in return for their "loyal cooperation" in the future. He admitted that the strategy was "quite fragile and full of unknowns." How to predict the nationalist response or make scrutable the Makhzen's intrigues? Still, there was a chance for success. The sultan was "young and vain," worried about his dignity, and jealous about his place; in addition, Grand Vizier el-Mokri and Si Mammeri, the sultan's tutor, were firmly in the French camp.[14]

But would the European community countenance a policy of concessions to those whom it had dismissed as little more than walking "digestive tracts"? The answer to that question should never have been in doubt. When the nationalists' Plan of Reforms was made public late in 1934, *L'Afrique française* called it "tendentious, empty, and incoherent." Even Ponsot tagged it "a thesis for a law degree" rather than a plan for action.[15] The language may have been different but the impact was the same: the nationalist proposal was immediately rejected by the government. The episode effectively discredited Ponsot in European eyes as an expert in native affairs.

The main reason for Ponsot's recall, however, was rooted in his determined opposition to the colonists' demands for revision of the 1906 Act of Algeciras, which fixed the tariff rate at 12.5 percent ad valorem, preventing the protection of domestic produce and manufactures and any bargaining for reciprocal commercial advantages.

Ponsot admitted that the Algeciras system was "unjust and out-dated," but amid the world economic turmoil of the mid-1930s he judged the time unripe for change. Any modification of Algeciras, he said, was "impossible and perhaps even undesirable." In addition, he was cold to the notion, pushed hard by many influential business-men, that Morocco should move closer to France to form an imperial economic bloc. He made no friends by bluntly telling the Conseil du Gouvernement that the integration of the Moroccan economy into the French economy was a "utopian idea" and ought not to be taken seriously.[16]

Thus, Ponsot was equally unsuccessful as advocate for native af-fairs or as guardian of the colonists' welfare. A career diplomat (who had negotiated successfully with Abd el-Krim in 1926), he spoke for the ministry of foreign affairs. Revision had been ruled out by Paris, but bilateral negotiations with the Algeciras signatories were still possible. The catch was that the tariff freedom would have to be paid for by commercial privileges to the treaty powers at prices that most Europeans found too high: increased living and labor costs. There would be no gains to Moroccan trade abroad to offset these losses. Over time, when the clock on concessions ran out, Morocco would know true tariff liberty, but few colonists wanted to wait. What Pon-sot proposed was clearly unacceptable: a protectionist plan that raised new money for the administration through customs revenues but postponed relief for the colonists.[17]

Not surprisingly, the Ponsot plan did not stay the agitation for re-vision, which climbed to a fever pitch in 1934 and took on a nasty ad hominem tone. Obviously there was more to this than Algeciras—personality and politics had a share in the dispute as did dissent over budget allocations and native policy—but economic interest was the touchstone that brought the chambers of agriculture and of com-merce and industry into coalition. Finding Ponsot unmovable, the colonists pressed to transform the Conseil du Gouvernement from a consultative body to a deliberative body where votes would be taken (a giant step toward a legislative assembly) and lobbied for a *conseil économique* as well. Both would have given the colonists more clout in Rabat and their opinions additional weight in Paris. Both were firmly rejected by Ponsot.[18] Ultimately, the colonists played Romans in an Aventine secession that succeeded. The Conseil du Gouvernement refused to sit for the December 1935 session, and, following Casablanca's lead, all the members of all of Morocco's chambers of commerce and industry resigned. When Paris had had enough, Ponsot was told to prepare for his leave-taking and was promoted to ambassador of France, that ambiguous mark of past success or failure.

Marcel Peyrouton, who took Lyautey's cape from Ponsot, came the closest to the colonists' *beau idéal*. A respecter of work, talent, and money, a tough advocate of colonial interests, a no-nonsense adversary of native nationalism, and a ruthless budget trimmer and foe of spendthrift government, he possessed an energy that was as compelling as his views were harsh. He too had his favorites. He was soft on farmers and businessmen, hard on low-level bureaucrats (*fonctionnaires*) and trade unionists, and he never had a kind word for those of the political Left. On balance, however, he probably spoke for more Europeans than his predecessors had, for the times were ripe for this stern speaker of plain prose. Even the sultan was intrigued by his austere, aggressive plans for economic recovery.

Peyrouton wasted no time in expanding settler participation in the affairs of the protectorate. He set up regional administrative councils and economic committees, the Comité Permanent de Défense Économique to be consulted on virtually every question of an economic nature, and the Comité Supérieur d'Action Sociale et du Travail to advise on matters pertaining to the labor force. Although there were native members of all these groups, Moroccans were heavily outnumbered. The net effect was to entrench Europeans firmly in areas where Lyautey—and poor Ponsot—had tried to hold them at bay. Coupled with the extension of credit to farmers and merchants and delays for "debtors of good faith," the flurry of *dahirs* and *arrêtés* made Peyrouton a popular man.[19] Consciously or not, he was stacking the deck against the Popular Front, making a reformist game, should the government decide on it, difficult to play. For what Peyrouton had given no man or government could take away with ease.

Peyrouton had been appointed to the Residency on the advice of colonists who wanted an experienced economic problem-solver. He came with a good track record in Tunisia and was told on his arrival that no leader had been more impatiently awaited, for it was a moment of urgency, expectation, and trouble. Morocco—so said the president of Casablanca's Chamber of Agriculture—was at "a decisive turning point" in its economic history.[20] What so worried the colons was the lack of export markets for their farm products. The complaint was familiar: it reflected a difficulty international in origin, inflicted without purpose or malice on the sharifian empire, which had raised a universal hue and cry among the farmers of the world's agricultural-exporting states. But Morocco's lament was laced with bitter irony. Stunning Europe and America by the strength and rapidity of its economic growth, Morocco had won a place in foreign markets for its grain, garden produce, wines, oranges, canned goods, and palm fiber (*crin végétal*), only to see what had been created begin to stagnate and die, what had been conquered, surrendered. The pain of it all was eloquently conveyed by one *vieux Marocain* whose roots went back before the protectorate: "With the sweat of our brows and at great sacrifice, we transformed Morocco's wastelands into fields, orchards, and vineyards. In twenty years we accomplished the work of two generations. But, having created new riches at a time when economic conditions frustrate their distribution, each day we become poorer and poorer." The anger was expressed by Marcel Chapon, president of Casablanca's Chamber of Commerce, who had led the fight against Ponsot: "We are proud of our products, concerned about our markets, and scandalized when commercial practices, against which we are powerless [i.e., the dumping of foreign goods], condemn us to selling at a loss, to stagnation, and to unemployment." Said many ways, it all amounted to the same thing: Algeciras had left Morocco naked to its enemies, an unprotected "free city," Noguès later called it, in a walled world of tariffs.[21]

Part of the blame for Morocco's misfortune was assigned to France, which was accused of having forgotten Morocco in its economic negotiations with other countries. "Too often, [Morocco] has been shunted aside, isolated, even sacrificed."[22] In direct Franco-Moroccan trade agreements, the criticism was also on the mark, judging by the shrinking size of the quotas of Moroccan produce permitted entry into France. But it was hardly fair, for metropolitan farmers were struggling with low prices and contracting markets, just as their Moroccan confreres were, and certainly deserved the small break that the exclusion of Moroccan goods brought. The real villain of the Franco-Moroccan piece was the system of subsidized agriculture in Morocco, which required state aid of some form or another to turn a profit. In good times the cost of this aid was written off as necessary to the prosperity of the colonial community in order to encourage and make permanent the French presence. In hard times it was a burden increasingly resented by metropolitan producers and taxpayers.

A loaf of bread and a jug of wine tell the tale. With wheat, what had once seemed a good cash crop to ease Europe's hunger had grown into a stiff competitor for the favor of France's bakers. Until 1928 France had bought all the wheat that Morocco could produce at higher prices than could be obtained in Casablanca. The happy situation ended with the worldwide overproduction of 1929 and the surpluses of the 1930s. Nevertheless, true to its imperial vocation, France permitted an annual quota of Moroccan wheat to enter duty free into the Metropole throughout the years of hardship. This was generosity, not stinginess, even though colonial farmers, overloaded with wheat, still plunged into debt. Winegrowers, virtually swimming in rivers of wine, expected similar life preservers. If denied them, "several hundred" European and "numerous" native winegrowers would drown. But despite intense lobbying, France refused to admit Moroccan wine to French tables. In consequence and with great reluctance, the protectorate itself was forced to step in to prohibit the planting of new vineyards, to control domestic sales, and to purchase the excess production. Angry winegrowers accused France of turning its back on them, although they had been warned repeatedly against extending the cultivation of wine grapes.[23]

There could never be a satisfactory resolution to these irritating questions, which at desperate moments pushed some colonists to utter the vague, threatening demand for economic "liberation" from *all* the "internal and external mortgages" on Morocco.[24] It sounded like a declaration of independence. But could European agriculture in Morocco survive in a free and open world market without protectorate or French support? Since farming was "characterized by high costs, by an insistence upon high profits, and, as a result, by high-priced products," one economic historian has concluded that without "heavy" subsidy Moroccan exports would not have stood a chance abroad. A contemporary report confirmed that judgment.[25] Was there any choice? With subsidies no longer certain, a step toward the world market was forced by circumstances. There was even a certain brave defiance about it.

It seemed as if the colonists were now united in a vision of their land and its future: its resources had been developed enough (at least for the moment); now the need was to find buyers for its products. Peyrouton's role was to be the champion of Morocco's commercial independence, the architect of its economic transformation, the seller of its goods. He was eager for the assignment. Lyautey's effort, he explained, had been to pacify and create; his would be to pull together and revitalize. "We are experiencing growing pains, a *crise de croissance*, not always the least serious of ailments." But he welcomed "tough tasks"; with the colonists' help, disciplined thought, and determined action, he was certain of the "ultimate triumph."[26] Of course, he would not be permitted to play the colonial Carnot, organizing for economic victory, because the Popular Front had slated him for early retirement. But the hopes he had encouraged remained, adding to the bitterness felt by his removal. The Blum government was wise to fire him in Paris, to refuse to let him return to Rabat, for it was said that the colons would never have given him up if he had returned.

Under such tense circumstances, Noguès arrived in Morocco, his ceremonies of reception separated from those for Peyrouton by only four months. Those who greeted him did not disguise their contempt for the partisan politics that had felled Peyrouton and for the government that had shown by this act such small regard for their concerns. "How many Frenchmen," asked *La Bougie de Fès*, "have spent a good part of their lives in the colonies to get away from all the nauseating filthiness of the so-called civilized life of the Metropole, renouncing numerous pleasures in favor of the satisfaction of a liberated existence through hard work, far from the repugnant stupidities of partisan politics."[27] This was strange and strong stuff, particularly from those pledged to bring the benefits of French "civilization" to Morocco, and it could hardly have fostered respect for France's delegates among the native elite.

Although Noguès was billed as the shining example of continuity, the parade of residents—three in as many years—gave the lie to any Paris attachment to permanency in the protectorate. Moreover, no one had forgotten that when Paris police chief Jean Chiappe was fired in February 1934 (the prelude to the street fighting of 6 February), he had been offered the Residency in Morocco as compensation. On the other side, Noguès was a hard man to fault even though he came under the sign of Blum. "He has all the qualities of intelligence, of heart, of experience, of wisdom, and of bravery needed to direct France's enterprise" across the Mediterranean. "With General Noguès the tradition, the doctrine, the soul of Lyautey return to Morocco."[28] In addition, the international reasons for Noguès's nomination were apparent, even to those most outraged by the change. The military uprising in Spain, triggered by the army's takeover of the Spanish zone in July (while Peyrouton was still in Rabat), posed a threat to the security of the French zone as serious as that of the Rif rebellion. In fact, this was the official explanation for taking on the "new pilot," and Noguès was the first resident since Lyautey to be given both political and military powers. Seen in this light, one might even applaud the Popular Front's imperial vigilance rather than condemn its lack of "colonial spirit." Even the fussing over the question of "residential instability," touted as so "prejudicial to the interests of the country," was dismissed by *Le Petit marocain* as childish prattle. "We have no need of someone to take us by the hand and lead us to our destiny. It would make no difference who our guide was, if we were clear-sighted enough to direct ourselves. Our wisdom, our prudence, our unity of vision, our concerted action, our devotion to the interests of our own social community should enable us to withstand without any great harm this governmental instability which is important only to the degree that we make it so."[29] This was a wise and realistic statement, asserting publicly the private force of colonial society.

In his initial contacts with the colonists, Noguès sought to reassure them by praising Peyrouton, an attempt at political stroking that the nationalists interpreted as Blum's betrayal of promised colonial reform. It is true that there would be no reform of the hundred days sort. It would come only after order and confidence had been restored in all quarters, and then, slowly and deliberately but surely. Aesop's unheroic, victorious tortoise might have been a fitting and not unkind symbol of the Popular Front's reform intentions. At the same time, Noguès never stopped saying that his first concern was for the welfare of the native population, not the colonial community, the kind of statement that twenty years later would have brought angry European mobs into the streets to hoot and spit at the resident. That it did not can be attributed to Noguès's recognized skill in the touchy matters of human relations and to the colonists' grasp of the realities of the moment.

The dramatic difference in priorities was in part a result of a change in the weather. In May only one of the spokesmen who greeted Peyrouton thought to mention the serious consequences for the harvests of the twin terrors of drought and flood.[30] By October, however, the fullness of the calamity had been made manifest. The disaster in the fields now surpassed the export market crisis as the protectorate's chief worry. Coupled with the nationalist-led disruptions at Casablanca and Fez in November, native questions clearly took precedence over other cares. Still, Noguès linked the welfare of the native population to the economic prosperity of the protectorate as a whole. Working for the well-being of the native population was "the surest way" of working for the prosperity of the Frenchmen in Morocco. In this European farmers could find some comfort.

Noguès's public remarks did not contain as much encouraging news as Europeans would have liked. In his tour of the cities in 1936 and 1937, he said that the protectorate would do all in its power to mitigate the effects of the economic crisis so as to protect the "admirable achievement of Moroccan colonization." But whatever was promised was counterbalanced by reminders of present and future problems. "The budget restrictions that the present situation demands, the imperious and urgent aid that the misery of a large number of our protégés requires, [and] the obligation to harmonize our economy with those of the Metropole and our Algerian neighbors must remain constantly before our eyes."[31]

Noguès did reveal to Meknès producers that the French government had established "a certain number" of new quotas for "several categories of agricultural products," thereby creating more outlets for farm produce. Yet the creation of a wheat office meant that those who had struggled to find high-priced export markets for their grain would now be forced to sell it in Morocco at government-regulated prices. Even the stunning domestic price rise—for soft wheat, a rise from 69 francs a quintal in 1935 to almost double that (132 francs) in 1937—did not fully compensate or satisfy producers, according to the president of Casablanca's Chamber of Agriculture, who pointed to the farmers' unbalanced account books and debts of the past.[32] What they wanted were new markets abroad and free markets at home to reap the gold from the grain that they felt was their due.

It might be argued that these were merely the whinings of Morocco's greedy Silas Marners, well-off misers who played the pauper. But this interpretation did not seem valid to Lucien Paye, a teacher at the Collège Moulay Youssef at Rabat and later France's minister of national education and first ambassador to the People's Republic of China. Paye tramped the countryside around Fez in 1937, interviewing colonists and leaving them questionnaires to fill out so he could better understand the economics of colonial agriculture. He discovered that farmers who had borrowed money to buy their land and equipment and to build their homes and farm buildings prior to 1932 were indeed caught by the collapse of land values and farm prices. By mid-decade what they owned was worth a third of what they had paid and what they produced was unwanted in France or abroad. To continue farming meant still more loans for seed and running expenses. Debts to private banks and public institutions piled up; beginning in 1934, defaults were not uncommon, and they were soon followed by demoralizing property seizures and sales. There was little here to cheer colonists or to serve as an example for native farmers.[33]

Like Arthur Young, the English agronomist who traveled through

France on the eve of the Great Revolution, Paye let the colonists speak for themselves. They had a lot to say. They told him they were tired of being tagged colonial *cul-terreux*, wealthy clodhoppers enriched by exploiting the natives, leading a "château life" among the palms: "If, instead of thinking of us as middle-class farmers made rich by the work of others, people would see us for what we are, look at how we live, and understand our worries and burdens, they would come to our aid." They readily admitted that there were those who wanted a fast fortune and had no love for the land or its people. The majority of the colonists, however, were of another kind—honest, hardworking men of the soil who saw no easy road to riches and were committed to making Morocco their home. Nor were they out to soak the government by having it bail them out in rough times. "The cherished dream of every colonist is one day to be able to live up to his contractual obligations." But frankly, without government help, the colonist was sunk and he knew it. Some farmers had debts that would take sixty years to repay. "Many of us are over fifty years old. We will all be dead before we are debt free."[34]

The way out lay with the government. The colonists, contradicting their modest manners, suggested that the government cancel the farm debt (estimated at 126 million francs) owed to the Caisse Fédérale de la Mutualité et de la Coopération Agricole, the state farm bank, or revalorize the land by valorizing their crops; price supports on such a truly revolutionary scale would enable them to pay off their debts.[35] Staggering in their financial implications, these solutions were never seriously considered. However, it was possible to do more of what the government had done before, namely, guidance in introducing new crops, aid in finding markets, and more credit on better terms—tried and true remedies, albeit undramatic ones. The one bright spot was that the government now assured the colonists that it would press for revision of the Act of Algeciras to pry open foreign markets and pave the way for a better economic relationship with France. One of the labors of Peyrouton was reassigned to Noguès.

Commerce was the other side of the colonial coin. The European business community, which Gallissot has called the "dominant element of the protectorate," was both formidable and vulnerable, as the events of 1936 proved.[36] It had toppled Ponsot and promoted Peyrouton. But it had been stunned by the Popular Front's victory in France and unprepared for the wave of summer strikes in Morocco. The military revolt in the Spanish zone and the drought and famine in the French zone, coupled with the announcement of Peyrouton's dismissal, completed its demoralization. Angry and apprehensive businessmen met the new resident at dockside in September. In Noguès they found a conciliator who promised to help them as best he could in return for their support and cooperation. His success with the *patronat* was largely a result of his skillful repair of damaged relationships between the colons, the Residency, and France. What he wanted was an end to the agitation for the *voix délibérative* in the Conseil du Gouvernement and no protest over the plans for native welfare. What he offered in exchange was a closer relationship with government.

Noguès's city speeches in 1936 and 1937 mixed warnings against "blind optimism" with kind words and small favors. Everywhere an olive branch but little money. Tourism was to be promoted in Marrakesh, and plans were made to beef up the military garrison and build a naval air station at Port Lyautey. The main purpose of these projects was to help out "small commercial enterprises" by supplying them with new customers. In fact, when money was tight, French legislators usually suggested this sort of remedy for places past their prime. For the merchants of Oujda, however, there were only promises: Noguès would try to iron out the difficulties blocking Moroccan exports through the port of Nemours (Morocco's Algerian outlet to the Mediterranean) and to work out with Algerian authorities the questions of transit and markets for Moroccan goods. At Safi plans to enlarge the fishing port, aid the export of manganese, and increase the supply of city drinking water were shelved; only the expansion of foreign markets for Safi's specialty, canned sardines, was being vigorously pursued. With Mazagan it was tourism again, a pledge for small water projects, and authorization for a bond issue of 4.5 million francs for municipal works to be floated locally without the Residency's participation.[37] For the moment at least, there was only a trickle of cash flowing from Rabat to the European cities. Commerce would be forced to ride out the crisis with no more than what Peyrouton had done.

What sweetened a tart pill was Noguès's handling of urban unrest and labor matters. The firm repression of city violence in 1936 and 1937 reassured the colonists that order remained the password of the hour and that the feared economic and social reforms would not come about as a result of popular pressure from the streets. On the other hand, Noguès began to convince them—if the strikes and riots had not—that native progress was a prerequisite to their own prosperity and France's security. The call for labor corporations and Noguès overall policy of "good works" in dealings with the native working class provided the *patronat* with a unity of purpose, a clean conscience, and a doctrine. Above all, Noguès seemed to be someone commerce could count on over the long haul, for he believed that the state should be an associate to business and industry. "To the formulas that characterize the action of the state—the state-as-judge, the state-as-policeman—we are glad to be able to add that of the state-as-partner," he told those who attended the closing banquet of the 1938 Casablanca International Fair. "The interests of private individuals and the public interests of the state are, in effect, interdependent. This need for solidarity is clearly apparent in a country like Morocco, which is going through a period of economic growth and whose structure plainly shows the interpenetration of all the economic forces at work. Here the state has the fundamental role of supporting enterprise without stifling its energy and vigor by a tutelage that is too rigid."[38]

Noguès expected businessmen to pledge a share of their time and money to the protectorate's projects in return for a slice of the profits. This was what Roches Noires was all about. If they overreached themselves, he pulled them back. When it became obvious, for example, that they were disregarding the 1941 law on the minimum wage, he ripped the matter from their hands and gave it to his regional heads to enforce. The stranglehold that the *patronat* tried to put on the protectorate—judging by its list of requirements in July 1940—was fought off.[39] In fact, during the Vichy regime, colon institutions either were muzzled or disappeared altogether. The Conseil du Gouvernement was suspended in December 1940, then abolished in March 1941; the municipal commissions were dissolved in September 1940; and the chambers of agriculture, commerce, and industry were made appointive. Peyrouton's famous Comité Permanent de Défense Économique and Comité Supérieur d'Action Sociale et du Travail were both suppressed at the end of 1940. The protectorate, now running on Vichy time, turned the clock back to 1919. *Patronat* influence survived, of course, through a restricted Comité Central Économique (set up in 1941 without a clearly defined membership or function), small budget committees, and the celebrated Groupements Économiques, which were established as a wartime measure prior to France's defeat.[40] But these were dwarves' cottages, hardly fit meeting houses for a strong, argumentative, and diverse business community. Agricultural interests were complaining about the Groupements Économiques in 1941 long before the democratic breezes of 1943 made such complaints obligatory.[41] Even the private power it brought to certain leaders lacked the force of

Meknès, June 1942. *Photo Jacques Belin*

Meknès, October 1942. *Photo Jacques Belin*

public *patronat* expression that had been decisive in the feud with Ponsot.

Still, with a resident who was sympathetic and shrewd, there was little reason to buck his authority. In fact, amid inner turmoil and external threats of both the economic and political kind, Noguès was more and more recognized as the long-awaited *chef*, capable of leading the protectorate from chaos to order and of enforcing the "entente among all Frenchmen in Morocco." He regarded such an

Meknès, October 1942. *Photo Jacques Belin*

entente as "indispensable" to safeguarding French interests, and few
settlers needed to be reminded of the colonial facts of life. "Never
forget that we are only a handful of French families in this land,"
Noguès said in his 1941 New Year's message, a "weak minority" that
can only carry out its mission by remaining "tightly knit," by con-
stituting a "bloc without fissures."[42] The unity of the colonial community that Noguès pursued and Vichy later prized was a result of
circumstance, personality, and colonial good sense. Best of all, it
worked for Noguès rather than against him.

What surely won the hearts of all the colonists was Noguès's part
in the assault on Algeciras (the millstone that had sunk Ponsot) and
in the ending of the British capitulations. Both symbolized outside
intrusion in France's affairs in Morocco, the "open door" pushed

wide in matters of trade and extraterritorial rights exercised by rivals, in this case, Great Britain and the United States. Even older than Algeciras were the capitulations imposed on the sharifian empire to snatch Europeans and those in their employ from the clutches of native justice; it was a humiliating lever used to press for political and economic concessions. France's drive to end them preceded the establishment of the protectorate. At the time of the Anglo-French declaration of 1904 on Egypt and Morocco, both parties tried to work out a mutual surrender of capitulatory rights, France forgoing its privileges in Egypt in exchange for Britain's forbearance in Morocco. The "prolonged negotiation," as a later British memorandum put it, came to nought.[43]

For a long while, Lyautey's attitude on capitulations was surprisingly relaxed. He viewed the consular courts and the *protégé* system as infringements on the sultan's sovereignty and France's prestige but considered them things he could live with because they did not really interfere with the functioning of the protectorate. Before he left Morocco, however, he had changed his mind. He told the foreign minister that the majority of Britain's native *protégés* were "secretly hostile" to French influence and would lash out against France every time an opportunity presented itself. In addition, as commercial agents, they did what they were paid to do—encourage the British import trade. This bothered him and worried his successors as well. Steeg wondered aloud whether the *protégés* were not being "selected and shaped" to be future leaders of a "party" opposed to French authority. But this was much too conspiratorial to be taken seriously and was far from Britain's more modest commercial aims. Even Steeg pulled away from his own "hypothesis" by saying that he did not have a shred of evidence to back it up. On balance, he guessed that commercial rather than political impulses moved the *protégés*. He was right to exonerate the British but wrong to pass over the *protégés*. Their later involvement in the protest over the Berber *dahir*, in the nationalist movement, and in the city unrest in 1936 and 1937 showed that these men needed no one to pull their strings. Despite a speculation that was wide of the mark, Steeg's conclusion of 1928 stood the test of time: abolish the capitulations "as soon as possible."[44]

For close to a decade, the twin problems of the capitulations and Morocco's economic regime failed to make the agendas of international gatherings. Then, in March 1937, Viénot telegraphed Noguès that the British government had indicated its willingness (after French promptings) to renounce its capitulations in Morocco if

France reciprocated in Egypt. A linkage between capitulations and commerce was clear from the start. Before any convention on capitulation surrenders went into effect, Britain wanted a new commercial treaty with Morocco. France was glad to be a party to the drafting, to use it to batter down the Algeciras system.[45]

The meetings went off without a hitch. France subscribed to a document drawn up at an international gathering at Montreux ending its privileges in Egypt, and then the English and French met à deux in London to arrange for what the French considered the more serious business, the English withdrawal from Morocco. The Convention for the Abolition of Capitulations in Morocco and Zanzibar was signed by the end of July. "You were a thousand times right to insist on a quick negotiation," Morize wrote Noguès, who was still in France; and he added that the convention was having a "great impact" in Morocco. Although a final commercial treaty was still a year away, Noguès reported home in triumphant terms. The end of British capitulations had begun the "burning of the international mortgages that had impeded Morocco's progress"; it had loosed the bonds of the past, freeing Morocco from "a very old international enslavement," and now permitted the sharifian empire to turn toward the future with confidence.[46] It also moved Noguès a step closer to fulfilling the protectorate ideal.

As always, Noguès was alert to the political ramifications. Ridding himself of the *protégés* was a blessing that he did not disguise. "Henceforth, there will be no more British *protégés* nor British *mokhalets* in the French zone of Morocco," he told the Moroccan section of the Conseil du Gouvernement. "About 150 *censaux* and 300 *mokhalets* will once again fall under the absolute sovereignty of His Majesty the Sultan." The verb was well chosen, for bringing them under sharifian jurisdiction meant an end to their political free flight above the heads of the French. Even closing down the British post offices in the French zone, which had provided the world's philatelists with a diverting collecting field for over fifty years (Frenchmen strong among them), was a political plus. Noguès told Delbos why. "It is through the British post that the banned newspapers, brochures, and tracts containing anti-French propaganda are sent. It is through the British post that the connections between the Tetouan nationalists and their correspondents of the French zone are established in complete security. It is through the British post that the recruiting agents receive their instructions and their funds."[47] These were lethal letter boxes. Now *protégés* and postage stamps were no more.

Britain's amiability was correctly seen as part of an overall plan of cooperation with France in Europe, the Mediterranean, and the Far East. The conflict in Spain brought Britain and France closer together, for both sought to contain it and neither wanted to intervene. Although Blum refused to fight for the Spanish republicans, he would not cozy up to their enemies; when Italy intervened on the nationalist side, therefore, the French connection snapped. Italian activity on both sides of Gibraltar now took on a new and menacing aspect. Italian warships in the Balearics, at ports in the Spanish zone, in the strait, and along the protectorate's coast en route to friendly stations in the Canaries testified to the need for a more militant North Africa. To the traditional titles of reservoir of men and supplier of goods were added wager of war, defender of the western Mediterranean, protector of France's southern shore. Those charged with France's defense were now forced to plan on Italy's hostility in case of a general European war. This too united Britain and France, a vigilant union against any "Italian mad-dog act."[48] From these joint concerns (and others as well) flowed Britain's "friendly collaboration" in Morocco. Noguès was quick to acknowledge it. He saluted England's representatives for making his task easier "at this particularly difficult moment" (he was writing in May 1937), for helping to bolster France's prestige, and for contributing to the "common policy of the two countries." The English view from Paris, where British support had been carefully cultivated, was the same. At year's end, the British ambassador was happy to note the "cordiality" that had marked France's relations with Great Britain.[49] Appropriately, the last British commemorative stamp for use in the French zone (overprinted MOROCCO AGENCIES) was the handsome coronation issue for George VI and Elizabeth, sovereigns whose state visit to France in July 1938 would seal what many hoped would be a new Entente Cordiale.

For the discussions to follow on a commercial treaty, Noguès had already stated the colonial case. He viewed the "essential objective" of any negotiation to render the protectorate "complete control of its tariff policy" by abolishing both the 10 percent tariff clause of the 1856 Anglo-Moroccan Treaty of Commerce and Navigation and chapter 5 of the Act of Algeciras, which regulated taxes. It was the Anglo-Moroccan treaty that blocked any increase in Morocco's tariffs; coupled with Algeciras's law of economic liberty without any inequality, it held the rate for all nations at the relatively low 12.5 percent ad valorem (the additional 2.5 percent had been approved at Algeciras). In addition, Noguès believed that it would be "desirable" if Britain were to recognize Morocco's right to establish import quotas, thus ending the unrestricted dumping of the past, and—the best of all the possibilities—to renounce the notion of "economic equality" altogether, contenting itself with most-favored-nation treatment. All this would liberate Morocco from a "permanent limitation on its sovereignty," give the protectorate a "freedom of action that would better correspond to its needs," and permit metropolitan and overseas France preferential advantages of the "imperial" sort.[50] Noguès could not have expressed the settler sentiment in economic matters more precisely.

Part of what Noguès wanted was achieved at the signing of the capitulations convention. In the letters exchanged by Ambassador Charles Corbin and Foreign Secretary Anthony Eden, mention of the "principle of reciprocity" in the forthcoming negotiations for the trade treaty implied the junking of Algeciras because reciprocity had been impossible under Algeciras. The British hesitated to state it so baldly; the most they would admit was that the abolition of capitulations had created "a new situation of fact which is bound to operate to the advantage of the French." Still, they were acting as if Algeciras and the "old British status in Morocco" were no more. One Foreign Office official told the American chargé d'affaires in London that Britain expected "at least most favored nation treatment as regards any third power in Morocco" and contemplated the institution of quota provisions as the "only possible way" to protect its textile trade. He was under no illusion, he said, about France's desire to achieve primacy in the Moroccan market and was not sure if anything could be done about it.[51] These were hardly phrases from a man on top.

Japan, not France, was Britain's chief commercial competitor in Morocco. Japanese sales of textiles were squeezing Britain's share of the Moroccan market so much that Britain was willing to abandon the opportunity of a free marketplace for the security of a controlled one, provided its situation was guaranteed. Even given an equal percentage of a fixed import quota, Britain's trade position could actually improve at the expense of Japan's. In addition, France was so determined to modify Algeciras, legally or otherwise, that Britain felt obliged to fall in step. To justify the desired quota system, the French had begun to interpret the famous "economic liberty without inequality" formula to mean "non-discrimination in treatment as between importing countries" rather than "the absence of any restriction on liberty of import for the individual country." If Britain marched with France on this issue, France was prepared "to consolidate duties," that is, bind them at a fixed rate for the life of the treaty "on goods of interest to the United Kingdom and to consult the wishes of His Majesty's Government as to quotas." If not, not. Britain could little afford to let the moment pass.[52]

The Anglo-Moroccan commercial treaty, signed in mid-1938, was no surprise: tariff autonomy and reciprocity for the protectorate, most-favored-nation status for Great Britain. Separate from but connected to it, in the form of an exchange of letters between British Ambassador Sir Eric Phipps and French Foreign Minister Georges Bonnet, was the quota system, which was intended to restrict the imports of specified commodities to Morocco. Each importing nation was to be assigned a percentage of the global amount of the quota based on its trade statistics with the protectorate over a set period of time. In this system, Britain was thrice favored. Items of importance in its Moroccan trade, those vulnerable to foreign competition (such as woolens and cottons), were placed on the quota list first, with Britain's share determined by the most desirable years of reference. (With cotton cloth, for example, Britain would be granted about 37 percent of the import quota compared to the 12 to 15 percent allotted to France.) Articles secure from competitors were unlisted and would not be put on the list without Britain's prior consent. Furthermore, Britain was guaranteed that its share of the quota of any particular article would never be less than 5 percent.[53]

In the dealings over rates, France agreed to bind duties on goods of which Britain provided an important share of Morocco's imports and promised that future increases in internal taxes (a favorite French source of revenue) would not wipe out these advantages. The effect was to increase the then current 10 percent tariff to 12.5 percent and even 15 percent on a wide variety of items; this did not include the additional 2.5 percent special tax instituted at Algeciras, which would continue to be collected separately. Moreover, with the internal taxes, the French still figured that they had "a considerable margin of increase." The British reciprocated by admitting articles of special interest to Moroccan export duty free into Great Britain. However, despite French pressure and special pleading, there would be no preferential treatment for French exports to Morocco. Such proposals were "dropped," Delbos explained, because of their "political nature." The British simply would not have it. The door to these discussions remained ajar, not closed; it might be pressed open whenever the "general situation" offered a "favorable opportunity."[54]

Noguès was guarded when he spoke about the treaty to the Conseil du Gouvernement. It marked "an important date in the history of Morocco's international status," a "step in the direction of economic liberation," yet he cautioned against expecting too much too fast. Besides, it had to be "completed by other negotiations, already under way." [55] The mystery was heightened when he omitted any reference to the treaty in his remarks to the Moroccan section a week later. Frankly, the agreement was in trouble. Added to a delay in ratification while Britain consulted the Dominion governments was the opposition from the United States, seconded by Belgium and Italy, which threatened to undo the agreement altogether. These three were signatories of Algeciras, and America was the sole surviving holdout on capitulations. What bothered them all was the fear of losing their share of the Moroccan market or of being forced to buy in Morocco as much as they had been wont to sell. (In 1937 Belgium sold twice as much as it bought, the United States over four times as much.) The Belgian ambassador to Washington said it squarely: The Anglo-French treaty would "gravely affect the favorable international régime from which foreign Powers benefit in the Sheriffian empire." [56]

America's economic creed was uncomplicated. "Our essential interest in Morocco," emphasized Secretary of State Cordell Hull, "is one of trade. We want maintained the existing principles governing Moroccan trade, namely 'economic liberty without inequality.' This means equality with all, including France. Anything less . . . means the dissipation of a large percentage of our existing exports to Morocco." This was a ringing declaration of support for Algeciras and for keeping the capitulations, for they provided barter for commercial concessions and prevented the protectorate from using administrative decrees and regulations to give France an economic edge. To tamper with the status quo, to permit Algeciras to slip into history's dustbin, would require "real guarantees" for Yankee trade. Even a quota system implied the favoritism that the Americans said they could not stomach; and it was restrictive and cumbersome to boot. In State Department prose, quotas were put down as "a hindrance to that normal and free development of international trade most conducive to the upbuilding of world economy." Still, in circumstances of a "compelling and exceptional nature," such as both France and Britain claimed, the United States would not be "obstructive," provided it was "not deprived of the share of trade which it has enjoyed in the past or which it might reasonably expect to share in the future." [57]

America's fussing surprised the French. They had assumed that they would encounter no resistance from the Americans and that once an agreement was reached with the British, their transatlantic cousins would follow suit. Earlier in the year, Viénot had written Noguès that they could count on Ambassador Bullitt, who was "very well disposed" toward France, to argue the French case before Roosevelt.[58] But Washington was uninterested in making a change and in consequence unenthusiastic about negotiations. When pressed, America would drag its feet, complain it had been ignored in the bilateral Anglo-French discussions, and stand on its treaty rights. The British kept the Americans informed on the progress of the talks and quietly passed along America's reservations to the French as part of their own strategy to get the best bargain that they could. When the subject was quotas, they promised that nothing would be final without Washington's consent. By the time the French turned to deal with the United States, America was even less inclined to be cooperative. It refused to consider capitulations apart from a commercial treaty, as the British had done. The French lamented that this showed "no confidence" in their ability to deal fairly with American trade and scant regard for political problems in Morocco. Moreover, America continued to harp on "economic liberty without any inequality," which annoyed the French no end, for it was just this "absurd régime" that they wanted eliminated. To compose the differences, France promised guarantees "equivalent" to those made to Great Britain. But when this appeared to be far from enough, France offered more: protection for American interests for thirty years (the Anglo-Moroccan treaty was for a seven-year period) in exchange for a total surrender of American rights.[59]

Now the State Department was ready to negotiate. The architect of France's discomfort, Wallace Murray, chief of the Division of Near Eastern Affairs, had finally come around. "It seems to me that these binding proposals, if they can be written into a clear and unequivocal treaty, will give us adequate and satisfactory guarantees during the next generation." Who could ask for anything more? Not surprisingly, someone did. Under Secretary of State Sumner Welles's initial reaction was that the thirty-year period was "rather short."[60] In the end, time rather than tempers was decisive. Five weeks after Secretary of State Hull recommended pressing on with the negotiations, France was at war with Germany. The trade talks were suspended indefinitely. France made one last desperate request for a separate capitulations convention. It was to no avail. The American consul general at Tangier cabled Washington his opinion: "Separate conclusion of capitulation convention fatal error."[61] In short order and despite protests from Washington, France adopted measures to protect itself in Morocco: restrictions on imports and exports and preference for the entry of French goods, precisely what it had labored without success to achieve in peacetime.[62]

What Britain had seen as so important—the strengthening of French power in the Atlantic and the Mediterranean—was lost on the Americans. References to the protectorate as "one of the principal factors of peace in Africa" or to the "vital necessity" of developing the North African littoral if France was to remain a "world power" were brushed aside as colonial palaver. The State Department thought it knew what the French were really up to: roping Morocco to France just as Algeria and Tunisia were tied. For that there was no sympathy. Whether the French and Moroccan economies would benefit from such a relationship was of no importance. Even on defense, America was uninterested in making it easier for France to get what it might need from Morocco in case of a European war.[63] This was economic self-interest with an anticolonialist vengeance. It demoralized the French. They understood economic haggling: in return for the closed door, they were willing to accommodate American commerce. But America's lack of heart for the protectorate's predicament and the requirements of France's defense took its toll. Noguès never forgave nor forgot the unhappy episode. Who could blame him? Ending Algeciras was to have given the protectorate new life, new freedom, and a new relationship with France. America had frustrated that design.

In truth, America's concerns about Morocco spinning ever more tightly in the French economic orbit were not wholly justified. Only if France was granted a preference in Morocco, which the French had reluctantly conceded would not happen soon, could its economic control increase significantly. To be sure, this is what most metropolitan businessmen hoped for; the Confédération Générale du Patronat Français and the Marseilles Chamber of Commerce anxiously anticipated the day when France's trade deficit (on the rise since 1931) might finally be wiped out, giving France its rightful return on a sizable investment.[64] But dreams and plain facts are two different things. Among the latter must be counted the post-Algeciras economic course that the protectorate was charting, a course that would have made it less dependent upon French markets, merchants, and money.

Money had always made the protectorate more of a colony than anyone wanted to admit, linking Rabat with Paris by chains of paper notes. Lyautey might insist that Morocco was an "autonomous state," but when French investors loaned it money, they thereby increased French control. Outsiders even claimed that France maintained the fiction of sharifian sovereignty only to use the Moroccan government as a mechanism for French investment, skirting the provisions of Algeciras. A decentralist in empire matters, Lyautey feared the centripetal pull of Paris through public loans, that is, bond issues authorized by parliament and guaranteed by the French state.[65] But it could not be resisted. "Morocco's development up to now," Noguès confessed in 1938, "has been made possible almost entirely because of loans." In the previous quarter century, three-fourths of the expenditures for public works projects had come from monies raised by long-term loans on the French market. With the tight money of the 1930s, France could no longer be counted on for support of this sort on which the protectorate had come to depend. "You all know how much the Moroccan economy has benefited from defense spending and from loans that have financed major public works projects," Noguès told the Conseil du Gouvernement. We have been "hit hard by the continued reduction of these two items, so important for our balance of payments."[66]

The financial burden of empire was simply too much for the Republic to bear. "Judged by trade alone," concluded an American economist in 1937, "the French colonial empire has evidently been an expensive national luxury during the depression period."[67] For saying this aloud in French and starting to make the colonies pay for themselves (if not for ending the empire), the Popular Front deserves much credit. The change, however, sometimes came with unexpected brutality. At the end of 1937, the protectorate was barred from floating new loans. To frantic questions, Noguès replied: "You know the policy of the government of the Republic on this point: regardless of our desires or our rights, our access to the money market has been blocked." The reason, Algeria's Governor General Georges Le Beau had been told, was so that such bond issues would not "prejudice the possibilities of the absorption of metropolitan loans."[68] This was a simple statement of France first, empire second.

The ax also fell on quotas. Morize never forgot his sessions at the ministry of agriculture in spring 1937. What he imagined would be a rubber-stamp renewal of past import quotas turned into a donnybrook, a "tough battle" with the government hacking away at Moroccan imports. French and Algerian vegetable and fruit growers would no longer tolerate the competition; as far as they were concerned, Morocco was a foreign country. He survived, narrowly averting the "catastrophe" he was certain would have caused "a revolution in the Moroccan economy." But it had been neither easy nor pleasant. "The life of a salesman," he confided with characteristic understatement, "whether he sells tomatoes, sardines, or himself, is without charm."[69]

The handwriting was on the wall, put there by Delbos in legible if gentle script. "The quota system for the sale in France of Moroccan produce seems to have reached its maximum extension. The difficulties encountered in Paris last April during the negotiations for the renewal of the annual quotas lead us to believe that these quotas are not capable of being appreciably increased." In consequence, the government refused to pay for any development projects unless their produce could be sold in places other than France. European farmers in the Souss region east of Agadir were out of luck. The same went for miners of manganese in the Atlas. Business and industry would have to foot the bill (or a stiff portion of it) for the desired roads, railroads, and port facilities. New funds would be forthcoming only when justified by the needs of the native population or military defense. "The economic outfitting of Morocco for the profit of Europeans," Delbos concluded, "seems to have reached a level that ought not to be passed without a strict concern for the 'return' on these ventures. The back interest on the debt takes too important a part of the budget for the state to continue to run the risk of further expanding an economy based on loans (*économie d'emprunt*)."[70]

Morize got the message before being told. If the protectorate wanted to continue its economic expansion and retain some decision-making independence, it would have to rely on its own resources. If it wished to avoid an agonizing economic restructuring to make its production complementary rather than competitive with France (the imperative in any imperial connection), it would have to count on increased foreign trade and markets.[71] The first step was to "slash away energetically" at the protectorate's budget, to tighten its purse strings before they were yanked shut by Paris. "I am convinced that with careful planning the protectorate can live by its own means . . . and that it is in its interest [to do so] as soon as possible." He made a virtue of necessity. "Only at this price can the resident general escape a tighter and tighter control from the Rue de Rivoli [the ministry of finance], which experience proves is always sterile. Only at this price can anything of *lasting importance* be accomplished since it will be independent (not dependent upon the changes of the political climate in Paris) and lasting because it is adapted to the resources and progress of the country, and because, in a word, it is not artificial."[72]

The road to financial freedom lay in a balanced budget, argued

Morize, which was "perfectly possible" if the current budget was stripped of "extraordinary expenses" and provided with "a little more" tax money from those who could afford to pay. He was not of the soak-the-rich school, which saw hundreds of millions of francs flowing from the pockets of the well-to-do into the coffers of the state. But he estimated that 15 million francs could be raised and that would suffice.[73]

Noguès accepted the diagnosis but brewed his own home remedy for the cure. The "new financial policy" that he unveiled to the Conseil du Gouvernement at the beginning of December 1938 had as its goal a balanced budget, "not obtained by the compression of essential expenses, nor by the increase in taxes, but by the increased productivity of the country, by the increased number of taxpayers produced by prosperity; in short, a budget linked to the economic life of this country." Instead of abandoning economic development, Noguès made it his first priority. The wealth of the land and its people, aided by foreign investment and the post-Algeciras prospects of trade, would make self-financing a reality.[74] Followed to the letter, the plan would have made Morocco less a colony and more an independent state, where Frenchmen, if not France, still would retain their pride of place. Its success depended upon breaking Algeciras.

Noguès's optimistic outlook coincided with the worldwide economic recovery, which eased the protectorate's financial pinch. He talked as if all his economic worries were at an end: the "five years of crisis" were over, the "rugged test" had been passed. Although the 1938 harvest was only "average," it ended three years of crops ruined by weather. Gone were the "devastated regions"; some grain could be stockpiled, even exported. The report from the cities was equally assuring: artisans to architects found business improved, and this was reflected by contracts, commissions, and cash. Statistics on commercial and industrial activity provided the numbers to verify what Europeans and Moroccans knew was true.[75]

Morocco still remained a buyer of goods with a negative trade balance, the permanent reminder of its weakness in production and trade agreements. But Noguès saw the sunny side: Moroccan consumption had stayed steady despite the economic crisis (a positive sign), and exports were on the increase, reducing the deficit. Among private fortunes he detected an improvement, so much so that he predicted the liquidation of the colonization debts that once had seemed insurmountable peaks of paper.[76] These were happy prospects in the fall of 1938 but they would soon be comprised by America's obstinance and Hitler's war.

As it emerged from the other side of the 1930s, French Morocco, or more precisely, Le Maroc des Français, was more fragile than at any time in the protectorate's history. The power of the colons had been tempered by nature and man. The curses of bounty and dearth had taken their toll, amputating fortunes and altering the relationship with France, most significantly by kicking out the supports under colonial commerce and agriculture. The long march toward the world market, part defiance, part desperation, had bogged down in the mud of Algeciras. Strikes, street marches, and nationalist agitation among the tribes challenged colonial control and elicited the dual response of cash and cold steel. Neither really comforted the colons: the first shifted funds from the European to the native community, not merely for a short-term emergency but for the long trek to a prosperous native economy; the second showed what would happen in the factories, medinas, and souks if the colons balked or the natives failed to respond.

On the other hand, with Noguès the Residency regained the stature it had lost when Lyautey departed. Paris and Rabat were united on the path to follow, reaching back to revive the early hopes for native betterment while at the same time containing and educating the colons (neither discouraging nor disparaging them) for the protectorate partnership of the future. Here Lyautey's colonialism with a soul and Jaurès's humanist socialism converged. Both were paternalist, populist, and patriotic; and Noguès and Blum, their pupils and successors, made the most of these points of contact. Neither man was under any illusion, however, about the ease of selling his wares to sneering capitalists at home or skeptical colonists abroad. There was good reason. Declining fortunes encouraged resistance, not generosity. Just as the gap between workers and bourgeois widened during the days of the Popular Front, so the gulf grew between Frenchmen and Moroccans in the 1930s. Never a pessimist, Noguès thought the negative signs were reversible. In time he believed that the protectorate would emerge, as Lyautey had intended, as France's greatest colonial venture. It was just the darkness in Africa before the dawn. For the faint-hearted, the marshal even had words of encouragement from beyond the tomb: "Worry and anxiety are the indispensable seasonings for action, that holy, divine action that we cannot do without!"[77]

FIVE

Three Tangled Zones

Morocco, the diplomats said, was a mare's nest. Its political complexities, like those of the fabled Schleswig-Holstein question, required expert advice and a good memory, and they produced their share of scares as well as successes for France. Along the slow,unsure march toward the protectorate came the incidents that reputedly poisoned the spas of prewar Europe—the kaiser's speech at Tangier, a German gunboat off Agadir. These were significant enough to rate in the textbooks as the "first" and "second" Moroccan crises and as "causes" of the Great War.[1] What Frenchmen considered meddling in their private affairs was probably only justified German concern over France's violation of the spirit of the international agreements on Morocco and over its growing political and economic hegemony in the sharifian empire. The Germans were not the only ones involved. From the beginning, Morocco was a topic for world gatherings, not a two-sided tug-of-war. Thirteen nations had signed the 1906 Act of Algeciras and not one of them considered it a bill of sale to France.

With the establishment of the French protectorate in 1912 came the partition of the empire into two zones (and the provision for a third, Tangier), an internationally sanctioned division designed to preserve the sultan's state by providing it with two guardians instead of one. By treaty it was only a one-power protectorate, but France immediately turned over the mountainous northeast to Spain (as a kind of leased subprotectorate officially called the *zone d'influence espagnole* by the French) in order to gain British approval of the deal. All of this had been worked out on paper eight years before, with the British insisting that Morocco's northern coast across the Strait of Gibraltar remain in the hands of a weak power.[2] Spain was thus chosen to be Britain's Belgium in the western Mediterranean, but at far smaller reward. The king of Italy's table remark comparing Libya and Morocco could be applied to the French and Spanish zones: France's share was the loin of the chop, Spain's portion the bone.[3] Still, despite Spain's initial reluctance to accept such an unpromising bit of land, much less than had once been pledged, "Spanish Morocco," as it came to be known, partly fulfilled the hopes for a North African mission. What is more, it kept Spain alive as a European power. In the words of Conde de Romanones's celebrated remark, "Morocco was for Spain her last chance to keep her position in the concert of Europe."[4]

The scars of the long negotiations did not disappear. Spain never forgot France's whittling away at its territorial aspirations south of Agadir and north and south of the Sebou River from the Atlantic to the Moulouya and its preference for arrangements with Britain and Germany behind its back.[5] In 1911 some Frenchmen even wished to deny Spain the "Atlantic horn" of its northern domain and others to cut Spain out of Morocco altogether. But that would have put an unreconcilable enemy on the Pyrenees, the last thing France needed in case of war across the Rhine. Spain's friendship was not worth much, Ambassador Jules Cambon admitted with arrogant candor, but its enmity could be fatal.[6] It did not necessarily follow, however, that a Spanish zone in the north would make Spain less of a potential adversary. From the start, Spain interpreted its place in Morocco as equal to that of France, a protector state with pretensions to sovereignty.[7] Interzonal friction rather than fraternity was the result, so much so that each zone really lived its own life jealously separate from the other. The French ignored Spanish Morocco as impotent and irrelevant; it was tolerated rather than accepted. The Spaniards responded in kind, blotting out as best they could the colossus to the south.

After 1936 the northern zone could be forgotten no longer. The July military uprising in the Spanish zone, which began the civil war, brought Morocco back into Spanish politics and preoccupations as it had not been since the days of Miguel Primo de Rivera and the Rif. Spanish Morocco was the jumping-off place for the soldiers in rebellion against the government on the mainland. It was a base of operations, a storehouse of men and materiel, all of which caused the French to worry about the consequences to the protectorate of the victory or defeat of either side.[8] What would happen if the military revolt failed? Peyrouton predicted a "severe movement of repression" by the government, beginning with the cities, then spreading out into the countryside among the rural tribes. In addition, native troops fighting for Franco in Spain would be subjected to "particularly rigorous measures," which would have an impact on their brethren at home. Both would surely pose a "danger" for the French along their northern boundary and perhaps require a "police action" extending well into the Spanish zone. However, if Franco emerged on top, what price would Germany and Italy exact in payment for services rendered? Unsaid but understood was that Morocco would figure somehow in the final reckoning. What of the returning Moroccan soldiers armed to the teeth and exhilarated by their triumph on European battlefields? Peyrouton thought they would create "foyers of anarchy" in the north. Regardless of the outcome of the Spanish conflict, France risked "being obliged to intervene." "However you look at it," he concluded, "General Franco's uprising seems loaded with troubles for the future."[9] He was correct. From the moment of Franco's victory to the end of the protectorate some sixteen years later, Spain, more confident and secure than it had ever been in North Africa, would exploit any and every French weakness in Morocco to right what it considered the wrongs of the past.

As it turned out, France never intervened in the Spanish zone, but in its efforts to sever the zone at war from the zone at peace, it came uncomfortably close to the conflict. Realizing that this would be so, the government in Paris was all the more eager to push a soldier into Peyrouton's place. The situation even seemed to have some of the makings of a third Moroccan crisis because once more it brought the European states face to face over questions of power and influence in the sharifian empire.

As always, the French spoke through the sultan. In September he issued a proclamation lamenting the strife in the north, regretting his people's participation in a war that was not their own and promising to act in cooperation with the French government to safeguard the unity and sovereignty of his empire. *Dahirs* in August and September restricted and then halted the shipment of goods across the frontier, slicing the Spanish zone's normal routes of supply. The traffic in men was also shut down because the exodus of tribesmen from the French zone to serve in the armies of the north had reached "troublesome proportions."[10] The lure of money, food, and firearms (and perhaps a career in the army) was hard to resist. These were time-honored enticements, particularly attractive given the economic crisis of the French zone. Cities bulging with hungry refugees were ideal recruiting centers where migrants from the south were encouraged to continue their trek farther north. After the sultan's verbal appeals fell on deaf ears, he put his seal on a *dahir* forbidding his subjects to join Spain's armed forces in Morocco or on the mainland, but illegal departures and enlistments and a veritable black market in men continued until the casualty lists drowned out the recruiter's calls.[11] France's aim in all of this was not to smother the rebellion but to deny it the fuel, human and otherwise, that might cause its flames to spread.

Outside intervention posed a second peril. Italian activity was concentrated in the Balearic Islands, not in Morocco proper, but since the archipelago lay across the communications route between France and North Africa, France could not remain "indifferent" to what looked like "de facto control" under the "cover" of Spanish sovereignty. It upset the status quo in the western Mediterranean, which the French were resolved "to have respected," and affected the "most vital interests of France."[12] Here the French were alive to the danger posed by the transport of colonial troops from North African ports to Marseilles, an essential element in the metropolitan mobilization plan in the event of a war in Europe. There could be no doubt as to the anti-French thrust of the Italian intervention in Spain and the Balearics. Whether Mussolini really expected to make the Mediterranean an Italian lake and, as Ciano said, to lay in Spain the foundations for a "Roman Mediterranean Empire" is an open question, but he surely desired to strengthen Italy's strategic position at the expense of France by blocking France's land and water links through Spain and across the Mediterranean.[13] "If we use the base in Majorca, that in Pantelleria and others already in existence and equipped," Mussolini told Ribbentrop in November 1937, "not one negro will be able to cross from Africa to France by the Mediterranean route."[14]

With France's formal protest to Italy about the Balearics buildup came the suggestion to England, ever concerned about its maritime communications on the way to Egypt or India, of a joint demonstration of naval strength in the roadsteads of the Balearics.[15] Foreign Secretary Anthony Eden was alarmed, suggesting to the cabinet in December that Italy might be preparing to establish a protectorate over the islands, but no one else seemed to be. The military chiefs of staff had determined in August that Italian bases in Majorca did not constitute a threat to Britain's vital interests and saw no reason to revise their opinion. The Anglo-Italian "gentleman's agreement" (signed on 2 January 1937), wherein both parties pledged to respect the "*status quo* as regards national sovereignty of territories in the Mediterranean area," was designed to put the mind of official England at rest.[16] But the words did not square with the facts: even as the documents were being signed, Italian involvement in Spain was on the increase. Perhaps the suspicious editors of *L'Humanité*, the voice of Jacobin communism in France, were correct to interpret the agreement as recognition of Italy's predominance in the western Mediterranean and Britain's in the eastern Mediterranean, a situation in no way favorable to France.[17]

Although France opposed Italian involvement in Spain (which was the chief reason for the deterioration of relations between the Blum government and Rome), the threat to Morocco was slight. Off-course aviators crash-landing at Oujda, hydroplanes touching down at Melilla, and Italian flags in the northern ports did not add up to a permanent presence. Neither Mussolini nor the frenzied crowds in the Piazza Venezia ever added Tangier, Rabat, or Casablanca to the chant of places marked by history as Italian.[18]

With Germany the problem was more serious. From the start of the military insurrection in Spain, the Germans were credited with seeking "a privileged position" in the Spanish zone that would permit them "to reestablish their commercial and even political influence in the sharifian empire," an influence lost as a result of the Great War. German naval vessels made frequent visits to Ceuta, Melilla, and Larache; furthermore, the Germans had abused the docking permission granted by the French and, together with the Italians, had turned Tangier into "a kind of naval base." Some ships carried military supplies to the nationalists; others brought only *deutscher Gruss*, German goodwill. In neither case was there any attempt to mask the German presence. Elaborate ceremonies attended their comings and goings, and these alarmed the French more than furtive activities would have since they paraded German might before the impressionable native population. "The Moroccans have been all the more taken with this continuous demonstration of German power," Delbos wrote to Corbin, "because it comes after an absence of twenty-two years."[19]

The French discounted the rumors that the Spanish payoff to Germany would be in the form of territorial cessions in the Spanish zone. Such a transfer violated the 1912 Franco-Spanish treaty and would precipitate French intervention, a risk that neither the Spaniards nor the Germans wanted to run. Equally important, it ran counter to Spanish colonial aspirations in Morocco. German aid was to be purchased with iron ore under conditions that would give Germany "complete control" over the mining resources of the Spanish zone. This did not mean that the Germans would be content with economic rewards. According to the French, the Germans were behind the suggestions of autonomy for the Spanish zone, whispering words of "self-government" into Muslim ears; these were certainly the right words to win some native hearts, especially since they came less than two years after France had slammed the door on the Moroccan nationalists' reform proposals. Such suggestions also had the effect—which the Germans counted on—of humiliating and undercutting the French by weakening the unity of the empire (which the French were pledged to preserve) and opening it up to outside penetration.[20]

Whatever the German interest in Morocco, it jeopardized the security of French North Africa. Germany's prewar activity had left its bad memories. Might not the recollections of kaisers and gunboats create an "uneasiness" among the Muslim population? This, Delbos admitted, "usually worked to the detriment of French authority . . . and in difficult circumstances, such as in the case of a mobilization, it would surely degenerate into a dangerous agitation." France would be obliged to strengthen its occupation troops in Morocco as well as the forces needed to protect its military transports in the Mediterranean.[21]

However, the German threat—which the French admitted was more a future fear than a present danger—could serve, much as it had at the time of Tangier and Agadir, to push the French and British closer together, which is precisely how the French.used it. A common menace always moved them closer to joint planning, which was the prelude, Delbos knew, for any concerted action, an indispensable requirement for French security in Europe and for any major maneuver abroad. Morocco was thus tailor-made. Neither England nor France wanted a "first-rank military power" to have a foothold in the Spanish zone, and neither wanted the security of Mediterranean sea lanes compromised, either north-south or east-west. "This preoccupation," Delbos could safely say, "has always been at the base of Anglo-French solidarity in Moroccan matters."[22]

Regardless of Germany's intentions, Blum believed that war might have come over Morocco in January 1937, and Viénot was told to sandbag the protectorate just in case. Noguès reported that German troops were expected in Tetouan, Ceuta, and perhaps Larache after the tenth of the month. Reconnaissance units had already reached the Spanish zone, preparing for the arrival of "several thousand" men (according to "diverse sources"), presumably en route to Spain. Such an event, so "filled with consequences," wrote Noguès, began a flurry of diplomatic activity. The resident's information was passed immediately to Britain, with Delbos adding cryptically that what Germany was up to might be the prelude to a "much larger operation" coming fairly close on its heels. The Spanish were questioned at Tetouan, and Delbos spoke personally with the German ambassador in Paris to call his attention to the "trouble" that any mass landing of German volunteers in Morocco would create for Franco-German relations.[23]

The British were taken by surprise. Ambassador Charles Corbin reported to Delbos that Eden seemed "rather stunned" by the news, perhaps because British consular reports were not nearly as alarming as Noguès's and also because of the Foreign Office's tendency to discount the French view of the seriousness of events in Morocco and the Near East.[24] The British seemed to have been correct in downplaying the Moroccan happenings. After a long and frank discussion with Colonel Juan Beigbeder, the interim high commissioner in the Spanish zone, Jean-Claude Serres, the French consul at Tetouan, came away convinced that the matter had indeed been blown out of proportion. Beigbeder assured him that there were no German troops in Morocco and none expected. "[T]he colonel told me that he was well aware that the landing of a German-speaking unit of the [Spanish foreign] legion would touch off a European war" in which the nationalists, weaker in numbers and materiel than their republican adversaries, would be the "first victim."[25] Just to be on the safe side, Beigbeder claimed, he had refused to let *any* foreign unit come to Morocco. He added that Franco was completely aware of the international "catastrophe" that foreign troops in Morocco would cause. Certainly neither he (Beigbeder) nor Franco wanted to shoulder the responsibility for creating a situation whose dangers they both understood so well. Moreover, once the Italians or Germans got into Morocco, Beigbeder was not sure when, or if, they would leave. He had no desire to compromise Morocco's future. On all this, Beigbeder said that France could count on the "political sense and intelligence" of Franco. After so satisfactory a conversation (in which Beigbeder even offered to telegraph Franco for authorization to put what he had just said in writing), Serres could only wonder aloud how the rumors of a massive German landing had found their way into the French press.[26]

One imagines that on receipt of Serres's report the French might have been willing to let the matter die. In fact, it is rather surprising that information was passed to the British and a protest lodged with the German ambassador before the Spanish high commissioner had been questioned. As Beigbeder talked, he pulled the rug from under the French. When the British heard the story, they had yet another bit of evidence to prove that the French got riled too easily on Morocco. Even Corbin worried that exaggerated press reports of what the French intended to do to counter a German move in Morocco— invade the Spanish zone, for example—was creating "a certain uneasiness in English public opinion." Neither the Foreign Office nor the Admiralty had been able to confirm the French reports, and in the face of German denials, it appeared that Berlin had been needlessly poked by Paris. Corbin was left to argue lamely to Britain that it was just this French "firmness" that had "perhaps" prevented Germany from carrying out its plans.[27]

German documents show that there was indeed a unit of German volunteers at Melilla but no mass landing of German troops in the works. Since Melilla was not part of the protectorate set-up with France (it had been Spanish since 1496), Foreign Minister Constantin von Neurath could tell the German ambassador in France that he should "energetically dispel the fears of the French" with the words: "There are no German volunteers of any kind in the Morocco zone." Here there was room to quibble. But seen from Berlin, Germany was innocent, France guilty of stirring up a fracas.[28]

Berlin pushed its advantage by beginning a press counteroffensive. The language in the French newspapers, wrote the French ambassador to Germany (after surveying the German dailies on the morning of 11 January), was "pale and timid" compared with the "fiery calumnies" that were being shot France's way. Rhetoric aside, the substance of the matter was that Germany had thrice denied France's accusations and still the French press continued to print reports of German infiltration in Morocco. "In the last twenty-four hours," the ambassador judged, "the atmosphere has been considerably charged with electricity." But within sixty minutes of his telegram, André François-Poncet tapped out better news. At a reception for the diplomatic corps, Chancellor Hitler had made a point of giving him the "formal and absolute assurance" that Germany had no intention of setting foot on land belonging to Spain nor of establishing any bases. He hoped that the foreign press would calm down and not further injure Franco-German relations. "You know," he added wistfully, "we are counting on being represented at the Paris Exposition this coming spring; it would be too bad if we could not participate." Von Neurath, standing near the chancellor, repeated that it was "absolutely false" that German units had been or were being sent to Spanish Morocco. As a follow-up, François-Poncet met with von Neurath in the afternoon to ask that Hitler's words be made public, offering in return a French declaration to respect the integrity of Spain and the "statute" on Spanish Morocco. A short communiqué containing both messages was released in Paris and Berlin.[29] It ended the three-day war of words.

The "third" Moroccan crisis was over except for the retrospective on why it had happened and what it all meant. The French explanation was simple. Germany had been caught in the act of slipping into Spanish Morocco. Under the bright lights of world scrutiny, it had retreated, claiming that it had been framed. "France and the peace of the world had been threatened," read the Moroccan column in *L'Afrique française*. "The government reacted decisively, quietly, calmly, secure in its right and conscious of its duty, and the entire country, in spite of domestic quarrels, rallied around it. Was this another Marne?"[30] It certainly was not. But Frenchmen thought it was a step back from the brink of war. In addition, the French chargé at Berlin volunteered that the overall political strategy of the Reich had been compromised. As a result of the fuss over Morocco, tensions had emerged between London and Berlin, suspicions raised between Berlin and Burgos. What happened on the London-Berlin line was the more absorbing news for Paris. "We know that the axis of [German policy] runs less through Burgos than through Rome and London. It is not by running afoul of British interests in the Mediterranean at Gibraltar that Germany will realize its dream of extending the Italo-German entente to England, thus isolating France."[31]

Precisely because Germany's political designs were well known, the French indictment was suspect. Had Morocco been made in France to expose the fascist danger to a Britain that had just signed a "gentleman's agreement" with Italy? Was it a French attempt to make history repeat itself, sealing Anglo-French relations over a German scare in Morocco? There was a real possibility for some French diplomatic points from the crisis. It was exploited by France but not conjured up in Paris. Its roots lay in Berlin. No German government could have been ignorant of the fact that German troops anywhere in Morocco, for whatever purpose, would alarm the French. For over a quarter of a century, the French in Morocco had been possessed by the fear of sighting German gunboats off the coast, iron demons that refused to be exorcised. The very phrase "coup d'Agadir" had entered the French political vocabulary of the day.[32] German ships, planes, and soldiers in the north made reality of those phantoms and were bound to release emotions bordering on hysteria. But Morocco in the headlines of France's newspapers (for the last time until the desperate days of 1940) turned out to be good press for Germany, for this time, unlike 1905 and 1911, the French came off as little boys who cried wolf.[33]

When asked to summarize the evidence against Germany and to evaluate France's reaction, Noguès reviewed the reports he had sent to Paris. He was convinced that *Weltpolitik* continued to direct German aspirations, although less certain of Morocco's precise place in the scheme. Were the troubles in Spain an opportunity for Germany "to set foot once again in this corner of Africa, which figured so large in its prewar policy and ambitions," or was German activity in Morocco merely the consequence of aiding the Spanish nationalists? What he did know for sure was that soon after it had recognized the Franco government at Burgos, Germany had acquired a "virtual moral and material dominion" over the Spanish zone. Although it was "difficult to measure the extent of the economic advantages accorded Germany," he thought it "undeniable" that the Germans were holding a kind of "economic mortgage" on the country that would be hard for the Spaniards to pay off. In addition to the politics and economics, there was the anti-French propaganda of German inspiration, distorting the acts of the French and sharifian governments and hinting that Morocco's prosperity and freedom would only be restored after "the occupier or rather the French usurper is kicked out."[34]

In January, Noguès recounted, German activity had become "more intense, almost feverish," and all "credible information" pointed to the fact that Germany was committed to making the Spanish zone a "solid base of operations" to aid Franco in winning the civil war and thereafter "to implant" itself firmly in Morocco, confronting Europe once again with a fait accompli. In Noguès's opinion, France's strong protest, the furious press campaign, the hurried meetings of the French general staff, and the immediate calls for British support had stopped Berlin and Burgos dead in their tracks, barring them from the "dangerous road" that they had "without doubt" chosen for themselves. Within days the German ships and sailors, planes and airmen, technicians and engineers had disappeared from the Moroccan strand. If this was what had been expected from the French plantings, then they had "borne fruit." For the moment, German military plans had been shelved, even though the campaign against France and the propaganda among the native population continued. "Therefore, we must remain vigilant. The collusion between the rebel and Hitler authorities is too tight, the strategic situation of Morocco, especially in time of tension or in case of war, is too tempting and the attraction that this country has exercised on Germany since the beginning of this century is too powerful for us not to remain on our guard. The distant and the recent past demands it, if we want to remain the masters of our destiny."[35]

Noguès laid out the facts in this final report just as he had done in the telegrams preceding the crisis. The issue was one of interpretation, and he championed the continuity theme, understanding German policy in terms of a timeless fascination with Morocco: Germany was the moth, Morocco the flame. But although Hitler traded on the kaiser's dreams, he was never a German-Morocco enthusiast, even though he may not have been adverse to using German activity in Morocco to draw French men and minds from the Rhine to the Sebou, from a spot where Germany had important interests to a place where it had none. Guided by Noguès, supersensitive to every German twitch, the ministry of foreign affairs stumbled. The British brushed off the matter as French bluster and the Germans won some sympathy as hapless victims of the *furia francese.*

Once satisfied that the foreign danger to Morocco had passed, the French took a closer look at what the Spanish themselves were doing in their zone. In April 1937 Colonel Juan Beigbeder was appointed high commissioner (equivalent in authority to the resident general in the south), the sixteenth since 1912 in a line of soldiers and civilians to hold the post. Although Beigbeder's rank might have been the tip-off to a downgrading of the slot (usually the job went to a lieutenant general), the opposite was the case. Beigbeder was an *africanista* of long standing, a brilliant if somewhat eccentric soldier who had spent most of his army career abroad and had found in Morocco a sympathetic country and culture that shaped his own intellectual interests. He spoke Arabic and the Rif dialect of Berber and was well read in Islamic history and civilization. Without doubt, he was "the most culturally distinguished of the *africanistas.*"[36] Here was someone who knew his Morocco. Equally important, he knew his Germany too. He had served as military attaché to Spain's embassies and ministries in Germany, Austria, and Czechoslovakia. In spring 1936 he had secretly toured German weapons factories with the nationalists' designated commander-in-chief, General José Sanjurjo, and after the July revolt, Beigbeder was the contact between Tetouan and Berlin, arranging for transport and arms for Franco's forces. Reports put him down as pro-German, which, even if a surface sentiment and not a deep-down conviction, was a requirement for any *franquista* in Tetouan. When he was interim high commissioner, Beigbeder had handled the Spanish side of the January Moroccan crisis, convincing France's representative that all was quiet on the northern coast and that no German soldier had or would set foot on Spanish sod overseas. It was a virtuoso performance and established him as more than a lightweight in matters diplomatic. Taken together, these assets boosted his appointment, which would prove one of the smartest that Franco ever made.

Beigbeder's charge was to keep Morocco solid for Franco, to persuade the Muslim elite of the Spanish zone that its interests and those of the Spanish rebels coincided, and to supply Franco's armies with Morocco's men. From the beginning, Beigbeder showed that he was the right man in the right spot. In the frantic hours of the military revolt on 17–18 July and in the days that followed, he was credited with overcoming native hesitations with private promises and dramatic radio appeals. Once won over to the rebel cause, tribal leaders were turned into recruiting sergeants, overseen and guided by Beigbeder himself. Tally sheets recorded the success: between 1936 and 1939, over sixty thousand Moroccans served in Franco's forces, about 6 percent of the manpower of the Spanish nationalist army.[37] What made such numbers easier to come by were Beigbeder's close personal relations with Muslim leaders and his overall approach to the Spanish zone. He gave native leaders, including homegrown nationalists and those in exile from the south, greater autonomy than they had ever had in the past and hinted that with the Franco victory might come an independent Moroccan state. He sounded like T. E. Lawrence. Obviously this conflicted with the international agreements on Morocco, made a mockery of the vaunted unity of the sharifian empire, and came close to enthroning the khalif (the sultan's representative in the Spanish zone) as the sultan of the north. For all this to have happened would have taken more than Beigbeder saying so. In the end nothing did. It was all just a word game to outbid Spanish republicans for Morocco's support, but Beigbeder played it to Franco's advantage.

The buildup of the khalif's authority strengthened the independent stance of the Spanish zone and correspondingly weakened the pull of the sultan and the French. This was important, given Burgos's reliance on Morocco's men and Rabat's hostility to their participation in the civil war. At the same time, it was compensation to the native command for its support of the military rebellion. The French reported a "frightening" increase in the power of native leaders, particularly over the collection of taxes, with a corresponding decrease in the authority of the Spanish tribal administrators, the *interventors*. This would create future problems for the Spaniards. But it was a clever counterweight to the new prominence of Moroccan nationalists. The French grudgingly admitted that it was "one of the most remarkable aspects" of the native policy of the Spanish zone.[38] Beigbeder was also convinced that the nationalists were easier to watch above ground than below. In return for toleration, jobs, and money, Beigbeder expected and got kind words, some measure of cooperation, and a steady stream of nationalist invective directed toward the south. Nevertheless, all nationalist activities were monitored by the police, and the government quietly exploited their personal rivalries and political feuds to its own advantage. In a sense, Beigbeder had become both comrade and assassin of the national cause.

Some of what Beigbeder did was inspired by the Lyautey example—in fact, he said he was following in Lyautey's footsteps—and at times he went the French one better.[39] The display of Hispano-Moroccan fraternity, the respect for Islam and Arab civilization, and the deference to Muslim leaders were novel in the north. Native education, culture, and religion were emphasized as they had not been before. Mosques and schools were built or repaired, centers of religious instruction opened, and the Institute for Moroccan Studies created (named for the khalif and a counterpoise to Lyautey's prestigious Institut des Hautes Études Marocaines). Most remarkable of all, Arabic was made the sole language of instruction in the public schools (unthinkable in the French zone), the curriculum was "Arabized," and teachers were chosen by Muslim community leaders, all of which prevented education from becoming the symbol of a divided and conquered society that it was for southern nationalists. Unlike the French, Beigbeder encouraged cultural contacts between Morocco and the Middle East; he invited foreign visitors to tour the zone, and in 1938 the government built "Morocco House," the Casa de Marruecos, as a home away from home for Moroccan students in Cairo. Moroccan pilgrims were sent to Mecca on ships provided by Burgos, Muslim festivals were celebrated as general holidays throughout the zone, and Spanish officials feted the faithful and gifted the poor. It is small wonder that some observers thought that in spite of the war (actually because of it), Spanish Morocco had become *la zona feliz*.

In matters of social and economic development, Beigbeder practiced Lyauteyism on a shoestring. The hospitals, schools, and highways that were the pride of the French protectorate could not be matched in the Spanish zone, even though Beigbeder did what he could. The commitment was there, but the cash was lacking. Since Lyautey and Noguès believed that France's future in Morocco depended in the long run on the material well-being of the native population, one might wonder if Beigbeder's policies were destined to founder on the rocks of poverty. Here the high commissioner was at his most creative, for he explained Spain's connection with Morocco in racial and cultural rather than in material terms. History and blood counted for as much as progress and prosperity. Beigbeder recalled that Spanish and Muslim societies had interpenetrated during the Middle Ages. Spain was therefore not alien but a living part of modern Morocco. Beigbeder emotionally baptized his Muslim listeners, calling them "brothers," the physical and cultural stock of the same family tree. The "new Spain" led by *africanistas* understood that better than others, he insisted; the only conquest it sought was of the "heart." It aspired to something far more important than the exploitation of men, markets, and materials: the "renaissance of Arab culture, Arab expression, Arab letters and of a civilization which is an integral part of Spain. We want Cordoba to rise again from its ashes." Beigbeder interpreted the Hispano-Moroccan contact as a source of human reconciliation and spiritual greatness that could alter the nature of Spain's mission in North Africa, transforming a dark and bloody ground into a bright field of amity and union. There was a world task as well. The empire that Spain coveted was "something analogous" to the intellectual imperium of ancient Greece. Spain wanted to present a "new ideal" to humankind. Said Beigbeder: "It is the reign of Don Quixote in the world."[40]

Regardless of his flights of fancy, there is no doubt that Spaniards appreciated Beigbeder's accomplishments. "In less than three years Juan Beigbeder has transformed the life of Morocco," wrote an enthusiast in *España*.[41] He was considered an "architect" of Franco's victory and named foreign minister in 1939—neither the job nor the time for a dreamer—largely as the result of what he had done in Morocco. It is easy to fault him for Machiavellianism, particularly in regard to the Moroccan nationalists. But his was the dilemma of every colonial administrator from Lyautey on down: how to fit the aspirations of the native population (or a small segment of it) into the overall designs of the Metropole. For Beigbeder it was almost a question of Spanish survival; until 1938 the victory of the Spanish nationalists depended on what went on in Morocco.

For the French, Beigbeder was an unmitigated disaster. This was Lyautey used against France at a time when Noguès had been forced to abandon some of the marshal's gentler precepts. At moments it reduced the French, who were unaccustomed to this sort of thing, to reacting to Spanish initiatives. Most serious was the Spanish traffic with the nationalists, which the French considered a perilous and disgusting business. Permitting the attacks against the French protectorate to go unchecked amounted to encouragement of sedition and revolt. To be sure, when Meknès exploded in September 1937, Beigbeder began to move more circumspectly, fearing the spread of the violence, but the nationalist press was still allowed to hammer away at the criminal responsibility of the French. Relations deteriorated to the point where the Spaniards began to fear armed French intervention in May 1938.[42]

No one in Paris needed to be reminded of Jules Cambon's musing on the havoc that a hostile Spain could wreak in the event of a European war. Once the Franco forces triumphed on the battlefield, the Third Republic recognized Burgos as Spain's legal government and appointed Marshal Pétain its ambassador, a hoped-for symbol of the cooperation it now so earnestly desired.[43] But the victorious nationalists were in no mood for a quick reconciliation. Distant grievances, compounded by close unfriendly encounters with official France, meant that Spanish goodwill, once dismissed as of slight value, would now have to be purchased. Not surprisingly, Morocco figured as part of the price.

France first moved to make concessions to Spain on Morocco's "third zone," Tangier, whose special international status had created as many problems as it solved. Designed as a separate urban enclave, Tangier had been carved out of Spanish land in the north, depriving Spain of the city, port, and hinterland that might have permitted Spanish Morocco to turn a profit. In terms of human and physical geography, there was neither rhyme nor reason for the amputation, but the French and British believed Tangier was far too important commercially and strategically to be left to Spain. It was a wound of purse and pride that never healed. At the time of Algeciras, Cambon predicted nothing but trouble by keeping Tangier from the Spaniards; he put it down as a "serious political mistake."[44] Three decades later, the Spanish foreign minister erupted to the American ambassador with words that recalled Hitler on Danzig: Tangier's status had been a "legal fiction and a monstrosity."[45]

What France had in mind in April 1940 (seven months after the outbreak of the European conflict) was surrendering the administrative headship of the zone. Since the establishment of the 1923 Tangier statute, Tangier's city manager had been a Frenchman, and although Pierre Le Fur routinely got high marks from the *tangerinos* (including the Spaniards among them), there was no doubt of his private loyalties. The French were privileged insiders, and Le Fur, who had learned the ropes in the French administration of the southern zone, kept it that way.[46] Noguès was strongly opposed to this concession. He argued that any change at Tangier could lead to "unforeseen difficulties" hurtful to France. Here was an opportunity for "third powers" to fish in troubled waters or for the Spaniards to whittle away at the sultan's authority. What would be the reaction of the native population or the consequences to the economic life of the zone? In the end, Noguès imagined that a change would only make relations with Spain worse.[47] Like Lyautey, he was cold to the idea of working with the Spaniards in good times or bad.

Whatever the merit of Noguès's worries, the issue was Spain's amity or enmity in the contest between France and Germany. French reports indicated that native criticism of the Spanish regime in Morocco had increased since Beigbeder's promotion to foreign minister and the end of the civil war, that there were serious economic difficulties, and that Spain now looked for some Franco-Spanish accord to set things straight.[48] In addition, Beigbeder was on record as opposing Spanish intervention on the Axis side, preferring to sit out the conflict and barter with France on the quiet for modest concessions in Morocco. On the other hand, Beigbeder's eventual successor as foreign minister, Ramón Serrano Suñer, was cut from different cloth; he was convinced that Spanish imperial designs at their most grand—Tangier, Gibraltar, French Morocco, western Algeria— would only come through blood sacrificed in comradeship with Italy and Germany. He had no love for the "Anglo-French group" that had condemned Spain to be a "country of the third rank."[49] Serrano Suñer's pressure on Franco, the Spanish consul general at Rabat told Noguès, was becoming more "energetic and effective" and it was aided by Italian coffee conversation of an imminent Allied strike at Tangier, Melilla, and Ceuta. It was now up to France, he warned, to "strengthen" Beigbeder by pulling closer to Spain, making it clear to the Spanish government "all the advantages that neutrality would bring for the reconstruction of the country" in the aftermath of the civil war. Might they not include the economic aid of France and Britain?[50] What was needed was some concrete gesture to Spain, a move toward a Franco-Spanish reconciliation.

None was forthcoming until June, a time when German armies had bottled up Anglo-French forces at Dunkirk—hardly the moment for France to pretend that this was generosity based on strength. Even then, the most France would offer was a mixed Franco-Spanish security force for Tangier. Noguès did not like that either, although it was surely preferable to the unilateral takeover bruited about by the Spaniards: "We must not forget that the occupation of Tangier by Spain without our participation or at the very least without an express mandate from us would result in a considerable loss of prestige, which would be strongly resented by the native population and the sultan."[51] Of course this was too little and too late. Probably taking Italy's declaration of war on France as a sign of the desperateness of France's plight, Spain announced the occupation of the zone. To save face, France agreed to the occupation, but no one was fooled. Morize had been telephoned at Rabat on the morning of 14 June and told unceremoniously that "Spanish military forces would occupy Tangier within ten minutes." It caused "a considerable sensation" throughout French Morocco. The Spanish press observed that Tangier had been taken the same day that Paris had fallen to the Germans.[52] Like Paris, Tangier was a prize of war.

Within days Beigbeder was back with more blueprints for change. Acting on the inside information of France's request for armistice terms from Germany and concerned lest they parcel out Moroccan territory, Beigbeder pressed France for a quick, spontaneous cession to Spain: "If you have to lose a piece of your North African empire," he told Robert Renom de la Baume, French ambassador at Madrid, "better that it go to Spain rather than Germany." What Spain wanted was an adjustment of the zonal frontier to extend Spanish control over the Beni Zeroual in the north and the Beni Snassen in the east. As with Tangier, Beigbeder wished the transaction to be carried out in accord with France, the public reason being a "disturbing agitation" among the tribes that the Spaniards had volunteered to quell.[53]

At Bordeaux, where it had been chased by advancing German armies, the French government played for time to examine the conditions of both the German and Italian conventions (then unknown) and to solicit Noguès's reaction to the Spanish initiative. Neither armistice document projected a German or Italian occupation of Morocco. Responding from his wartime post at Algiers, Noguès wrote: "I am convinced that the government will not give effect to such an improper maneuver as that of Colonel Beigbeder. Moreover, any cession of territory to Spain would be dishonorable for France and cause, after the Tangier occupation, a new and more serious wound to the pride of the sultan and the Moroccan people. Their guns would literally fire themselves and we would be obliged to go to the aid of our tribes or risk having all of Morocco turn against us."[54] With France's defeat in Europe, Noguès leaned more heavily on intangibles to keep the peace—France's prestige, the sultan's moral authority—and certainly wanted nothing to undermine them.

There could be no outright rejection of Beigbeder's scheme. Slapping Spain might trigger another Tangier or, even worse, push Spain down the alley of alliance with Germany and Italy. Moreover, to put it plainly, Vichy (the government was en route to Vichy from Bordeaux) was too weak to insult Madrid. The foreign ministry staff, headed by its newly appointed secretary general François Charles-Roux (a hard-nosed Huguenot who had spent the previous eight years as France's ambassador to the Vatican), set a course between "the desire not to say yes and the impossibility of saying no" by accepting the notion of a summer negotiation in the hope that it would be long and inconclusive. Every step of the way, Noguès was to be kept informed, consulted, and listened to. In fact, "waiting for Noguès"—a time-consuming effort given his command responsibilities, the distances involved, and a government on the move—was elevated to an operating principle of the foreign ministry staff, not only because it made sense, but because it took time. As Charles-Roux remembered it, Noguès was a "brake," the government an "accelerator." "He kept us from the weaknesses of the government, subjected to the pressure from Spain, and from our own frailty, subjected to the pressure from the government."[55]

From the first, any deal that turned over the Beni Snassen to Spain was ruled out. It would have put the Spaniards on the Algero-Moroccan border across the line from the Oranais (which the Spanish press was agitating for) and abandoned much of eastern Morocco, severely truncating the French zone. But the foreign ministry was willing to "give way" on the Beni Zeroual if a final determination of borders was left to a general peace settlement at war's end, which was then thought to be not far off. The hope was to "handle" (*ménager*) Spain, to fortify Beigbeder, and to build some vested interest in Franco-Spanish solidarity.[56] The concession was not made cavalierly, for it would bring the Spaniards nearer Fez. Still, it was not a bolt out of the blue. The 1912 boundary had placed the Beni Zeroual entirely within the Spanish zone even though the tribe was to be administered by the French for security reasons. During the Rif war, France had occupied the region, and although the Franco-Spanish boundary accord of 1925 called for a French military withdrawal and an administrative transfer to Spain, an exchange of notes postponed both indefinitely.[57] So what France offered in 1940 was to make good on a fifteen-year-old pledge.

Noguès was furious. Privately he warned: "If, bolstered by vague promises, the Spaniards try to penetrate our zone, it will be war. The Beni Zeroual want to stay with us and will defend themselves." Officially he even raised the specter of internal rebellion: "I repeat: at the present moment any tangible concession before a treaty of peace is signed would run the risk of starting a war and turning the entire native population against us." To ask Spain to wait was clearly unacceptable because Beigbeder's strategy depended upon a fast bilateral settlement. He was dealing behind the Reich's back and did not know how long it could remain secret. "It is with France that [Beigbeder] wants to settle the question," Ambassador de la Baume had insisted, "without waiting for it to be submitted to the goodwill of the Reich in the future peace negotiations. If we put off the solution until later, we will force Spain to ask Germany, in exchange for certain services rendered, for what we ourselves have not wanted to give now." The counsel was divided, the dilemma real: either to destroy what Lyautey had created in Morocco or to toss Madrid into the arms of Berlin.[58]

Noguès's "energetic protests," transmitted as "precautions" to take in the event of a negotiation, doomed the possibility for a quick deal. All of his points were incorporated into the foreign ministry's bargaining strategy. Whatever the results of the talks with Spain, nothing would take effect until after the European war had ended. Nothing would be done that "by its extent or nature" might compromise the future of the French zone. No land would be ceded to Spain if it had not been the subject of prior agreements known to the Makhzen (which restricted the discussion to the 1925 accord). And the region in question would be carefully delimited; under no circumstances would it extend south of the Ouergha, where it might compromise the security of Fez. Finally, in return for a concession by France, Spain would be "invited" to declare that it had no further aims in Morocco or French Africa, what was called a *quitus général* in Quai d'Orsay Latin. Still, Noguès was far from sanguine. Even as he deluged the foreign ministry with a flood of paper—memoranda and maps on the Beni Zeroual, notes on the 1925 accord—he persisted in questioning the very idea of a territorial cession.[59]

In the end, the foreign ministry staff added a further item to the package to be presented for Spain's consideration: the renunciation of France's prerogatives in Tangier in return for the retrocession of Ifni by Spain. It was said that Madrid could never accept the retrocession of Ifni, which had been Spanish since 1860, nor an agreement that in toto looked more like an exchange than a surrender; and that was precisely what the foreign ministry wanted. But Noguès was worried enough about the whole matter to come to Vichy, his first visit to France since the German invasion. He made sure that the government understood the "delicate and fragile" nature of the protectorate and of the possible consequences of any rupture in the political status quo. There was also talk of the benefits to Germany of the maintenance of the Pax Gallia in Morocco. Finally, with Noguès's blessing, the foreign ministry underscored the permanence of the French installation in Morocco: "Whatever fate has in store for Morocco," read the prayerlike prose, "we must conduct ourselves as if there were no threat to its future. Circumstances might even force us to declare ever more loudly how permanent we intend our establishment to be. In the political and economic scheme of things, this concern must take priority over all others." It was a statement designed to hide the awful truth, that the bargaining on Morocco, to which Noguès had given his "resigned consent," had begun.[60]

The final draft of the proposal to Spain was not in Foreign Minister Paul Baudouin's hands until the end of August. What he saw was something even less generous to the Spaniards with regard to the Beni Zeroual than the 1925 agreement had been, for Noguès had excised the ridges north of the Ouergha and a bit of territory known as the Gherouaou Basin for defensive purposes. Even the foreign ministry conceded that the concessions might seem "small" to Beigbeder. Here was a gift once given, then taken away, now offered again but shriveled in size. Fearing that this would do nothing for Franco-Spanish friendship and anxious about a German or Spanish preventive pounce on North Africa in light of the dissidence in French Equatorial Africa, Baudouin rejected the draft as "too stingy." "The project gives almost nothing to start with," the foreign minister noted in his day book, "and invites counterproposals. It will lead to haggling." What Charles-Roux had seen as helpful hedgerows, Baudouin saw as stumbling blocks. The result was a new streamlined offer that promised Madrid the "complete execution" of the 1925 boundary agreement. The insulting *quitus* clause was dropped in favor of a request for Spain's public assurance of support and solidarity in Morocco. In lieu of a lengthy document were two short notes, one on the Beni Zeroual cession, the other on the Ifni-Tangier exchange.[61]

Baudouin assured Noguès that he realized the extent of the "sacrifice" that he was proposing and that the tribe's "disappointment" might well have serious repercussions on the native population. But it was clear that Noguès was on his own to devise whatever measures he could to handle the situation. He accepted the decision obediently but without enthusiasm. As solace he convinced himself that at issue were far-reaching foreign policy matters of which he could not be the judge.[62]

While the French thrashed out the terms and tactics on Morocco, the Spaniards were debating the questions of war and peace. The well-publicized visits of Serrano Suñer to Berlin and Rome in September–October 1940 seemed to mark the victory of the war party in Madrid. As if to confirm the inner struggle, Beigbeder confided to the French ambassador: "I am opposed to the armed intervention of my country and I hope it will not happen." When questioned closely on Morocco, he reiterated the views that had always been his. He desired the status quo in the protectorate with any adjustments to be made through bilateral Franco-Spanish negotiations. Only if France ceased to have an independent existence would Spain seek a major change—all of Morocco for itself—but the idea of a partition with Germany or Italy was excluded.[63]

Although Beigbeder had said all of this before, his message took on a special urgency for Baudouin, who was surrounded by fresh evidence that Madrid was on the verge of entering the war. To Baudouin, Beigbeder had become the last, best hope for a reasonable settlement on Morocco that would keep Spain at peace. This was why he broke impatiently with the spidery Quai d'Orsay strategy to tell the Spanish ambassador that France was now "favorably disposed to the pure and simple application of the 1925 accord." It did no good for Beigbeder. Even though Serrano Suñer's visits abroad did not bring Spain closer to a military alliance with the Axis, Beigbeder was sacrificed to the false front of harmony and replaced by Serrano Suñer in mid-October. There would now be no negotiation with France, not because force had won out over persuasion, but because (so reported the French ambassador) Spain now feared that Germany desired to be the arbiter of matters Moroccan. In fact, Ciano had told Serrano Suñer that although Hitler and Mussolini supported the Spanish claim to Gibraltar and agreed in principle to some changes in Morocco, these could not be determined precisely until after the war was over.[64] The danger to Morocco of a belligerent Spain appeared to have been replaced by that of a German shadow. Ultimately, Spain's firm decision to remain neutral in the European war worked to France's advantage in Morocco. All that Spain now offered Germany was its friendship, not enough to justify colonial concessions. Moreover, Hitler believed that promising Morocco to Spain would push the French into the arms of the English. Even if the Spaniards did occupy the French zone, could they hold on to it? Hitler thought not. They would probably call for Germany's help in the event of an English attack.[65] Better to keep Morocco French and have the French, past masters at beating back the English, defend it themselves.

The Vichy French proved that they were willing and able to hold on to their empire, even if it meant fighting against their former allies. They resisted the British fleet at Mers-el-Kebir in July and defended Dakar against Anglo-Gaullist invaders in September. For his

part, Noguès throttled a Churchill-inspired attempt in June to encourage the formation of a French government in North Africa to
carry on resistance to Germany. The purpose, of course, was to prevent the shrinking of Vichy's assets. But the French recognized that
the empire's disintegration was "an immediate danger not only to
French interests, but even to those of Germany and Italy." This was
an important place where French and German interests overlapped.
It was one reason why Vichy, determined not to let the colonies slip
away or be pried loose, first spoke of collaboration. France would defend its empire if Germany provided the weapons.[66]

The broad collaboration that the French sketched in the fall of
1940 was in essence to be Germany's Mediterranean and colonial
partner in the new Europe. With all that it implied in the economic
and political realms, this was surely not what Hitler had in mind.
But collaboration in Africa, that is, reduced German restrictions on
the colonial army in return for a vigilant French imperial defense,
made sense.[67] Even then there was no German guarantee of French
sovereignty at home or overseas, what Laval labored so long and so
hard to obtain. Hitler did not hide this. At the Montoire meeting
with Pétain (24 October 1940), he acknowledged the "necessary territorial modifications in the existing French colonial domain," but
he also promised that "in the final accounting" at war's end, France
would retain an African empire "essentially equivalent to what she
possesses today."[68] This was probably just part of the "grandiose
fraud" that Hitler engaged in to resolve the conflicting colonial interests of the Mediterranean powers, but it was apparently enough to
encourage the French to believe that good works piled one on top of
the other would bring about the empire's salvation.[69]

Silence on Morocco, then, was part and parcel of what has been
called Hitler's "new policy" toward France, Germany's willingness
to collaborate in some areas. In North Africa it meant "a tacit choice
of France over Spain."[70] Although the "new policy" was dead in Europe by the end of 1940 (when for the Reich's planners the Soviet
Union replaced Great Britain as chief enemy), it continued to live on
in Africa until the Allied invasion of 1942. Still, Spain never gave up
completely on a Franco-Spanish negotiation, and there was always
the "danger" of a Spanish offensive against the French zone backed
by the Germans if Germany should decide to buckle up the western
Mediterranean.[71] As the war dragged on, however, Franco-Spanish affairs improved. Spanish High Commissioner General Luis Orgaz
told Noguès in February 1942 that he "sincerely desired to preserve
the *status quo* in the western Mediterranean."[72] Gone were the fears

of Spanish military adventures in the southern zone or of a new Moroccan partition presided over by Germany, if only France kept Morocco quiet and out of the war.

All of this was good for France. But it was distressingly apparent that the considerations of policymakers in Berlin and Madrid counted for more than those of Vichy and Rabat. France had been struck dumb in Morocco. As the sultan's foreign minister, Noguès had stood mute (and begged the sultan to do likewise) while the Spaniards flouted sharifian authority in the north, absorbed Tangier, and pressed for land to the south and east. What stopped Spain's progress was not French military action or political pressure but an appeal to Germany. France's defeat in Europe, coming hard on the heels of the troubles brought by the Spanish civil war, had neither completely untangled the empire's zones (although now there were two instead of three) nor unraveled the protectorate. But it had sapped French confidence and diminished France in the eyes of the sultan and his subjects.

SIX

The Fall of France and the
Vichy Change

On the eve of the eclipse of France as a European power, Charles Noguès was at the pinnacle of his military career. In addition to holding France's most coveted diplomatic post overseas, he was a member of the Supreme War Council and designated wartime commander-in-chief of the North African Theater of Operations. In Morocco he was hailed as the long-awaited *chef*, the marshal's true successor, and in France his counsel was valued, particularly as storm clouds formed over the Mediterranean. Among the colonial military, it is safe to say that he had no peer. He was recognized as the architect of Morocco's revival. With Noguès at the helm, the protectorate had weathered drought and famine, survived riots in the cities and sedition among the tribes, skirted the shoals of the Spanish conflict and foreign intervention in the north. Paris's motto could have been taken as its device: *Fluctuat nec mergitur*. Moreover, there were encouraging signs of a new inner strength brought about by an upswing in the native and colonial economy, a commitment to urban and rural improvement, affirmation of the authority of the native elite in the souks and medinas, and renewed reliance on the sultan.

The last is worth special mention, for Noguès prided himself on restoring the close relationship between resident and sultan that Lyautey had nurtured with Moulay Youssef and that the marshal had seen as so important to French success in the sharifian empire. Like the father, the son—Sidi Mohammed ben Youssef—had been handpicked by the French (in 1927) and tutored by servants faithful to France, the Algerian Si Mohammed Mammeri and the Grand Vizier Mohammed el-Mokri. Although they dutifully put words in his mouth, he yearned for his own voice. Caught between those who wanted a marionette and those who wished for a real, live champion, he played a double role, at times responding to the pull of the French, at times resisting it. Seen in retrospect, his aim was to secure an independent place for himself, safe from any group, party,

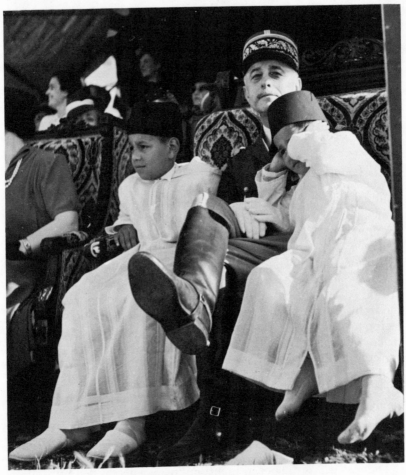

Left, Moulay Hassan; *center,* Noguès;
right, Moulay Abdallah. Fez, 1940.
Courtesy French Embassy, Rabat.

people, or clan. "This young, proud, personable sovereign," recalled Charles de Gaulle, always a shrewd analyst of men and their missions, "did not conceal his ambition to be at the head of his country on its march toward progress and, one day, toward independence. Watching and listening to him as he spoke, sometimes ardent, sometimes prudent, always skillful, one felt that he was ready to come to an agreement with whoever would help him play this role, but that

Left, Moulay Hassan; *center*, Sultan Sidi Mohammed ben Youssef;
right, Moulay Abdallah. Ifrane, September 1941.
Photo Jacques Belin

he was capable of bringing a great deal of obstinacy to bear against those who wished to oppose him in this design."[1]

The pretensions of the nationalists, their disobedience, street violence, and attacks on the native hierarchy kept the sultan near to the French during the Noguès years, although he did not disguise his sympathy for some of their grievances nor his solicitude for their persons at anguished moments of their struggle. For the time being, he was "very loyal," Noguès confided, "but he has become too adept at politics and one day that could be dangerous."[2] Noguès never had the sultan's total allegiance, but he managed to keep an edge on all other competitors. It was a confident bond based on trust, affection, and mutual self-interest. Only twice did Frenchmen see the sultan weep in public, at the news of the fall of Paris in 1940 and at Noguès's leave-taking three years later. Even de Gaulle, no friend of Noguès's, acknowledged the resident's happy influence over the sultan at the ebb tide of France's fortunes.[3]

The outbreak of the European war in September 1939 took Noguès to Algiers to coordinate Mediterranean activities. Morize was left at Rabat to handle the day-to-day affairs of the protectorate, which had increasingly been placed on a war footing since the Czechoslovakian crisis of a year before. The spirit of the Moroccan population was "excellent," its loyalty unquestioned.[4] As was the case at the time of Munich, the sultan promised "cooperation without reserve" as a witness for all that France had done for Morocco. For those who felt less than thankful, he added a warning: He "who fails to be grateful . . . runs the risk of banishment."[5] One by one the nationalists, released from prison or brought home from exile, expressed their fidelity to France. As moving as these professions of faith could be and as welcome the halt in political agitation, the French were under no illusions. It was only a "temporary withdrawal" from the field of battle dictated by the uncertain political climate of the moment; the opponents would reappear as soon as "favorable weather" permitted it. In addition, during a war anticipated to be "long and hard," there would be ample opportunity for political disruption, prompted at home or provoked from abroad. As ever, the Germans had pride of place among foreign agitators: "German propaganda, handled with great tact and a perfect understanding of the native mentality, will be particularly dangerous." Political calm could therefore be maintained only "at the price of constant vigilance and great strength."[6]

Noguès's mission was to provide the Metropole with the troops required by France's strategy in a contest with Germany. He discharged this duty with energy and skill. From the first week in September 1939 to the third week of April 1940, he sent the equivalent of six divisions to France, more than 150,000 combat-ready troops with the best equipment, training, and officers in North Africa.[7] Supplying soldiers was only part of his responsibility. Protecting his patrimony from Spanish or Italian attack was the second, and offensive operations the third. The third responsibility would disappoint Noguès the most, initially because of the eight months of quiet on the western front and in the Mediterranean, later because the Maghreb was denied the chance to enter the fray.

What Europe called the sitzkrieg had its counterpart in North Africa, but its impact went beyond a concern for the morale and fighting spirit of front-line troops. Here the rules of the game were different. "In North Africa, more than elsewhere, he who does not attack is considered the weaker and our inaction will cause an uneasiness among the native population capable of producing internal troubles."[8] For this reason, even after months of shipping soldiers to France had drained off his forces, Noguès advocated offensive action against the Italian army in Libya if Italy should declare war. "I prefer to put myself in a difficult military situation than to resign myself to a surrender of territory, ruining our prestige with the native population in North Africa and opening the door to agitation that would create for us an inside danger to add to that from the outside." What he did not want was to let the Italians march unopposed into Tunisia from the Libyan frontier to his defensive fortifications on the Mareth line, a distance of some 150 to 200 kilometers. Even so, with his forces decreasing and those in Libya on the increase, there was slim chance that an offensive could amount to more than "showing soldiers" on the border and encouraging "small uprisings" in the mountains. "If the enemy went on the offensive and I could not hold him back, I would fight step by step," he assured his commander-in-chief, General Maurice Gamelin, "until I reached the Mareth line—the limit of our pullback—which would then be defended with no thought of retreat." Any real advance against Libya—the taking of Tripoli, the conquest of its western sector (the Tripolitania)—would require reinforcements from France. But Noguès pledged Gamelin that he would grasp any opportunity that presented itself to press forward "to the maximum."[9]

A month later, after two divisions were subtracted from the five that Noguès counted on for an offensive and sent to France, all hope was gone for a forward encounter. His forces were "scarcely sufficient to assure [Tunisia's] internal security and to stop the enemy at the Mareth line." In Morocco he had only eighteen battalions, of which twelve to fourteen were needed to defend the northern front against the five divisions of the Spanish zone. Overall his troop strength was so weak that he turned down the Metropole's request for another division, explaining that to honor it would be all the encouragement that Italy needed to intervene. He could not do more than he had already done. On 30 May, when asked to send three regiments to France, he announced that his forces were "insufficient" to handle both internal and external defense. The "very serious risks" to North Africa at a time when Italian belligerency appeared imminent outweighed in his mind the "relatively feeble support" that the regiments could provide.[10]

No oracle was needed to foretell the outcome of an invasion from Libya. An Italian air raid on the naval base at Bizerte (after Italy's entry into the war on 10 June) brought no French response because the aircraft in Tunisia were so few in number that a reprisal was "impossible." In the air the North African situation was "precarious" and Noguès pleaded for the return of the fighter groups that had flown to France. On the ground Tunisia's troops were stretched thin, reduced to what Noguès euphemistically called an "active defense."[11] But ultimately there never was a full-scale Italian invasion and Tunisia's defenses remained unbreached. The Italians had wisely decided not to fight for what the Germans had already won for them in Europe.

At the time, Noguès's refusals and requests must have seemed unreal amid the crisis in France. Due to reverses in the northeast in May, Gamelin had been replaced by General Maxime Weygand, commander of the Middle Eastern Theater of Operations, now charged with the national defense. Despite the confidence he inspired in mid-May, Weygand's inheritance was already spent. The day he took over, the nineteenth of the month, the situation was "irremediable."[12] But buoyed up by "Fochian optimism," he was unwilling to admit defeat. He tried to execute a holding operation along a defensive line from the Somme to Montmédy that had only a faint chance of success, for it required a relaxation of German pressure and massive British air support. Neither materialized. Implicit in the scheme was that there would be no fallback if it failed. Therefore, by 26 May Weygand had quietly ruled out a withdrawal to North Africa if the home front collapsed and a continuation of the war by other means as well.

His decision not to move the military bridgehead outside of Europe demonstrated his inability to make a "revolutionary departure" from traditional European warfare. It was something no modern commander had ever done or even contemplated. What was left was an armistice, the customary end to a continental conflict. So when the time came on 12 and 13 June—a week after the military situation looked "hopeless," a day before the Germans trooped into Paris—he first requested, then demanded, that the government seek Germany's terms. As if to close off any other option, he said he would not leave France if the government (en route to Bordeaux) should decide to flee abroad. He also rejected a compromise proposal that the government move to North Africa and he stay in France to surrender only the ground forces. Finally, he made no offer to resign. These defiant, rebellious acts, the second accompanied by loud, angry outbursts at members of the cabinet, pushed Paul Reynaud to resign as premier on 16 June, finishing forever the debate on the armistice.[13]

On 17 June Marshal Philippe Pétain, Reynaud's successor and Weygand's confederate in the cabinet, announced from Bordeaux that it was "necessary to stop the fighting." Responding to what he took to be a radio command, Noguès ordered his forces to halt offensive operations but to guard "with force the absolute integrity of the national territory." Then the North African commander telegraphed Weygand to ask that he be permitted "to continue to fight" to save North Africa's "honor" and to keep North Africa French. He explained: "Even if North Africa is left to us [by the terms of an armistice], we would forever lose the respect and confidence of the native population if we do not make a gesture of this sort. I am ready, if the government has no objection, to take on the full responsibility of [battling on] with all the risks that it entails. It could even be a factor of some consequence in the [armistice] negotiations. With the help of the fleet and the air force units that I have been told to count on, we can hold out."[14]

To make certain that his proposal was understood, Noguès dispatched his liaison officer with the high command, Major Marius Guizol, by night flight with a personal letter to Weygand. In it he asked for "authorization to disobey" Pétain's call for an end to the hostilities, and, concerned lest Weygand interpret this as insolence, he told his senior by nine years: "I have no desire by this act to step in front of anyone else. Send whomever you wish. I am ready to serve in the ranks wherever you want me."[15]

The purpose in all of this was not to refuse to deal with Germany by escaping to North Africa (which Pétain and Weygand had no interest in) nor to pretend that France was not defeated by dancing across the globe. It was purely a matter of Noguès's savvy in North African politics. To stop without a struggle, to quit before a *baroud d'honneur* would forfeit France's prestige in the Maghreb. Even worse, if a chunk of North Africa was to be handed over to the enemy without a fight, there would be no way of containing the fury of the native population, "who will quickly sweep us out of Tunisia and Morocco and Algeria as well." [16] Reinforced by men and materiel from the Metropole, North Africa could not reverse the result of the contest in France, but it might prevent the disintegration of the empire.

Pétain's announcement had had a chilling impact on the colon population as well. Unlike the sense of relief in France that the fighting was finally over, there was only dismay and apprehension among the settlers, for North Africa was not the Metropole but land up for grabs in the event of France's defeat. The Spanish march into Tangier trumpeted the beginning of the redistribution, and for days thereafter the French anxiously awaited the expected Spanish rush into the protectorate. To struggle on was more than just the honorable thing to do, more than mere sensitivity to the Muslim mentality, it was a requirement to protect the colonial situation, the futures and fortunes of Frenchmen abroad.[17]

On the afternoon of the seventeenth, Admiral François Darlan, minister of the navy and commander-in-chief of France's naval forces, broke Bordeaux's silence by ordering Noguès to continue "with fierce energy" all air-sea operations "regardless of the news from whatever source." [18] But there was nothing at all from Weygand. While he waited, Noguès passed along the information he was gathering at Algiers, in particular the British encouragements to continue the fight. Here was the beginning of one misunderstanding, for the British interpreted North Africa's combativeness as a desire to break away from the Metropole in imitation of the Dutch and Belgian empires, not at all what Noguès had in mind.[19] He spelled it out once more in a telegram addressed to Pétain because Weygand had still sent him no sign. Because he knew that the government was weighing a gift of Moroccan territory to buy off Spain, he referred directly to the Moroccan and Tunisian protectorates: "To envisage their surrender to a foreign power without their consent and without having done battle would be considered treason. If we do not defend North Africa, we will have a hard time keeping any real authority over what our enemies leave us *at the final reckoning*, for a government that is scorned cannot function." Perhaps heartened by the evidence of support around him, he boldly suggested that the fight might be more than just a *baroud d'honneur*: "With our fleet intact, the aircraft now crossing the Mediterranean, and some additional reinforcements in men and materiel, we can hold out for a long time and without doubt do well enough to be able to contribute to the defeat of our enemies. So with a respectful but burning insistence, I ask the government in the name of the most vital interests of our country to pursue the struggle (or let it be pursued) in North Africa, if it is no longer possible to do so on the Continent. This is the only way for France to keep its Muslim empire."[20] Yet despite the phrases worth quoting, phrases seeming to echo the London broadcasts of dissident General Charles de Gaulle, Noguès still defined the struggle in narrow North African terms.[21]

Noguès's messages received no full reply. Weygand's first sound was in response to the general's order to suspend offensive operations. It was a crisp one-liner. Ignoring the confusion created by Pétain's words, Weygand said he was "astonished" at Noguès's communication and informed him that French troops continued to resist everywhere in the Metropole.[22] The following day Weygand acknowledged the resident's "moving" telegrams and explained that the government had asked to enter into armistice discussions with the Germans and Italians because the "situation of the army and the population demand it." "But this does not mean an end to the fighting and, still less, capitulation. The armies of France, although separated and sorely tried, continue to fight magnificently and with fierce energy. For the moment a cease fire is out of the question."[23]

Noguès's messages coincided with a renewed interest among the political leaders to send representatives of the government to North Africa, if not to continue the fight, then at least to negotiate in greater freedom. If dealing with Germany proved impossible, North Africa would be the escape. Pétain was still unwilling to make the trip himself but was amenable to delegating his powers to a member of the cabinet. Noguès's zeal to hold out and yet remain obedient to the government fit in perfectly with this plan. Still, Weygand's answer did not spell this out. There was nothing about the transfer of men and materiel to North Africa in case of military collapse in the southwest or an unsatisfactory response from the enemy. For another full day, Noguès remained in the dark as to the government's intentions.

When Major Guizol returned to Algiers, he reported Weygand's assurance that the government would do nothing contrary to honor. Guizol ventured that if the armistice conditions were "too heavy," the government seemed prepared to carry the fight to the empire and had made contingency plans to that effect, but in the meantime it preferred to remain mum. Darlan alone put it in writing: "We are ready to come to North Africa, if it is necessary to continue the fight." The request for terms was only a "gesture" to make it clear to the country that the government would not prolong its "immense sufferings" unless there was no other alternative. As for the fleet, it would fight on until a regularly constituted government *"indepen-dent of the enemy"* ordered it to stop; and the fleet would never be surrendered. On the other hand, Guizol did not conceal his severe measure of the men he had talked with. Nowhere had he found ex-citement for the message he carried. Everywhere he had witnessed confusion, a lack of enthusiasm for the fight, and suspicion of No-guès's motives and loyalty.[24] In spite of Weygand's change in temper and Darlan's note, Noguès could now have no doubt of his shaky footing with his commanders. Worse, he still had no clue as to what course to steer.

Playing the pirate, Noguès began to beg, borrow, and steal the rein-forcements in arms and equipment that a continued struggle would require. He ordered the unloading of all supply ships en route to Bayonne or Bordeaux that stopped at Casablanca for refueling. He contacted French purchasing agents in Washington about credits and war materiel, and queried the head of the British liaison mission in Algiers about aid from London. He sent staff officers to Port Vendres, Sète, and Marseilles to supervise shipments from the Metropole. In addition, he bought fifteen thousand contraband Mauser rifles from black marketeers in Tangier.[25]

The English encouraged Noguès to continue the fight. They also pressed General Eugène Mittelhauser, commander-in-chief of the Middle Eastern Theater of Operations in Beirut. Mittelhauser too was inclined to battle on. He telegraphed Weygand on 20 June that "whatever happened," the Army of the Levant, together with the French and English fleets and the English army, would "pursue its mission without mental reservation and with the last ounce of its energy." Better informed on the spirit of Bordeaux, Noguès knew that "whatever happened" was farther than Weygand would let him go. He cautioned Mittelhauser that although the military chiefs in France believed that the empire had to be defended, "in the interests of the cause we serve they ask that until further notice we use great prudence in any declaration we make in regard to the position that we plan to take in the future."[26] Already Noguès was repeating the language of the new Girondins, if not out of conviction, then out of obedience.

Once broken out, however, the colonial resistance fever was hard to contain. The prefect of Constantine reported that many officers believed that North Africa had to fight "even alone at the side of our Allies." Should the Metropole capitulate, there was sure to be a "break" whose effects would be hard to measure. Through the press and radio, Noguès tried to firm up the discipline in both the civilian and military populations. He called for an end to all "demonstrations" in favor of continuing the war that might "hinder the government's action." "We must remain calm. This is the characteristic of true courage. Remain united, resolute, and disciplined behind the government and your leaders, who like you have no other wish at this moment than to defend the destinies and the honor of France and its empire."[27] This was pure Weygand, phrases couched in conditions allowing the government to do what it wanted but the governed only the freedom to obey.

The effervescence at Algiers was both useful and unsettling. The stronger the will of the empire to resist, the more likely that Germany would present less stringent armistice conditions designed to coax it into submission. It was in Bordeaux's interest to "manage" this imperial stubbornness, to plan for the transfer of the government and its armies abroad, even if it was a fraud. Pétain and Foreign Minister Baudouin understood this; they let the Germans know that if they wanted an armistice with France, they had better hurry up or the government might skip the country.[28] On the other hand, with one rebel already on the loose—General de Gaulle had refused Weygand's order of 20 June to return to France from London—the loss of the empire through disobedience or the dissidence of its chiefs was a live threat. From Guizol's report, Noguès knew that he was suspected of tottering dangerously close to rebellion. Thus, when he was asked on 21 June to "come to Bordeaux today by the most rapid route," he agreed, then had second thoughts, fearing that Weygand might be "planning a Peyrouton" (bringing him to France with no intention of letting him return to North Africa). What he told Weygand was that it was impossible for him to leave his post for fear of triggering "very serious events," always the code word for popular disturbances. It was no secret that he was not having an easy time keeping North Africa behind the government. Pétain's speech of 20 June, which revealed that French emissaries were at that very moment meeting with the Germans to learn their terms for an armistice, had stunned a population "still untouched by the struggle and unwilling to admit defeat." "As soon as my departure is known," he continued, "the news will spread like wildfire that the government is abandoning North Africa and that I am deserting my post." The certain result would be "serious disorders" involving almost the entire population, including the soldiers, which the government would be incapable of preventing. In sum, "total collapse." "If the government has an important message to communicate to me, it is better that it send a qualified emissary here."[29]

Weygand accepted Noguès's decision and asked the two crucial questions by telegram: "Given the almost absolute impossibility of the Metropole to reinforce you and to supply you with munitions, in your opinion what are: (a) the possibilities of the length of resistance in Algeria, Tunisia, and Morocco, taking into account a possible Axis intervention through the Spanish Rif, (b) the possibilities and the effectiveness of land and air offensives from Tunisia?" Noguès was told to answer "urgently." General Louis Koeltz of Weygand's staff was dispatched to Algiers to gather any "additional information."[30]

Noguès had already posed the problem of Axis intervention to General Jules François, the commander of Morocco's ground forces. Not surprisingly, François answered that to meet an attack of that sort he would need "very important reinforcements." Moreover, he thought that there was a real likelihood of Axis intervention if France should continue to resist. Within six or seven days Germany could transport the required invasion materiel from the Pyrenees to Spain's southern ports. To be sure, crossing the Mediterranean would present "real difficulties." Spain's merchant marine was small and only Cadiz and Malaga could handle the loading of tanks and other heavy equipment. Once at sea, the transports would encounter the British and French fleets. All of this reduced but did not eliminate the danger. Darlan for one was convinced that the "precondition" for any continuation of the struggle from North Africa was a "very rapid takeover of the Spanish zone."[31] Whether or not Hitler would have followed retreating Frenchmen into North Africa—and in retrospect it seems that he had neither the inclination nor the capability to do so—is beside the point.[32] French commanders thought it was a distinct possibility and to counter it believed a war with Spain unavoidable.

Answering Weygand, Noguès said that with his present forces, the reinforcements in aircraft that were crossing the Mediterranean, and the support of the fleet he could hold out "for a long time." To check the danger from the Spanish zone, he recommended a preventive strike as soon as the first Italian and German units set foot on Spanish soil; this could be carried out by the forces currently under his command in Morocco and reinforced by units transferred from Tunisia. His trump card, played from the Lyautey deck, would be "an effort along political and religious lines" directed at the native population of the northern zone. The chances of success would be "greatly increased" if he could have immediate reinforcements in tanks, antitank weapons, antiaircraft batteries, and "eventually" complete units. But if the operation failed, the Sebou and Ouergha rivers would constitute a good defensive line. With regard to an offensive against Libya, he suggested a September or October attack spearheaded by North African units that were "reinforced by new units created as a result of British and American cooperation"; this effort would be supported by a simultaneous English action against the Italians in eastern Libya (the Cyrenaica) and Ethiopia.[33]

Noguès's optimistic estimates of 22 June were in stark contrast to the dismal declaration of a month earlier, when he complained of being badly outnumbered across the line in Morocco and could barely protect Tunisia's internal security. What had happened? According to his own charts, the only change was the lateral shift of some forces from Tunisia to Morocco.[34] What made the difference—and Noguès pointed it out to Weygand—was the six hundred aircraft that had flown the middle sea, making it possible for North Africa to "support" land and sea operations and "to intervene very effectively against vital points in Libya and Italy." But everywhere Noguès wrote the word "indispensable." It was "indispensable" that supplies of weapons and fuel be sent from the Metropole, England, or America as soon as possible; it was "indispensable" that France make a "final effort in the coming days to send all possible troops, personnel, and materiel." Even Noguès's note, hand delivered by Koeltz to Weygand, listed the Maghreb's "most indispensable" needs.[35]

All of this must be seen in light of Weygand's insistence that it was absolutely impossible for the Metropole to reinforce North Africa. He had no need to deceive the cabinet, as it was later claimed that he did, about the response from Noguès. He had only to subject it to a careful explication de texte and to repeat what Koeltz had told him, that Noguès complained of being "impoverished" in resources and desired the restitution of all that had been taken away from him.[36] In spite of the brave words, the deeds to back them up depended upon supplies and reinforcements from France and upon starting a war with Spain.[37]

No doubt Noguès realized that his telegrams were encouraging resistance to the armistice, making it difficult for Weygand and Pétain to achieve what they thought was imperative. But he took the risk to keep hold of North Africa. With enough fuss and tough talk, the empire might be spared the fate of Germany's colonies after World War I, might at least not be bartered away. It was a fight to salvage the empire amid the wreckage of the state.

France signed the armistice late on the afternoon of 22 June. Noguès was in the dark as to the terms, but he, Algeria's governor general, and Tunisia's resident general were determined not to abandon North Africa without a fight, although they agreed there was "no thought of any isolated action on the margin of the government's directives."[38] All they knew of the armistice was what Koeltz could tell them: there was no mention of North Africa in the conditions, but the army would surely be demobilized. Once more Noguès lifted his voice in protest. He telegraphed Weygand that the demobilization of the North African army was "not possible," for it, together with the air force and the navy, was the "last guarantee" of an "honorable peace." Once we are disarmed, he continued, "the demands of Germany would grow every day until we are completely enslaved," precisely the way de Gaulle had explained it on British radio the night before.[39] If the armistices with Germany and Italy were not accompanied by the government's declaration that the integrity of North Africa would be maintained intact, the people of North Africa would reject them; they, joined by "almost all of the armed forces," would continue "with or without their leaders" to struggle on to the bitter end. It would be an "irreparable disaster" for France. "If the government is unsure of getting honorable peace conditions to protect the future of our country, it must pursue the fight in Africa." Germany "still fears us because of our Mediterranean forces" and wants this armistice to sew up the victory that could unravel "if we hold out for several more weeks." Privately he urged Weygand to come to Algiers as proof that France was not abandoning its North African empire. "Your presence will rally everyone to your side and your position as a member of the government will make the Metropole's decisions stick."[40]

To this Weygand replied that for the moment signing the armistice with Germany had changed nothing because it would not go into effect until the conclusion of the negotiations with Italy. "In consequence, hostilities continue on all fronts." He let Foreign Minister Baudouin handle Noguès's concerns. Baudouin insisted that there was "no basis whatsoever" for the rumor that the government would hand over all or part of North Africa to a foreign power without a fight. It just would not happen. In addition, a military occupation anywhere in North Africa had been "ruled out." As for the demobilization of French troops in North Africa, the government was not "inclined" to agree to it. In short, Noguès's fears were exaggerated. "The government knows it can count on your devotion," he concluded, "in order to ensure in the countries under your authority the maintenance of cohesion, national unity, and discipline . . . more necessary than ever in [these] circumstances." When Baudouin later interpreted the armistice to France's representatives abroad, he called it "the least uncertain way of preserving the colonial empire from the covetousness of the powers that fought against us." As for the government's failure to relocate in North Africa, he said that French public opinion "would not have understood it." To have been justified from the military point of view, a continued fight would have had to be based on some "new fact," such as American entry into the war or the armed intervention of Turkey and the Balkan states, neither of which had been in the offing.[41]

Once signed, the Franco-German armistice, which violated the promise to England not to stop the fighting without its consent, put an end to the Anglo-French alliance. Although Churchill and Eden could sympathize with the French decision, the prime minister felt obliged to blast the French for the agreement, which he said could not have been signed by a government "which possessed freedom, independence, and constitutional authority."[42] Noguès reported that General Eric Dillon, head of the British liaison mission, had read him a declaration inviting France's leaders abroad to join in the struggle against Germany in spite of orders to the contrary from Bordeaux.[43] Weygand wasted no time in calling this an attempt to foment "rebellion" and ordered the mission to quit North Africa "in the briefest time possible." In the same vein, the minister of the interior wired the governor general of Algeria to make it impossible for Britain's consular agents to carry on agitation, propaganda, or recruitment; and Morize received a similar instruction from the ministry of foreign affairs.[44] The second Entente Cordiale, the limestone of France's interwar foreign policy, already badly cracked, simply eroded away.

The conclusion of the armistice with Italy and the ending of hostilities in all theaters of operations after midnight on 25 June was the expected and anticlimactic finale to the days of furious telegramming. Baudouin had paved the way by assuring Noguès that no Italian military occupation was planned for North Africa or the Levant and that demobilization and troop reductions would be placed in the hands of a commission that would take "internal needs" into careful consideration. Weygand detailed that in southern Tunisia and along the Algero-Libyan border there would be demilitarized zones but no

Italian soldiers. He chided both Noguès and Mittelhauser that, so far from home, they had neither been able "to judge the situation faced by the government nor to appreciate the decisions that this situation imposed, none of which is contrary to the country's honor." But he appealed to their "spirit of duty . . . to maintain the strictest discipline in your troops and to promote a mood of concord and confidence in the government."[45]

Mittelhauser turned to Noguès, his senior in rank and command, one last time: "It is the empire's turn to speak." The voice from Algiers was hoarse. "In spite of numerous energetic and anguished dispatches . . . I have been unable to get an agreement, even a tacit one. General Weygand and Admiral Darlan have taken a firm position in favor of accepting the armistice. Under these conditions—given the impossibility of any effective fight without the navy and given the government's assurance with regard to the overseas territories—so as not to split France in two at this hour of its adversity, I have resolved with despair in my soul not to continue the struggle."[46]

Weygand may have breathed a sigh of relief when Noguès and Mittelhauser heeded the cease-fire order. But, as has been shown, he really had no cause to worry. Neither was a rebel. Bound to the government by the soldier's professional code, Noguès shrank from assuming any national authority in an illegal manner. Mittelhauser followed Noguès's lead.[47]

Noguès did feel strong enough, however, to argue his case in firm, dramatic language. His dispatches still make stirring reading. But once a decision was made, he accepted it. Like Weygand, he believed passionately in the cohesiveness of the army, its close identification with the nation itself, and its role in preserving national unity. In this scheme of things, divisiveness came near to being a form of treason. It is impossible to say for sure what he would have done if the armistice terms had included a cession of territory to Germany or Italy, for here Noguès clearly had won what he wanted. Once informed by Baudouin that there would be no surrender of land, no military occupation of North Africa, he released the foreign minister's exact words in a public proclamation. Since the message had come in code, his military chief of staff rightly protested that it should not be waved about. "I don't give a damn," the general replied. "What I want is to get the government's statement on record before the entire world."[48]

Weygand's insensitivity to Noguès's plight amid a populace clamoring for war, his silence on Noguès's appeals for instructions and information, and his curt directives all took their toll. Noguès did not hide his grief at not being allowed to continue the fight nor did he mask his concern about the future dangers the government might encounter. He had been under intense pressure "to take command of the unconquered forces of the empire," and he warned that if the government's promises were not or could not be kept, North Africa would explode. The native population was "profoundly troubled" by the events in France and with the armistice "we have lost all our prestige since we did not fight on to the limit of our abilities." He argued against any hasty demobilization of the native troops for military, economic, and psychological reasons, all of which would compromise French rule. He cautioned that any German or Italian "controllers" in the empire would "make manifest our humiliation and provoke incidents that could reopen the armistice question altogether." In response to Weygand's cutting put-down that he had had insufficient information to appreciate the situation that had brought about the armistice, Noguès accused the government, "in an atmosphere of panic," of failing to assess the moral and physical strength of North Africa, which, joined with that of the navy and air force, could have resisted France's enemies until they were "worn down." Not having done so, he added, would be "bitterly regretted." "We remain ready to march if, as is probable, the Germans in short order present us with new demands. That would be the salvation of the country." "Personally," he concluded, "I shall stay at my post as long as a danger exists in order to carry out this sacrificial mission, which covers my face with shame, so as not to cut France in two. But as soon as I judge that calm is assured, I shall ask you to relieve me of my command."[49]

Weygand rejoined that he found Noguès's remarks on the government "inadmissible." As for resigning his command, Weygand had already ordered that the theaters of operations would cease to exist as of 1 July; it was understood that Noguès would return to his post as resident general in Morocco. It was a graceful way of pushing the belligerent commander out of Algiers and packing him off to Rabat. Noguès excused the "violence of his words" as an "ardent desire to serve his country" by underscoring those local elements that he considered of "extreme importance" at a grave moment in France's history. "The fervent wishes of the troops and the people of North Africa should be taken into consideration in all the decisions made by those authorities responsible for France's destiny." Concerning political unrest in North Africa, he reported that at the moment there was no organized movement against the government.[50]

The ending of resistance was in no small part Noguès's own doing in obedience to the government's wishes. It certainly was no happy task. With despair in his soul, he had resigned himself not to continue the struggle. Now he would become the instrument for the extinction of the fighting spirit in North Africa.

His reports to Bordeaux on North Africa's combativeness, particularly his fear of "a general uprising against the government," were not exaggerated. Europeans at Casablanca declared openly that they hoped the armistice conditions would be so onerous that the government at Bordeaux would have to reject them. Despite the press censorship, there was a clear sentiment to go it alone if the French government made a decision "judged unacceptable." Moroccans in general were "dumbfounded and overwhelmed" by the news of France's misfortunes on the battlefield, particularly the notables, who were terrified that France's defeat would spell the end of the protectorate and thus their end as well. Here too there was sympathy for the continued struggle, even if it was contrary to the commands coming from France. On the other hand, the grand vizier told Morize that although he was a partisan of resistance, it had to be legal, ordered by the government. Either way, prolonged fighting might have jeopardized the protectorate's inner peace. If Morocco battled on, the grand vizier asked Morize, were the French certain of the loyalty of the tribes, particularly those in the mountains? "We must not be faced with fighting both an external and an internal enemy at the same time." To counter these worries and to preserve calm and control, the French reinforced their surveillance and called General Jacques de Loustal out of retirement "to coordinate native questions" in the Middle Atlas and Tafilalet.[51]

When the armistice confirmed the status quo, however, the resistance spirit subsided in both communities. By preserving the colonial situation, it eased the pain of the defeat and ensured social peace. But every step of the way, Noguès was important as example and guide. He was portrayed as a leader who "alone" understood all the parts of the "tragic problem" and would make a decision in the best interests of France and North Africa.[52] Imitating his disciplined obedience, North Africa was led into the Vichy fold.

In addition to smothering the resistance fire in Morocco, Noguès snuffed out the flame brought from France to Casablanca on the steamship *Massilia*, which carried what might have been the advance party of the government's transfer to North Africa. Among the passengers was former Minister of the Interior Georges Mandel, the man most opposed to an armistice and most committed to continued resistance to Germany. "I shall go on fighting in North Africa," he told Churchill's personal representative in France a month before the armistice. "You may be sure that so long as I have the power to do so, I shall advocate fighting on to the bitter end everywhere." Mandel conferred with British Consul General Leonard H. Hurst at Rabat, then telephoned Noguès at Algiers to discuss plans for a resistance government. Noguès promised to come to Rabat on 26 June and counseled patience until he had word on the armistice (signed while the *Massilia* was still at sea) and instructions from Bordeaux. Mandel was in no mood for this sort of delay. "Bordeaux," he told Noguès, "represents nothing." [53]

In the meantime, London dispatched a top-level team—Minister of Information Alfred Duff Cooper and General John Lord Gort—to Rabat to encourage North African resistance. When Noguès learned of the impending visit, he made it clear that this was not for him. He would have no contact with the English agents without authorization of the French government, and he ventured that a dissident government, proclaimed at Rabat or Casablanca, would encounter the hostility of the local populace and provoke a German or Spanish attack. [54]

Face to face with the unwanted guests, Morize expressed his "sharp astonishment" at their unauthorized presence in the protectorate (they had come from Gibraltar by hydroplane and landed in the Bou Regreg River). After hearing Duff Cooper's intentions in full—to discuss with the Massilians, in particular Mandel, "the ways and means of continuing the resistance in French North Africa"—he protested as gently as he could that it was "really an intolerable breach of conduct" for a member of the British government to attempt such a mission. He added that the passengers on the *Massilia* were persons "without mandate," "without a particle of authority" in North Africa, just "unexpected travelers in transit," not the nucleus of a resistance regime. Recognizing the futility of their mission, the Englishmen returned to Gibraltar the following morning. [55]

Once Mandel learned of Duff Cooper's arrival, he tried in vain to reach him. His exit from the *Massilia* was blocked, all telephone communication with the ship was cut, and at dawn on the twenty-sixth the ship was moved into the harbor so that "any contact with the outside world was rendered impossible." Morize told Bordeaux that he regretted having to act with such severity toward the *Massilia*'s passengers because their behavior, Mandel's excepted, had been "quite correct." [56]

When Noguès arrived in Rabat, Consul General Hurst asked that the political leaders on the *Massilia* be allowed to leave for England on a British destroyer. "I expressed my surprise and my indignation at such a request and formally rejected it," Noguès cabled Bordeaux. Hurst explained that Mandel had made the request at their meeting on 24 June, to which Noguès replied that to his knowledge (and he was correct) Mandel was only speaking for himself and that his colleagues "ardently desired" to go back to France (because the government had finally decided not to emigrate and Africa would not fight on alone) or to stay in North Africa. In any event, Noguès gave no one freedom of choice: in the name of the French government, he "forbade" Mandel to depart for England and, through an intermediary, told Mandel that "at the first incident, the slightest attempt to get in touch with the English consular agents, I would not hesitate to have him arrested." [57]

Piecing together what Hurst had told him and what Morize had learned from Duff Cooper, Noguès concluded that Mandel had been the initiator of the British connection. This is precisely what he reported to Bordeaux: "The remarks of the British consul general as well as the investigation made into the trip of Duff Cooper to Rabat prove that since his arrival in Casablanca, the former minister of the interior made contact with the British consuls [in Casablanca and Rabat] and that the minister of information undertook his journey at his, Mandel's, instigation." Later Mandel would deny that he ever asked for a British official to come to Morocco (in truth, he had not) and Noguès would back down, admitting that there was no way to be certain exactly what Mandel had said to Hurst. But even if Noguès's hurried judgment was wrong on how the British got there, there was no doubt about the fact that Mandel was eager to talk with them and wanted to embark for England. There was nothing surprising or illegal about that. Britain was not yet the "perfidious Albion" it would become after the 3 July attack on the French fleet at Mersel-Kebir. To have permitted it, however, would have been to aid Britain's recruitment of French diehards and to add another voice to the dissidence abroad. Noguès would not be a party to that. It would not serve England's cause, Noguès told Hurst, it would only increase the "misunderstanding" between the two countries. [58]

Considering the matter closed, Noguès permitted the passengers to leave the *Massilia* but sent Mandel under police surveillance to Ifrane, a summer resort town in the mountains. He later explained that this was done at the request of the director of public security and the commandant of the Casablanca region, who, given the angry mood of the quayside crowd, feared for Mandel's safety. There was probably good reason for the concern. Politicians, Jews, and Freemasons were already being blamed for France's misfortunes. Mandel was guilty on the first two counts. But his forced exile was also intended to end his political activity and to prevent his departure abroad. As far as Noguès was concerned, the Duff Cooper affair was just another Mandelian "intrigue."[59]

For those whose road to Morocco had been the *Massilia*, the odyssey was just beginning. For most it led to Algiers and a long wait for permission to return to France. When repatriation came, it was accompanied by false accusations of emigration and desertion. What had begun as a patriotic journey to North Africa was now depicted as akin to a traitor's flight abroad. When Mandel reached Algiers, he finally spoke to Noguès. Both Noguès and Georges Hutin, the resident's right-hand man, remembered it as a "cordial" encounter. Mandel declared "spontaneously" that he "very well understood" why Noguès had prevented his meeting with Duff Cooper. Interpreting this in a positive way, Noguès added that it had probably turned out for the best, making nonsense of the charge, bruited about at Vichy, that he had plotted with the British to undermine the security of the state. Yet three days later, Vichy announced that an investigation would take place into Mandel's activities and the former minister of the interior was returned to Casablanca under guard.[60]

Noguès's part in the inquiry was limited to providing the tribunal copies of the telegrams that he and Morize had sent to France and to testifying before the court. He later asserted that despite the pressure put on him when he visited Vichy in August to furnish "conclusive evidence to the prosecution," his testimony was not damning. But at one point, obliged to inform Vichy on how the investigation was going, he accused the tribunal's presiding officer of not prosecuting the case firmly enough. Although the investigation resulted in a dismissal of the charges, Mandel was returned to France in the custody of the Sûreté Nationale for prosecution under "special jurisdiction."[61] He would never go free. After years of prison in France, he was shot by the Milice, Vichy's security force, in 1944.

Without dark motive Noguès believed that he was "in no way responsible" for Mandel's fate.[62] Convinced of Mandel's collusion with the British, he had done only what he judged was required. But there was a surprising lack of sympathy for Mandel, whose crimes were precisely those that all North Africa had begged Noguès to commit in June. Perhaps that was the clue to explaining the ambiguities of

Noguès's role in the matter. Mandel earned the title of France's "first resister," but Noguès became Vichy's bloodhound, tracking down and stamping out the resistance that he had done so much to inspire.

Despite Noguès's desire to quit Algiers and Weygand's apparent eagerness to be rid of him, the general was told to remain at his post until mid-July to preside over the repatriation and demobilization of North Africa's forces. On his own he persuaded Weygand to prolong the life of the Algiers command past that date because, once dissolved, there would be no single authority over all the Maghreb to provide the "firm action" and the "direct and permanent control" that he considered "indispensable." It was not only a question of internal security. Weygand too was worried by the daring British attempts to pry the empire from Vichy's hands. In a premonition of disaster, he told the armistice commission that he was against any disarmament of North Africa, especially the naval bases at Mers-el-Kebir (Oran's main port) and Bizerte, in order to be able "to oppose any possible English enterprise." That same day the Royal Navy appeared off Mers-el-Kebir and, after a day of talking, crippled or destroyed what amounted to one-fifth of the entire French fleet, claiming nearly 1,300 lives. Seen by the British as a regrettable albeit necessary measure to prevent the ships from falling into German hands, it recalled the ruthless "Copenhagening" of the Danish fleet during the Napoleonic wars—Churchill actually described it as such—and provoked a wave of Anglophobia throughout France and North Africa, doing more to discredit the partisans of continued resistance alongside the English than anything else could have done. It was to Frenchmen what Pearl Harbor would be to Americans. Due to the emergency, Noguès was informed that his command would be extended "so long as the crisis started today by England lasts."[63]

The month was not an easy one. In agreement with the Germans, the French government installed itself at Vichy; Marshal Pétain, voted full powers, was authorized to set up a new regime—the État Français—and to proceed with a program of national reform and renewal. At the end, the Third Republic had few friends and fewer mourners. Even those who opposed the establishment of a government at Vichy were not necessarily warm partisans of its defunct predecessor. What is more, at first it was hard to say what Vichy was or how permanent it would be. Vichyites came from many camps, from diehards to defeatists, from monarchists to socialists, from technocrats to advocates for peasants. It was soon clear, however, that the armistice would not be followed by a general treaty of peace.

Unlike the French prediction that England's neck would be wrung like a chicken's, Britain survived the German onslaught from the sky, forcing Hitler to abandon the early conquest of the island. Churchill crowed: "Some chicken! Some neck!" Britain's holdout ended the French hope for a short war and quick peace but not their belief in an ultimate German victory.

To prepare for the future Germany demanded air bases in Morocco to cover the Atlantic approaches to Gibraltar and the western Mediterranean. It was a clear violation of what had been agreed upon at Rethondes and confirmed Noguès's worst fears. With Weygand in the lead, the French protested vigorously.[64] The Germans wisely backed down, probably out of concern for pushing the empire into dissidence but also because the French volunteered to do what the Germans wanted done, namely, protect the African coasts from British infiltration. It was probably not the best bargain, for the French refused to go on the offensive and the Germans never trusted Weygand or Noguès. But in the changed circumstances of the war, it was not a bad one. Germany had the satisfaction of watching Noguès and Weygand, both fiercely anti-German, become Anglophobes as well.

In July also came the first indication of difficulties in command authority in North Africa, revealing Vichy's continuing distrust of Noguès. In the planning for an air strike on Gibraltar, Noguès was accused of "hesitation," of holding back on the planes needed for the raid. It was true. But what he objected to was the navy's direction of an operation that rightly belonged to North Africa's air commander and in general the navy's irritating habit of making decisions affecting North Africa's forces without telling him. In sum, interservice rivalry writ large. That the admiralty attributed his stalling to a lack of zeal, however, showed the label stuck on his lapel. He was someone to be watched, lukewarm on the policy changes in France and capable of jumping ship. Still, Noguès was the sole survivor of the prewar administrative trio in the Maghreb, the others having been replaced by admirals. But even with the imposing title of commander-in-chief of North Africa, he had been reduced to keeping the peace, watching the Franco-Spanish boundary, and supplying whatever the navy needed. After 1 August, when his post was officially abolished, he was appointed inspector general of the North African army. This was a paper command, charged with demobilization, reorganization, and the execution of the armistice clauses.[65] Although all military matters were to cross his desk, the fact that he would be in Rabat, not Algiers, was the telltale sign. Moreover, in

Morocco he was left only civil power, having been stripped of the dual authority awarded by the Popular Front, another testimony to his diminished stature.

Leaving Algiers at the beginning of August, Noguès went straight to Vichy to protest the foreign ministry's plans for a land deal with Spain in the protectorate. Charles-Roux remembered that the visit was not comfortable for Noguès because of the rumors that he would be asked to resign. What saved him was his already legendary Moroccan expertise. He stayed in the spa-turned-capital for five days and received his new marching orders. "What do I think of the new constitutional and administrative organization of France? The very future of France depends on it." This benediction pronounced on Radio France came from a man who had fought the armistice tooth and nail and was now trying to save his career in the protectorate. Of all the things that weighed France down, the "bureaucratic routine" was the most "suffocating." Marshal Pétain, testified Noguès, "has done away with it." "What I found at Vichy . . . were hardworking men unconcerned with formalities and willing to take responsibility. This is truly a revitalized administration." Morocco was to undergo an administrative "rejuvenation and simplification" as well. "The French government has given me its entire support. I will devote all my energy to the task. The coming days will be fruitful in accomplishments in every sphere of activity."[66]

Seen from overseas, the need for a metropolitan revival was an imperative, the sine qua non of imperial preservation. France's force and prestige were at an all-time low and destined to sink deeper. "Our welfare, our families, the future of France and Morocco are at stake," Noguès cried. "Nothing will stop me from protecting them. The stakes are too high to tolerate even the slightest weakness. Everyone must work with dedication and recognize that now is the time for unity, obedience, and duty."[67] Was it more difficult to shield the protectorate than France? Some thought so. If the protector was incapable of affording shelter, might not the protectorate simply cease to exist?

The reform program outlined by Vichy demonstrated that France had no intention of abandoning its North African mission. The objective in Morocco was to strengthen the loyalty of the native population and increase its attachment to France by tight cooperation with the sultan, the native hierarchy, and all those, the nationalists included, who were not blind opponents of the protectorate. Foreign Minister Baudouin characterized it as a "widely comprehensive and humane policy" intended to bring about "an era of liberalism and clemency."[68] None of this was new to Noguès, except perhaps the open hand to the nationalists, which he himself had first extended in 1936 but then had been forced to withdraw. Under the circumstances it was the right move to make, a follow-up of the sultan's leniency in 1939 and early 1940, and the resident may have even suggested it to Baudouin. But, as always, it was something to handle with care. What heartened Noguès was the emergence of a native "neonationalism" around the sultan and the Makhzen, quite unlike the anti-French variety of 1937. He interpreted it as a search for inner assurance in the face of a future with a question mark, a quest encouraged by a sultan who worried that a change in the status quo might undermine his personal situation. It boosted him to the head of the decapitated national movement of which he had formerly been both beneficiary and victim. The new nationalism was "reasonable and progressive," opposed to revolution and still without a program of reforms. For the moment, it sought only to give Morocco a feeling of its own "strength," which would be measured by the prestige of its sovereign, now acclaimed as both spiritual and temporal leader of the country. To be sure, this could one day be difficult for France, depending on the rise and fall in French fortunes, but Noguès saw no immediate danger. In fact, these sentiments worked to France's advantage. "Our rights to Morocco, to protect it and keep it within our empire, will be strengthened if Morocco represents a force on its own, if it acts like a state in control of its own destiny whose aspirations, preferences, and will ought not to be challenged."[69]

For Frenchmen reform would require an attitude of courage and confidence. No wholesale exodus to the Metropole would be tolerated from either Tunisia or Morocco. The residents were to reassure the colonists of France's determination "to protect their homes and their interests." If that failed, they were to make it difficult for them to sell their property and leave. There could have been no better indication of the connection between colonists and colonies. Protectorate administrators were counseled to conduct themselves in a manner above reproach, particularly in regard to the management of public funds, and the residents were ordered to take whatever measures were necessary to punish the heedless. At the same time, they were to undertake an "administrative reshuffling" to purge and reduce the numbers of their staff. As described by Baudouin, it came off as a crusade to pull down the citadels of privilege and greed. "The resistance you encounter must be completely broken. The hierarchies and private fiefdoms will henceforth no longer thwart the general welfare, which demands sacrifice and discipline from everyone." Finally, it was up to the resident to balance off the gains and losses of each individual or group in the economic and political life of the protectorate. The Jewish question merited "attentive study" because of the "already rumbling" anti-Semitism among the Muslims. His advice was to make certain that the Jews shared in the sacrifice by giving up "anachronistic privileges." In conclusion, Baudouin promised the government's full support in this "mission of harmony, rapprochement, and purification."[70]

The Vichy change took many forms. It meant mandatory early retirement for army officers, civil servants, and native affairs officers, thus clearing places for others and cutting the payroll. Ignoring Lyautey's lesson that longevity was the key to accomplishment, *La Vigie marocaine* welcomed the regulations because of the "real fatigue" that came with any "prolonged stay" in Morocco.[71] Rejuvenation was often a cover for the political housecleaning that usually followed a major ministerial shake-up, but such reshuffling had not affected Morocco since 1936. Morize was the most important casualty. Named *délégué général* by the Popular Front and privately known as a Delbos man, he did not survive, despite Noguès's strong recommendations. He had the satisfaction, however, of being replaced by two men: Jacques Meyrier, a career diplomat who took the title of *délégué général*, and Emmanuel Mönick from the ministry of finance, named to head the resurrected secretariat general. Neither selection was controversial. Mönick's appointment was especially wise, given the new economic setting of the protectorate. He was a realist in matters of finance and, having served as an economic attaché to the embassies at Washington and London, was committed to a world view of the commercial role of France and its empire. If anyone could adapt the protectorate's economic needs to the dictates of the moment, he could. In one of Lyautey's favorite English phrases, he was "the right man in the right place."[72]

Weygand's appearance in Algiers in October 1940 as the government's delegate in French Africa was the unexpected result of infighting at Vichy and the logical consequence of the need for imperial unity and security. Ousted from the cabinet as part of a political trade-off, Weygand was handed an administrative and military command the likes of which no one had ever seen. As commander-in-chief of all African land and air forces and coordinator of the continent's political and economic activities, his authority stretched from Tunis to Casablanca and from Algiers to Dakar, and there was no doubt that he intended to exercise it. Every governor in Africa was

Left: General Maxime Weygand,
government delegate in French Africa. Fez, October 1940.
Photo Jacques Belin

to report directly to Weygand, including the resident generals in Tunisia and Morocco, who previously had had privileged correspondence with the minister of foreign affairs. Even the powers of the residents, defined by treaties with the sultan and the bey, were expressly "entrusted" to Weygand, who in turn delegated "part" of them to his subordinates. Noguès was quick to complain that bit by bit Weygand was taking total control of North Africa.[73]

It was a revolution in the relations between Morocco and France because it made the sharifian state more a part of the empire than it had ever been. All the coordinating plans of the Popular Front's Haut Comité Méditerranéen were just so much paper compared to Weygand's bolting of the protectorate into place. For Noguès it broke the direct Rabat-Vichy line by requiring a mandatory stopover at Algiers. It all but destroyed Morocco's special identity, fencing in the open range that both Lyautey and Noguès guarded so jealously. Some of this was inevitable, given the war and France's collapse, but all of it injured Noguès's pride and wounded his authority. The change was too fast and taking place without his counsel.

Among his attributes, Weygand was charged with the "purification of the bureaucracy," the role of scourging angel whose sword he took up with conviction. Deeply committed to a moral regeneration of France, he set about casting out the evildoers, the unbelievers, the faithless, by which he meant Freemasons, Gaullists (a term that encompassed a multitude of sins), Jews, and Anglophiles.[74] After an inspection tour of Morocco, Weygand accused Noguès of building a wall behind which "nothing had changed." The "profound transformation" that he had hoped for and that was implied in the program of "national renovation" had not happened; "the occult influence of the Freemasons remains as powerful as in the past." In addition to being tortoiselike in instituting the "needed reforms," there was evidence that Noguès was less than a complete collaborator. Weygand ticked off his grievances: the incomplete dossiers supplied by Moroccan authorities in recent treason cases, Noguès's persistence in excusing the "serious errors" of members of his staff, and the instructions given some of them to conceal things from Weygand. He sent Noguès the names of a dozen persons who were to be retired, suspended, or transferred immediately, adding that this was only a beginning. For the national renewal to become a reality, Noguès had to commit himself fully to the task. "At stake is my confidence in you."[75]

Noguès had already protested to Pétain's aide General Émile Laure that Vichy was becoming a "regime of cabals, of informers, of secret reports," all "very dangerous for the morale of the army and the country." It in "no way" tallied with the marshal's intentions and would bring the national revival to a "screeching halt" and "demolish" the army to boot. With Weygand he confessed that he was at his wit's end. Everything Weygand did seemed calculated to weaken the resident, to make more difficult his task in Morocco. During his nine-day tour of the protectorate, Weygand refused to have Noguès travel with him except when he visited the cities and that only after much pressure. What Noguès considered "indispensable"—since his absence would be taken as a sign of his disgrace by the Muslim population—troubled Weygand not at all because he was out to conduct a private investigation. All along the way, he excluded Noguès from the tête-à-têtes with French officials, who were urged to speak freely about the state of the country and to communicate any grievances they had directly to Algiers. "I do not understand what would make a leader undermine the authority of his subordinate in a country where authority is, more than elsewhere, indispensable, especially in the present circumstances." He bridled at the general's cavalier interference in matters Moroccan, particularly on such touchy issues as the choice of one's closest collaborators. And he resented how he was being handled. "I do not deserve to be treated in this way."[76]

Certainly Weygand's mistrust was a legacy of the fussing over the armistice, of the hard words exchanged by telegram, of the suspicion that Noguès was less than 100 percent behind the government. In defense Noguès claimed that the "great majority" of Frenchmen and the entire native population now supported the marshal and were ready to follow him, something for which he took a generous slice of the credit. But he cautioned that in Morocco the native question "comes before anything else," and it was wrong to assume that what worked in France would work on the other side of the Mediterranean.[77]

Given the difficulty with Weygand, Noguès toyed with resigning. But he did not. Call it pride of place, duty, or just plain stubbornness. Morocco was his *pays d'élection*, and he would not be routed into retirement as Lyautey had been. Sadly ironic, Weygand was the soldier Lyautey had once considered a fit successor, Pétain the one who had humbled him. "The marshal knows very well that he can count on my absolute devotion (which doesn't date from yesterday) and call upon it without reserve. My past and the position I took at the armistice by preventing the empire from splitting away from him, even though I burned with the desire to continue the fight, show that I am capable of understanding situations and of obeying." If he was to continue, however, something would have to be done about Weygand, for he could not stand by and watch the progressive diminution of his authority. "Unity of direction and uncontested authority are indispensable to keep the upper hand in this country, which is never easy."[78]

Noguès's running battle with the Légion Française des Anciens Combattants de l'Afrique du Nord, Vichy's veterans organization, which presumed to make political demands on the resident and to go over his head to Algiers and Vichy, exemplified the sort of problems he now encountered at every turn. He had resisted its creation, fought its pretensions (which he told Darlan bordered on those of a "state within a state"), and battled its leaders, all to no avail. Weygand ordered it set up at Rabat and told Noguès to leave it alone. Even the relations between Noguès and General François, the legion's president who made no secret of his availability to replace the resident, were so bitter that Weygand tried to force a reconciliation. Noguès would have none of it. The legionnaires would not have been fooled: they refused to take their oath of allegiance before Noguès, whom they knew was a thorn in their side. It was a feud that later stood Noguès in good stead, for rightly or wrongly the Légion des Combattants was ranked as one of Vichy's most unsavory creations.[79]

Weygand and the Légion des Combattants were both bona fide instruments of the national revolution. Both were resisted by Noguès. The issue was not one of ideology or loyalty but of his authority over Morocco. In a private letter to Admiral Darlan, then newly named deputy prime minister and minister of foreign affairs, Noguès argued that it would be "impossible" for him to carry on unless the "attributions" of the Légion des Combattants were modified and it was placed under his control. At the same time, he blasted the "progressive centralization of all power" at Algiers as "disastrous." Weygand and his staff simply could not keep tabs on local questions nor judge the decisions of the Residency from such a distance. "A period of crisis is no time to try to unify North Africa, to fool with experiments. Our primary task is to live, to survive." His staff needed to devote its full attention to this effort and not "waste its time with innumerable reports." But the "biggest danger" to French rule in Morocco was Weygand's appeal for "direct communications" from the rank and file outside of the chain of command. It undermined authority, which he thought was being "systematically disrupted" throughout the country, and caused confusion among the followers over whose orders to obey. "The native population understands very well what is going on. They witnessed all this at the start of the Popular Front, and of all things it bothers them the most." Although the Moroccans remained "devoted" to France, coming so hard on the heels of a period of "unprecedented security and confidence," these changes had provoked a "secret uneasiness" among all groups in society and in the Makhzen. What was needed to meet the threat was the reinforcement of the resident's authority. To account for this covert criticism of his chief, Noguès cited his "duty" and "absolute dedication" to Pétain and Darlan.[80]

Weygand's recall in November 1941 was Pétain's personal decision, made under German pressure, but Darlan, who was a bitter rival of Weygand, had a hand in his fall. At the very least, Noguès supplied the admiral with ammunition. There had never been real cooperation between Noguès and Weygand. Too much had passed between them and they were men out of different molds: Weygand, opinionated, impulsive, rigid, often unkind; Noguès, moderate to the point of seeking (so said Léon Blum) "too close, too exact a balance," cautious, supple, a man who tried to be on good terms with everyone.[81] There is no mystery why throughout his career Weygand had to pound on the gates of the Third Republic while Noguès was given the key to the keep. Weygand's kingdom was partitioned, divided into a North and West African command. The governors and resident generals were released from their tutelage, free to report directly to the colonial or foreign ministry as in the past.

In a final report to Pétain, Weygand praised Noguès in a generous paragraph. "On several occasions I have asked that General Noguès be allowed to remain in Rabat. He is an intelligent and flexible administrator brought up in the Lyautey tradition. He has a deep understanding of the native population of Morocco and the confidence of the sultan. . . . I remember that in August 1940 the government considered replacing him with General [Alphonse] Georges. I was told to inform Georges of his impending appointment, but he refused it on the grounds that he knew too little about native affairs to replace Noguès, who knew so much. Several days ago, after the word from Vichy was that there might now be a change at Rabat, General Juin said about the same thing, that such a move at the present time would be a great disadvantage." There was probably no intention of removing Noguès, just a rumor started to cover the unpleasant fact that Weygand alone was to be axed. But Weygand had made good on what he had told Noguès privately some days before, that "it would be folly to put Morocco in the hands of someone unfamiliar with the men and matters of the Makhzen and of the native population."[82] Unfortunately, this appreciation of Noguès and his concerns came at the end of a long proconsulate that had frustrated the resident by his inability to convey to the general the realities of a land so different from France.

The good that Noguès found in Vichy's national revolution was trumpeted far and wide. Marshal Pétain became a cult figure in Morocco rivaling his apotheosis in France. Before July 1940 *le maréchal* had always meant Lyautey, but after that time it referred to Pétain. "There could be only one marshal," Maurice Martin du Gard, the empire's chronicler at Vichy, explained wryly, "for whom the heart of empire panted."[83] This was less substitution than combination, and Noguès adroitly painted each portrait on a panel of a diptych, the one mortal, the other immortal. At the annual ceremonies marking Lyautey's death, Noguès pledged: "We promise to remain faithful to your ideas, to follow in your footsteps, and to practice those virtues that will remake the grandeur of France as they once made the grandeur of Morocco. Have confidence in us, *Monsieur le Maréchal*, as we have confidence in Marshal Pétain, our illustrious leader into whose hands the country has placed its destiny."[84]

Vichy's values, beginning with Work, Family, and Country—the substitute for the Republic's Liberty, Equality, Fraternity—were more in touch with the colonial mentality and imperial realities than the democratic triad. Discipline, obedience, order, duty, hierarchy, unity—these words that saturated Pétain's speeches had always been part of the language of the empire builders. There is no doubt that by preference Frenchmen abroad were politically much more conservative than their metropolitan cousins and few in North Africa had difficulty adjusting to the political complexion of the new regime in France. It more closely resembled the authoritarian style in the colonies than did the Republic. For the military men, Vichy was a dream come true. It was the first modern French regime that was unabashedly khaki in sentiment.

Morocco's future, Noguès told the representatives of the Conseil du Gouvernement the day after the British attacked Mers-el-Kebir, depended on "strength" provided by the "unity of all Frenchmen"; it was an essential ingredient for Franco-Moroccan union. "If Morocco continues to form a solid and resolute bloc, it can look to the future with confidence." This unity, he explained to a Rabat crowd, meant putting an end to political opposition and divisiveness, silencing the groups on the Right and the Left, and forgetting the foreign sympathies and hatreds of the past: "In time of war, whoever does not think strictly French is a traitor. It is the same today when the danger is perhaps even greater than when we were fighting." Mimicking the moralists at Vichy, he repeated the Vichy diagnosis of France's defeat and prescription for revival. France had been "laid low more by its own faults than by its enemies." "The tragedy of 1940," he said in a later reflection, "capped off twenty years of individualism and frivolity." Like the saints of old, France would only be "purified by its suffering." "Has not our sweet and beautiful France already paid too much for the intense commitment that pressed it forward to make of itself the champion in the world of the ideal and of the just? Now it has the right to weigh its decisions carefully, to take up the single task of defending its unity and the integrity of its empire. . . . The path we follow is a straight one in respect to the pledges we have made. The marshal's orders . . . will be obeyed."[85] To visitors on a junket from France, Noguès repeatedly swore Morocco's fidelity to Pétain, the guide and guardian of France's resurrection. To Jean Borotra, former tennis star and commissioner general for education and sport: "You can repeat with ever more force to the marshal that he can count on Morocco." To Jean Berthelot, minister of communications: "You can tell the marshal that Morocco is completely behind him and ready to prove it whenever the time comes."[86]

Noguès said that the protectorate administration would be reshaped in the "image" of the French state and in important ways this was true. But cost cutting was also on his mind. He acknowledged the purge of the bureaucracy and immediately implemented designs to simplify and make more efficient the French services. Much was merely a regrouping of what had existed before, but three directorships were eliminated: the Office Chérifien de Contrôle et d'Exportation and the Office Chérifien du Tourisme, reflecting wartime realities, and the Office Chérifien Interprofessionnel du Blé, the Popular Front's most controversial creation. In addition, Noguès reorganized the Direction des Affaires Politiques and the secretariat general of the protectorate to ensure his "immediate and personal action" more effectively. Most significant, the number of administrative regions was halved, reduced from fourteen to seven. In consequence, the powers of the regional heads were increased. Regional administrators were to draw up their own budgets and were given authority to handle matters that previously had to be forwarded to Rabat for action. This produced an invigorating sort of local rule, something that neither Rabat nor Vichy opposed so long as the authorities on the edges of the empire remained loyal to the center.[87] Unrelated to Vichy directives or to saving money was the transformation of the *officiers des affaires indigènes*, the soldier-administrators in the field, into *contrôleurs civils*, members of the civilian native affairs corps. Although a step down in prestige, the purpose was to camouflage the number of French soldiers in Morocco from the prying eyes of the Germans and Italians.[88]

In political matters, the protectorate followed Vichy in abolishing elective institutions (the Conseil du Gouvernement was no more), replacing them with appointive councils and committees such as the Conseil Économique, which assembled delegates who spoke for different economic interests. The Vichy preference for representation by function also required setting up economic and professional corporations, some already established because of wartime hardship. None of these political or economic restraints was foreign to Morocco, where the residents constantly had to remind their countrymen that this land was not their land. This time the gentle reminder was replaced by an order from Vichy.

The social ideology and policy of the protectorate, as they affected Frenchmen, were also imports from the Metropole. Agencies proliferated to back up the emphasis on work, the family, and country: the Conseil Central de la Famille et de l'Assistance, the Office de la Famille Française, the Conseil Central de la Jeunesse et des Sports.[89] The restrictions on Freemasons, Communists, Jews, and Gaullists were copied from laws adopted at Vichy. The dissolution of secret societies was aimed at the masonic lodges.[90] The law suppressing Communist and anarchist activity, which also netted the "antinational" Gaullists, set up special sections of military and naval tribunals and civilian courts of appeal to try offenders for deeds committed before they were crimes.[91] The Jewish statute barred Jews from a host of professions, government jobs, and public offices.[92] How strictly this legislation was enforced is a matter of opinion and depended on the circumstances. At the end of the war, an impressive number of highly placed Freemasons and Jews testified that Noguès was a friend, not a foe.[93] But there were individual cases of great tragedy, such as that of the lawyer Félix Guedj, who died in prison while serving a five-year sentence for loaning a small sum of money to three young men en route to England to join de Gaulle.[94] Vichy's laws were on the books in Morocco, and Frenchmen were the worse off for it.

With Vichy's blessing, Noguès continued the ambitious program of economic improvement and urban reconstruction begun before the war. Port facilities at Casablanca and Agadir, a road and rail line in the south leading toward Senegal and in the southeast leading toward Algeria, electric power plants at Oujda and Agadir, a dam at Infout, the irrigation of the Beni Amir perimeter, and the construction of native housing were part of the resident's want list. To these he added job-retraining centers for unemployed native workers and veterans.[95] The price tag of 225 million francs was only slightly less than the total increase in government spending from 1941 to 1942.[96] It brought Noguès to Vichy for authorization to float a bond issue, a return to a financing practice disallowed by the Popular Front and that had been seen at the time as a salutary renunciation. It was the second bond issue since the beginning of the war, made necessary not only by Noguès's determination to get on with his economic and social projects but by price inflation, the needs of internal security, and a drop in tax revenues, the result of the protectorate's British-blockaded commerce.[97]

Witnessing France's fall and Vichy's ascent from afar, Noguès had momentarily feared that the protectorate's days were numbered, its fate sealed on the battlefields of northern France, its lands surrendered abjectly by an impotent and frightened regime. Preserved by the armistice, however, it was given a second life that Noguès believed could endure the crisis of war and even a treaty of peace. To do so required careful handling of the Vichy changes, incorporating them into France's ongoing reform in Morocco, stressing their connection with what had been done before, and minimizing the risks to the control and authority he had built up since 1936. It called for a vigilant watch on the German victor as well. Perhaps most important, Noguès was convinced that it demanded his own political survival, the man indispensable to Morocco's safe emergence on the other side of the conflict. Above all, he could not envision a Morocco without France. Whatever alternative he posed—a German protectorate, a unified and independent Morocco under nationalist rule—he rejected as provoking internal resistance and anarchy.[98] To his mind France alone could manage Morocco. He was determined to let no one else try.

SEVEN

The American Road to Morocco

In spite of the cold comfort that America gave the protectorate on the eve of the Second World War and in June 1940, once France was flat on its back, there was new American interest in Morocco and in fact in all French Africa. Ironically it came at a time when Algiers was doing its best to stamp out the fires of dissidence and while Dakar was beating back an Anglo-Gaullist attack. What is more, it centered on Weygand, the high priest of obedience to Vichy and loyalty to Pétain, but whose part in setting up a regime of resignation was overshadowed by his anti-German reputation. Even Churchill hoped that Weygand could be persuaded or prodded into bringing North Africa back into the war.[1] The American desire to do something in North Africa stemmed from a sincere sympathy for France—the celebrated Lafayette tradition—made all the more tender because of France's crushing defeat. But calculations of far-off political and military advantage also counted. There was a commercial incentive as well. France's fall and Britain's ouster from Morocco created an opportunity for economic and strategic place that could not be passed up. To defend and advance American interests, the State Department worked to restore its ties with the protectorate. The French, having begun to reassess their lot in the world, eagerly encouraged the American attention.

Before Emmanuel Mönick left Vichy to take up his post as secretary general at Rabat, he impressed upon the American chargé d'affaires his desire for "closer economic relations" based on the terms and tempo of the past. Under the circumstances, France could no longer continue as the "principal supplier of Morocco or as its leading market." America was asked to fill the breach. The Algeciras cord that France had wished to cut in 1937 was now pulled to draw America nearer. With Britain Mönick hoped that things would get better, not worse.[2] This was a 180-degree turn from the traditional attitude toward American commerce and from the Anglophobia of June and July. It reflected new and sober realities. French vessels of commerce had been swept from the Atlantic and the Mediterranean—even the French Line's majestic *Normandie* lay tied up in

New York harbor—and the ships of the undefeated French navy, once the empire's maritime protector, rode at anchor in now silent naval stations across the globe.[3] Dependent for survival on the sea, on distant markets and foreign purveyors, Morocco needed the life-line abroad. Mönick unashamedly petitioned for American aid and intercession with the British to lift the blockade of the protectorate's ports.

To Wallace Murray, Morocco's prewar nemesis in Washington, nothing could have better vindicated his stubborn defense of anach-ronistic rights nor suited his vision of American commercial and po-litical expansion. He was ready to make North Africa an outpost of American influence, both a frontier fort capable of defense against Axis encroachments and a fortified camp in the Lyautey sense whose main purpose was pacific penetration through trade. The guiding precept was that providing Morocco with the necessities of life would encourage the Vichy administration to hold the line against Germany. The amount of trade might be tiny, but its political significance could be great. "From our larger defense interests," went a November 1940 memorandum from the State Department's Near Eastern Division, "it is important that French Morocco should not fall into hostile hands, and anything done to bolster the morale of the authorities and people of that area and to avoid the collapse, whether economic or political, of French Morocco is all to the good." Mönick made clear that he understood the political implications and welcomed the opportunity to keep Morocco out of the Reich's eco-nomic reach to maintain its "freedom of action." He even suggested that Morocco might be able "to sever the link that bound the French Moroccan franc with the French franc and to establish an indepen-dent currency." Whittled away by the war, Morocco's vaunted "inde-pendence" was still worth fighting for.[4]

For the same reasons, the British too were interested in the Moroc-can trade, especially the supply of tea and sugar in exchange for phosphates. If they reached an agreement with the French, they pro-posed to raise their blockade and to invite America to sail under as well. But they wanted some say as to the goods imported. Under no circumstances did they desire a spill of petroleum products, so des-perately needed by the protectorate. Who could be sure that the oil pumped into storage tanks at Fedala would not eventually grease Hitler's machines? But Washington, having seen its Syrian trade as-phyxiated by the British blockade, was in no mood for London's rules, particularly when they operated to England's commercial ad-vantage and to the detriment of American commerce.[5]

At the direction of Under Secretary of State Sumner Welles, the State Department initiated "exploratory conversations" with Mö- nick and Weygand, expanding the topic from Moroccan-American trade to the provisioning of all North Africa. But there was never wholehearted agreement in Washington on the wisdom of this course. The head of the Division of International Economic Affairs opposed it as liable to prejudice the forces fighting the Axis. The Treasury Department and the Bureau of Economic Warfare were also unsympathetic and placed roadblocks in the path of the economic exchanges.[6] This was surely one reason why President Roosevelt, in- trigued by the African project, named a personal envoy to expedite the negotiations, pulling the matter above and beyond official dis- agreements and departmental rivalries.

The White House emissary, Robert D. Murphy, was a protégé of the former ambassador to France, William C. Bullitt. Murphy had worked out of the Paris embassy for ten years, but apart from the time spent in France, he had no special qualifications for the task. He had never been to North Africa and knew little about France's African empire. He was unskilled in economic and military matters and once admitted that "with luck" he might be able "to distinguish a battleship from a submarine on a particularly clear day." Even he wondered why he had been chosen, picking up on Roosevelt's com- ment, presumably made in earnest, that perhaps he and Weygand could go to mass together.[7] In Murphy's favor were his closeness to French politics, his command of the French language, his prior ser- vice in Germany and familiarity with Franco-German relations, his genial personality, and his energy and ambition. Being a Ro- man Catholic and Irish-American was no liability, either, although the British would later see his heritage as a factor that weighed against them.

Assigned to construct a building blueprinted by the State Depart- ment, Murphy conferred with no one there before leaving Washing- ton for Vichy, a telling discontinuity in a policy that has often been seen as of one piece. This was to be a White House operation. To keep a hand in the matter, Murray posted one of his own men, James Rives Childs, to the Tangier legation, the most important American mission in Morocco and soon to be the center of American intel- ligence for all North Africa. Childs had been the most forceful advo- cate of aid to the protectorate, the hand behind the memoranda and reports written to convince the higher-ups in Washington.[8]

When Murphy first visited Rabat at the end of December 1940, Mönick told him that the economic situation was "dangerous," not so much because of the shortage of food stuffs, although tea and sugar were always in demand, but because of the lack of gasoline, Morocco's "life blood." Tractors and trucks, vital to European agriculture for the last fifteen years, stood dead in their tracks for lack of fuel, raising alarms for the March planting.[9] Highway caravans, more important than railroads for moving goods and people, were disappearing from the roads, bringing commerce to a halt. Industry stagnated. French officers, welded to their cars, jeeps, and small aircraft, were returning to the horse and camel. Like a Hollywood set, Lyautey's Morocco was being recreated. Despite the pleasure for some in reliving the rough old days, the efficiency and tightness of French control suffered. So did France's prestige. The French had laid a wager on modernity, more so in the colonies than in the Metropole, and France's stake went with its retreat. For the pashas, *caïds*, and tribal chieftains gifted with automobiles as symbols of their standing with France, there was resentment at the empty gas tanks. This was no trifle. Amid the turbulence at Fez in 1937, the business of a new car once threatened to break the cooperation between the pasha and the French authorities.[10]

Both Mönick and Noguès schooled Murphy in these colonial facts of life. The "reasonable contentment" of the native population was their most serious concern and the Germans would exploit any discontent to their advantage. Weakened by the British blockade, French Africa might conceivably fall apart. Strengthened by American supplies, it might be preserved to "play a vital role in the decision of the present European war." Mönick hoped that Britain could be made to look upon French Africa as a "friendly element capable of great utility in the future, rather than a dubious force to be dealt with harshly, deprived of means and subjected to adverse propaganda." Murphy was persuaded that the French were sympathetic to the British cause but resented Britain's intemperate talk, aggressive action, and apparent inability to comprehend their need to keep the empire intact. He was impressed with their "surprisingly firm control" over Africa in spite of "defeat and chaos in France." Furthermore, he was convinced after talking with Weygand that the general's aim was eventual "independent military action against Germany and Italy." But Weygand would only act if the Germans violated the armistice, which he had urged on France and was honor bound to defend. For Murphy it was good enough: at the very least Weygand was pledged to resist the German domination of Africa. With these words he endorsed the French requests for economic assistance.[11]

In nonbelligerent Madrid and neutral Lisbon, Noguès's men, Léon Marchal and Robert Marjolin, had been meeting on the quiet with David Eccles, a representative of Britain's ministry of economic warfare, to hear England's terms for the passage of ships to Morocco's ports.[12] Murphy was sent to listen in because lifting the blockade was a requisite of American aid.[13] Britain required that the protectorate sell its strategic minerals to England alone, that it release the ships of British registry held in Morocco's ports, and that it supply the Spanish zone with food. The final point—and as the French understood it, the "essential" one—was the most surprising. But Eccles explained that British trade agreements with Spain had already made Franco more friend than foe. In anticipation of military conversations with Spanish soldiers in Tetouan, England would assume the cost of the grain and dried vegetables sent north if France would tend to their delivery. Eccles seemed to think that if the German army in France should cross the line at Saint-Jean-de-Luz, Spain would resist, fighting on in Spanish Morocco, if need be, at the side of the British. Marchal thought the whole thing "strange." Be that as it may, here the tangle of zones could have worked to France's advantage, even bettering north-south relations.[14]

Each of the British conditions posed a difficulty. Berlin would balk at any exclusive British purchase of Moroccan cobalt and molybdenum, and the release of British vessels would never clear the desks of the armistice commissioners at Wiesbaden. Supplying the Spanish zone would be next to impossible with the surplus of the southern harvests earmarked for the Metropole. Nevertheless, Noguès recommended pushing ahead with the negotiations because of Morocco's serious economic needs. He also speculated on the disastrous consequences that a unilateral British supply of the north might have on a still-blockaded south; the contrast between the haves and the have-nots "would dangerously influence the spirit of our population."[15]

One of the happy surprises that came out of the Lisbon talks was seeing Murphy in action. He let the French in on his private chats with Eccles and exerted a "very effective pressure" on the Englishman in France's favor. In fact, Eccles may have been pushed too hard. "If it is in our interest to have the Americans put a little friendly pressure on the English," Marchal cautioned, "it should only be done with a good deal of discretion." Rough-edged with the British, Murphy was soon tagged a "Vichyphil" and Anglophobe, and Eccles warned that he could be dangerous; he was more interested in cozying up to the French than defeating the Germans.[16]

At a subsequent meeting between Marchal and Eccles in Tangier, where Murphy sat in as a full partner, Eccles proposed an Anglo-French agreement worked through Spain to furnish North Africa with its most pressing needs while the protectorate supplied the Spanish zone with food. The triangular arrangement had the advantage of skirting the objections of the armistice commission and keeping Britain out of the northern zone, which Noguès wanted to do at all costs. Moreover, America was to be permitted to pass the British blockade to supply North Africa directly. In this final point, the French detected a reluctant British concession to a commercial rival. Whatever disadvantages the scheme had, such as diverting protectorate stocks from Vichy to Tetouan, were more than made up for by the prospects of increased agricultural production and social peace in Morocco.[17]

Weygand's endorsement to Vichy characterized the accord as essential to the life and political tranquillity of French Africa. Any stones that strewed its path he cast aside as "secondary considerations" or turned into useful steps. Although the release of British ships in Moroccan ports was "not acceptable," it was probably unnecessary if the protectorate was to handle the shipments to the north and the carrying trade for its own imports. The exclusive sale of strategic minerals to Britain was no longer being demanded; London merely asked that Rabat do "everything possible" to prevent their export abroad. Finally, linking the supply of Spanish Morocco to the economic recovery of the French zone would serve Vichy's policy of rapprochement with Madrid. What excited Weygand was that the "principle" of supplying Morocco had been accepted by the British and that the provisioning of the rest of the empire was being examined in a favorable light. For all this, he gave Murphy a generous portion of the credit. America had become the empire's "firm support."[18]

However pleasant the plans, the Anglo-French negotiations in the end came to nothing. The French speculated that neither the British ministry of economic warfare nor the war cabinet had ever been seriously interested in an accord but had pursued the talks under American pressure. On this score, the most the British would ever admit was that Murphy had "endangered" the negotiations. The crux of the matter, they told Washington, was the release of British ships, despite the fact that it had never been put as such to the French. Since the French had been unable to handle that item, the negotiations had ceased. What really bothered London was that it had failed to elicit any response from Weygand on political or military collaboration with Britain. As a result, Churchill reluctantly concluded that North Africa's stability favored Germany, chaos favored England.[19]

The British change of mind was dramatic. When Secretary of State Hull announced that America was "going forward" with its plans to supply French Africa, the British response was to call it "a great gamble" because there was "no way of telling whether a strengthened French force in that area might not attack the British instead of helping them." The embassy's first secretary put it plainly: "His Government was extremely reluctant to take any chances on restoring the economic system in French Africa and that he personally regarded it as a great risk." However explained, the Anglo-French talks stopped because the British wanted them to, not "unaccountably" and not because the French were ordered to break them off by the Germans.[20]

For America the effect of the negotiations was to have unlocked the Maghreb. By negotiating with Vichy, the British had been forced to admit that although their policy was "to blockade Morocco like any other territory owning allegiance to Vichy," it would be subject "to such relaxations as may be desirable for specific reasons." Through this loophole climbed the State Department, arguing that to prevent "a disintegration of the situation in Morocco," which it found favorable to America, it was imperative to provide the "necessities of life." Petroleum was counted chief among them. With real anxiety, therefore, Britain accommodated America's determination to provision Morocco and consented to include Algeria and Tunisia in the bargain. In return, Britain thought it "essential" that American officials be stationed as monitors in North Africa's ports to watch over the shipments and guard against their reexport. America agreed with this. But as for making a Franco-American accord contingent upon the release of British shipping, America would have none of it, knowing full well that the French could not meet that condition.[21]

Judged in the light of America's prewar concerns over restrictions on its commerce and political privileges in Morocco, its wartime attitude was consistent and made sense. Worried lest Britain violate its own blockade yet keep it watertight for others, the State Department reacted with the same words that had been used on the French in 1939. Although the American government was in sympathy with Britain's fight against the Axis and in many cases pursued a policy of "parallel action" to achieve certain common objectives, it reserved its "complete freedom" in economic negotiations with foreign states.

It refused to accept Britain's restrictions and rejected its conditions. In genesis, then, the future Franco-American economic accord in North Africa could in no way be considered a weapon in Britain's war with Germany. Quite to the contrary, it was a purely American instrument to further Yankee interests in the Maghreb and employed, some said, at Britain's expense.[22]

Murphy was instructed to tell Weygand that America was ready "in principle" to cooperate with French North Africa. In turn, Weygand's delegate in Washington, sent there in the first place by Noguès to act for Morocco, assured the State Department that "he was prepared to cooperate with us in every respect, to give any assurances or guarantees that might be required, and to follow our wishes in every way." But at this crucial juncture came the alarming reports, waved about by Britain's representatives, of "serious German infiltration" in Morocco. Sumner Welles called the news "disquieting" but turned it around by arguing that American aid might well be the best defense against the German progress. Hull merely registered his "concern" with Pétain. Murphy pegged the news as just so many "false rumors and reports" and urged that Washington "not be dissuaded from any plan of economic cooperation with French Africa."[23]

Doubtless the German flutter was designed as a counter to American activity. In the main, it consisted of replacing the Italian control commission at Casablanca with a German one. Noguès fought it as hard as he had every German move since July 1940, but without success. French assertions notwithstanding, Germans on the streets of Casablanca did not violate the armistice. Although he complained bitterly to Vichy that nothing good could come of the German presence, Noguès downplayed what was going on to the Americans. He told Murphy that the purpose of the German team was to verify military supplies, survey economic resources, and prevent the development of any anti-German French organization. He pledged to watch every move the Germans made, to track their every step. He did. There was certainly no need to fear a German takeover (as the British did), for he said it would take the Reich twenty years, the time it had taken the French to pacify Morocco, to bring the country under its control.[24] Weygand told Leahy that the Germans would undoubtedly try to spread propaganda among the native population and that he would do his best "to control and circumscribe their activities." To help Washington justify sending aid, he volunteered that American assistance would constitute the best bulwark against German propaganda by enabling France to satisfy the natives' essential needs. Perhaps that did the trick. In any event, neither Britain nor

Germany could break America's enthusiasm for the economic accord that Weygand initialed on 26 February and Vichy ratified on 10 March. In fact, their efforts had the opposite effect. Instead of scaring the Americans off, it made them more determined than ever to wave the Stars and Stripes in Casablanca. "If the French are to resist German efforts to penetrate further into Morocco," wrote Wallace Murray, picking up on the Weygand line, "I believe that we should at once commence our program of economic collaboration."[25]

Nevertheless, for six weeks implementation of the American plan was stalled by ever-increasing evidence of German activity. Not only Casablanca but Rabat, Fedala, Fez, and Marrakesh were to have German commissioners. Noguès was "considerably worried." At the armistice commission in Wiesbaden, General Paul Doyen argued to his German opposite that the "massive installation" of control commissions threatened to undermine French authority and encourage disorder. Malaise had begun to grow among the native population, and he predicted "the most serious events." "We cannot forget that a good part of Morocco has only recently been pacified and that any insurrection in this country is capable of rapidly reaching considerable proportions, witness the Rif insurrection in 1925 that took the combined efforts of the French and Spanish armies to put down." "Of all our colonial empire," he told General Oskar Vogl, "the part that worries us the most is the Moroccan empire." He put in a pitch for togetherness, suggesting once again that it was in the "common interest" of both Germany and France that calm and order be maintained.[26]

Much of this the Germans dismissed as something the French had dreamed up to keep them out of Morocco. But French reports indicated otherwise. Among the working class at Casablanca, in particular those workers who hailed from the Souss region east of Agadir, there was much pro-German, anti-French sentiment and wild talk of liberation from the French "yoke." With the young and educated of the city, there had always been a strong Germanophile current. After counting heads, Casablanca's police chief had to admit that "the majority of Muslims of Casablanca admire Germany."[27] In this Casablanca was not unique. Morocco's director of public security confirmed a "quasi-general" sympathy for Germany among the native population, a sympathy based on the belief that France was now under Germany's thumb and encouraged by economic discontent and anti-French propaganda from the Spanish zone.[28] Even American reports showed that German agents were "creating difficulties" in the area east and south of the Atlas mountains along the Oujda-

Tafilalet-Agadir line, a region that Noguès counted on to be resistant to Teutonic influence.[29]

When Noguès sorted it all out, he explained to Vichy that the increased German activity, coming at a time of the Reich's military success in the eastern Mediterranean (the capitulation of the Yugoslav army, the invasion of Greece, and the reoccupation of the Cyrenaica) and coinciding with the protectorate's economic distress, had shaken the native population's faith in France.[30] Most visibly touched were the sultan, the members of the Makhzen, and the urban elite. Sidi Mohammed confessed his "great concern" to Noguès and "seemed very affected by the course of events and the uncertainty of the future." Still, Noguès could "ensure that at this moment we can count on him." This went for the aged grand vizier as well. But others of the Makhzen were less dependable. "Their support will last only as long as we are capable of ensuring the security of their situation." Certain pashas and *caïds* of the cities felt the same way. But France could rely on the "great majority" of the *caïds* in the countryside, particularly among the Berber mountain tribes. Almost alone among city dwellers, the nationalists remained reserved about the German presence and worried about its political designs and racism, yet they were prepared for "any eventuality," even "active collaboration" with France. "We are encouraging this tendency," Noguès was quick to add, "which will permit us to channel the movement."

In sum, the resident acknowledged that despite his efforts to limit German influence and to prevent the disaffection of the population, France had "lost ground and the slope is becoming dangerous. . . . We can no longer say that Morocco is a solid bloc behind us and would follow us blindly on any adventure. Only if its territory is invaded, in particular by the Spaniards, would the country recover its will to resist. Our prestige can still be defended and we have substantial trumps in our hands. But once the natives sense that we are powerless to resist an infiltration and progressive takeover by the Germans, a large part of the population will move to the side of the master of the moment and our situation will become very precarious." To keep Morocco for France, he recommended that Vichy negotiate an end to the increase of German operatives and propaganda. For his part, he would clamp a "hermetic" seal on all German action. Both were vital as well to continue the economic supply program with America. There could be no doubt of its importance in his mind. "The state of the country's spirit and perhaps its future are a function of the success of our efforts in this area, and several tons of cotton goods, outside of sugar, tea, and oil, would do more to combat German propaganda than all the internal measures that we can take."[31]

Noguès purposely exaggerated the effects of the German presence to Vichy. He told Weygand that there was no threat of outright "treason" by the native population. In fact, the country as a whole remained "healthy and devoted but a bit uneasy." Only in the case of "serious incidents on our borders" would there be a risk of internal unrest. The sultan, however, was shaky. Fear of losing his throne had made him susceptible to "every evil influence." Noguès had to hold his hand—"more and more I need to be near him"—and escort him around the empire to raise his spirits, for "the joy of appearing in public and being acclaimed makes him forget all his worries."[32] This was part of the reason for the pilgrimage to Tafilalet in May to pray at the tomb of his ancestors. He would be the first sultan since Moulay Hassan to venture so far south, and in the company of the French there was an obvious political message. Despite the Germans, France was still at the sultan's side.

In Washington Hull was forced to admit that the Germans in Africa had caused "very serious concern," and he instructed Ambassador Leahy to tell Pétain that if his government could not prevent the German infiltration of North Africa, then the United States would not be able to honor its initials. All Pétain could reply was that he had Germany's promise (for all that was worth) that the members of the German armistice commission in Morocco would never top two hundred. In short, he could do nothing, leaving Weygand and Noguès, like vigilantes on the frontier, to impose their own law, which they did with a vengeance.[33]

The British were frankly delighted at the turn. It had come about according to the upstaged and contrite Eccles because of America's "overestimation of the French Government's liberty of action." Vichy was impotent in the face of Germany's demands. With the arrival of the Germans in French Africa, Pétain's "only card" had been grabbed from his hand. Economic assistance plainly had no power to induce North Africa to resist. What Eccles recommended was an Anglo-American military expedition, with or without French invitation, to seize Casablanca and Dakar, a reprise of the ill-fated Operation Menace of September 1940, this time with American participation.[34]

Nothing of the sort figured in American calculations. From Childs at Tangier came the word that Noguès and other high protectorate officials were still strong for the United States and Britain and had

Left, Weygand; *center*, the sultan;
right, Noguès. Ksar es Souk, May 1941.
Courtesy French Embassy, Rabat.

recovered from the initial shock of the arrival of the German troupe. "Our willingness to give them economic aid has greatly encouraged them." He implied that they would be lost without it. To Consul General Felix Cole, both Weygand and Mönick stressed the "larger general political considerations" that ought to propel American action. Mönick called for American "countercollaboration." Why shouldn't America wage a peaceful battle with Germany over Morocco? It was in its own interests to do so and would "force [the] average Frenchman and high French officials in North Africa [to] choose definitely between Germany and the United States." After "careful thought," Leahy too recommended going ahead with the supply program. He reasoned that the increase in the number of Germans in North Africa should not in and of itself cause its cancellation. If it later proved that German encroachment threatened the Maghreb's integrity, there would still be time for America to reverse itself.[35]

Washington accepted the advice of those closest to the project and that of its own men in the field. Murphy was designated director of the American control commissioners, supervisor of the consulates in French Africa, and reporter to the State Department on all matters of political, economic, and military interest. In short, he would be an American "High Commissioner for French Africa," second only to Admiral Leahy in the lands where French was spoken. Weygand was telegraphed word of the approval of French purchases in the United States, the unblocking of French funds by the Treasury Department, and the shipment of goods on French vessels, with their control at journey's end by American agents on the spot. "This government," Hull declared, "is glad to offer these facilities because it believes that this method presents the possibility of preventing the economic disintegration of French North Africa and of preserving the French administrative control in that area." The general cabled his "sincere thanks."[36]

During the negotiations on the economic agreement, Noguès took a back seat to Weygand and to the protectorate's secretary general, Mönick, who as the most enthusiastic local promoter of the accord had become a kind of economic éminence grise to Weygand. From his contemporary conversations with Americans and from his memoirs, it is clear that Mönick intended the agreement to be the first step toward political cooperation, later followed by military alliance. In April, for example, he angled for an American declaration to the effect that any change in the African status quo would be seen as a "menace to the security of the Western Hemisphere," a Monroe Doctrine for French Africa. He also urged the Americans to approach Weygand on military matters, for he wanted Weygand by hook or by crook to develop into the leader of a resistant North Africa. Even Murphy, who nurtured the same dream as Mönick, wished that Weygand would act more like a prima donna instead of being content with membership in the chorus. He never did. Weygand was too loyal to Pétain to sing out on his own. To be sure, he was always interested in what the United States was up to and valued the channel across the ocean for the goods it brought the empire and the clout at Vichy that came with it. But he never desired political or military conversations. He always regretted that politics got mixed up with the economics of the American accord.[37]

Mönick called Noguès "Maître Renard"—the fox—an appropriate handle for a man with political impulses. He even looked like a fox, Mönick remembered. "And in moral terms—I later discovered—the resemblance was all the more striking. He had a taste for ruse, a sense for long detours, an instinct for slow approaches, like the fox carefully sniffing the baited trap." Mönick doubted Noguès's commitment to the American supply program and was certain he was uninterested in moving from petroleum to politics. But Mönick misinterpreted Noguès's silence as secretiveness, his reserve as hostility. He did favor the economic exchange with America, although he had his private reservations about the way it was being managed and was irked by its on-again, off-again character. "The Americans should realize," he wrote Weygand, "that it is in their interest to let us survive and not to depend entirely on the goodwill of the Germans."[38] Like Weygand, he wanted the aid without political strings attached.

The difficulty in gauging French intentions was rooted in the Vichy predicament. Like it or not, France had been politically "Polandized," reduced to a state of the third rank, trailing behind Italy and Spain in importance, reacting to events rather than shaping them. Once they admitted defeat, signed the armistice, and trekked to Vichy, its leaders had no recourse but to press for collaboration with Germany and seek a place among the victors as France had done so skillfully after Waterloo. Laval, in fact, styled himself the new Talleyrand, and he was not alone.[39] Collaboration was not a one-man show but a succession of performers each trying to outdo the other to capture the eye of Berlin in order to play in Paris. The problem was that more often than not Berlin was bored and uninterested in the presentation set before it. It was easy for an outsider to be deceived. Because of the patriotic pedigree and anti-Germanism of so many who clustered around Vichy, it was hard to believe that collaboration was the top priority of the French state. In addition, the fleet and the empire gave France the semblance of strength. But no state with three-fifths of its territory under enemy occupation and close to 2 million of its soldiers in prisoner-of-war camps could bridle at collaboration. Most Frenchmen were willing to walk the penitent's path to a reconciliation that would liberate their lands and their sons. The message that America never deciphered was that France would not swing toward the Allies unless all hope of collaboration with Germany was gone or until German defeat was certain. For Pétain and Laval that time never came.

Algiers was not Vichy, and if geography counted for anything, it was right to expect that North Africa's leaders would have a different attitude toward Germany. They did. Publicly and privately, Weygand and Noguès were rough and rude to the Germans. Neither ever promoted collaboration that strayed beyond the bounds of the armistice nor volunteered anything in Africa to the Germans. But they were forced to reconcile their commitments to the Maghreb with their loyalty to Vichy and its wider view of Franco-German relations. Noguès had been through it all before. The tension between the two produced the conduct that puzzled Frenchmen as well as Americans and gave rise to words and deeds that alternately heartened and discouraged Washington.

For North Africa the German threat was greatest in 1941, when Darlan was foreign minister. The admiral assiduously sought a breakthrough in relations with the Reich. When the Germans requested the use of French airfields in Syria to rush aid to anti-British rebels in Iraq, Darlan granted it and used the occasion to press for far-reaching cooperation. He greeted Hitler at Berchtesgaden with the message that the French government was convinced of the need for a "lasting entente" and that he personally saw collaboration as an "irresistible historic necessity." Back at Vichy, he argued that this was the "last chance" to seek a rapprochement with Germany. If France favored England, it would be "crushed, dislocated, and cease to be a nation." If it tried to straddle the fence, Germany would create a "thousand difficulties." With a German victory, France would lose a great swath of territory in the northeast, along the Mediterranean coast, and Corsica, Tunisia, and Morocco as well. If, however, France collaborated, it would be saved as a nation and play an honored role in the Europe of the future. "For me," Darlan concluded, "my choice is made: it is collaboration and I will not be sidetracked by the conditional offer of a boatload of wheat or gasoline." So much for the Murphy-Weygand accord, which Darlan saw of small value.

As always, Darlan left himself an out. The military intervention of the United States might change things. But he was convinced that due to American military unpreparedness it would take "many years" before an American soldier could set foot in Europe. Moreover, the admiral thought American society was in "a more advanced state of decomposition than we were in 1939." France's interest was that the war be short in order to survive it and still remain a great power. Given the world situation and France's "formidable" defeat, the admiral saw no other solution than collaboration to safeguard his country. On the copy of the admiral's remarks circulated to top French representatives abroad was the final line that made it more than one man's decision: "The Council of Ministers presided over by Marshal Pétain unanimously approved the declaration of Admiral Darlan."[40] The next day Pétain made it public: he announced the second wave of collaboration, promising that if the negotiations with Germany succeeded, France would preserve its rank as a European and colonial power.[41]

In the wake of Darlan's "Montoire," Weygand reminded the government of its pledge to defend Africa against all comers. He warned that "if the Germans or Italians succeeded in obtaining from us the use of military, naval, or aerial key positions in one of our African possessions, this broken pledge would create unrest whose consequences would be impossible to foresee. Africa can only be defended by our own forces." Weygand was imitating Noguès, now feeling for the first time the resident's fear of summer 1940, when Bordeaux's actions almost broke the chain of words that bound the Maghreb to the Metropole. Weygand was not opposed in principle to collaboration (just as Noguès had not been opposed in principle to the cease-fire or the armistice), but he wanted guarantees and, like Noguès, wanted them to be public.[42]

To be sure, Noguès was in accord. As far as he was concerned, the opening of Syrian bases to Germany was not a happy sign of future cooperation but unpleasant evidence of French weakness, the German "knife" at the throat of the empire. There was no way of comparing what had been received—"certain small advantages" in France—to what had been given. The only interesting thing about Darlan's collaboration (and Weygand and Noguès saw it right away) was that it might result in a strengthening of French forces in North Africa. "The first dividend that we must draw from the profound sacrifice that this present policy imposes on us is to be able to increase our potential for resistance for that day when the promises that have been made to us are broken and our country is once again in danger."[43] These were sentiments apparently not yet shared by Darlan.

When Murphy inquired whether the announced policy of collaboration would affect Africa, Weygand "solemnly" assured him that it would not and "denied emphatically" the rumor that Tunisia was now being used as a German base of military operations. What he did not know was that the Franco-German negotiations under way in Paris (which resulted in the protocols of 27 May) would open Dakar to the German navy, air force, and merchant marine and would make Bizerte and the Bizerte-Gabès railroad line available to the German army in Libya.[44] This was Darlan's doing. However, a note signed by him and Otto Abetz, the German ambassador in Paris, specified that before the protocols could go into effect, Germany had to grant France political, economic, and military concessions.

Summoned to Vichy to be briefed on this infringement of his patrimony, Weygand "protested with the greatest energy" against the agreement. It went beyond the armistice and was "entirely contrary to the mission he had been given to defend North Africa for France." It made of him a liar to Murphy and would finish off any hope of American economic aid. "It would make me belie everything I have declared in agreement with the government. The government is changing its policy; a new policy requires a new man." There can be no doubt that Weygand fought hard against the protocols and he took credit for blocking them. He told Mönick that he had "succeeded in calling a halt to the proposed adoption of the new policy. The council took no decision on it."[45]

Lest there be confusion over the word "policy," it is clear that Weygand only meant opening African bases to Germany, not collaboration in general, which, as a member of the government and then as the government's delegate, he had accepted from the beginning and which he implicitly endorsed again by not resigning. Even then, pressed hard by Pétain, he was willing to accept the Bizerte deal (which he, not Darlan, called military collaboration), if the price was right. First, he wanted a "frank and open declaration of French policy" explaining in no uncertain terms that such a military arrangement was required "in order that France may live." Second, he wanted Germany's prior consent to a political and economic counterpart in a signed, ratified, and published treaty. Darlan's blunder to Weygand's mind was that he had signed a secret document before knowing what the Germans would give in return; the vague reference to unspecified concessions to France in the Darlan-Abetz note was no good at all. Darlan was prepared with a proposal to the German government. According to Weygand's summary, Darlan would ask for the ending of the armistice regime as a preliminary to a peace treaty, a German guarantee of the territorial and colonial integrity of France, the step-by-step but continuous return of the prisoners of war, France's release from the costs of the occupation troops, the transformation of the demarcation line into a simple map mark separating the occupied and unoccupied zones, the reduction or elimination of the control commissions, and the suppression of the *Ostland*. In addition, Germany would be asked to grant North and West Africa the troop strength and materiel to defend themselves against a possible American or English reaction to the Franco-German agreement.[46] Had they been accepted, the conditions would have amounted to a revolution in Franco-German relations.

When the meeting at Vichy broke up, Weygand returned to Algiers with the written assurance that his mission remained unchanged, knowing that for the moment nothing had been conceded to the Germans and Italians in North Africa. A final decision on the African bases was to be put off until November, when the issue would be reassessed in light of the "evolution of events" and the German response to the French note. Before a month had passed, however, the English had attacked Syria, the Germans Russia. Faithful to the mood of the Council of Ministers, Darlan declined the proffered German aid, but without it the French could not hold. Damascus fell on 21 June and Vichy forces surrendered at Saint-Jean-d'Acre on 14 July.[47]

Despite Syria, Weygand still maintained that to go forward with any military cooperation with Germany, particularly in view of the German war in Russia, would be to expose Africa to English reprisals. Moreover, to welcome Germany anywhere in Africa would incur the "disaffection and hostility" of the colons, result in France's "complete loss of prestige" in the eyes of the native population, and paralyze the action of French authorities everywhere by bursting the bonds of trust and confidence. In short, it would provoke "a great movement of revolt and dissidence." "It is a risk that we cannot afford to run. To act otherwise seems folly to me and can bring about the loss of Africa." Weygand tagged on a final consideration that he called the "American factor." America's "sincere desire" to supply Africa militated against setting the United States "against us." Even in a Europe dominated by Germany, it was in France's interest as well as America's to keep the connection, "for regardless of what happens, we must not risk at any price remaining alone with the Germans, even as friends."[48] In addition, the American factor worked for Weygand at Vichy, something in his pocket so he need not come powerless and penniless to the Metropole.

None of this meant that military collaboration in Africa with Germany was forever out of the question. But "let her pay for it," Weygand insisted, already sensing how costly Russia had become for Germany, "and in cash." He recommended continuing with the negotiations already begun—there had been no response to the French conditions to the protocols—but "to hold high our political demands and stick it out." "We are in no hurry."[49]

Weygand was called back to Vichy for a meeting on 12 July with Pétain and the military chiefs to discuss the continued German pressure to use Bizerte. "I expected a very tough fight," he told Noguès. "But I must say that I had little to quarrel with. Admiral Darlan explained the German request and the several notes summarizing the meetings that he or Benoist-Méchin had had with the Germans. In short, they are insisting on getting what they need. But they are in no hurry to pay for it. The government realizes their bad faith and the risk it would run if it gave in to these demands, which would compromise our situation in French Africa. That is why the course adopted was what my note [of 11 July] demands and backs up: no reduction in our political demands; no haste to reach an agreement. A meeting of the Council of Ministers that I did not attend decided to send a new note to the Germans whose terms I am ignorant of but which I believe to be in accord with the position that I have set forth."[50]

This, then, was the background to Darlan's *note verbale* of 14 July to the Germans, which Robert Paxton has called "the most ambitious French proposal of the Vichy period." It certainly was. But it came not as a new Darlan initiative but as a retread of an earlier unanswered communication in part pressed on the admiral by Weygand. As with its predecessor, there was small chance that it would be accepted. Pierre Laval, the Germans' enfant gâté, spent his life as foreign minister trying to extract a guarantee for France's lands at home and abroad without success. Darlan's note asked for much more. July was in fact a less likely month than June for the Germans to have warmed to such a proposition because the loss of Syria to the British could be used to show how much the French needed Germany, not vice versa. Ribbentrop saw it as "a naive French blackmail attempt," planned to rupture negotiations over Bizerte.[51]

Being the bearer of old and soon to be twice-rejected tidings did nothing for Darlan's ego, his feelings for Weygand, or his genuine desire for a breakthrough in Franco-German relations. To resist the total collapse of his credit with the Germans, he ceded privately what he could not volunteer publicly. At Bizerte and along the rail line from the port to Gabès, concessions were granted for the transport of food, fuel, and military supplies which eased down the road of African collaboration. Weygand complained that the government gave lip service to the principle of keeping the Germans out of Africa but violated it in practice. In turn, Darlan accused Weygand of disloyalty and demanded "total" authority to carry out the government's program, reaching for what General Laure called an "absolute dictatorship." At the height of the fray, Weygand defiantly announced that whatever the result of the diplomatic overtures to the Germans (and they had already been rebuffed by Berlin), he would "never agree to the occupation of Bizerte."[52] This completed the rupture between the two men.

To bolster Weygand in what seemed a Vichy-Algiers tug-of-war, Murphy recommended some signal from President Roosevelt on a program of military assistance. At the least, he thought it would "hearten" the general; at the most, it might encourage him to contemplate independent responsibility. But these requests for "definite assurances of support" went unanswered as well as the suggestion that Weygand be told that America had "decided to act should France lend Mediterranean or Atlantic bases to the aggressor powers."[53] Even had Washington given such assurances, would they have been believed? Léon Marchal, now negotiating for the protectorate in America and a stalwart of the aid program, admitted the "uncertainty" surrounding all of America's plans. "The United States is not materially or morally ready to enter the war. Will it ever be? I doubt it. Europe is far. The life here is easy." He added to his friends in Morocco that it would be a mistake to rule out a reconciliation between America and a German-dominated Europe.[54] This was from a pro-American on-the-spot observer! No wonder Darlan was seeking an honorable place in Hitler's "new order" and those who thwarted him were likened to Benedict Arnolds.

One by one Darlan's opponents in North Africa fell. Mönick was removed at the end of August, proud of his reputation as the Germans' "public enemy number one" in Morocco. His close identification with the American aid program and his nearness to Weygand sealed his fate. Noguès did nothing to spare him and was even rumored to have requested his recall, for the two men never had a good working relationship.[55] Since Mönick's first loyalty was to Weygand, Noguès was deprived of a confidant at the summit of his administrative staff. With Darlan's private coldness toward America and his feud with Weygand, Mönick was more a liability than an asset. The irony is that American assistance had given and could have continued to give the protectorate the margin of freedom that Noguès prized. But the signs in summer were unclear. Forced to choose between the admiral and the empty sea, he chose the admiral.

Although Weygand understood that by October Darlan was less infatuated with the prospects of Franco-German collaboration than he had been in June, it was not so. In fact, the admiral was doing all he could to pry open the door that the Germans had slammed shut. Believing that he would soon have total control of France's armed forces, he told Ambassador Abetz that he was finally ready for military collaboration, putting a gloss on the Bizerte accord that Weygand had always read into it. He added that it was only a matter of time before he was rid of the obdurate general. But Germany had lost interest in haggling over Bizerte, Weygand or no Weygand, because it involved political concessions that Darlan could not or would not abandon and because Darlan had given most of what they wanted anyway. By the time Weygand was forced to retire under fire of the Germans and the admiral, Bizerte had been dry-docked as a point of departure for Franco-German cooperation.[56]

One immediate consequence of Weygand's fall in November was the suspension of the North African trade program. This bothered the admiral not at all, for the aid was of little material importance and its chief political value had been to buck up Weygand and anger Germany. "You should not trouble us so in Africa," Darlan scolded the first secretary at the American embassy at Vichy; "you just arouse German suspicions, whereas if you would reduce your activities there, they would never go into Africa." It was an argument that may have made some sense for Morocco and Algeria but none at all for Tunisia. It was not the Americans who drew the Germans to Bizerte but the German need to supply Rommel's Afrika Korps. Africa aside, both Pétain and Darlan still believed that a negotiated peace in Europe might not be far off and in that process Germany counted for all, America nothing. There was, to be sure, no desire for a break with America. Looking beyond the war, Vichy saw itself as the intermediary between the United States and Germany in the Europe of the future.[57]

The elimination of Weygand raised Noguès's standing once again. Now no one in the Maghreb was his match. Childs immediately spoke up for Noguès as a successor to Weygand as an American hopeful. He suggested a "modified program" of economic aid to the protectorate alone, where America had treaty rights and consequently more leverage than elsewhere in North Africa. The problem was that in reports home Noguès had come off as an opportunist, a timeserver, a man without fixed principles, a politician. An early sentence summed it up: "The best opinion here is that Noguès is a 'political' general and that he will keep his eye pretty well glued to the weather vane." Childs turned the description to Noguès's advantage, venturing that only a "consummate politician could have survived the storms of the past year" and that Noguès had proved to be "skillful and dexterous in maintaining himself." He explained Noguès's link to Lyautey, that Morocco was his sole passion, and that its disintegration would mean the "loss of his life work." His great value was in his skill in native affairs and it was this that accounted for his esteem at Vichy. Pertinent to Washington was the "very advanced position" that Noguès had taken in favor of con-

Center: Admiral François Darlan,
commander-in-chief of French sea, ground, and air forces.
Casablanca, 1942.
Photo Jacques Belin

tinued French resistance in 1940 and that he had never betrayed an
anti-Allied sentiment. Although discreet, he was still "unmistak-
ably friendly disposed" to the democratic cause. Childs had no clue
as to Noguès's current feelings but thought that the general would
be ready to take "any reasonable risks to safeguard France's position
in Morocco."[58]

Noguès was not a difficult man to assay. His entire career was one
of implacable defense against the German danger to Morocco. He
strongly seconded Weygand's vigorous protests on the Reich to
Vichy, repeating the litany of broken promises and the crisis of
French authority. He kept a tight surveillance over the Germans in
the protectorate and boasted that no German had ever dined at his
table. In loyalty to Pétain he was Weygand's equal and also in his
commitment to the American economic agreement. Privately he
confided that because Weygand was a "universally known soldier,"

the ballyhoo accompanying the accord had compromised its effectiveness; if Noguès had been alone in the negotiations, he was sure that they would have been more discreet and fruitful. On matters of administration and internal affairs, he and Weygand parted company. The centralization and control of the proconsulate at Algiers were stifling. He was glad to be rid of them. "Algiers is dead" were the words passed through the protectorate on Weygand's retirement, "Long live Rabat."[59]

Resurrected Rabat, however, had little room to move. Here men counted for less than the stagnating economy and the dependence on the Metropole's money. In any event, Darlan was not about to release the strings. Five days after Weygand had been removed, Darlan informed Noguès that the government had decided "to pursue a constructive policy through rapprochement with Germany," which alone would "maintain intact" the political situation in North Africa and permit France to strengthen its military defenses. "I am therefore asking you to set your political line of conduct to conform with this information and in particular to take care that the relations with the German control commission are normalized and free from useless bickering. As far as economic relations with foreign powers, this is to let you know that the government is alone entitled to decide on them. No special diplomatic representation will be assigned to you for this matter." Darlan's reasons for rapprochement were familiar, although now he argued that the armistice itself had implied some entente with Germany. Not to seek it would bring about a rupture in relations, the total occupation of France, the loss of the empire. In short, this was not just the "most favorable" policy for France to follow, it was the only one. In Africa he approved the Weygand-Noguès practice of defense against any assault but assumed that the Allies, not the Axis, would be the enemy: if France failed to keep its guard up, he warned, then Germany would send its own sentries.[60]

Murphy recognized that the "doors of French Africa [were] now open to the Germans." But he still argued in favor of the aid program to keep an observation post in the western Mediterranean. When he saw Noguès, the resident gave no hint that things had changed. He urged continuation of the supply program, for even the "small trickle" of goods was important in light of Morocco's desperate needs. As always, he refused to discuss politics. Murphy concluded correctly that Noguès was "as well disposed as ever but it is obvious that we cannot count heavily on him for independent resistance to Vichy decisions in favor of German influence in Morocco." On this point Childs had to agree. From Noguès on down, French officials in North Africa had neither the will nor the means for anything but "passive resistance" to the Germans. Paradoxically, Germanophobia among other Frenchmen in the Maghreb was strong, the result of the German success at sacking Weygand. "I do not think I have ever found the feeling in Rabat so pronouncedly anti-German nor have I found at the same time such uncertainty as to the future." The one permanent element in French public opinion in the protectorate, bred from years of remembering Agadir and Tangier, was the anti-German sentiment. This was now expressed as hostility to the notion of collaboration (so Noguès had told Darlan squarely in April), precisely what the resident was being told to talk up.[61]

While Vichy pushed for collaboration with Germany, North Africa was ordered to do nothing to encourage the Americans. Noguès transmitted the message to Childs by emphasizing how disastrous war would be to Morocco, how much he wanted the protectorate to stay outside the combat zone. He repeated what Weygand had always said, that Morocco would defend itself against any attack from whatever quarter.[62] Murphy cast about for other sources of support for a pro-American policy. Now that the efforts to work with a "friendly French administration" and to encourage its resistance to the Axis appeared to have failed, he confessed he was "at sea." Finally he was authorized to broaden his contacts. But moving away from official North Africa was done with great reluctance by Washington. When the consul in Tunis, in despair over the collaboration, suggested getting up an Arab revolt against the French, he was sternly put down: "Our policy in French North Africa is directed to building up the confidence of the French authorities and the French population in general, and to induce them to support the democratic cause in one way or another. It is obvious of course that what counts in this connection is the friendly attitude of French military officials, and if anything were done to destroy such favorable sentiment as we may have aroused, our entire objective would be defeated."[63] Despite dismal reports, Washington still stuck to Vichy, American barnacles on the French ship of state.

America's fighting fraternity with Britain and the Soviet Union, brought about by the Japanese attack on the Pacific fleet in the Hawaiian Islands, caused no change in Vichy policy toward the United States. Neither Darlan nor his successor as foreign minister, Pierre Laval, sought any rupture with America and were in fact glad to maintain cordial relations. But the Americans were still unwelcome in North Africa. Pétain made it official: his government would "resist invasion by British, Gaullists, Germans, or Americans." As ever, the hope for an understanding with Germany took precedence over any desire to join hands with the Allies, even though the Allied side was growing stronger. Laval candidly told Ambassador Leahy that a Franco-German accord would bring "lasting peace" to Europe, thus revealing his narrow notion of the war, and volunteered that a "German victory (or possibly a negotiated peace) [was] preferable to a British and Soviet victory" because the latter would spread bolshevism across the continent. This was the closest that anyone ever came to telling Leahy that he hoped his side would lose.[64]

The American aid program all but dried up after Weygand's dismissal. Suspended in November 1941 as a protest over the general's forced retirement, it was resumed in April 1942 after a third blowup over Bizerte. This time it was Noguès who journeyed to Vichy to argue that the German supplies snaking through Tunisia had jeopardized the resumption of American aid, causing him to face criticism from Europeans as well as the native population. Welles called it the "most serious" crisis that had developed in United States–Vichy relations to date. Under pressure Darlan agreed to stop the flow of supplies and by so doing squandered the last bit of credit he had with the Germans.[65] His failure to bridge the Rhine forced him to resign as foreign minister. Weygand and Noguès had built the barricades on Darlan's path to Berlin via Bizerte, and both had used American stones.

Laval succeeded Darlan in a turn that stunned America, for his reputation and record on collaboration were worse than his predecessor's. The aid program was promptly suspended, just eight days after it had been resumed. But Noguès was unflapped at the change at Vichy. Laval was uninterested in Africa, and by that time, so were the Germans.[66] Like a harassed householder whose noisy neighbors were on vacation, Noguès celebrated the quiet. Murphy and Childs pressed for continuing the economic assistance despite Laval. Murray called it a useful propaganda and psychological instrument of economic warfare. He underlined the military and strategic importance of the control officers. "Their continued functioning is perhaps the most important single advantage to be derived by the United States from resuming shipments to North Africa."[67] The aid program began once more in June and was allowed to limp along until the Allied invasion of November put American assistance on an entirely new footing. But it had long ceased being considered a cornerstone for Franco-American countercollaboration in French Africa. Now it was justified on the grounds that it gave Americans the right to roam through North Africa and preserved some prestige for the American flag in the Maghreb. Stopping the program altogether would have destroyed this advantage completely.

The economic road to Morocco turned into a dead end because of the hesitations of Washington, the fears of London, the coldness of Vichy, and the outright hostility of Berlin. Only Algiers and Rabat gave the program wholeheated support, and even that was often compromised by the play of personalities and politics. Murphy admitted that the material basis of the program had been "exceedingly flimsy," the volume of trade never really important, and this certainly had something to do with results.[68] But the major problem was the different expectations of the partners. As its relationship with Europe changed from neutrality to belligerence, America wanted the economic tie with North Africa to do likewise, to assume a partisan political and military character. Noguès wanted none of it. The balance in Morocco was hard enough to maintain without frightening Vichy and angering Germany by tipping the scales toward America.

Throughout 1942 Noguès acknowledged the pro-American, anti-German sentiment in Morocco but warned against any American intervention. "Morocco is very favorably disposed to the United States," he told Childs, "but we shall resist any effort which may be made to attack us and I hope you will emphasize this to your Government." Nothing would bring the Germans in force to Africa quicker than the "serious chance of an Anglo-American landing." He also told Murphy straight out that an Allied intervention would ruin the French position in Morocco. The native population "could not be trusted" and would take advantage of the situation to attack the French and perhaps the expeditionary force as well. Chaos would result, doing no one any good. What he wanted then was the preservation of the status quo in the protectorate.[69]

Noguès's reference to the unreliability of the native population was something new to Murphy but only to be expected after two years of a steady barrage of English, Spanish, and German propaganda, all undermining French control, and an economic situation that was not at all satisfactory in the cities and the countryside and that the small American aid had done precious little to improve. In some ways, it was a return to the conditions of the mid-1930s. In 1941 there were bumper crops in wheat and barley, yet nothing could be sold abroad, and the prices set by the government for grain sent to France were at unprofitably low levels. For native growers there was no incentive to sell because the cash could no longer buy consumer goods. Cotton cloth was even used as a premium to get the natives to sell their grain at market prices. Mother nature reduced cereal production in 1942—heavy rain in the north, dryness in the south, and locusts south of Safi. Reductions were no where near famine proportions, but yields were less than anticipated, causing some distress and pushing prices upward.[70] French prestige was at an all-time low. It is a wonder that the French managed the cities in such explosive circumstances, particularly in light of the troubles of 1936 and 1937, and to their credit that they did as well as they did. For Casablanca, with over two hundred thousand native inhabitants, the garrison was judged "completely inadequate," and the police force should have been "five times stronger" than it was. The urban scene was "unsettling" and could become "suddenly tragic." "Our situation demands that we carefully avoid giving rise to opportunities for trouble and demonstrations of all sorts." Maintaining order in the protectorate had become "very difficult."[71]

What Noguès concealed was his growing concern over the American part in weakening French prestige. He had evidence that Murphy's men, the overseers of the aid, were mixing with the native elite and proselytizing for America. Five months after the first vice-consuls had arrived, General de Loustal, Noguès's roving informant on native affairs, brought him news on the political business being transacted in the souks. "One of the promises having the greatest impact in native circles is to abolish the protectorate and return to a regime of capitulations favorable to the Makhzen." In addition, the word was that both Moulay Larbi, the sultan's cousin and judicial khalif of the pasha of Marrakesh, and Ahmed Bennani, the secretary to the grand vizier, had implied in conversation with an American vice-consul that Morocco might welcome an American protectorate. Although none of this had Washington's cachet of approval, it had gone on nonetheless and left a mark.[72]

American reports had it that the sultan was "delighted" at the prospect of an American protectorate but could and would do nothing to hurry its creation: "If they do come," he was quoted as saying, "I shall be the first to welcome them, but first let them come." These were words that hinged on events, not unlike those of Weygand to Murphy or Darlan to Leahy. Abderrahman Bargach, pasha of Rabat, was also put in the pro-American column. Even Hadj Thami el-Glaoui, the puissant seigneur of the Atlas, pasha of Marrakesh, and close friend of Noguès, was slated as "favorably disposed" to the United States. Among the tribes, the Beni Ouriaghel, resistant to both Spain and France in the Rif war, was targeted as "psychologically prepared for friendship with the Allies." What was decisive in rallying the natives, explained the Office of Strategic Services, was the show of force, the display of power, the manipulation of tribal antagonisms, and the disbursement of "money, loot, and food."[73] In short, regardless of who was suitor and who was being wooed, America was present in Morocco, making up lists of its friends and foes, and ready to play Lyautey if the casting called for it.

Murphy was surprised and embarrassed during his June trip to the protectorate by the anti-French talk among the native troops and Arab leaders in southern Morocco, some of it attributed to Axis action and some to rumors of an American invasion. He was confronted with spontaneous and effusive statements of native support for the United States and had heard of native soldiers refusing to obey their French officers because they knew the Americans were coming. All this infuriated Noguès and was proof positive of what might happen if the Allies attacked.[74] Now the Americans, not the Germans, were candidates for the protectorate's new centurions.

Precisely because pro-American feeling was running high, protectorate officials were more prudent, cautious, and reserved than ever. It was hardly what Murphy or Childs had hoped for, and it placed Noguès in an unhappy but familiar predicament, tamping down spontaneous war spirit, this time with an anti-French flavor. Even worse, as the likelihood of an American attack increased—and Pétain told the Germans he thought it was "inevitable"—Vichy suggested the cooperation of the German army to prevent it. Noguès wanted no part of that.[75]

Noguès chose to sit tight. He "expressed his satisfaction" with Laval as head of government, saying that he was "far better qualified and intelligent than Admiral Darlan" and that he intended to give him his "wholehearted and active cooperation." Laval was "above all a good Frenchman." What figured heavily in Noguès assessment and pledge of fealty was the foreign minister's promise (so members of Noguès's staff whispered to Murphy) that the resident would remain "undisturbed" in Morocco and that there would be no major administrative shifts. Noguès's "tenacious affection" for his spot was part of it, but so was Laval's commitment to a neutral North Africa, which had been so endangered by Darlan's Bizerte projects.[76] Keeping North Africa out of the war and everyone out of North Africa was more necessary than ever in 1942.

This was completely opposite to the American direction. Murphy's talent hunt for the elusive man on a white horse who could rally Africa for the Americans had finally fixed on General Henri Giraud, leader in 1940 of the ill-fated Ninth Army, who was captured by the Germans and incarcerated in the fortress of Königstein-an-der-Elbe. In April 1942 he escaped in Errol Flynn fashion, making his way across southern Germany and into Switzerland. When he surfaced at Vichy and his exploit became known, he was dubbed the first French hero since the armistice. His feat embarrassed Pétain and Laval, who wanted him to return voluntarily to Germany. He refused. Available and ready for action, Giraud, who had fought in the Rif under Lyautey and served with Noguès in the Atlas, agreed to conspire with Murphy to bring North Africa back into the war. As worked out, the plans called for a political and military coup d'etat at the moment of an American landing and Giraud's assumption of the French command in the Maghreb.[77]

Giraud and his confederates were free from the commitments and ignorant of the fears that bound Noguès to Vichy and forced him to keep at arm's distance from the United States. All they wanted to do was fight Germany. Giraud—who turned out to be the least competent political soldier of his day—and Noguès were kilometers apart. To speed the Allied march to Tunisia, Giraud even favored buying off the Spaniards with land in the French protectorate up to the Ouergha River, something that Noguès could never have done or accepted.[78]

What made Murphy's cloak-and-dagger dealings with Giraud more than play acting was the Allied determination to invade North Africa before the year was out. The decision was made official in July and was explained to Murphy in detail when he visited Washington the following month. Eisenhower was named military commander, and Murphy the president's representative charged with the civil and political end of the invasion and occupation. Frankly, Murphy was surprised at the suddenness of the decision and how little time it gave him to make final arrangements. His task was doubly difficult because he was forbidden to reveal the November landing date to his French friends.[79] In the days that followed, he would find himself webbed in conflicting commitments. Through it all he nursed the hope that Vichy's team in North Africa might still join the American side, making the tricky amphibious operation more a marine regatta than a naval assault.

What encouraged him were the discreet contacts made by emissaries of Darlan and Juin in the wake of rumors of an imminent American aggression and talk of German countermeasures. The admiral was now ready to cross to the Allied side and, like Gulliver, pull the fleet behind him if the United States would supply "large-scale" aid. Opportunism, ambition, and grudges pushed him forward. He had been jettisoned in favor of Laval and would now use his rank and command to buy a place for himself aboard the craft of the opposition. Juin too inquired if the Americans would back him if he tried to resist a German invasion from the Libyan-Tunisian border, where Axis troops and aircraft had been massed. Even Noguès was thought to be approachable. Nothing worked out. Darlan broke off communication. Juin turned dumb, then apparently had second thoughts, but it was too late. And Noguès, asked point-blank what his reaction would be to a major American military expedition, exploded: "Do not try that! If you do, I will meet you with all the firepower I possess. It is too late for France to participate in this war now. We will do better to stay out. If Morocco becomes a battlefield, it will be lost to France!"[80]

But America now wanted precisely that—a ground from which to battle the Axis. Gone were the friendly field of economic cooperation and the peaceful observation tower that Weygand and Noguès had once encouraged. America had "gone British." It resolved on military intervention and planned to destroy the protectorate's precarious neutrality. For Noguès bringing Morocco back into the war meant reliving the terrible days of summer 1940 and spring 1941 and facing the horror of a native insurrection against France. Having preserved French control in Morocco despite defeat, dissidence, and Darlan's deals, is it any wonder that when the Americans reached the end of the road, Noguès himself barred their way?

EIGHT

Casablanca and Beyond

The most difficult days of Noguès's residency came in November 1942 when an American task force, unannounced and uninvited, spilled its soldiers on Morocco's beaches. What the general had hoped would not happen had. In accord with the plans for coastal defense, Admiral François Michelier, charged with the security of the Atlantic shore, resisted the invasion, but once the enemy reached the littoral, the command automatically passed to Noguès, who had been given back the military responsibilities denied him since the armistice. He held out for three days and inflicted serious casualties on the Americans, making good on France's word and completing his commitments to Vichy. He later explained that the "solemn promise" made to defend the empire against everyone was the "only way" of preventing the Germans from taking over its defense and of keeping the army intact. It had saved the empire; even more, it had been the "keystone of North Africa's resistance" to the Reich.[1] True or not, Noguès was convinced that he had no choice but to oppose America. An Allied move in Morocco would bring an Axis force to Tunisia, and at the first sign of French complicity in an American landing, Germany would revenge itself on France, unleashing ANTON (the plan for total occupation) to swallow up what was left of the Metropole. What he found inconvenient to remember was that he feared the Americans as much as the Germans. North Africa would fall like dominoes to those who pushed harder, destroying French authority in the Maghreb forever.

As was the case at Oran and Algiers, where Allied invaders also battled ashore, the French were ultimately unequal to their adversaries. At the signal from Algiers, Noguès concluded a second armistice; then, like the leaders of metropolitan France in June 1940, he offered to collaborate with the enemy to salvage what he could of France's prestige and power. This was not to be a full-fledged military partnership but a "benevolent neutrality" similar to the kind of relationship that he and Weygand had wanted Vichy to maintain with Germany in Hitler's war against England. Like the Germans, the Americans encouraged collaboration in Africa because it fit in with their own immediate military plans and far-off political designs. Noguès did not greet America as liberator but as a Goliath to be handled circumspectly until a French David should step forth.

The November invasion was sudden and terrible. Two hours after midnight on the eighth, Noguès was awakened with the news that the Americans would be landing on Morocco's beaches before dawn. General Antoine Béthouart, commander of the Casablanca Division and part of the Giraud conspiracy, explained by letter to Noguès that he had assumed the military command of the protectorate in order to welcome the invading forces. "I would be infinitely grateful if you would give me your support," he wrote. As proof of what was about to happen, Béthouart sent along copies of letters exchanged between Murphy and Giraud containing America's pledges to the general, Giraud's order to aid the Americans, and a sketch of the military intervention in North Africa. Thunderstruck, Noguès dismissed them as unauthentic and incredible given what he knew of the state of the American war effort and maritime transport and the hazards of amphibious operations, which were considered impossible in winter along the Atlantic coast. Convinced that Béthouart had been the victim of a hoax and outraged at having been unceremoniously deposed, Noguès prepared to recover the authority that was being stripped from him. By violating the orders to oppose an invasion from whatever quarter, Béthouart not only threatened to upset the delicate Franco-German balance but also to imperil the internal security of the protectorate. Noguès's first thought was for the reaction of the native population. But his overriding concern was for what Germany might do. If the Allies landed unopposed, he imagined that "the Germans would arrive instantly."[2]

Béthouart's troops sealed off the Residency and cut the telephone lines, but Noguès was not taken into custody. Using a secret line to naval headquarters, Noguès informed Michelier of his plight and discovered that the admiral knew what was going on. He had concluded independently that the Béthouart documents "merited no consideration whatsoever." The whole thing was just a bad joke. Based on information from the admiralty and his own coastal surveillance stations, the admiral assured Noguès that there was "no indication of any foreign presence [or] foreign warships off the Moroccan coast."[3]

Nevertheless, Noguès ordered an alert in all the defense sectors, asked the admiralty what General Juin in Algiers was doing about the invasion alarm, and contacted the military commanders at Meknès and Marrakesh to countermand Béthouart's orders and direct the suppression of the "military mutiny." Meanwhile, Michelier had checked once more and reported that "there were no Americans on the ocean." "If there is something there," he ventured, "it can only be a commando group." But he called back within the half hour to notify Noguès that the Americans had in fact attacked Algiers and later to say that Oran was under siege as well. Darlan (trapped in Algiers while visiting his hospitalized son) and Juin were showing their fists rather than opening their arms, defending North Africa against the Allied invaders. When asked a third time about an American armada off Morocco, Michelier replied that there was "not a single ship within 100 kilometers of the Moroccan coast."[4]

Noguès finally reached Béthouart by phone, accused him of rebellion, and warned that he would be responsible for civil war if the dissidence should continue. Béthouart had expected the Allies off Rabat two hours after midnight. There was still no sign of them. Unwilling to hold out any longer and bear the burden of fratricidal fighting, he surrendered, repentent and confused. Shocked at Béthouart's disobedience and the scope of the armed revolt, Noguès bundled him off to the military prison at Meknès.[5]

Amid the confusion of the attempted coup and its suppression, the American vice-consul at Rabat came to the Residency carrying a letter from President Roosevelt officially announcing the landings in Morocco. Noguès had him sent away. When Noguès called Michelier to report the contact and to say that he had refused the "ultimatum," he learned of the attack on Safi, south of Casablanca. "We will resist with all our forces and with all the means at our disposal," he told the admiral. As he talked, the first American bombs fell on the Rabat airstrip within three hundred meters of the sultan's palace. The Americans were attacking all along the coast "by surprise and very brutally."[6]

Despite the signs of an invasion, Noguès was caught off guard. The rumor was that the Americans would land under the guise of responding to an appeal by the sultan. Noguès took it seriously. On Darlan's visit to Rabat at the end of October, the sultan was asked to reiterate publicly his fealty to Pétain and the French state, and at the ceremonies for the admiral at Fez, Noguès made it clear that he would repel any invader: "Whoever counts on a pleasant welcome here is in for a cruel disappointment."[7] But he really did not believe that an American operation could come before spring 1943. Before then the most that could happen would be another raid on Dakar. Reinforcements to meet this threat had already been sent from Morocco to West Africa, and the troops that bolstered Morocco's shoreline defenses in summer had been sent to winter barracks at Meknès, Fez, and Taza.[8]

This was certainly why Darlan wired the admiralty that he did not think "a deliberate assault on French territory was presently planned by the Anglo-Saxons" when he was informed of the convoys passing Gibraltar. Rather, he imagined that the ships were headed for action against the Germans in Libya. To be on the safe side, the admiralty cautioned Michelier to be "particularly attentive and vigilant" to any Allied threat. But up until the end, the admiral remained unconvinced that he would soon be under attack.[9]

The sighted convoys were in fact bound for Algiers and Oran. Landings there were to be followed up by a rapid land march to Tunisia and a hoped-for link with the British in Libya. Later trans-Mediterranean strikes would batter the southern gates of Axis Europe, the so-called peripheral strategy for the liberation of the continent. Arrayed against Morocco were the unseen ships of the Western Task Force—over one hundred in number and carrying a fighting force of thirty-three thousand men—under the command of General George S. Patton, Jr., whose mission was to capture Casablanca and secure communications between that city and Oran. To avoid a costly frontal assault and spare the important port facilities from damage, the plan was to land north and south of Casablanca at points from which the American forces could advance overland to their target. The main infantry attack was to be at Fedala, northeast of Casablanca, with a second landing at Mehdia–Port Lyautey, 60 miles farther north; the third debarkation site was at Safi, 140 miles south of Casablanca.[10]

The invaders anticipated a hostile reception, although it was hoped that the French would have little stomach for the fray and quit the fight when they realized that the odds were against them. The negotiations with Giraud were also counted on to have some effect, at the very least to cause disorder among the French forces; this is precisely what the Béthouart "rebellion" did in Morocco. True to character, Patton wanted the French to resist, for his troops needed "blooding" and, as he confided to his diary, it would be better for his "future prospects."[11]

Michelier and Noguès did not disappoint him. Everywhere the French obliged with first fire. American troops wading ashore before daylight at Safi were met by an artillery and machine-gun barrage. The Fedala greeting was equally inhospitable, with Casablanca's defense forces joining the battle at sunrise. Nevertheless, American superiority in the air and at sea was decisive. By evening Safi and

Fedala were in enemy hands and at Casablanca one lone shore battery remained in operation. The landing at Mehdia–Port Lyautey encountered the most trouble. Confusion and poor communications, coupled with stiff French resistance, jeopardized the entire operation. Hours after the successful landings at Fedala and Safi, the Port Lyautey group was still struggling to secure firm footholds on unfamiliar beaches. The French made the most of their adversaries' predicament, counterattacking on the afternoon of 8 November and rushing reinforcements to the area from Rabat, Fez, and Meknès. The battle for the Port Lyautey airstrip continued all day on 9 November with seesaw attacks and counterattacks. It finally turned in the Americans' favor on the morning of 10 November, but all resistance was not ended until late in the afternoon.[12]

Once Noguès was in full command of Morocco's defenses, he telegraphed Vichy that although the fight ahead looked tough, both Frenchmen and Moroccans were prepared to make the "necessary sacrifices" to maintain Morocco's integrity. He reported that he had lost what aircraft he had to Allied bombardments of his airfields and called for reinforcements from West Africa or France. He moved his headquarters from Rabat to Fez on 9 November and adopted a coastal containment strategy to block the enemy advance along interior roads and ordered reserve units to assemble at Petitjean and Khémisset (from Fez and Taza) to close the main route to Fez and Oran and at Marrakesh (from Agadir) to seal the way to the south. Wherever possible, the French went on the offensive to try to halt the Americans' forward movement or to divert them from Casablanca. At Safi and Fedala, counterattacks were brushed back by the Americans and French troop reinforcement frustrated. But at Port Lyautey, the French almost succeeded in driving the Americans into the sea. Even an account sympathetic to the Americans concluded that their situation after the first day's action was "insecure and even precarious."[13]

Unlike the troubles in Morocco, the landings at Algiers proceeded without a hitch. A successful pro-Allied military putsch and a civilian coup d'etat captured the city, squelching any possibility of resistance.[14] The only sensible course for Darlan was to make the best deal he could with the Americans, who were eager to negotiate a suspension of arms for all North Africa, particularly since neither Giraud's name nor his person had been able to work any magic at all. Darlan was thus placed in an enviable spot: even though he had been defeated, he was still offered his former command if he would only cooperate. Characteristically, he hedged, apparently unsure which way to turn, and claimed that his every order needed Pétain's approval. He did authorize a cease fire for the city of Algiers but told Pétain that his plan was not to negotiate with the Americans, only "to listen and report back." He had already split the North African command, giving Noguès authority over the Oran region of Algeria so that resistance might continue. (On the morning of 9 November, Noguès was also given command of the troops of the Algiers Division—those not included in the city armistice—which extended his authority to Constantine and the southern territories.) He also wired Resident General Pierre Estéva in Tunisia and the military commanders at Bizerte that since the Americans had invaded North Africa first, they were the "adversaries" and "we should fight them alone or with assistance," leaving the door ajar to a German partnership at the very place where he had been stymied in the past.[15]

As for Noguès, although pressed by the Americans and some of his own staff to seek a truce, he refused. "I did not have the right," he asserted, "to give the cease-fire order before having the authorization of my superior at Algiers or my superior at Vichy." In other words, he would not break with the strict discipline of the chain of command. The reflex was understandable. His one move toward disobedience in 1940 had caused him great personal anguish and endless political difficulties, and almost cost him his job. In addition, he foresaw dire military and political consequences if he acted on his own. What would happen to France and the army if he parlayed without authorization? "Above all, I had to maintain the unity of the army and its connection with France not only in Germany's presence but also in the presence of the United States, thereby preserving France's prestige with the Moroccans at this grave moment." As always, Morocco dominated his thoughts. There was nothing to gain in an unauthorized truce, much to lose. Even in a deteriorating military situation, he could at least hope to strengthen the bargaining hand of Darlan and Juin at Algiers.[16]

Throughout the day of 10 November, Noguès's strategy remained the same: to impede the American advance while seeking instructions from Algiers or Vichy. But there was no doubt of the outcome. "Given the crushing imbalance of troops, it became impossible to oppose the occupation of the country. Moreover, the Allies possessed sufficient forces to hold on to Africa." The Americans were in North Africa to stay. He wrote the battle's epitaph: "We had kept our word." Now, however, he was ready for a cease-fire and quickly. He dispatched an envoy to Pétain to report that the military and political situation was "serious." French resistance had been reduced to "sacrificial missions" and the fighting men seemed to have no heart for the combat. Some junior officers even offered to guide the American march on Casablanca to hurry the end of hostilities. Noguès delicately confirmed all this to Pétain by recording that the troops were fighting "magnificently" but "without enthusiasm." "Their feelings would have been very different had the aggressors been English." Moreover, the civilian population wanted a swift conclusion to the fight, fearing that its continuation would "compromise the country's future." Despite the gloomy picture, Noguès let the facts speak for themselves and held back a written recommendation. It was for Pétain to determine what was in France's interest and how Morocco might best be preserved. "As long as I am at the helm, your orders, which are those of France, will be obeyed." Privately, however, Noguès had told his envoy to urge Pétain to authorize a cease-fire "to save Africa."[17]

Darlan finally did the deed in the marshal's name. But word of the cease-fire passed slowly. Noguès heard it third hand, and although he immediately told his commanders to avoid all clashes with the enemy, given the "gravity" of the message, he waited until he had the official communication directly from Juin before he halted the fire. Only then did he ask Patton for a meeting to discuss terms. Michelier, on the other hand, fussed about accepting the order in any form, for he figured that Darlan was now a prisoner of the Americans with a Colt .45 at his head. He cabled Vichy for instructions and was told to battle on "as long as possible." But further resistance was futile. At long last the admiral gave up, telling Vichy that he had held out as long as he could and was now following in Noguès's footsteps, the best way to cover his own tracks.[18]

Although the guns were silent, the political chatter over the cease-fire continued. As Michelier had rightly suspected, Darlan's order had been extracted under pressure. Eisenhower's deputy, General Mark W. Clark, had told Darlan that if he refused to issue the order, he would have Giraud do it. Tired of the endless checking and doublechecking with Vichy, Clark was prepared to dump the North African regulars and take a chance with the rebels. Under this threat, the admiral caved in, wrote out the order, and relayed it to Vichy. Pétain answered by repudiating both the order and its author. "I gave the order to resist the invader. I maintain this order." He named Noguès his "sole representative" in North Africa. At the worst possible moment, Noguès was given the rank and the authority of a Weygand. Humiliated, Darlan tried to retract his order, but Clark would not have it. The on-again, off-again writ was kept in force.[19]

By the time Noguès learned of his appointment and the situation in Algiers, he had already agreed to the cease-fire. He apologized to Vichy that he had acted in the belief that Darlan had spoken for Pétain, implying that had he known Pétain's true wishes, he would have continued to fight. He could not have wanted that. Fortunately for Noguès, what was done was done. He reported that he would be meeting with the Americans at Fedala on the afternoon of 11 November, the anniversary of that other, happier armistice when the French and the Americans had been on the same side of the table.[20]

For resisting the Americans and in consequence aiding the German invasion of Tunisia, Noguès was later condemned by the Haute Cour de Justice to twenty years of hard labor, "national degradation for life," and the confiscation of all his wealth and property. He was never imprisoned, for he went into exile in Portugal in 1943 and remained there until 1954, when he returned to France and requested a retrial. Tempers had cooled by then and the burning issue of the day was no longer collaboration but decolonization. In the changed circumstances, Noguès was remembered as the link with Lyautey, the counselor of Sidi Mohammed ben Youssef, the preserver of France in Morocco. The press was sympathetic to the efforts of a broken old man to clear his name. Even so, the government prosecutor was unbending, the verdict ambiguous. The court imposed a penalty of "national degradation," which it immediately lifted in consideration of Noguès's understandable concern for the German reaction to an American landing and because he had built up secret military forces "capable of contributing to the national resurrection," for use on that day, as Noguès had told Weygand in 1941, when Germany would break its promises.[21]

During the trial, Noguès's lawyer argued that once the resident realized that the American attack was more than a commando raid, his resistance was just "a clever pretence, an extraordinarily astute game" designed to prevent massive German intervention in North Africa and reprisals on metropolitan France. (At the time, German Foreign Minister von Ribbentrop had actually called it a "vast deception.") He noted that Noguès repeatedly refused the offer of German air support, even threatening that French antiaircraft batteries would fire on German planes should they attempt to join the battle. The resident warned Vichy that German intervention would have "a very bad effect on the spirit of the army and on the European and native populations," and perhaps lead to "important defections" among the troops. Instead, he requested aircraft from Dakar; General Augustin LaHoulle, commander of Morocco's air fleet, testified that Noguès knew they could never arrive in time to fly against the Americans. In addition, he forbade counterattacks at Port Lyautey, Casablanca, and Safi; and his area commanders swore that he had ordered them not to be aggressive. Furthermore, on his withdrawal to Fez to organize the defense of the interior, he left the sultan and his ministers, the protectorate administration, and most of the general staff at Rabat and Casablanca. Taken together—so said the counsel for the defense, André Viénot—this would have been "a serious imprudence" if Noguès had really wanted to hold out to the bitter end.[22] Whether gamesmanship or stubborn resistance to an unwelcome guest, the court was convinced that Noguès was constantly checking on Germany over his shoulder. Shooting at Americans had been necessary to keep Frenchmen from becoming German targets.

Testifying on his own behalf, Noguès insisted that he had not wanted to fight the Allies at all. Had he been informed in advance of an invasion in strength, he would have greeted the Americans enthusiastically. Witness after witness vouched for Noguès's pro-American, anti-German sentiments, including the top American diplomatic officer in Morocco, James Rives Childs, who blamed himself for not having pressed Washington to send a soldier of general rank or a senior foreign service officer to brief Noguès immediately prior to the landings. Childs said it was "the greatest mistake" of his career. Had Noguès been warned, he speculated, "the most he might have done would have been to offer a purely token resistance." But Childs himself admitted that the resident had never "held out the least promise that we might count upon the unopposed reception of Allied troops in Morocco; on the contrary, he many times emphasized that it was his intention to defend Morocco from attack from whatever source it might emanate." Given what Childs had to go on, it is hard to accept his self-criticism as anything but a misplaced mea culpa. To be sure, it is impossible to know what Noguès would have done in the face of a certain significant American intervention, but it is unlikely that it would have changed his initial reaction. In addition to the worrisome German factor, there was the question of the protectorate. By attacking, America was not only exposing Morocco to the vicissitudes of war once again but to the possibility of internal revolt. Noguès could never have welcomed the Americans with ease. Fourteen years after the events, he took pains to point out to the court that American and French interests were not one and the same. The Americans had come with "pretensions that we could not accept."[23]

What Noguès meant was made crystal clear in his first meeting with Patton. After an exchange of pleasantries, he was handed terms that were "more severe" than those of the 1940 Franco-German armistice. When added up, they established an American military government in the protectorate. To Noguès they were "absolutely unacceptable." He protested furiously, arguing that they were tougher than those imposed on Darlan at Algiers, in violation of Morocco's international statute, and would spark a native revolt. If the latter occurred, the responsibility for restoring order would be placed on American shoulders.[24] It must have been a virtuoso performance, for Patton and his staff were impressed. Patton was persuaded rightly or wrongly that the French had not really wanted to fight. In addition, he wanted nothing at all to do with an "Arab uprising." He concurred with Noguès's conclusion that discrediting France would serve no useful purpose, particularly since the French seemed ready to aid the Allied cause. "Had I insisted on disarming the army and removing the navy from the ships and shore batteries," he explained to Eisenhower, "I would have dealt such a blow to the prestige of the French that I am personally convinced a revolution would have eventuated." In sum, Patton decided for collaboration based on no more than the "age-old friendship between France and America." He tore up the draft armistice and shook hands on a "gentleman's agreement" with terms similar to those in force at Algiers. The French were to retain their arms and control of Morocco. "I realize that I am taking a chance," Patton admitted, "but feel convinced that the end justifies the means. We do not wish to occupy this country and pacify it."[25] These were Noguès's words translated into English.

Patton was taken to task for having been conned by the smooth-tongued resident. Perhaps he was. It can be argued that the choice was not between "Noguès or chaos," not between working with the Vichy French or ousting the French from Morocco. The issue was the replacement of Vichy's North African team with "a reputable group of French patriots who were untainted by collaboration with the Nazis and fully committed to the Allied cause, and who now waited in the wings to take over." But Patton was worried about the safety and strength of his troops, the attitude of the Spanish, the retaliatory power of the Germans, and his future military role in the North African campaign. His thoughts were on who would win the war in Africa and Europe, not on who would govern in Morocco. He thought it to be "the height of inexpediency to get mixed up in politics."[26] This was the American attitude everywhere. The official army historian wrote: "The past political sympathies of officeholders were to be treated as of small significance compared with their ability to discharge the technical duties of their respective positions." The verdict on Noguès was: "For lack of a substitute, General Noguès was more necessary to the Americans than those who protested against his retention."[27] It should come as no surprise. Working with Vichy hierarchs was part of the American strategy in French Africa, an extension of the gamble on Vichy begun in 1940.

Although Patton was impressed with the French military style and the "colonial razzle-dazzle," he was never hopelessly beguiled by Noguès. After meeting with the resident, he wrote home: "Noguès is a crook—a handsome one." He repeated this crude assessment, which was not without a trace of admiration, to Eisenhower. He knew that Noguès's pleas to leave the French command intact were merely the opportunistic prattle of a man in a tight spot. With the enemy inside his gates, he was forced to make amends to hold on to as much as he could. But for the time being, Noguès's expertise and the French willingness to cooperate "heartily, promptly, and loyally" served Allied interests. "I realize," wrote Patton, "that some of them, perhaps all of them, are serving their own ends, but nevertheless they are doing so in a manner to facilitate our operations, which is really the only point of importance."[28]

Moreover, the surprises and mysteries of Morocco were less disconcerting with the French as go-betweens, interpreters, and guides. American soldiers had been led to expect a dignified, aristocratic native population—the "First Families of Virginia in bathrobes," as Samuel Eliot Morison put it—but on the beaches they met beggars, thieves, and pimps, a jolt to their handbook introduction to the sharifian empire. Patton's advisers knew that the native scene could be bewildering. "Throughout the entire complex native pattern of friendly, semi-friendly, and potentially hostile tribes of Arab, Berber, and Arabized Berber collectivities of city, plain, and mountain, their caids and pashas, their individual peculiarities, their local customs, their deep-seated xenophobia, continuous control and a very sure touch is essential. Noguès has it!" The resident bore "watching," but he knew "his Morocco, his Arabs, his Sultan, and his job."[29]

For Noguès what counted was that French sovereignty had been respected and the civil and military structure maintained "in such a way that the Muslim populations . . . have the impression that nothing has changed."[30] What is more, Giraud and the rebels had been pushed aside in favor of the Vichy command. At first Noguès gave less than complete cooperation to the Americans. He continued to consider them interlopers. He told Pétain (in a message that was sure to be read by the Germans) that any resumption of hostilities was out of the question since he had no way of mounting "any useful resistance" and in any event renewed warfare would only lose the advantages already obtained. But under the "pretext" of making way for American forces, he withdrew his troops from the coast to the interior for employment as a "means of pressure" against them. And he wanted the troops loyal to Giraud to be separated out of the forces pledged to Pétain, so that only the former would actually fight alongside the Americans in the anti-German drive into Tunisia.[31] In this way he implemented the "strict neutrality" formula that had been written into the Algiers cease-fire agreement and that remained at the core of his North African policy. Patton was aware that Noguès, caught between the Americans and the Germans and still faithful to Vichy, had no real desire to come out strongly for the Allied cause. The Germans were not yet down and out in North Africa. "General Noguès's adherents are of the opinion that the Germans will soon run us out of Morocco," Patton explained, "and that they therefore do not wish to commit themselves."[32]

In the days that followed the armistice, Noguès participated in the adjustments to the French command caused by the appearance of Giraud, who had been promised the top spot in North Africa. Yet Darlan commanded the obedience of both the civil administration and the military. "You can see I now have two Kingpins. . . ," Clark wired Eisenhower at Gibraltar, "but hope to wiggle out of it somehow." In the end, Darlan and Giraud agreed to share power, the former handling political affairs, the latter military matters. But nothing could be final until Noguès, still the marshal's annointed representative, could bless the union. Even Juin, who had taken it upon himself to order French forces in Tunisia to resist the German airlift and who seemed about to strike out on his own, wanted Noguès's hands on his head. Before coming to Algiers, Noguès had decided to surrender his power to Darlan to shore up the Vichy side. To keep Darlan in disgrace, Noguès argued to Pétain, "would greatly diminish our authority vis-à-vis the Americans and risk compromising the results already obtained." All Clark wanted was a quick settlement of the leadership issue that had taken up too much of his time. "It is absolutely essential that we get an established leadership here without further delay. I have played along in hope of getting the fleet and knowing that Darlan could issue orders." He hoped that

Noguès would readily consent to the Darlan-Giraud combination. But if not, he proposed to arrest the "uncooperatives" and enthrone Giraud as the "supreme authority" in North Africa.[33]

When Noguès appeared in Algiers on the afternoon of 12 November, he made things more difficult, not easier. He wanted nothing to do with Giraud, treating him as a traitor and rebel. When Giraud denied that he had ordered French officers like Béthouart to disobey their superiors, Noguès spit out: "You are a coward and a liar." But faced with Clark's threat to impose a military government if the French could not compose their differences, Noguès reconciled himself to working with the "dissident" general. After hard conversations, a new arrangement emerged. In this scheme Darlan would lead North Africa and Giraud, apparently alone eager for combat with the Germans, would be given the command of a volunteer force recruited to serve with the Allies. Everyone else would remain in place. Shortly after midnight, Noguès reported to Pétain that the "agreement in principle" maintained "the present military, political, and administrative structure" and denied Giraud the post of commander-in-chief promised by the Americans. Insulting as this would later appear, Giraud—ever the soldier—accepted his demotion and banishment to the battlefield with the men loyal to him weeded out of the North African command. As for the regular army, Noguès, still committed to keeping North Africa out of the war, stuck to the notion of "benevolent neutrality."[34] These troops would have as their sole mission the defense of North Africa, in particular the northern Moroccan frontier. That was not easy to do. He recognized the growing pro-American sentiment in the army and among the French and native population. Even Giraud's star was shining a bit brighter. It frightened him. "It is essential to keep North Africa united under the marshal's authority and not under that of the dissidents, thereby holding the present structure in place so as not to upset the natives and encourage them to seek protection elsewhere." But with or without the marshal's badge, Noguès was no longer in charge. "In truth," he admitted, "this is a real occupation against which we are powerless."[35]

The agreement among the French did not stick. According to Noguès, Giraud reconsidered his lot and on the morning of the thirteenth refused it, demanding instead the leadership of North Africa, as he had been promised. Frankly, the Americans would not have permitted the total eclipse of the man they had chosen to rally the Maghreb. This time, however, he was sustained by a group of army officers, among them Juin, who, now willing to fight the Germans and to serve under Giraud, rejected Noguès's neutrality as timid and demeaning.[36] In this Juin showed the courage and common sense that would mark his later career and win him a marshal's baton. Noguès backed down. But he persuaded Clark and Giraud to keep Darlan at the helm, emphasizing the admiral's usefulness and the need for continuity. Giraud was given command of the armed forces, although it was decided on Noguès's recommendation to delay the announcement because of the adverse effect that Noguès said it might have on the army and public opinion. All this was confirmed by Eisenhower and duly proclaimed in a statement, as carefully phrased as a finely worded act of succession, that established Darlan's right to rule.[37] Once again Pétain denied Darlan. "You should have defended North Africa against American aggression. The decision you have taken in violation of my orders is contrary to the mission that you were given. I order the Army of Africa not to act against the forces of the Axis under any circumstances and not to add to the misfortunes of the country."[38] By that time Pétain's words no longer counted. Once the Germans invaded unoccupied France (as they had done on 11 November), the marshal was considered a prisoner in his own house. Regardless of what he said, Darlan would govern in his name.

The new Darlan government, styled the Haut Commissariat de France en Afrique Française, explained the November events with surprising candor, if not complete accuracy. The Anglo-American landing had been resisted "with all the vigor and heroism" expected of troops following their orders to the letter. But because they were outnumbered and without sufficient materiel (recalling Pétain's lament of 1940), they could not hold. Once it was determined that the landing was in such strength as to rule out any Axis reprisals (at least in the Maghreb), there was no need to, for the Allies had proclaimed that they would restore France and its empire to its prewar greatness, and the United States had put it in writing to Giraud. Knowing this, Noguès ended a resistance that had become "both sterile and purposeless." Through it all, the Vichy chain of command remained unsevered. Although publicly disavowed by Pétain, Darlan claimed to be the true interpreter of his thought by virtue of his rank and his nearness to the marshal—his named successor, his "first lieutenant." The orders he now gave were "to fight alongside the Americans and their allies for the defense and liberation of our territories and the integral restoration of French sovereignty."[39]

Right: General Henri Giraud, commander-in-chief
of French forces in North Africa. Rabat, December 1942.
Photo Jacques Belin

Given the circumstances—Americans at Algiers, Germans at Marseilles, the fleet at the bottom of Toulon harbor, the metropolitan
armistice army disbanded—it was a good bargain.

"We are now wholly with you," Noguès told Childs when he returned to Rabat, revealing that for a while he had only been half
there. He meant what he said, but despite all the public pronounce-
ments of Franco-American friendship, he could never be trusted.
Eisenhower tagged him the "sail-trimmer" who "now believes that
his best interests parallel ours. His protestations of cooperative intent are most emphatic, but he is unquestionably 'slick.'" After
Darlan was assassinated in Algiers on Christmas Eve and the French

once again clamored for Noguès (for he was Darlan's designated replacement), Clark did not even want to let him know that the admiral was dead, much less bring him to Algiers. He had been through all of that once before. Eisenhower's reaction was the same. He specified that Noguès was not even to be considered for the succession; Giraud was the "only possibility."[40] With Giraud back on the white horse, American apprehensions about the faithfulness of their North African allies eased.

The Americans had a strong impact on Morocco. Patton gleefully reported on his meetings with the sultan, which he handled with panache and tact, careful not to upstage the French, yet eager to stake out a claim on Moroccan affections. "My relations with the Sultan have also been very friendly and I believe that he is wholly on our side." More than once Moroccan notables approached him to "talk politics," not unlike the experiences of Murphy before the landings. He enjoyed the attention and watching the French squirm at such encounters. At public ceremonies his reception was overwhelming: "Driving back from the review, I had a regular ovation. It is quite thrilling to have about a hundred thousand people cheering, yelling, and clapping and shouting 'Vive l'Amérique.' I kissed my hands to them which had the effect of arousing them still more. Even some of the veiled women waved at me which is quite unusual and I believe immoral. I feel that if the worst comes I shall run for sultan." Basing his opinion on the public cheers and private chats, he concluded: "You could get up a revolution here for a dollar." However, he understood the limits of his popularity. "The French have lost face and the Arabs are all for us—as long as we are winning."[41] There is little mystery why Noguès found it so hard to express genuine enthusiasm over the American accomplishment. Even the grand vizier, France's faithful ally for three decades, moaned about his imminent demise, for that might come to pass if the Americans set up their own protectorate.[42]

On the other hand, Noguès's enemies worried that he was cooperating too well and too closely with the Americans. Both the British and the Gaullists, who found it hard to work with men who had fought them every step of the way since 1940, railed against Noguès's power in the protectorate. Britain's man in Algiers, Harold Macmillan, saw Noguès as totally unsympathetic and, worse, a double-dealer who bad-mouthed the Americans to the British, then belittled the British to the Americans. He told Churchill that it was a "monstrous thing" the way Patton had been taken in by Noguès and how little concern the American commander showed for the way Noguès

Right foreground: General George S. Patton, Jr.,
American military commander in Morocco. Rabat, January 1943.
Photo Jacques Belin

treated the friends of Britain and America.[43] It was true that Noguès
was reluctant to open his arms or his jails. Béthouart was released
only at American insistence. At the March meetings of the Comité
de Guerre, chaired by Giraud, Gaullism and "Gaullist propaganda"
were still being discussed as problems to be resolved.[44] The American invasion had not erased the bitter memories of the British at
Mers-el-Kebir or the Anglo-Gaullists at Dakar and Damascus.

From British and Gaullist sources Casablanca took on the sinister
character of the city depicted in the 1942 American film, alive with
Axis plots and governed by Hitler's henchmen. Patton was particularly annoyed when Clark rushed to Casablanca in mid-December to
track down a story that Noguès and his "pro-German staff" were
sabotaging the war effort. He confided to his diary: "I am convinced
of the loyalty of the French and only wish others in high places
would be less impressed by half-baked rumors from irresponsible
persons."[45] The charges were frivolous. But even Childs, who was
partial to Noguès, was taken in, distressed at finding "little quis-
lings," who before the landings had been "in league with notori-

ous German agents in Tangier," quoted in the Moroccan press. On firmer ground, he noted the "unaccountable passiveness" on the part of Moroccan officials to prosecute the war. Here the habit of staying on the sidelines was hard to break. In his dispatches to Washington, Childs revealed the frustrations and fears of those who had expected an Allied invasion to end Vichy control but witnessed instead its further entrenchment "with the consent of the American authorities." This was the unavoidable effect of the deals with Noguès and Darlan, the latter made firm in the Clark-Darlan agreement of 22 November, which enshrined the political and ideological status quo.[46]

Guided by Clark's prose and Patton's praise, Noguès assumed that Morocco's internal affairs were of complete indifference to the Americans and he governed accordingly. Even so, the changes in the protectorate were enormous. Morocco was now open again to the markets of the world, and no one, least of all Noguès, could regret that. Moreover, lend-lease from America promised to supply the goods and military equipment that the French counted on to recapture their influence with the native population.[47] Under the Haut Commissariat, Morocco had more attributes of an independent government than ever in the past. Noguès said it was simply a return to the prewar system, which had permitted "great initiative" on the part of overseas administrators. But it was rather a North African federalism, different from either the colonial centralization of the Third Republic or the tight control of Vichy.[48] Without the Americans, it might have come close to Lyautey's *beau idéal*. Yet French authority depended upon American arms, and Noguès was eager to get some firm commitment on politics not only to bolster France in Morocco but also to increase the influence of the Vichy contingent in the contests for power in the empire and later at the liberation of the Metropole.[49] Patton would have none of it, saying that politics could wait until the war was over. Roosevelt felt the same way: he characterized the link with Vichy (through the person of Admiral Darlan) as a "temporary expedient" and repudiated Murphy's agreement with Giraud, which guaranteed the integral restoration of France and its empire as of 1939 and which Darlan and Noguès counted as part of their dowry.[50] At the same time, the president hinted broadly to Sidi Mohammed during the Casablanca Conference in January 1943 (in which Noguès had only the smallest part) that America desired greater independence for Morocco and much tighter American-Moroccan trade relations.[51] It was all precisely as Noguès feared. While Juin and Giraud battled the Germans, he was left behind the lines to fight the Americans to preserve North Africa intact and under French dominion. This time, however, he wore not France's flowing cape but Vichy's fraying mantle.[52]

It was Vichy, not the empire, that unraveled. De Gaulle's price for the union with Giraud, earnestly desired by both the British and the Americans, included the purge of Giraud's North African team, the "psychological shock" to split the Vichy past from the Free French future. Noguès led the list of those to be removed.[53] At first Giraud balked. But the increasingly vociferous public support for de Gaulle in America and Britain was hard to resist. Noguès argued that Gaullist progress in North Africa was nothing more than "clever propaganda" designed to make Giraud concede to his rival for political leadership. He counseled the general to stiffen his position and force de Gaulle to come around. "The marching wing of Gaullism is made up of extremists for whom disorder in the streets is considered the surest way of pressuring those in power, and they will not hesitate to use it." He assured Giraud that in Morocco and West Africa he could count on the Muslim population, on the army, and on the great majority of the French population. "You have 400,000 soldiers behind you and a population almost as numerous as that of the Metropole." Counting noses did not work, nor did Noguès's direct appeal to Roosevelt, sent along with an album of Moroccan stamps for the president's collection. Those who surrounded de Gaulle he labeled "professional politicians and propagandists" who were upsetting the native populace and had but one aim, "to organize a government in Africa in order to impose it afterwards on France," precisely what Roosevelt was determined to prevent.[54] Noguès's moves failed to checkmate de Gaulle, and he was soon reduced to making overtures to Gaullist emissaries, all of which were rebuffed.[55] The axe fell on 3 June, day one of the Comité Français de la Libération Nationale that brought de Gaulle and Giraud together at last. Giraud delivered the blow: "Ever since the start of our interviews and conferences, General de Gaulle's attack against you was more ferocious than against anyone else. You can guess his arguments. General Georges and I have defended you as best we could. This morning in committee a vote was taken and we were beaten. I must ask for your resignation as resident general of Morocco."[56]

What Noguès had helped to preserve did not slip into the American pocket but into the hands of other Frenchmen just as committed to the perpetuation of the empire. "Men leave," he said at his farewell, "France and Morocco remain."[57] At that moment, it was a wish, not a statement of fact. But it came true. In part it was because, despite the sleepless nights America gave the protectorate's leaders, the United States did nothing to break French control. Colonial liberation, which might have worked to America's economic and political advantage, would have weakened France in Europe, where it was counted on as America's partner in continental reconstruction and defense. In short, the global alignments of the postwar world took precedence over the principles of the Atlantic Charter and the Four Freedoms.[58] It was nothing new. During the Great War Wilson's words had captured the imagination of Europe's peoples, but the texts of treaties determined their fate.

Noguès's successor was Gabriel Puaux, the former high commissioner of Syria and Lebanon who had followed Noguès in obedience to Vichy in 1940, then later resigned. He was seconded by Léon Marchal, a Noguès stalwart until April 1942. This was scarcely the triumph of the "pure and the hard." Outside of a few men at the top, the Gaullist broom raised little dust. Within four years, General Alphonse Juin, then General Augustin Guillaume, both Noguès men, would be called to Morocco as France's resident general, much as Noguès had been in 1936, to work the mentor's magic in a changed and troubled sharifian empire. Both failed. By then the Americans had gone and the native nationalists had resumed their feud with the protectorate. They were emboldened by the open support of the sultan, himself encouraged by the events and outcome of the war.[59]

The sultan's switch was neither surprising nor unexpected. He had always been both collaborator and resister of the French, depending on the circumstances. The task of every resident, and Noguès's main effort, had been to keep him on France's side. "What is most important," Noguès reminded Guillaume, "is that the protectorate can only operate in agreement with the sultan, and not against him."[60] Noguès had not always found that easy to do, and Juin and Guillaume would find it impossible because Sidi Mohammed wanted Franco-Moroccan relations set on foundations other than those of the Treaty of Fez. Once this formula—the sultan and resident working as a team—was discarded, the protectorate was doomed. The exile of Sidi Mohammed to Madagascar and his replacement by a pro-French puppet was the sign of defeat, not victory. It brought back the tumultuous days of the Berber *dahir*, which had stretched into months made violent by acts of native terror and French counterterror. In 1930 the faithful had pleaded not to be separated from their Berber brethren; now they prayed in the name of their absent spiritual commander. They would not be put off—not by men or money, not by promises or reforms. In the end, France agreed to the sultan's restoration, the prelude to terminating the protectorate.[61]

After full sovereignty and independence came to Morocco in March 1956, the sentiment against France made Lyautey's tomb an unwanted reminder of the colonial past. The marshal's body was returned to France to lie close to Foch and Napoleon in Les Invalides. Fifteen years later, King Hassan II, the prince who had once trailed after Noguès through the corridors of the Residency and sat at his side during so many ceremonies, remembered his father's friend who had tried to serve France and Morocco at the same time. Morocco's funeral tribute to Noguès, a delegation headed by Morocco's ambassador to Paris, was in stark contrast to the absence of official France. In honoring Lyautey's disciple, the one who had assimilated and applied the marshal's lessons "on the highest level," Hassan saluted Lyautey and France one final time.[62]

NINE

The Lyautey Legacy

By naming General Charles Noguès to the Residency at Rabat, France reestablished the Lyautey line in Morocco. From 1936 until 1943, he provided the protectorate and French colonial policy with purpose and authority, and restored the Lyautey priorities to what he considered their rightful rank.

From the first, Noguès gave precedence to native affairs, which had been neglected by Lyautey's successors. He revived the entente with the sultan and firmed up the governing partnership with the native elite. To the anxious and disgruntled nationalist bourgeoisie he promised political and economic reform, and he inaugurated an ambitious program of urban and rural improvement to win friends for France among the artisans and tribesmen. Everywhere he counted on good works and prosperity to keep the peace and to preserve France's stake in Morocco.

The Noguès strategy had its limitations and contradictions. Strengthening the sultan did not necessarily ensure lifelong faithfulness to France. Given the social turmoil and political uncertainty that accompanied the Berber *dahir* of 1930 and the street riots of 1936 and 1937, it is not surprising that Sidi Mohammed ben Youssef was both partisan and foe of the French. That he became Morocco's first king at independence is a tribute to his political instincts, his ability to follow his own course, not one charted by others. By the same token, economic and political reform did not make a Moroccan partnership certain and actually weakened the influence of France's "old friends." Noguès reluctantly concluded that the nationalists could never be appeased and was pushed against his will to use force to halt their progress in the cities and among the tribes. With the artisans and tribesmen, fidelity was linked to prosperity, something that even France could not guarantee.

Native challenges to French rule and the protectorate's economic hardships pointed to the fragility of French Morocco. Noguès told Europeans that their future and that of France depended upon Franco-Moroccan solidarity, the "keystone" of the protectorate.[1] He set the style in his direct contacts with the Moroccan people. So vigorously did he denounce the racism of the past that critics tagged him the "Résident des Marocains."[2] To be sure, he never neglected the colonists or the French investment in Morocco—his struggle to break Algeciras and to win a place at France's table for Moroccan produce proved that—but he refused to coddle his countrymen. Amid the crisis of the colonial economy, he insisted on bettering the lot of the native population first, arguing that this would help knit the two communities together for good times and bad.

Noguès exemplified the authoritarian paternalist tradition in French colonialism. He possessed an unwavering conviction of the blessings of France's presence overseas and a deep, emotional attachment to a people and land far from home. This was part of Lyautey's legacy in Morocco and an important component of the "new colonialism" or "colonial humanism" of the 1930s, which was embodied in the reform plans of the Popular Front. Although the political Left emphasized the liberating and humanitarian aspects of their programs, they contained a bit of France as well. No government in France was prepared to accept "separatist" nationalism, nor did any government wish to move so fast with political and economic change as to upset the native elite loyal to France or distress the European colonists. In fact, because of the Metropole's economic difficulties and the threats to peace in Europe, the empire was seen as a source of strength, something to be treasured and held tightly rather than given away. Without doubt, a renewed sense of responsibility for the colonies came with the Popular Front, which explains the increased economic aid, the schemes for commercial and industrial development, and the funds for public works. Here too, however, France was to be the ultimate beneficiary. Empire policy—which might be called colonialism with a human face—was as much inspired by Lyautey as Léon Blum.[3]

During the Second World War, Noguès interpreted his mission as the defense of the protectorate, even when a colonial deal or imperial dissidence might have better served France. He refused to purchase Spain's friendship with Morocco's land or to accept a Franco-German or Franco-Italian armistice that would alienate any part of France in Africa. As much as anything else, it was Noguès's reluctance to lay down his arms that postponed the colonial reshuffling desired by France's enemies. For Noguès collaboration with Germany depended on maintaining French sovereignty overseas and keeping the Germans out of the colonies. At the same time, he was deaf to the appeals of Mandel and de Gaulle to continue the war once the French government had ordered otherwise; he heard only

Albion's siren song urging Frenchmen to bend the empire to Britain's purpose. Later, although he encouraged economic aid from the United States, he fretted about America's political impact and military designs on the protectorate. If Morocco was forced to rejoin the war, he feared a native insurrection against France and the conquest of the protectorate by America or Germany. In sum, he wanted to sit out the war while defending Africa against everyone. When America invaded, he resisted, but when he was overpowered, he tried to make the best bargain to preserve French sovereignty in North Africa.

Noguès was one of the last of a vanishing species, the "compleat colonial officer" for whom the empire was a vocation and whose career was identified with a particular spot on the globe. He admitted that he had spent "the most wonderful and productive years of his life in Morocco," the country he had come to consider "a second homeland."[4] This too was part of the Lyautey legacy, and it may have encouraged a narrow Moroccan "particularism," led to mistaken judgments in colonial affairs, and blurred the true relationships between France and Morocco.[5] Making Morocco the highest form of French colonialism often demanded the sacrifice of the interests of Moroccans and those of Frenchmen as well.

Notes

ONE

1. [Simoneau], "De Lyautey à Noguès," pp. 150–72.
2. Lyautey to Noguès, 6 February 1924, Noguès Papers; Noguès quote in *L'Afrique française* 46, no. 10 (October 1936): 511.
3. Lyautey, "Politique du protectorat," 18 November 1920, Charpentier Papers. There are differences between this text and that found in Lyautey, *Lyautey l'Africain*, 4:25–36. I quote the Charpentier text throughout.
4. Lyautey to his sister, 16 November 1894 and 1 September 1896, in Lyautey, *Lettres du Tonkin et de Madagascar*, 1:71–72; 2:81. Also see Betts, *Assimilation and Association*.
5. Lyautey, "Note à M. André Tardieu sur la politique indigène," November 1913, in Lyautey, *Lyautey l'Africain*, 1:253.
6. Lyautey, *Paroles d'action*, p. 195.
7. Lyautey to his sister, 16 November 1894, and Lyautey to Antonin de Margerie, 15 August 1896, in Lyautey, *Lettres du Tonkin et de Madagascar*, 1:72–73, 2:45.
8. See Durosoy, *Avec Lyautey*, p. 59.
9. Harris, *France, Spain, and the Rif*, pp. 193–94.
10. [Simoneau], "De Lyautey à Noguès," pp. 157–58.
11. [Simoneau], "De Lyautey à Noguès," p. 158; Goulven, *La France au Maroc*, pp. 24–25.
12. Lyautey, "Politique du protectorat," 18 November 1920, Charpentier Papers.
13. Lyautey, "Politique du protectorat," 18 November 1920, Charpentier Papers.
14. Scham, *Lyautey in Morocco*, p. 193.
15. Julien, *Le Maroc face aux impérialismes*, pp. 95–127.
16. Lyautey, "Politique du protectorat," 18 November 1920, and "Décision," 25 May 1921, both in Charpentier Papers.
17. Lyautey, "Politique du protectorat," 18 November 1920, Charpentier Papers.
18. Lyautey, "Aux personnalités venues pour l'inauguration du grand port de Casablanca et du premier tronçon de chemin de fer à voie normale de Rabat à Fès," 4 April 1923, in Lyautey, *Paroles d'action*, p. 395.
19. Lyautey to Noguès, 23 October [1923], Noguès Papers.
20. Noguès, "Préambule" and "Plan général," n.d., Noguès Papers. These were preliminary notes for a book manuscript that Noguès never wrote.

21. Georges Hutin to Père René Point, 10 September 1971, in letter from Point to the author, 22 March 1977; Haute Cour de Justice, Ministère Public c/ Général Noguès, Audiences du 23, 24, 25, 26 octobre 1956, Archives Nationales, Guillaume testimony, 2:114 (hereafter referred to as Haute Cour de Justice [1956], AN); *Paris*, October 1947. The complete results of the *Paris* poll were:

	Noguès	68%
	Steeg	18%
	Ponsot	8%
	Peyrouton	4%
	Saint	2%

22. Noguès, "Plan général," n.d., Noguès Papers; Point, "Le général Charles Noguès (1876–1971)"; Point to the author, 9 April 1977.

23. Noguès, "Plan général," n.d., Noguès Papers. Also see Ministère de la Guerre, "État des Services de Auguste, Paul, Charles, Albert Noguès," 27 July 1920, Noguès Papers.

24. Noguès, "Préamble," n.d., Noguès Papers.

25. Noguès, "Discours à la Municipalité et les trois collèges de la Région d'Oujda," 25 January 1937, Noguès Papers.

26. Noguès, "Plan général," n.d., Noguès Papers.

27. Lyautey to his sister, 5 December 1914, in Lyautey, *Choix de lettres*, p. 311.

28. Ministère de la Guerre, "État des Services," 27 July 1920, Noguès Papers.

29. Noguès, "Plan général," n.d., Noguès Papers.

30. For example, see Lyautey to Noguès, 28 January and 7, 9, and 11 March 1924, Noguès Papers.

31. Lyautey to Noguès, 6 February 1924, Noguès Papers.

32. Chambrun to Noguès, 17 March 1924, Noguès Papers.

33. Lyautey to Noguès, 29 March 1924, Noguès Papers.

34. Woolman, *Rebels in the Rif*, p. 157.

35. Jacques, *L'aventure riffaine*, p. 64, cited in Woolman, *Rebels in the Rif*, pp. 169–70.

36. Rivet, "Le commandement français," pp. 119, 123.

37. Woolman, *Rebels in the Rif*, p. 170.

38. Lyautey to Minister of Foreign Affairs, 29 April 1925, Archives Diplomatiques, Maroc, 1917–38, Ministère des Affaires Étrangères, 498:85–86. Hereafter referred to as MAE, Maroc.

39. Lyautey to Noguès, 11 May [1925], Noguès Papers. Lyautey referred to Premier Paul Painlevé; chief of the general staff, General Eugène Debeney; Foreign Minister Aristide Briand; and Secretary General of the Ministry of Foreign Affairs Philippe Berthelot.

40. Lyautey to Noguès, 11 May [1925]; Ordre général No. 515, 2 December 1924, and Ordre général No. 559, 13 July 1925, in "Citations au Maroc: Noguès," all in Noguès Papers.

41. Durosoy, *Avec Lyautey*, pp. 165–68.

42. Lyautey, *Lyautey l'Africain*, 4:343; Lyautey to Premier Paul

Painlevé, 4 and 6 July 1925, and Lyautey to Foreign Minister Aristide Briand, 31 July 1925, all in Lyautey, *Lyautey l'Africain*, 4:345, 352–53, 360; Durosoy, *Avec Lyautey*, pp. 167–73.

43. Noguès, "Plan général," n.d., Noguès Papers.

44. Members of the Medjlis to Noguès, 14 October 1926; Members of the Medjlis to Steeg, 16 November 1926, both in Noguès Papers.

45. Durosoy, *Avec Lyautey*, pp. 189, 198.

46. Lyautey to the Président du Conseil, 14 June 1925, in Lyautey, *Lyautey l'Africain*, 4:330.

47. Loustaunau-Lacau, *Mémoires d'un français rebelle*, p. 63, cited in Griffiths, *Pétain*, p. 112.

48. See Griffiths, *Pétain*, pp. 114–15, and Rivet, "Le commandement français," pp. 125–27.

49. Ordre général No. 57, 28 August 1925; Ordre général No. 455, 19 November 1925; "Rapport du Général Billotte, commandant le secteur centre, sur les faits qui motivent la proposition pour le grade du commandeur de la Légion d'Honneur en faveur du Colonel Noguès," 21 July 1925, all in "Citations au Maroc: Noguès," Noguès Papers.

50. Noguès, "Plan général," n.d., Noguès Papers.

51. Lyautey to Noguès, 19 December 1925, Noguès Papers.

52. Steeg to the Minister of War, 2 July, 7 August, and 7 November 1926, all in Noguès Papers.

53. *L'Afrique française* 46, no. 10 (October 1936): 511.

54. Saint to the Minister of War, 25 June 1932, Noguès Papers. Also see General Antoine Huré, Commandant Supérieur des Troupes du Maroc, Ordre No. 34, 31 December 1931, Noguès Papers.

55. Noguès, "Plan général," n.d., Noguès Papers.

56. On the Sétif riot, see the file "Événements de Sétif," Noguès Papers.

57. See Jacques Ladreit de Lacharrière, "Le differend marocain," *L'Afrique française* 46, nos. 1, 2 (January and February 1936): 20–28, 80–86.

58. Sidi Mohammed ben Youssef to Albert Lebrun, 8 June 1936, MAE, Maroc, 413:175–79. Also see Peyrouton, *Du service public*, pp. 52–59.

59. Noguès, "Plan général," n.d., Noguès Papers.

60. Noguès, "Plan général" and "Préface," n.d., Noguès Papers. "Préface" was part of Noguès's uncompleted book manuscript.

61. Noguès, "Plan général" and "Préface," n.d., Noguès Papers.

62. Julien, "Léon Blum et les pays d'outre-mer," 397.

63. Ministry of Foreign Affairs to the Residency at Rabat, 15 September 1936, MAE, Maroc, 426:214.

TWO

1. Urbain Blanc to Minister of Foreign Affairs, 12 August 1930, Noguès Papers. The *délégué général des affaires étrangères à la résidence générale*

was the foreign ministry's representative in Morocco. The text of the Berber *dahir* is printed in Halstead, *Rebirth of a Nation*, pp. 276–77.

2. General Henri Simon, "Notre politique berbère, rapport de mission du Général H. Simon," 8 January 1931, Noguès Papers.

3. Saint to Minister of Foreign Affairs, 20 June 1930, Noguès Papers.

4. Lyautey to Minister of Foreign Affairs, 10 October 1925, MAE, Maroc, 427:52.

5. Quoted in Bidwell, *Morocco under Colonial Rule*, p. 250.

6. Saint to Minister of Foreign Affairs, 20 June 1930, Noguès Papers.

7. Montagne, "Les tendances du Jeune Maroc," CHEAM report, 15 July 1929; Le Tourneau, "La jeunesse marocaine," CHEAM conference, 30 June 1938. Montagne taught at the Institut des Hautes Études Marocaines at Rabat and later was the director of the Centre des Hautes Études d'Administration Musulmane in Paris. Le Tourneau taught at the Collège Moulay Idriss in Fez from 1930 to 1935 and was its director from 1935 to 1941.

8. Saint to Minister of Foreign Affairs, 20 June 1930, Noguès Papers; Montagne, "Les tendances du Jeune Maroc," CHEAM report, 15 July 1929.

9. See Brown, *People of Salé*, pp. 92, 198–202, 205–6.

10. Urbain Blanc to Minister of Foreign Affairs, 12 August 1930; Direction Générale des Affaires Indigènes, "Note sur l'agitation créée autour du dahir du 16 mai 1930 sur la justice berbère," 10 August 1930, both in Noguès Papers.

11. Urbain Blanc to Minister of Foreign Affairs, 12 August 1930, Noguès Papers; Mohammed el-Mokri to the pashas and khalifs of Fez, Salé, Meknès, Casablanca, Rabat, and Marrakesh, 8 August 1930, and Sidi Mohammed ben Youssef to the notables, 8 August 1930, both attached to the Blanc letter of 12 August 1930.

12. Urbain Blanc to Minister of Foreign Affairs, 12 August 1930, Noguès Papers.

13. Urbain Blanc to Minister of Foreign Affairs, 4 September 1930, Noguès Papers.

14. Saint to Minister of Foreign Affairs, 23 September 1930, Noguès Papers.

15. Urbain Blanc to Minister of Foreign Affairs, 4 September 1930, Noguès Papers.

16. "Note sur l'attitude de sujets ou de protégés étrangers au cours du récent mouvement d'agitation dans les grands centres musulmans," 6 October 1930, Noguès Papers. Also see Wendel, "*Protégé* System in Morocco," pp. 48–60.

17. Saint to Minister of Foreign Affairs, 6 October 1930; "Note sur l'attitude de sujets," 6 October 1930; "Note sur le comité syro-palestino-moghrébin établie d'après des informations de sources diverses," n.d.; "Note sur l'attitude des Espagnols au cours de l'agitation qui s'est manifestée en zone française," 13 October 1930, all in Noguès Papers.

18. "La réforme judiciaire marocaine et la réaction musulmane," n.d., Noguès Papers.

19. Saint to Minister of Foreign Affairs, 6 October and 3 November 1930; "Note relative à la campagne menée par la presse d'Égypte contre le dahir de Sa Majesté chérifienne en date du 16 mai 1930 organisant la justice dans les tribus de coutume berbère," n.d., both in Noguès Papers.

20. Le Tourneau, "Le nationalisme marocain," CHEAM conference, 1 December 1945; Brown, *People of Salé*, p. 128.

21. Urbain Blanc to Minister of Foreign Affairs, 4 September 1930, Noguès Papers.

22. Urbain Blanc to Minister of Foreign Affairs, 12 August 1930 and 4 September 1930; Saint to Minister of Foreign Affairs, 23 September 1930, all in Noguès Papers.

23. Direction Générale des Affaires Indigènes, "Aperçu sur la situation politique intérieure à la date du 1ᵉʳ septembre 1930; Direction Générale des Affaires Indigènes to the Commanders of the Civil and Military Regions, 5 September 1930, both in Noguès Papers.

24. Saint to Minister of Foreign Affairs, 23 September, 6 October, and 3 November 1930, Noguès Papers; Le Tourneau, "Le mouvement nationaliste marocain de 1930 à 1937," CHEAM report, 1937. The *dahir* was maintained intact with the exception of article 6, which transferred criminal justice to French courts. A *dahir* of 8 April 1934 restored the jurisdiction of sharifian authorities to criminal cases in Berber territory.

25. "Note relative à la campagne," n.d.; Direction Générale des Affaires Indigènes, "Aperçu sur la situation politique intérieure"; "Note sur l'agitation," 10 August 1930; Urbain Blanc to Minister of Foreign Affairs, 6 and 12 August and 4 September 1930; Saint to Minister of Foreign Affairs, 23 September 1930, all in Noguès Papers.

26. See Matte, "Éléments d'une politique berbère au Maroc," CHEAM conference, 20 February 1937.

27. Noguès to Foreign Minister Yvon Delbos, 9 October 1937, Julien Papers.

28. al-Fāsī, *The Independence Movements in Arab North Africa*, pp. 141–42.

29. For the Popular Front, see Cohen, "Colonial Policy of the Popular Front;" for the Moroccan policy of the Franco government, see chapter 5.

30. Noguès to Delbos, 9 October 1937, Julien Papers.

31. Abdeljalil and el-Ouazzani to Viénot, 16 October 1936, Noguès Papers. The Syrian treaty was never ratified by the French parliament.

32. Viénot to Abdeljalil and el-Ouazzani, 23 October 1936, Noguès Papers.

33. Abdeljalil and el-Ouazzani to Viénot, 26 October 1936, Noguès Papers.

34. Abdeljalil and el-Ouazzani to Viénot, 26 October 1936, Noguès Papers.

35. Mohamed Diouri and Mohamed Ghazi to Noguès, 30 November 1936, Noguès Papers.

36. General Augustin Richert, Chef de la Région de Fès, to Directeur des

Affaires Politiques, 3 November 1936, Noguès Papers; Noguès to Delbos, 9 October 1937, Julien Papers. The Direction des Affaires Indigènes was renamed the Direction des Affaires Politiques in 1936.

37. I have found no evidence that French authorities spread the rumor of the sultan's message only to use it as an excuse to break up the meeting. See Julien, *Le Maroc face aux impérialismes*, p. 184.

38. Contrôleur Civil, Chef de la Région des Chaouïa, to Délégué Général, 18 November 1936; Commissaire Divisionnaire to Chef de la Région de Casablanca, "Note de renseignements," 15 November 1936, included in letter of 18 November 1936; René Thierry to Minister of Foreign Affairs, 15 November 1936, all in Noguès Papers; Noguès to Delbos, 9 October 1937, Julien Papers.

39. Commissaire Divisionnaire to Chef de la Région de Casablanca, "Note de renseignements," 15 November 1936, in letter from Contrôleur Civil, Chef de la Région des Chaouïa, to Délégué Général, 18 November 1936, Noguès Papers.

40. Thierry to Minister of Foreign Affairs, 16 November 1936, Noguès Papers.

41. See "Note sur le Makhzen Central," 25 January 1934, in letter from Henri Ponsot to Minister of Foreign Affairs, 10 February 1934, MAE, Maroc, 413:114–17.

42. Thierry to Minister of Foreign Affairs, 16 November 1936, Noguès Papers.

43. Viénot to Délégué Général, 17 November 1936, Noguès Papers.

44. Contrôleur Civil, Adjoint au Chef des Services Municipaux Ahmed, "Compte rendu," 17 November 1936, and Contrôleur Civil, Chef des Services Municipaux Jean Courtin to Contrôleur Civil, Chef de la Région de Casablanca, 17 November 1936, both in letter from Contrôleur Civil, Chef de la Région des Chaouïa to Délégué Général, 18 November 1936, Noguès Papers.

45. Commissaire Divisionnaire de Casablanca, "Note de renseignements," 17 November 1936, in letter from Contrôleur Civil, Chef de la Région des Chaouïa to Délégué Général, 18 November 1936, Noguès Papers.

46. René Thierry to Minister of Foreign Affairs, 17 November 1936, Noguès Papers.

47. Diouri and Ghazi to Noguès, 30 November 1936, Noguès Papers.

48. Thierry to Minister of Foreign Affairs, 17 November 1936; Contrôleur Civil, Chef de la Région des Chaouïa to Délégué Général, 18 November 1936, both in Noguès Papers; Noguès to Delbos, 9 October 1937, Julien Papers.

49. Thierry to Minister of Foreign Affairs, 18 November 1936, Noguès Papers; *La Vigie marocaine*, 18 and 23 November 1936; Ville de Casablanca, Commission Municipale, "Télégramme à Monsieur le Résident Général," 17 November 1936; Contrôleur Civil, Chef du Cercle de Chaouïa-Sud, "Bulletin de renseignements," 16 November 1936; Com-

missaire Divisionnaire de Casablanca, "Note de renseignements," 15 November 1936, all in letter from Contrôleur Civil, Chef de la Région des Chaouïa to Délégué Général, 18 November 1936, Noguès Papers.

50. Thierry to Minister of Foreign Affairs, 19, 20, and 21 November 1936; Viénot to Délégué Général, 21 November 1936, both in Noguès Papers.

51. Noguès to Minister of Foreign Affairs, 27 November 1936, Noguès Papers. Noguès wrote that Thierry had made all the necessary decisions with "firmness and prudence." "I have tested his devotion, his zeal, and the precision of his mind, all of which were taxed to the utmost during my recent trip to Paris." Noguès to Delbos, 4 December 1936, MAE, Maroc, 426 : 223.

52. "Discours du général Noguès," 28 November 1936, in report by the Contrôleur Civil Rosario Pisani, "Note de renseignements: Visite du Résident Général à Fès, 28–29 novembre 1936," 29 November 1936; Noguès to Minister of Foreign Affairs, 28 November 1936, both in Noguès Papers.

53. Pisani, "Note de renseignements," 29 November 1936; Noguès to Minister of Foreign Affairs, 28 November 1936; Viénot to Noguès, 30 November 1936, all in Noguès Papers.

54. Noguès to Minister of Foreign Affairs, 27 and 28 November and 6 December 1936; the Fez delegation to Noguès, 28 November 1936, all in Noguès Papers. Both Grand Vizier Mohammed el-Mokri and Si Mohammed Mammeri, the sultan's tutor, were strong partisans of collaboration with the French. Ponsot wrote that el-Mokri's "prudent wisdom serves us even more than it does his own personal interests" and that Si Mammeri was "the comprehensive instrument of a policy of collaboration" and "it was always possible to reach the sultan through his voice" ("Note sur le Makhzen Central," 25 January 1934, in letter from Ponsot to the Minister of Foreign Affairs, 10 February 1934, MAE, Maroc, 413 : 114–17).

55. Noguès to Minister of Foreign Affairs, 4 and 6 December 1936; Direction des Affaires Politiques, "Note" [Noguès's conversation with Ahmed Mekouar], 4 December 1936, all in Noguès Papers.

56. Direction des Affaires Politiques, "Note sur les incidents provoqués par les nationalistes marocains en novembre 1936," 24 November 1936, Noguès Papers.

57. Viénot to Noguès, 4 January 1937, Noguès Papers.

58. Morize to Delbos, 31 August 1937, Noguès Papers.

59. Halstead, *Rebirth of a Nation*, p. 245. El-Fassi's memoirs are important for this entire period. See al-Fāsī, *The Independence Movements in Arab North Africa*, particularly chapter 4, pp. 126–212.

60. Morize to Delbos, 31 August 1937; Morize to Noguès, 2 and 6 August 1937, both in Noguès Papers.

61. Morize to Noguès, 18 August 1937, and Morize to Delbos, 31 August 1937, both in Noguès Papers; Noguès to Delbos, 9 October 1937, Julien Papers.

62. Direction des Affaires Politiques, "Situation politique au 15 décembre 1937," n.d.; General André Lauzanne, Chef du Territoire de Taza to

Directeur des Affaires Politiques, 10 October 1937, both in Julien Papers. Also see the reports by Abadie, "Les tendances à l'insurrection en pays berbère," CHEAM report, 1939, and by Flye-Sainte-Marie, "Le nationalisme en pays berbère," CHEAM report, 1938, for the tribes touched by nationalism in the Middle Atlas and the Taza Gap regions.

63. Morize to Delbos, 31 August 1937; Morize to Noguès, 18 August 1937; Mellier to Noguès, 28 August 1937, all in Noguès Papers.

64. Morize to Noguès, 20, 24, and 28 August 1937; General Amédée Blanc to Noguès, 1 September 1937, all in Noguès Papers.

65. Noguès to Minister of Foreign Affairs, 11 October 1937, MAE, Maroc, 490:53; Direction des Affaires Politiques, "Situation politique au 15 décembre 1937," n.d., Julien Papers; Flye-Sainte-Marie, "L'évolution du nationalisme à Meknès jusq'en 1937," CHEAM conference, 9 June 1938; *L'Afrique française* 47, no. 10 (October 1937): 455; *Bulletin Officiel du Protectorat de la République française au Maroc* 26, no. 1268 (12 February 1937): 205–7 (hereafter referred to as *Bulletin Officiel*).

66. Noguès to Minister of Foreign Affairs, 11 October 1937, MAE, Maroc, 490:54; Flye-Sainte-Marie, "L'évolution du nationalisme à Meknès," CHEAM conference, 9 June 1938.

67. Noguès to Minister of Foreign Affairs, 11 October 1937, MAE, Maroc, 490:53–54; Direction des Affaires Politiques, "Situation politique au 15 décembre 1937," n.d., Julien Papers; Morize to Noguès, 29 August and [1 September] 1937, Noguès Papers.

68. Noguès to Minister of Foreign Affairs, 11 October 1937, MAE, Maroc, 490:54–55; Flye-Sainte-Marie, "L'évolution du nationalisme à Meknès," CHEAM conference, 9 June 1938.

69. Morize to Noguès, 3 September 1937, Noguès Papers; Flye-Sainte-Marie, "L'évolution du nationalisme à Meknès," CHEAM conference, 9 June 1938.

70. Noguès to Minister of Foreign Affairs, 11 October 1937, MAE, Maroc, 490:55.

71. *La Vigie marocaine*, 3 September 1937.

72. Flye-Sainte-Marie, "L'évolution du nationalisme à Meknès," CHEAM conference, 9 June 1938.

73. Morize to Minister of Foreign Affairs, 31 August 1938, MAE, Maroc, 491:5.

74. Noguès to Minister of Foreign Affairs, 11 October 1937, MAE, Maroc, 490:56–58.

75. Direction des Affaires Politiques, "Situation politique au 15 décembre 1937," n.d., Julien Papers.

76. Noguès to Delbos, 9 October 1937; Direction des Affaires Politiques, "Situation politique au 15 décembre 1937," n.d., both in Julien Papers.

77. Noguès to Delbos, 9 October 1937, Julien Papers.

78. Noguès to Delbos, 9 October 1937, Julien Papers. Throughout the Popular Front period, Noguès counted on Blum, Delbos, and Viénot to intercede in Socialist party circles and cut off criticism of French policy in

Morocco, which they apparently did without hesitation. See Viénot to Paul Faure, 18 November 1936, Noguès Papers.

79. Direction des Affaires Politiques, "Situation politique au 15 décembre 1937," n.d., Julien Papers.

80. *L'Afrique française* 47, no. 11 (November 1937): 519–21.

81. General Blanc to Noguès, 1 September 1937, Noguès Papers.

82. *L'Afrique française* 47, no. 11 (November 1937): 520–21.

83. On the Fez events, see Direction des Affaires Politiques, "Situation politique au 15 décembre 1937," n.d., Julien Papers; Le Tourneau, "Le mouvement nationaliste marocain de 1930 à 1937," CHEAM report, 1938; Le Tourneau, "Les émeutes de Fès," CHEAM report, 1939.

84. Direction des Affaires Politiques, "Situation politique au 15 décembre 1937," n.d., Julien Papers; *L'Afrique française* 47, no. 11 (November 1937): 519–20, 522.

85. Noguès to Minister of Foreign Affairs Georges Bonnet, 4 December 1938, in Ministère des Affaires Étrangères, *Documents diplomatiques français, 1932–1939*, ser. 2 (1936–39), 15 vols. to date (Paris, 1963–), 13:47 (hereafter cited as *DDF*).

THREE

1. Fogg, "Economic Revolution in the Countryside," pp. 123–29. Also see Bidwell, *Morocco under Colonial Rule*.

2. See Lyautey to Antonin de Margerie, 15 August 1896, in Lyautey, *Lettres du Tonkin et de Madagascar*, 2:44.

3. Urbain Blanc to Minister of Foreign Affairs, 9 October 1931, MAE, Maroc, 413:90–91.

4. "Discours prononcé par M. le général Noguès, Commissaire Résident Général de la République Française au Maroc à la session du Conseil du Gouvernement du Protectorat," 7 December 1938, p. 5; "Discours prononcé par M. le général Noguès, Commissaire Résident Général de la République Française au Maroc à la séance d'ouverture du Conseil du Gouvernement," 21 December 1937, p. 31; "Discours prononcé par le général Noguès devant la section marocaine du Conseil du Gouvernement," 28 December 1937, p. 17, all in Noguès Papers. Hereafter referred to as Noguès, "Conseil du Gouvernement."

5. Delbos to Morize, 6 August 1937, Noguès Papers.

6. "Réponse du général Noguès aux discours de Casablanca," 6 October 1936; Noguès, "Discours aux Européens," Taza, 13 February 1937; Noguès, "Conseil du Gouvernement," 25 June 1937, p. 6, all in Noguès Papers. Also see Noguès, "Conseil du Gouvernement," 21 December 1937, pp. 19–20, Noguès Papers.

7. Noguès, "Réponse au pacha de Fès," 19 October 1936; Noguès, "Réponse à trois discours européens," Meknès, 20 October 1936, both in Noguès Papers.

8. "Réponse du général Noguès aux discours de Casablanca," 6 October 1936, Noguès Papers. Lyautey's remains were later returned to France.

9. Noguès, "Discours à S.M. le Sultan," Rabat, 7 October 1936; Noguès, "Discours à la Chambre de Commerce," Fez, 19 October 1936; Noguès, "Réponse au pacha de Fès," 19 October 1936, all in Noguès Papers.

10. *Bulletin Officiel* 26, no. 1278 (23 April 1937): 562–63.

11. Noguès, "Conseil du Gouvernement," 25 June 1937, pp. 4, 11; Noguès, "Réponse au pacha de Fès," 19 October 1936; Noguès, "Réponse à trois discours européens," Meknès, 20 October 1936; Noguès, "Réponse au pacha de Meknès," 20 October 1936; Noguès, "Réponse aux Européens," Marrakesh, 25 October 1936; Noguès, "Réponse au pacha," Marrakesh, 25 October 1936, all in Noguès Papers. Also see Noguès, "Discours aux Européens," Mazagan, 8 October 1937, and "Discours du général Noguès à Oujda," 25 January 1937, both in Noguès Papers.

12. Noguès, "Discours à S.M. le Sultan," 7 October 1936; Noguès, "Réponse au pacha de Fès," 19 October 1936; Noguès, "Réponse au pacha," Marrakesh, 25 October 1936; Noguès, "Réponse aux Européens," Marrakesh, 25 October 1936, all in Noguès Papers.

13. "Discours du général Noguès," 28 November 1936, in report by Rosario Pisani, "Note de renseignements: Visite du Résident Général à Fès," 29 November 1936, Noguès Papers.

14. Pisani, "Note de renseignements," 29 November 1936; Direction des Affaires Politiques, "Note au sujet de l'opportunité d'une diminution de la fiscalité indigène," 24 November 1936; Noguès, "Conseil du Gouvernement," 7 December 1936, p. 5; Noguès to Minister of Foreign Affairs, 28 November 1936, all in Noguès Papers. Also see Pagès, "Les impôts directs urbains du protectorat marocain," CHEAM report, 1947.

15. Pisani, "Note de renseignements," 29 November 1936; "Réponse du Résident Général au Grand Vizir," 1 January 1937; Direction des Affaires Politiques, "Note sur l'amenagement de ressources budgétaires correspondant à la suppression des droits de marché," 25 November 1936, all in Noguès Papers. For the legislation and comment on it, see *Bulletin Officiel* 25, no. 1260b (22 December 1936): 1449–51; *L'Afrique française* 47, no. 2 (February 1937): 112; *Bulletin Officiel* 26, no. 1269 (19 February 1937): 235–36 and 26, no. 1272 (12 March 1937): 350.

16. Noguès, "Conseil du Gouvernement," 7 December 1936, pp. 3–4, Noguès Papers.

17. Noguès, "Conseil du Gouvernement," 7 December 1936, pp. 4–6, Noguès Papers; *La Vigie marocaine*, 5 December 1936. Also see *Bulletin Officiel* 26, no. 1278 (23 April 1937): 526–32. Cuts in the unemployment plan reduced Morocco's share to 50 million francs.

18. Noguès, "Conseil du Gouvernement," 7 December 1936, p. 8, Noguès Papers; Protectorat de la République française au Maroc, *Annuaire de la statistique générale de la Zone française du Maroc* 12 (1937): 37 (hereafter referred to as *Annuaire de la statistique générale du Maroc*).

19. *Petit Larousse*, 1961, s.v. "fonds secrets."

20. Morize, "Note pour M. le Résident Général," 4 August 1937, Noguès Papers.

21. A good place to begin sorting out the figures for 1936 is the excellent report in *Bulletin Officiel* 26, no. 1285 (11 June 1937): 800–807, on the financial effort of the Sociétés Indigènes de Prévoyance, the Caisses Régionales d'Épargne et de Crédit Agricole Indigènes, and the Caisse Centrale de Crédit Agricole et de Prévoyance Indigènes.

22. *Annuaire de la statistique générale du Maroc*, 12:33–36; Pagès, "L'Impôt agricole et les musulmans," CHEAM conference, 21 April 1947. Also see Stewart, *The Economy of Morocco*, pp. 82–85.

23. Morize to Minister of Foreign Affairs, 31 August 1938, MAE, Maroc, 491:13; Protectorat de la République française au Maroc, "Compte rendu des opérations organismes de crédit et de coopération en milieu marocain au cours des exercices 1938–1939 à 1945–1946," n.d., CHEAM, p. 9 (hereafter referred to as Protectorat, "Compte rendu des opérations organismes de crédit," CHEAM); Berque, "La question agraire au Maroc: Nouvelle politique rurale de la France au Maroc, CHEAM conference, 8 October 1945, pp. 9–10. Also see Bidwell, *Morocco under Colonial Rule*, pp. 224–28.

24. Noguès, "Conseil du Gouvernement," 25 June 1937, p. 9; Noguès, "Conseil du Gouvernement, section indigène," 30 June 1937, p. 2, both in Noguès Papers.

25. Assemblée Nationale, *Les événements survenus en France de 1933 à 1945: Rapport fait au nom de la Commission chargée d'enquêter sur les événements survenus en France de 1933 à 1945 par M. Charles Serre, rapporteur général*, 2 vols. (Paris, [1952]) and *Les événements survenus en France: Témoignages et documents recueillis par la Commission d'enquête parlementaire*, 9 vols. (Paris, [1951–52]), *Témoignages*, Blum testimony, 1:219. Hereafter referred to as *Les événements survenus en France*, followed by *Rapport* or *Témoignages*, the volume, and page.

26. Théodore Steeg to the Président du Conseil, 21 June 1937, pp. 8–9, 12, 21–28, Noguès Papers.

27. Noguès, "Conseil du Gouvernement," 25 June 1937, p. 3, Noguès Papers.

28. *Bulletin Officiel* 26, no. 1278b (26 April 1937): 565–69. Also see Résidence Générale de la République française au Maroc, "Rapport général sur le mouvement coopératif au Maroc en milieu autochtone, 1934–1950," 30 April 1950, CHEAM (hereafter referred to as Résidence Générale, "Rapport général sur le mouvement coopératif au Maroc," CHEAM).

29. *Bulletin de la Chambre d'Agriculture de Casablanca*, no. 91 (January 1938). Also see the *Bulletin de la Chambre de Commerce et d'Industrie de Rabat*, no. 66 (May 1938), for the opposition of Rabat businessmen.

30. For the legislation on the native wheat cooperatives, see *Bulletin Officiel* 26, no. 1278b (26 April 1937): 569–72.

31. Morize to Noguès, 2, 4, and 28 August and 1 September 1937; Noguès, "Conseil du Gouvernement," 25 June 1937, pp. 5–6, all in Noguès Papers.

32. Protectorat, "Compte rendu des opérations organismes de crédit," CHEAM, pp. 3–4; Noguès to Minister of Foreign Affairs, 16 May 1938, MAE, Maroc, 490:173; Résidence Générale, "Rapport général sur le mouvement coopératif au Maroc," CHEAM, p. 10; *Bulletin Officiel* 32, no. 1590 (16 April 1943): 307.

33. Noguès, "Conseil du Gouvernement, section marocaine," 14 December 1938, p. 39, Noguès Papers.

34. Bois, "La surpopulation rurale des Doukkala, les problèmes qu'elle pose," CHEAM report, 1938, pp. 50–52, 65; Flye-Sainte-Marie, "Le nationalisme en pays berbère," CHEAM report, 1938, p. 35.

35. Saulay, "Les coopératives oléicoles au Maroc," CHEAM conference, 11 June 1949, pp. 5–7.

36. Résidence Générale, "Rapport général sur le mouvement coopératif au Maroc," CHEAM, pp. 3–5.

37. Noguès, "Conseil du Gouvernement," 21 December 1937, pp. 21–22, Noguès Papers. Also see Noguès, "Conseil du Gouvernement, section marocaine," 28 December 1937, p. 6, Noguès Papers.

38. Noguès, "Conseil du Gouvernement," 7 December 1938, pp. 19–22, 25, Noguès Papers.

39. Noguès, "Conseil du Gouvernement," 7 December 1938, pp. 22–25, Noguès Papers. Also see Noguès, "Conseil du Gouvernement, section marocaine," 28 December 1937, p. 6, Noguès Papers.

40. Noguès's speech among the Beni Amir, 29 May 1938, Noguès Papers; Berque, "La question agraire au Maroc," CHEAM conference, 8 October 1945, p. 11; Tallec, "L'équipement hydraulique de la plaine des Beni Amir et ses incidences politiques," CHEAM report, 1941, pp. 1–8.

41. Tallec, "L'équipement hydraulique," CHEAM report, 1941, pp. 8–9, 12, 14–15, 21–23, 29–46. Also see *Bulletin Officiel* 26, no. 1265 (22 January 1937): 109 and 27, no. 1342 (15 July 1938): 932–33.

42. Tallec, "L'équipement hydraulique," CHEAM report, 1941, pp. 47–63; Noguès to Minister of Foreign Affairs, 1 July 1938, MAE, Maroc, 490:203–4. Also see Noguès's comments on the project to the Commission Coloniale du Parti Socialiste, in correspondence from Noguès to René Doynel de Saint-Quentin, "Note," 22 December 1937, pp. 200–202, Noguès Papers. A smaller sixty-hectare irrigated perimeter at Sidi Slimane (sixty kilometers east of Port Lyautey), where thirty families of the Hajjaoua had been set up, was considered a "complete success" without the unsettling political difficulties of the Beni Amir sort (Morize to the Minister of Foreign Affairs, 31 August 1938, MAE, Maroc, 491:14–15).

43. Berque, "Deux ans d'action artisanale à Fès," p. 8. For the procorporation view, see Moussard, "Les corporations au Maroc," CHEAM report, 1937, and Moussard, "De la coopération dans l'économie indigène au Maroc," CHEAM report, 1937. Also see the important report of André Tru-

chet, Contrôleur des Autorités Chérifiennes in Tangier to the Directeur des Affaires Politiques, 30 June 1936, Noguès Papers.

44. Noguès, "Conseil du Gouvernement," 25 June 1937, p. 4, Noguès Papers; Le Tourneau, "Les corporations au Maroc," CHEAM conference, 7 June 1938, pp. 6–7, 11–12.

45. Berque, "Deux ans d'action artisanale à Fès," p. 3. An excellent survey is in A. M. Goichon, "L'artisanat à Fès, crise actuelle, remèdes possibles," *Renseignements coloniaux et documents*, no. 11 (1937), supplement to *L'Afrique française* 47, no. 12 (December 1937): 113–20, and *Renseignements coloniaux et documents*, no. 1 (1938), supplement to *L'Afrique française* 48, no. 1 (January 1938): 7–14. Also see Ricard, "L'artisanat marocain," CHEAM report, 1937, and Paye, "Déchéance des corporations marocaines," CHEAM conference, 19 May 1937.

46. Berque, "Deux ans d'action artisanale à Fès," p. 8. Some of the prehistory of the credit policy is detailed in a Residency memorandum, "Crédit artisanal à Fès," 7 April 1937, Noguès Papers. See Noguès's description of the reorganization of artisan industries in Noguès, "Conseil du Gouvernement, section indigène," 30 June 1937, p. 3, Noguès Papers. For the legislation, see *Bulletin Officiel* 26, no. 1281 (14 May 1937): 670–77.

47. Le Tourneau, "L'artisanat en Tunisie et au Maroc," CHEAM conference, [1945], pp. 5–7; Le Tourneau, "Les corporations au Maroc," CHEAM conference, 7 June 1938, pp. 7–8; Blanc to Noguès, 1 September 1937, Noguès Papers; Berque, "Deux ans d'action artisanale à Fès," pp. 8–11.

48. Berque, "Deux ans d'action artisanale à Fès," pp. 11–12. The parallel with the SIP was conscious, for the French once considered creation of Sociétés Indigènes de Prévoyance Urbaines (SIPU) but abandoned them in favor of the *amin* and corporation councils (Direction des Affaires Politiques, "Note au sujet de la rénovation de l'artisanat indigène," 26 November 1936, Noguès Papers).

49. Berque, "Deux ans d'action artisanale à Fès," pp. 13–16, 20–23; Noguès, "Conseil du Gouvernement, section marocaine," 14 December 1938, p. 38, Noguès Papers.

50. Morize to Minister of Foreign Affairs, 7 September 1937, MAE, Maroc, 490:42.

51. Berque, "Deux ans d'action artisanale à Fès," pp. 18–19.

52. Morize to Noguès, 28 August 1937; Blanc to Noguès, 1 September 1937, both in Noguès Papers.

53. See Brown, *People of Salé*, pp. 135–49.

54. Blanc to Noguès, 1 September 1937, Noguès Papers; Le Tourneau, "Les corporations au Maroc," CHEAM conference, 7 June 1938, p. 12; Le Tourneau, "Le mouvement nationaliste marocain de 1930 à 1937," CHEAM report, 1938, p. 81.

55. Berque, "Deux ans d'action artisanale à Fès," p. 26; Noguès, "Conseil du Gouvernement, section marocaine," 14 December 1938, pp. 40–41, Noguès Papers; Noguès to Minister of Foreign Affairs, 12 February and 16

May 1938, MAE, Maroc, 490:109, 170–71; Morize to Minister of Foreign Affairs, 2 March and 15 April 1938, MAE, Maroc, 490:120–21, 140–41.

56. Bourgeois, "L'artisanat fassi depuis la guerre," CHEAM conference, 3 November 1941, pp. 5, 8; Le Tourneau, "L'artisanat en Tunisie et au Maroc," CHEAM conference, [1945], pp. 9–12; Théâtre d'Opérations de l'Afrique du Nord, État-Major, Bureau Politique, *Bulletin d'information*, no. 5 (2 October 1939), no. 6 (11 October 1939), no. 7 (17 October 1939), no. 19 (12 January 1940), no. 23 (10 February 1940), and no. 30 (2 April 1940) (hereafter referred to as TOAFN, *Bulletin d'information*).

57. Noguès to René Doynel de Saint-Quentin, "Note," 22 December 1937, pp. 210–12, Noguès Papers; Berenguier, "Le syndicalisme marocain sous le protectorat français," CHEAM report, 1955, p. 55. Also see Clément, "À propos de la revendication de droit syndical pour les musulmans marocains," CHEAM report, 1938.

58. Gallissot, *Le patronat européen au Maroc*, p. 111.

59. *Annuaire de la statistique générale du Maroc*, 12:76–79; Gallissot, *Le patronat européen au Maroc*, pp. 117, 128, 142, 186–87, 193–94; Berenguier, "Le syndicalisme marocain," CHEAM report, 1955, pp. 68–69; *Bulletin Officiel* 27, no. 1342 (15 July 1938): 929.

60. Berenguier, "Le syndicalisme marocain," CHEAM report, 1955, p. 34; Halstead, *Rebirth of a Nation*, p. 93.

61. See Gallissot, *Le patronat européen au Maroc*, particularly pp. 129–31, 181. Gallissot seems to believe that an alliance was possible, calling these years "a turning point in Moroccan social history" when the rupture between the two societies became total (ibid., p. 264).

62. Gallissot, *Le patronat européen au Maroc*, pp. 144, 147–48, 247–48, 265.

63. Gallissot, *Le patronat européen au Maroc*, pp. 206–7.

64. "Note sur les bidonvilles," 28 October 1936, Noguès Papers.

65. Roux, "Essai monographique sur le bidonville de la Cité Yacoub el-Mansour (Douar Debbagh)," CHEAM report, 1949, pp. 2–3, 20–21; Noguès, "Conseil du Gouvernement, section marocaine," 14 December 1938, p. 34, Noguès Papers; Noguès to Minister of Foreign Affairs, 17 September 1938, MAE, Maroc, 491:36. At Fedala, Port Lyautey, Taza, Fez, Safi, Agadir, Meknès, and Oujda, similar projects were under study or in progress; see Noguès, "Conseil du Gouvernement, section marocaine," 14 December 1938, p. 34, Noguès Papers. On the Comité de l'Habitat Indigène Urbain, see *Bulletin Officiel* 26, no. 1303 (15 October 1937): 1414. For a critique of the protectorate's city planning and slum clearance efforts, see Abu-Lughod, *Rabat*.

66. Édouard Gouin, "Rapport sur la cité ouvrière des Roches Noires," *Bulletin du Comité Central des Industriels du Maroc* (April 1939), pp. 6–8. For the instituting legislation of the Société Chérifienne de la Cité Ouvrière Indigène de Casablanca, S.A., see *Bulletin Officiel* 28, no. 1397 (4 August 1939): 1158–59.

67. *La Vigie marocaine*, 30 December 1940, 12 July 1941. "Première

pierre de la Cité Ouvrière Indigène de Casablanca: Réponse du Résident Général," 29 December 1940, Noguès Papers, also provides a summary of the protectorate's native housing program from 1937 to 1940.

68. Noguès, "Conseil du Gouvernement," 21 December 1937, p. 21; Noguès, "Conseil du Gouvernement, section marocaine," 28 December 1937, p. 11, both in Noguès Papers.

69. Consul General Leonard H. Hurst to the Foreign Office, 28 December 1938, Foreign Office Papers, FO 371/W17062/1629/28, vol. 22585, p. 153, Public Record Office, London. I am indebted to Brian Becharas for this reference.

70. Berque, "Deux ans d'action artisanale à Fès," p. 25; Saulay, "Les coopératives oléicoles au Maroc," CHEAM conference, 11 June 1949, p. 7.

FOUR

1. See "Extrait du procès-verbal du Conseil de Politique Indigène tenu à Rabat, le 14 avril 1925," Hutin Papers.

2. Andrew and Kanya-Forstner, "The French 'Colonial Party,'" pp. 99–128.

3. Lyautey to Antonin de Margerie, 4 February 1897, in Lyautey, *Lettres du Tonkin et de Madagascar*, 2:137, 142.

4. Lyautey to Antonin de Margerie, 4 February 1897, and Lyautey to his sister, 20 February 1897, both in Lyautey, *Lettres du Tonkin et de Madagascar*, 2:142, 151.

5. Lyautey to Henry Bérenger, 12 February 1897, in Lyautey, *Lettres du Tonkin et de Madagascar*, 2:148–49.

6. *Annuaire de la statistique générale du Maroc*, 12:64. On colonization under Lyautey, see Scham, *Lyautey in Morocco*, pp. 132–38.

7. Scham, *Lyautey in Morocco*, pp. 28–29, 89; Bidwell, *Morocco under Colonial Rule*, p. 202.

8. Noguès to the Association "Le Maroc," Paris, November 1938; Noguès, "Au banquet des Français résidant au Maroc avant 1917," 12 February 1937, both in Noguès Papers. See Knight, *Morocco as a French Economic Venture*, pp. 92–93, 186.

9. See Scham, *Lyautey in Morocco*, pp. 74–75, 84–85; Halstead, *Rebirth of a Nation*, pp. 41–42. There were parallel chambers of agriculture, commerce, and industry for Moroccans and native members of the municipal commissions.

10. See Brémard, *Les droits publics et politiques des français au Maroc*, pp. 23–24.

11. See Scham, *Lyautey in Morocco*, p. 75, and Halstead, *Rebirth of a Nation*, pp. 42–43. A Moroccan section of the Conseil du Gouvernement was set up in 1923.

12. Knight, *Morocco as a French Economic Venture*, pp. 60–61, 64.

13. Lyautey, "Réception offerte à M. Paul Deschanel, Président de la

Chambre des Députés," 3 May 1914, in Lyautey, *Paroles d'action*, p. 104.

14. Henri Ponsot, "Note sur le Makhzen Central," 25 January 1934, in letter from Ponsot to Minister of Foreign Affairs, 10 February 1934, MAE, Maroc, 413:114–17; Délégué à la Résidence Générale Jean Hellu to Minister of Foreign Affairs, 1 June 1934, MAE, Maroc, 413:122; Halstead, *Rebirth of a Nation*, p. 199.

15. Halstead, *Rebirth of a Nation*, pp. 62–63; Gallissot, *Le patronat européen au Maroc*, p. 64.

16. Gallissot, *Le patronat européen au Maroc*, p. 103.

17. The complicated struggle for tariff revision is explained in Knight, *Morocco as a French Economic Venture*, in particular pp. 134–75.

18. Knight said that the proposals amounted to a "revolution" in the government of the sharifian empire (ibid., p. 208).

19. See *Bulletin Officiel* 25, no. 1232 (5 June 1936): 662–63; *Bulletin Officiel* 25, no. 1236 (3 July 1936): 807–12; *Bulletin Officiel* 25, no. 1237 (11 July 1936): 854–55, 858.

20. *Bulletin Officiel* 25, no. 1235 (26 June 1936): 788–89.

21. *Bulletin Officiel* 25, no. 1235 (26 June 1936): 789, 795; "Allocution prononcée par le général Noguès au banquet de clôture de la Foire Internationale de Casablanca," 24 April 1937, Noguès Papers.

22. *Bulletin Officiel* 25, no. 1235 (26 June 1936): 788.

23. Stewart, *The Economy of Morocco*, pp. 88–91, 98–100. See Noguès, "Banquet des viticulteurs," 7 April 1937, Noguès Papers. For details on wheat quotas and price supports, see Knight, *Morocco as a French Economic Venture*, pp. 106–21.

24. *Bulletin Officiel* 25, no. 1235 (26 June 1936): 789.

25. Stewart, *The Economy of Morocco*, p. 100; Garcin, *La politique des contingents*, pp. 202–3.

26. *Bulletin Officiel* 25, no. 1235 (26 June 1936): 789, 791–92.

27. *La Bougie de Fès*, 17 September 1936. Also see *Le Journal de Casablanca*, 15 September 1936.

28. *Le Soir marocain*, 17 September 1936, quoting *Le Figaro* of Paris.

29. See Noguès, "Discours aux Corps Élus de la Région de Rabat," 7 October 1936, Noguès Papers; *Maroc-Matin*, 17 September 1936; *L'Information marocaine*, 16 September 1936; *Le Petit marocain*, 19 September 1936.

30. *Bulletin Officiel* 25, no. 1235 (26 June 1936): 790.

31. "Réponse à trois discours européens," Meknès, 20 October 1936; "Discours au Congrès de la Colonisation de Rabat," 15 April 1937, both in Noguès Papers. See the bittersweet assessment of the situation and prospects of the colonists in Goulven, *La France au Maroc*, pp. 47–49.

32. "Réponse à trois discours européens," Meknès, 20 October 1936, Noguès Papers; *Bulletin Officiel* 25, no. 1235 (26 June 1936): 790.

33. Paye, "L'Agriculture dans la Région de Fès," CHEAM conference, 2 June 1937.

34. Paye, "L'Agriculture dans la Région de Fès," CHEAM conference,

2 June 1937, pp. 15–16, 18–19. Also see Gadille, "L'Agriculture européenne au Maroc," pp. 144–58.

35. The Caisse Fédérale had already consolidated the farm debt and established payment schedules with easier terms. The total colonial debt (monies owed the Caisse Fédérale, the Caisse des Prêts Immobiliers, and ordinary commercial debts) was tallied at 550 million francs. Most farmers wanted the state to guarantee between two-thirds and three-fourths of it; see Knight, *Morocco as a French Economic Venture*, pp. 85–87, 121–25. Also see Oved, "Contribution à l'étude de l'endettement de la colonisation agricole au Maroc."

36. Gallissot, *Le patronat européen au Maroc*, p. 3.

37. "Discours du général Noguès à Oujda," 25 January 1937, p. 3; Noguès, "Discours aux Corps Élus," Port Lyautey, 18 December 1936; "Réponse aux Européens," Marrakesh, 25 October 1936; Noguès's speech at Safi, 8 December 1937; Noguès, "Discours aux Européens," Mazagan, 8 December 1937, all in Noguès Papers.

38. "Discours prononcé par le Résident Général au banquet de clôture de la Foire Internationale de Casablanca," 7 May 1938, Noguès Papers.

39. Gallissot, *Le patronat européen au Maroc*, pp. 235–38, 252–53. Among other things, the *patronat* wanted the Conseil du Gouvernement and the municipal commissions reformed to exclude representatives of political groups and parties, leaving the field free to the delegates of agriculture, commerce, industry, and labor; see *La Vigie marocaine*, 24 July 1940.

40. For the legislation, see *Bulletin Officiel* 29, no. 1468 (13 December 1940): 1159–60; *Bulletin Officiel* 30, no. 1481 (14 March 1941): 290; *Bulletin Officiel* 29, no. 1456b (23 September 1940): 910; *Bulletin Officiel* 31, no. 1533 (13 March 1942): 207–8; *Bulletin Officiel* 31, no. 1558 (4 September 1942): 769; *Bulletin Officiel* 30, no. 1471 (3 January 1941): 9; *Bulletin Officiel* 29, no. 1421 (19 January 1940): 107; *Bulletin Officiel* 29, no. 1468 (13 December 1940): 1151–53.

41. *Bulletin de la Chambre d'Agriculture de Casablanca*, no. 137 (January 1942).

42. Noguès, "Discours à la colonie française," 14 July 1938; Noguès, "Message, Jour de l'An," 1 January 1941, both in Noguès Papers.

43. Memorandum, 13 February 1925, in letter from Lord Crewe to Président du Conseil, 16 February 1925, MAE, Maroc, 566:30. The secret article 2 of the 1904 declaration set up the link between capitulations in Egypt and Morocco.

44. Lyautey to Président du Conseil, Ministre des Affaires Étrangères, 2 December 1920, MAE, Maroc, 564:60; Lyautey to Minister of Foreign Affairs, 28 July 1925, and Steeg to Minister of Foreign Affairs, 24 January 1928, MAE, Maroc, 566:74–75, 77–78.

45. Viénot to Noguès, 24 March 1937, MAE, Maroc, 563:98. See Ambassador in the United Kingdom Jonathan Bingham to Secretary of State Cordell Hull, 7 April 1937, in U.S. Department of State, *Foreign Relations of*

the United States: Diplomatic Papers, 1937–43 (Washington, D.C., 1955–64) (1937), 2:858. Hereafter referred to as *FRUS*. France agreed to this condition in a letter from French Ambassador Charles Corbin to British Foreign Secretary Anthony Eden; it went on to say that the "new treaty will be based on the principle of reciprocity and will replace the Treaty of Commerce of 1856." The letter is printed in *L'Afrique française* 47, no. 12 (December 1937): 597.

46. Morize to Noguès, 2 August 1937; Noguès, "Conseil du Gouvernement," 21 December 1937, p. 29, both in Noguès Papers.

47. Noguès, "Conseil du Gouvernement, section marocaine," 28 December 1937, p. 16, Noguès Papers; Noguès to the Minister of Foreign Affairs, 25 May 1937, MAE, Maroc, 566:102. *Mokhalets* were native farmers who sharecropped land owned by Europeans in return for the legal protection of the capitulatory regime. In 1937 British post offices operated in Casablanca, Fez, Marrakesh, Mazagan, Rabat, and Safi in the French zone; at Tetouan and Larache in the Spanish zone; and at Tangier, the head office. See *L'Afrique française* 47, no. 8–9 (August–September 1937): 435.

48. For the Popular Front's "freeze on Italy," see Young, *In Command of France*, pp. 134–38, 157.

49. Noguès, "Conseil du Gouvernement, section marocaine," 28 December 1937, p. 16, Noguès Papers; Noguès to the Minister of Foreign Affairs, 25 May 1937, MAE, Maroc, 566:102; Young, *In Command of France*, p. 157.

50. Noguès to the Minister of Foreign Affairs, 25 May 1937, MAE, Maroc, 566:99–100.

51. Minister of Foreign Affairs to Morize, 18 August 1937, MAE, Maroc, 563:158; Chargé in the United Kingdom Herschell V. Johnson to Hull, 25 September 1937, in *FRUS* (1937), 2:867; Confidential memorandum from the Foreign Office (dated December), in letter from Johnson to Hull, 7 December 1937, in *FRUS* (1937), 2:872–73. Also see Marchat, "Le régime économique de l'Acte d'Algéciras," pp. 18–30.

52. Confidential memorandum from the Foreign Office (dated December), in letter from Johnson to Hull, 7 December 1937, in *FRUS* (1937), 2:872–73. On Japanese competition in Morocco, see Knight, *Morocco as a French Economic Venture*, pp. 142–45, and Lévy, *Les conséquences du développement économique du Japon*.

53. Minister of Foreign Affairs to Noguès, 18 February 1938, MAE, Maroc, 568:230–31; French Ministry of Foreign Affairs press release, 5 August 1938, MAE, Maroc, 571:6–7; Johnson to Hull, 15 January 1938, in *FRUS* (1938), 2:847–50; Johnson to Hull, 27 January 1938, in *FRUS* (1938), 2:854–55; Ambassador in France William C. Bullitt to Hull, 3 February 1938, in *FRUS* (1938), 2:856–57. The French version of the treaty is printed in *Renseignements coloniaux et documents* (nos. 8–9), supplement to *L'Afrique française* 48, no. 7 (August–September 1938): 178–86.

54. Minister of Foreign Affairs to Noguès, 18 February 1938, MAE,

Maroc, 568:230–31; French Ministry of Foreign Affairs press release,
5 August 1938, MAE, Maroc, 571:6–7; Johnson to Hull, 15 January 1938,
in *FRUS* (1938), 2:847–50; Bullitt to Hull, 3, 7, and 9 February 1938, in
FRUS (1938), 2:856–58, 860–62; Counselor of Embassy in France Edwin C. Wilson to Chief of the Division of Near Eastern Affairs Wallace
Murray, 12 February 1938, in *FRUS* (1938), 2:862–64; Memorandum of
conversation by James Rives Childs of the Division of Near Eastern Affairs, 6 May 1938, in *FRUS* (1938), 2:877–80.

55. Noguès, "Conseil du Gouvernement," 7 December 1938, p. 8,
Noguès Papers.

56. Belgian Ambassador Count Robert Van der Straten-Ponthoz to Hull,
7 February 1938, in *FRUS* (1938), 2:860.

57. Hull to Bullitt, 13 April 1937, and Hull to Johnson, 11 December
1937, in *FRUS* (1937), 2:859, 874–76.

58. Noguès to Minister of Foreign Affairs, 25 May 1937, MAE, Maroc,
566:102; Minister of Foreign Affairs to Chargé d'Affaires de France à
Washington Jules Henry, 17 August 1937, MAE, Maroc, 563:166–70;
Viénot to Noguès, 4 January 1937, Noguès Papers.

59. Bullitt to Hull, 9 February 1938, in *FRUS* (1938), 2:860–62; Wilson
to Murray, 12 February 1938, in *FRUS* (1938), 2:862–64; Murray to Wilson,
10 March 1938, in *FRUS* (1938), 2:872–75; Memorandum of conversation
by the Chief of the Division of Near Eastern Affairs, 24 January 1939, in
FRUS (1939), 4:647–50; René Doynel de Saint-Quentin to Minister of Foreign Affairs, 25 January 1939, MAE, Maroc, 564b:4; Memorandum by
James Rives Childs of the Division of Near Eastern Affairs, in letter from
Hull to Roosevelt, 21 July 1938, in *FRUS* (1939), 4:660–62; Murray to
Bullitt, 21 July 1939, in *FRUS* (1939), 4:662–64.

60. Murray to Bullitt, 21 July 1939, in *FRUS* (1939), 4:663.

61. Hull to Roosevelt, 21 July 1939, in *FRUS* (1939), 4:660; Consul General at Casablanca Herbert S. Goold to Hull, 9 September 1939, in *FRUS*
(1939), 4:668–69; Diplomatic Agent and Consul General at Tangier Max-
well Blake to Hull, 13 September 1939, in *FRUS* (1939), 4:669. The United
States did not renounce its capitulations until 1956.

62. Hull to Blake, 15 September 1939, in *FRUS* (1939), 4:686; Blake to
Hull, 9 October 1939, in *FRUS* (1939), 4:688–92; Hull to Blake, 4 December 1939, in *FRUS* (1939), 4:692–93. Also see Morize to Blake, 9 January
1940, in *FRUS* (1940), 3:777. France sought to perpetuate the emergency
wartime controls on the Moroccan economy into the postwar period,
which revived the Franco-American dispute; the matter was ultimately
brought before the International Court of Justice at The Hague, which
ruled in favor of the United States; see Stewart, *The Economy of Morocco*,
pp. 131–33. An exhaustive analysis of that case is provided by Famchon,
Le Maroc.

63. French Chargé Jules Henry to Hull, 26 August 1937, in *FRUS* (1937),
2:864; Memorandum by James Rives Childs of the Division of Near East-

ern Affairs, in letter from Hull to Roosevelt, 21 July 1939, in *FRUS* (1939), 4:661–62; Murray to Johnson, 19 February 1938, in *FRUS* (1938), 2:864–66.

64. See Vice-Président, Délégué, Confédération Générale du Patronat Français to Minister of Foreign Affairs, 30 December 1937, MAE, Maroc, 568:151, and Chambre de Commerce de Marseille, *Le traité anglo-chérifien du 18 juillet 1938*, pp. 26–27. Between 1925 and 1934, France's share of the Moroccan market shrank from three-fifths to two-fifths. On the other hand, Morocco was sending more than one-half of its exports to France because of the favorable quota system; see Knight, *Morocco as a French Economic Venture*, p. 147.

65. Knight, *Morocco as a French Economic Venture*, pp. 34–35, 43, 56–57.

66. Noguès, "Conseil du Gouvernement," 7 December 1938, pp. 16–17; Noguès, "Conseil du Gouvernement," 7 December 1936, p. 7, both in Noguès Papers; Belal, *L'Investissement au Maroc (1912–1964)*, p. 25.

67. Knight, *Morocco as a French Economic Venture*, p. 196.

68. Noguès, "Conseil du Gouvernement," 7 December 1938, pp. 16–17, Noguès Papers; Haut Comité Méditerranéen, session de [8–12] mars 1938, séance du 8 mars 1938, CHEAM, p. 32.

69. Morize to Noguès, 14 May 1937, Noguès Papers. For Noguès's report on Morize's mission, see Noguès, "Conseil du Gouvernement," 25 June 1937, pp. 6–7, Noguès Papers. On the triangular Franco-Algero-Moroccan vegetable controversy, the "harmonization" schemes, and quotas, see Stewart, *The Economy of Morocco*, pp. 96–97.

70. Delbos to Morize, 6 August 1937, Noguès Papers. In 1938 the interest on the debt still absorbed 30 percent of budget resources; see Belal, *L'Investissement au Maroc*, p. 25.

71. Morocco was to be "welded" to France only on condition that it became an "economic collaborator" instead of a "competing firm"; see Garcin, *La politique des contingents*, pp. 203–4.

72. Morize to Noguès, 2 and 24 August 1937, Noguès Papers.

73. Morize to Noguès, 24 August 1937, Noguès Papers.

74. Noguès, "Conseil du Gouvernement," 7 December 1938, p. 14, Noguès Papers.

75. Noguès to the Association "Le Maroc" in Paris, November 1938; Noguès, "Conseil du Gouvernement," 7 December 1938, pp. 4–5; Noguès, "Conseil du Gouvernement, section marocaine," 14 December 1938, p. 29, all in Noguès Papers; Gallissot, *Le patronat européen au Maroc*, pp. 158–59.

76. Noguès to the Association "Le Maroc" in Paris, November 1938, Noguès Papers; Stewart, *The Economy of Morocco*, pp. 38–39.

77. Lyautey to his sister, 25 November 1897, in Lyautey, *Lettres du Tonkin et de Madagascar*, 2:220.

FIVE

1. On the diplomacy of the Moroccan question, see Andrew, *Théophile Delcassé;* Guillan, *L'Allemagne et le Maroc;* Allain, *Agadir;* Anderson, *The First Moroccan Crisis;* and Barlow, *The Agadir Crisis.*
2. Halstead, *Rebirth of a Nation,* p. 18; Trout, *Morocco's Saharan Frontiers,* pp. 170–73; Marchat, "Les origines diplomatiques du 'Maroc espagnol,'" pp. 101–70. The Spanish zone also included a strip of land in the south marked on French maps as southern Spanish Morocco (*Maroc meridional español*).
3. Stewart, *The Economy of Morocco,* p. 5.
4. Cited in Carr, *Spain,* p. 518.
5. See the map in Andrews, *Théophile Delcassé,* p. 224, for Spain's shrinking share in Morocco according to the draft Franco-Spanish treaty of 8 November 1902, the Franco-Spanish treaty of 3 October 1904, and the Franco-Spanish treaty of 27 November 1912.
6. Marchat, "Les origines diplomatiques du 'Maroc espagnol,'" pp. 132, 159, 164.
7. See Cordero Torres, *Organización del protectorado espagñol,* 1:82.
8. See Fleming, "Spanish Morocco and the *Alzamiento Nacional,*" pp. 27–42.
9. Peyrouton to Viénot, 5 August 1936, MAE, Maroc, 604:136–39.
10. Marchat, "La France et l'Espagne au Maroc," p. 90. The relevant *dahirs* are in *Bulletin Officiel* 25, no. 1242b (18 August 1936): 1029–30; 25, no. 1246 (11 September 1936): 1123; 25, no. 1247b (22 September 1936): 1157–58.
11. *Bulletin Officiel* 26, no. 1269b (20 February 1937): 261.
12. Delbos to the French diplomatic representatives in London and Rome, 5 December 1936, in *DDF,* 4:159.
13. Coverdale, *Italian Intervention in the Spanish Civil War,* pp. 76–77, 154–55, 383, 388–89.
14. Coverdale, *Italian Intervention in the Spanish Civil War,* pp. 127–28. Pantelleria was the island base between Tunisia and Sicily.
15. Delbos to the French diplomatic representatives in London and Rome, 5 December 1936, in *DDF,* 4:159.
16. Coverdale, *Italian Intervention in the Spanish Civil War,* pp. 148, 198–200; *L'Afrique française* 47 (1 January 1937): 10–11.
17. *L'Humanité,* 3 January 1937, cited in Dreifort, *Yvon Delbos,* p. 91.
18. Italian designs centered on Tunisia and eastern Algeria. Still, the Spanish high commissioner in Morocco revealed that the Italians were offering "anything" to get a foothold in Spanish Morocco; see Jean-Claude Serres to Delbos, 10 January 1937, in *DDF,* 4:457; Coverdale, *Italian Intervention in the Spanish Civil War,* p. 385.
19. Delbos to Corbin, 30 November 1936, in *DDF,* 4:88–89.
20. Delbos to Corbin, 30 November 1936, in *DDF,* 4:89.
21. Delbos to Corbin, 30 November 1936, in *DDF,* 4:90.

22. Delbos to Corbin, 30 November 1936, in *DDF*, 4:90.

23. *Les événements survenus en France, Témoignages*, Blum testimony, 1:219; Viénot to Noguès, 4 January 1937, Noguès Papers; Noguès to Delbos, 6 January 1937, in *DDF*, 4:417; Delbos to Corbin, 8 January 1937, in *DDF*, 4:438–39.

24. Corbin to Delbos, 8 January 1937, in *DDF*, 4:443.

25. Italian and German "volunteers" to the nationalist cause were enrolled in the Spanish foreign legion as a cover.

26. Serres to Delbos, 10 January 1937, in *DDF*, 4:457–59.

27. Corbin to Delbos, 11 January 1937, in *DDF*, 4:460, 462–63.

28. Chargé in Spain Wilhelm Faupel to the Foreign Ministry, 9 January 1937; Ambassador in France Count Johannes von Welczeck to Head of the Extra-European Section of the Political Department Otto von Erdmansdorff, 9 January 1937, both in *Documents on German Foreign Policy, 1918–1945*, Series D (1937–45), 13 vols. (London and Washington, D.C., 1949–64), 3:214–16. Hereafter cited as *DGFP*.

29. François-Poncet to Delbos, 11 January 1937, in *DDF*, 4:459–62; Memorandum by Foreign Minister von Neurath, 11 January 1937, in *DGFP*, 3:218–19.

30. *L'Afrique française* 47, no. 1 (January 1937): 13.

31. Pierre Arnal to Delbos, 13 January 1937, in *DDF*, 4:476–78.

32. *L'Afrique française* 46, no. 11 (October 1936): 530; 46, no. 8–9 (August–September 1936): 457, 459; 47, no. 1 (January 1937): 15.

33. An embarrassing footnote to the affair was the offer of the republican government in Spain to "examine" with the intent to modify the "present situation" of the Spanish zone "on the condition that the modification benefits no powers other than France and the United Kingdom." Britain rejected it out of hand; France did not. The reason given by François-Poncet was that France stood by its January declaration on the integrity of Spanish Morocco and saw no reason to respond to such "pretended offers." To end the matter, France published its note of 20 March to the Spanish government stating that "a problem of this magnitude" could only be handled after "order had been reestablished in Spain" and in conformity with the international agreements on Morocco. See Luis Araquistain to Blum, 13 February 1937, in *DDF*, 4:762–64; François-Poncet to Delbos, 18 and 19 March 1937, in *DDF*, 5:189, 202; *L'Afrique française* 47, no. 3 (March 1937): 162–63 and no. 4 (April 1937): 210–11.

34. Noguès to Delbos, 26 February 1937, in *DDF*, 5:55–56. For the German-Spanish economic connection, see Harper, *German Economic Policy in Spain during the Spanish Civil War.*

35. Noguès to Delbos, 26 February 1937, in *DDF*, 5:56–58. The best known of Morocco's Germany-watchers, Jacques Ladreit de Lacharrière, agreed with Noguès's conclusions but doubted that Germany was interested in any "durable political establishment" in Morocco. For Germany, Morocco would always be just the "medium of exchange" for something

else; see "La politique de l'Allemagne au Maroc," CHEAM conference, 26 June 1937.

36. Halstead and Halstead, "Aborted Imperialism," p. 55. My account of Beigbeder follows Halstead, "A 'Somewhat Machiavellian' Face," pp. 46–66. Also see Halstead, "Un africain méconnu," pp. 31–60.

37. Fleming, "Spanish Morocco and the *Alzamiento Nacional*," p. 30.

38. Clément, "L'Espagne phalangiste et le Maroc," pp. 31–34.

39. *L'Afrique française* 47, no. 3 (March 1937): 162.

40. Halstead, "A 'Somewhat Machiavellian' Face," pp. 51, 53–54; *L'Afrique française* 48, no. 7 (July 1938): 338; 49, no. 3 (March 1939): 77–78; 49, no. 7 (July 1939): 194.

41. *España*, 4 May 1939, cited in Halstead, "A 'Somewhat Machiavellian' Face," p. 63.

42. Noguès to Ministry of Foreign Affairs, 11 October 1937 and 16 May 1938, MAE, Maroc, 490:60–62, 175, 177–78; *L'Afrique française* 47, no. 10 (October 1937): 485.

43. *L'Afrique française* 49, no. 3 (March 1939): 64–66. Pétain was remembered for his generous statements and enthusiastic cooperation with the Spanish army during the Rif war; see *L'Afrique française* 49, no. 4 (April 1939): 122.

44. Auffray, *Pierre de Margerie*, p. 325.

45. Ambassador in Spain Alexander W. Weddell to Hull, 5 November 1940, in *FRUS* (1940), 3:787.

46. For references to Spanish criticism of France's privileged status in Tangier, see Halstead and Halstead, "Aborted Imperialism," p. 65 (nn. 13 and 14). On the administration of Tangier, see Stuart, *The International City of Tangier*, pp. 120–23.

47. Noguès to Diplomatie, Paris, 13 April 1940, Noguès Papers.

48. "Journal des marches et opérations du Quartier Général du Commandement en Chef du Théâtre d'Opérations de l'Afrique du Nord (2 September 1939–31 July 1940)," 14 February 1940, pp. 103–4; 29 February 1940, p. 112; 9 March 1940, pp. 119–20, Noguès Papers. Hereafter cited as "Journal des marches."

49. Serrano Suñer, *Entre Hendaya y Gibraltar*, p. 142.

50. Noguès to Ministry of Foreign Affairs, 17 April 1940, and Noguès to Guerre (Central Berlioz), 19 April 1940, Noguès Papers.

51. Noguès to Diplomatie, Paris, 3 June 1940, Noguès Papers; Weddell to Hull, 14 June 1940, in *FRUS* (1940), 3:783–84.

52. Blake to Hull, 14 June 1940, in *FRUS* (1940), 3:784; TOAFN, *Bulletin d'information* no. 40 (17 June 1940), p. 2; Halstead and Halstead, "Aborted Imperialism," p. 66 (n. 31).

53. Charles-Roux, *Cinq mois tragiques*, pp. 193, 224–25. The Spanish government considered using force against the southern zone but had second thoughts because of France's still strong air and sea power. Noguès purposely kept his troops in motion along the northern border to bluff the

Spaniards into thinking his strength was greater than it actually was. To make things easier for Spain in the future, Beigbeder pressed the Germans and the Italians to disarm the French in North Africa, suggested to Vichy that Noguès was less than loyal in an attempt to get him removed, and told the American ambassador that Spain would consider penetration of French Morocco by anyone as an act of hostility toward Spain. See Halstead, "Un africain méconnu," pp. 43–44, 47; General Étienne Buot de l'Épine (French military attaché at Madrid, 1940) to Maître Pierre Courteault, 10 November 1955, Noguès Papers; *Les événements survenus en France, Témoignages*, General René Bertrand testimony, 6:1793–94.

54. Noguès to Diplomatie, Bordeaux, 24 June 1940, in *Les événements survenus en France, Rapport,* 2:423; Charles-Roux, *Cinq mois tragiques,* pp. 225–26.

55. Charles-Roux, *Cinq mois tragiques,* pp. 226–28.

56. Charles-Roux, *Cinq mois tragiques,* pp. 227–28, 230.

57. Woolman, *Rebels in the Rif,* pp. 165, 208–9; Charles-Roux, *Cinq mois tragiques,* p. 229. For the 1925 military and boundary accords and the diplomatic notes (all dated 25 July 1925), see Gómez-Jordana Souza, *La tramoya de nuestra actuación en Marruecos,* pp. 82–86. I am grateful to Shannon Fleming for this reference.

58. Charles-Roux, *Cinq mois tragiques,* pp. 229–30.

59. Charles-Roux, *Cinq mois tragiques,* pp. 232–34.

60. Charles-Roux, *Cinq mois tragiques,* pp. 234–36.

61. Charles-Roux, *Cinq mois tragiques,* pp. 236–39; Baudouin, *Neuf mois au gouvernement,* p. 322.

62. Charles-Roux, *Cinq mois tragiques,* pp. 239–40.

63. Charles-Roux, *Cinq mois tragiques,* pp. 241–43.

64. Charles-Roux, *Cinq mois tragiques,* pp. 244–47; Puzzo, *Spain and the Great Powers,* p. 227.

65. Puzzo, *Spain and the Great Powers,* pp. 225–28; U.S. Department of State, *The Spanish Government and the Axis: Documents* (Washington, D.C., 1946), p. 17.

66. Warner, *Pierre Laval,* pp. 223–25; Paxton, *Vichy France,* p. 80.

67. Paxton, *Vichy France,* p. 62.

68. Schmokel, *Dream of Empire,* p. 134. German aims centered on Central Africa, not North Africa, except perhaps for German bases in Morocco.

69. Warner, *Pierre Laval,* p. 231.

70. Paxton, *Vichy France,* p. 81.

71. Piétri, *Mes années d'Espagne,* pp. 102–3; James Rives Childs, "Operation 'TORCH': An Object Lesson in Diplomacy," p. 52, Childs Papers; Weygand to Noguès, 25 April 1941, and Noguès to Weygand, 9 May 1941, Noguès Papers.

72. Childs, "Operation 'TORCH'," p. 76, Childs Papers.

SIX

1. De Gaulle, *Complete War Memoirs*, p. 446.
2. Villelume, *Journal d'une défaite*, entry for 2 February 1940, p. 181.
3. De Gaulle, *Complete War Memoirs*, p. 446.
4. TOAFN, *Bulletin d'information*, no. 3 (18 September 1939), Noguès Papers. From September 1939 until Noguès's permanent return to Rabat in August 1940, Morize was the resident general in all but name. Noguès praised his "qualities of calm and levelheadedness"; see Noguès to Diplomatie, Paris, 11 June 1940, Noguès Papers.
5. "Proclamation de S.M. le Sultan lue dans les mosquées," 4 September 1939, Noguès Papers.
6. TOAFN, *Bulletin d'information*, no. 9 (3 November 1939) and no. 20 (19 January 1940); "Journal des marches," 10 October 1939, p. 27, and 8 November 1939, p. 43, all in Noguès Papers.
7. Noguès to Gamelin, 23 April 1940, Noguès Papers. The combined total of North African troops sent to France or the Levant was probably closer to 170,000. See Noguès, "Raisons: Acceptation de l'armistice," August 1940, Noguès Papers (hereafter cited as "Armistice").
8. "Journal des marches," 10 October 1939, p. 26, Noguès Papers.
9. Noguès to Gamelin, 23 April 1940, Noguès Papers.
10. "Journal des marches," 25 May 1940, pp. 177–78, 180, and 30 May 1940, p. 183, Noguès Papers. André Truchet has sorted out the statistics in "L'armistice de juin 1940," pp. 40–43.
11. "Journal des marches," 12 and 13 June 1940, p. 190; Noguès, "Cahiers," no. 1: "Études," all in Noguès Papers. This notebook and a second, "Notes diverses," contain Noguès's writings in exile in Portugal from 1943 to 1954.
12. Chapman, *Why France Fell*, p. 255. On Weygand, see Bankwitz, *Maxime Weygand*.
13. Bankwitz, *Maxime Weygand*, pp. 293, 295–97, 309–12; Chapman, *Why France Fell*, p. 237.
14. Noguès to Weygand, 17 June 1940, in *Les événements survenus en France, Rapport*, 2:416. On 15 June Weygand had ordered what was left of France's air force to fly to North Africa.
15. "Relation de la 'liaison' effectuée auprès du général Weygand et du Gouvernement par le chef de bataillon Guizol du 17 au 21 juin 1940," 21 June 1940, pp. 4–5, Noguès Papers. Hereafter cited as Guizol report.
16. Guizol report, p. 5, Noguès Papers.
17. "Journal des marches," 19 and 20 June 1940, pp. 195–97; "Historique personnel du général Noguès concernant les journées des 17 au 27 juin 1940," 18 June 1940, p. 1, and 19 June 1940, pp. 1–2, all in Noguès Papers. For the fighting spirit of the European population in Morocco, see Truchet, "L'armistice de juin 1940," pp. 30–31.
18. "Historique personnel du général Noguès," 17 June 1940, p. 3, Noguès Papers.

19. See Noguès to Grand Quartier Général, État-Major, 18 June 1940, in *Les événements survenus en France, Rapport*, 2:417. For British encouragement of French colonial resistance and Noguès's pivotal position, see Woodward, *British Foreign Policy*, 1:316–21.

20. Noguès to Diplomatie (for Marshal Pétain), 18 June 1940, in *Les événements survenus en France, Rapport*, 2:417–18.

21. See the text of de Gaulle's radio addresses for 18 and 19 June 1940 in de Gaulle, *Discours et Messages* 1:3–5. The 19 June speech was geared for North Africa, which he baptized "the Africa of Clauzel, of Bugeaud, of Lyautey, of Noguès." By telegram de Gaulle offered to put himself at Noguès's disposal, "either to fight under your orders or for any other task which you deem useful." Noguès did not respond and censored the press so that de Gaulle's speeches would not be circulated, believing the appeals to be "inadmissible" so long as the French army continued to fight under Weygand's command; see "Historique personnel du général Noguès," 19 June 1940, p. 3, Noguès Papers.

22. Weygand to Noguès, 18 June 1940, in *Les événements survenus en France, Rapport*, 2:416.

23. Weygand to Noguès, 19 June 1940, in *Les événements survenus en France, Rapport*, 2:418.

24. Guizol report, pp. 23–25; Darlan to Noguès, 20 June 1940, both in Noguès Papers.

25. Noguès, "Armistice," p. 5; "Historique personnel du général Noguès," 21 June 1940, pp. 4, 6–7, and 23 June 1940, pp. 2–3, all in Noguès Papers. All of Noguès's efforts were fruitless. The navy protested his interception of cargo destined for the mainland; Washington and London were unwilling or unable to pledge immediate aid; and his officers in France ran afoul of the navy and war ministries; see Noguès, "Armistice," pp. 5, 7–8, Noguès Papers. Gates suggests that British "bankruptcy"—the inability to pledge men or equipment to fight in North Africa—might have been "*the* most important" concern of Noguès; see *End of the Affair*, pp. 319–21. Also see "Mission effectuée en Métropole au moment de l'armistice par le capitaine Loiret," in *Les événements survenus en France, Rapport*, 2:429–31. On the other hand, Truchet was impressed by the materiel obtained; see "L'armistice de juin 1940," pp. 43–47.

26. "Historique personnel du général Noguès," 21 June 1940, pp. 2–3, Noguès Papers.

27. "Historique personnel du général Noguès," 21 June 1940, pp. 4–5, and 20 June 1940, p. 1, Noguès Papers.

28. Warner, *Pierre Laval*, p. 179.

29. Weygand to Noguès and Noguès to Weygand, 21 June 1940, in *Les événements survenus en France, Rapport*, 2:418–19; *Les événements survenus en France, Témoignages*, General René Bertrand testimony (Noguès's *chef de cabinet militaire* in Algiers), 6:1788.

30. Weygand to Noguès, 22 June 1940, in *Les événements survenus en France, Rapport*, 2:419.

31. "Historique personnel du général Noguès," 22 June 1940, pp. 2–3; TOAFN, État-Major, 3ème Bureau, "Note au sujet des possibilités allemandes à travers l'Espagne," n.d.; "Historique personnel du général Noguès," 21 June 1940, p. 6, all in Noguès Papers.

32. Colonel Adolphe Goutard estimates that it would have taken four months for Germany to transport and put into place two divisions along the northern frontier in Morocco or along the Tunisian-Libyan border; see "La réalité de la 'menace' allemande sur l'Afrique du nord en 1940," p. 19.

33. Noguès to Weygand, 22 June 1940, in *Les événements survenus en France, Rapport,* 2:419–20.

34. "Historique personnel du général Noguès," 22 June 1940, attachment, Noguès Papers.

35. Noguès to Weygand, 22 June 1940, in *Les événements survenus en France, Rapport,* 2:420.

36. *Les événements survenus en France, Témoignages,* General Louis Koeltz testimony, 9:2814. Weygand told the postwar parliamentary committee that the proposals contained in Noguès's telegram "did not seem to be reasonable"; see *Les événements survenus en France, Témoignages,* Weygand testimony, 6:1782–84. Also see Weygand, *Mémoires,* 3:328–29, and Weygand, *En lisant les Mémoires de guerre du général de Gaulle,* pp. 76–93.

37. Foreign Minister Baudouin reported that the entire cabinet was against any military "adventure" that would result in war with Spain. For himself, he had decided that trying to continue the fight in North Africa was "chimerical" and that only the armistice could save the Maghreb from certain German invasion; see *Neuf mois au gouvernement,* entry for 23 June 1940, pp. 207–8. Once denied the support of the fleet and reinforcements from France, it was easy to make the case against battling on in North Africa; see Haute Cour de Justice (1956), AN, Noguès testimony, 1:34–35. In addition, there were serious doubts about the strength of Noguès's own forces; these cast another shadow over the general's optimistic estimates. For General Roger Pennès's bleak assessment of North Africa's air power, see *Les événements survenus en France, Témoignages,* General René Bertrand testimony, 6:1791; see also the retrospective note of Colonel Raymond Baufine-Ducrocq, Noguès's assistant chief of staff for supply, written in May 1945, which is attached to the letter from Baufine-Ducrocq to Maître Pierre Courteault, 10 May 1955, Noguès Papers. Gates argues that technical considerations played only a "minor role" in the French government's decision not to continue the fight from North Africa. What was decisive was the belief that Germany had won the war, that Britain would soon surrender, and that the government had to maintain order in France and in the empire; see *End of the Affair,* pp. 305–6, 313–17.

38. "Historique personnel du général Noguès," 22 June 1940, p. 4, Noguès Papers.

39. De Gaulle, "Discours prononcé à la Radio de Londres," 22 June 1940,

in de Gaulle, *Discours et Messages*, 1:5–7.

40. Noguès to Weygand, 23 June 1940 and 24 June 1940, in *Les événements survenus en France, Rapport*, 2:420–21, 423.

41. Noguès to Weygand, 23 June 1940; Baudouin to Noguès, 24 and 25 June 1940, all in *Les événements survenus en France, Rapport*, 2:422, 426–27.

42. Thomas, *Britain and Vichy*, p. 41.

43. "Historique personnel du général Noguès," 23 June 1940, p. 4, Noguès Papers. On British attempts to keep the French empire in the war, see Bell, *A Certain Eventuality*, pp. 165–90; on Britain's North African policy, see Gates, *End of the Affair*, pp. 303–12.

44. Weygand to Noguès, 24 June 1940, in *Les événements survenus en France, Rapport*, 2:424; "Historique personnel du général Noguès," 24 June 1940, pp. 2–3, Noguès Papers.

45. Baudouin to Noguès, 24 June 1940; Weygand to Noguès, 24 and 25 June 1940, all in *Les événements survenus en France, Rapport*, 2:424–25.

46. "Historique personnel du général Noguès," 26 June 1940, p. 1, Noguès Papers.

47. Noguès was automatically deferred to by other overseas commanders by virtue of his seniority in rank and command. He was also closer to the happenings in France than the others and thus better able to "see things more clearly." See *Les événements survenus en France, Témoignages*, General René Bertrand testimony, 6:1798.

48. Noguès to Weygand, 25 June 1940, in *Les événements survenus en France, Rapport*, 2:425; *Les événements survenus en France, Témoignages*, General René Bertrand testimony, 6:1793. Also see *La Presse marocaine*, 25 June 1940.

49. Noguès to Weygand, 25 June 1940, in *Les événements survenus en France, Rapport*, 2:425–26.

50. Weygand to Noguès, 26 and 28 June 1940; Noguès to Weygand, 28 June 1940, all in *Les événements survenus en France, Rapport*, 2:427–28.

51. Noguès to Weygand, 25 June 1940, in *Les événements survenus en France, Rapport*, 2:425; TOAFN, Direction du Cabinet, "Note sur l'opinion à Casablanca," 20 June 1940, Noguès Papers; Morize to Noguès, 22 June 1940, Noguès Papers; "Historique personnel du général Noguès," 20 June 1940, pp. 1–3, Noguès Papers.

52. TOAFN, "Note sur l'opinion à Casablanca," 20 June 1940; Morize to Noguès, 22 June 1940, both in Noguès Papers.

53. Noguès, "Note sur l'affaire Mandel," n.d., Noguès Papers; Spears, *Assignment to Catastrophe*, 1:207; Sherwood, *Georges Mandel*, p. 258.

54. Noguès, "Note sur l'affaire Mandel," n.d., Noguès Papers.

55. Morize to Diplomatie, Bordeaux, 25 June 1940, Noguès Papers. Also see Thomas, *Britain and Vichy*, p. 49; Cooper, *Old Men Forget*, pp. 282–84; Dillon, *Memories of Three Wars*, pp. 141–44; Woodward, *British Foreign Policy*, 1:327, 329–30. On his return to England, Duff Cooper argued for an expeditionary force that would land in Morocco and set up a

pro-Allied French administration. Despite Churchill's enthusiasm, the Combined Chiefs of Staff advised against it and the plan was dropped. See Gates, *End of the Affair*, pp. 323–24.

56. Morize to Diplomatie, Bordeaux, 25 June 1940, Noguès Papers.

57. Noguès to Diplomatie, Bordeaux, 26 June 1940, Noguès Papers.

58. Noguès to Diplomatie, Bordeaux, 26 June 1940, Noguès Papers.

59. Noguès to Diplomatie, Bordeaux, 26 June 1940; Noguès, "Note sur l'affaire Mandel"; Ivan Martin (Noguès's former *chef du cabinet civil*) to Maître Pierre Courteault, 14 April 1949, all in Noguès Papers; Tony-Révillon, *Mes carnets*, entry for 2 June 1940, p. 105.

60. "Plaidoirie de Maître Viénot," pp. 12–13; Noguès, "Note sur l'affaire Mandel," both in Noguès Papers. André Viénot was Noguès's defense counsel for the 1956 Haute Cour de Justice proceedings.

61. Noguès, "Note sur l'affaire Mandel"; "Plaidoirie de Maître Viénot," p. 13; Noguès to Diplomatie, Vichy, 11 July 1940, all in Noguès Papers; Sherwood, *Georges Mandel*, p. 265.

62. Sherwood, *Georges Mandel*, p. 262.

63. "Journal des marches," 28 June and 3 July 1940, pp. 206–7, 211, Noguès Papers. For the foreign ministry's reaction to Mers-el-Kebir, see Baudouin to Noguès, 6, 7, and 8 July 1940, Noguès Papers. For the reaction of the French in Casablanca, see Chef de la Région de Casablanca Louis Contard to Directeur des Affaires Politiques Louis Sicot, 8 July 1940, Noguès Papers.

64. Bankwitz, *Maxime Weygand*, p. 336; Weygand, *Mémoires*, 3:320–21.

65. "Journal des marches," 8, 9, 13, 23, and 31 July 1940, pp. 217, 219–21, 224, 232, 235–36, Noguès Papers.

66. *La Vigie marocaine*, 12 August 1940.

67. *La Vigie marocaine*, 12 August 1940.

68. Baudouin to Noguès, 4 September 1940, Noguès Papers.

69. Noguès, "Que deviendra le Maroc au traité de paix," n.d. [1940], Noguès Papers.

70. Baudouin to Noguès, 4 September 1940, Noguès Papers.

71. *La Vigie marocaine*, 31 August 1940.

72. *Bulletin Officiel* 29, no. 1454 (6 September 1940): 866. In addition to Morize, Noguès lost his Directeur du Cabinet, Georges Gayet; his Chef du Cabinet Civil, Ivan Martin; the head of his diplomatic staff, Vincent Broustra; and a member of his military cabinet, Colonel René Bertrand. Perhaps most precious, Noguès was deprived of his private secretary and factotum, Georges Hutin. Gayet and Martin owed their places to the former regime, Hutin was a Freemason, and Bertrand was accused of being a Jew and Anglophile. Noguès tried to save them all but without success; see Noguès to Laure, 4 November 1940, Noguès Papers; Pétain to Weygand, 9 November 1940, in Weygand, *Mémoires*, 3:app. X.

73. See "Instruction de mission pour M. le général Weygand," 5 October 1940, in *Les événements survenus en France, Témoignages*, 6:1670–72;

Noguès to Laure, 4 November 1940, Noguès Papers. On the inevitable personal conflicts between Weygand and the colonial governors, see Weygand, *Mémoires*, 3:359–60.

74. See Bankwitz, *Maxime Weygand*, pp. 243–45. Weygand accused Freemasons and Jews of spreading English propaganda and of involvement in "veritable dens of treason" throughout French Africa; see Weygand to Pétain, 10 November 1940, Noguès Papers.

75. Weygand to Noguès, 4 December 1940, Noguès Papers. Among those named were Chef de la Région de Casablanca Louis Contard; Chef des Services Municipaux de Casablanca Henri Bouquet; Premier Président Marcellin Cordier; Procureur-Général Gustave Huber; Présidents de Chambre Pierre Léris and Hippolyte Lidon; and Directeur de l'Office des Mutilés, Anciens Combattants, et Victimes de la Guerre Marcel Acquaviva. Next to Morize, Cordier was the most important victim of the purge; he had led the 1938 French delegation to London to negotiate the abrogation of Britain's capitulatory privileges in Morocco. In the end, only Léris was spared.

76. Noguès to Laure, 4 November and 8 December 1940, Noguès Papers.

77. Noguès to Laure, 8 December 1940, Noguès Papers.

78. Noguès to Laure, 8 December 1940, Noguès Papers.

79. Noguès to General François, 27 October 1940; Weygand to Noguès, 4 December 1940; Noguès to Darlan, 22 February 1941; Weygand to Noguès, 25 April 1941; Noguès to Weygand, 9 May 1941, all in Noguès Papers.

80. Noguès to Darlan, 22 February 1941, Noguès Papers.

81. Blum, *L'Oeuvre de Léon Blum*, 5:121.

82. Weygand, "Note," 18 November 1941; Weygand to Noguès, 15 November 1941, both in Noguès Papers. On Weygand's departure General Alphonse Juin was given command of North Africa's troops.

83. Martin du Gard, *La chronique de Vichy*, p. 117.

84. Noguès, "Anniversaire mort du maréchal, discours devant le mausolée," 20 July 1940, Noguès Papers.

85. Ibid.; *La Vigie marocaine*, 4 July 1940, 27 July 1941, 31 May 1942.

86. Noguès, "Voyage au Maroc du Commissaire Général à l'Éducation Générale et aux Sports," 20 April 1940; "Texte de l'allocution prononcée par le général Noguès à l'issue du dîner offert par le Résident Général dimanche soir aux personnalités venues pour l'inauguration du Méditerranée-Niger," 8 December 1941, both in Noguès Papers.

87. *La Vigie marocaine*, 6 July and 3 September 1940; *Bulletin Officiel* 29, no. 1456b (23 September 1940): 911–12, and 29, no. 1458 (4 October 1940): 946–49. Also see Montagne, "Un essai de régionalisme au Maroc," CHEAM report, 1941, and Brémard, *L'organisation régionale au Maroc*.

88. *La Vigie marocaine*, 18 January 1941. On the military camouflage directed by Noguès, see Jouin, "Le 'camouflage' des goums marocains," pp. 100–117.

89. *Bulletin Officiel* 30, no. 1480 (7 March 1941): 261–62, and 30, no. 1486 (18 April 1941): 458–60.

90. *Bulletin Officiel* 29, no. 1454 (6 September 1940): 868–70.

91. *Bulletin Officiel* 30, no. 1514 (31 October 1941): 1046–47. The prison terms of fifteen Gaullists sentenced in August 1941 ranged from eight months to fifteen years at hard labor; see *La Vigie marocaine,* 10 August 1941.

92. *Bulletin Officiel* 29, no. 1463 (8 November 1940): 1054–56. Also see *Bulletin Officiel* 30; no. 1503 (8 August 1941): 794–97; 30, no. 1504 (22 August 1941): 857; and 30, no. 1509 (26 September 1941): 947–48; Dutheil, "Les juifs au Maroc," CHEAM conference, 16 December 1941.

93. See Jean-André Cazemajou (assistant grand master of the Grand Orient de France) to Georges Hutin, 14 July 1948, Noguès Papers; Haute Cour de Justice (1956), AN, testimony of Louis Contard (former Chef de la Région de Casablanca), 3:11; letters in "La Politique juive du Protectorat," Noguès Papers. Also see "Plaidoirie de Maître Viénot," pp. 18–21, Noguès Papers; Haute Cour de Justice (1956), AN, testimony of Roland Cadet (former Conseiller Juridique du Protectorat), 3:16–24; Cadet to Maître Pierre Courteault, 6 February 1948, Noguès Papers.

94. Haute Cour de Justice (1956), AN, testimony of Madame Félix Guedj, 2:107–10; "Affaire Guedj," Noguès Papers. Also see *La Vigie marocaine,* 25 September 1941.

95. *La Vigie marocaine,* 21 September 1940.

96. The 1941 budget increased by 40 million francs over 1940; the 1942 budget, by 230 million francs over 1941; and the 1943 budget, by 307 million francs over 1942. See *Bulletin Officiel* 30, no. 1480 (7 March 1941): 234–35; 31, no. 1531 (27 February 1942): 166; and 32, no. 1578b (25 January 1943): 73.

97. *Bulletin Officiel* 29, no. 1433 (12 April 1940): 346; 30, no. 1480 (7 March 1941): 234–35; 31, no. 1531 (27 February 1942): 166; and 32, no. 1578b (25 January 1943): 73. On the bond issues, see *Bulletin Officiel* 29, no. 1442 (14 June 1940): 580, and 31, no. 1537 (10 April 1942): 298.

98. Noguès, "Que deviendra le Maroc au traité de paix," n.d. [1940], Noguès Papers.

SEVEN

1. Thomas, *Britain and Vichy,* pp. 54–55.

2. H. Freeman Matthews to Hull, 26 August 1940, in *FRUS* (1940), 2:579.

3. This began to change in December 1940 with the institution of escorted convoys between Casablanca and Marseilles. From 1940 to 1942 Moroccan trade was largely confined to exchanges with France, West Africa, the French Antilles, and Portugal; see Auphan, *La Lutte pour la vie,* pp. 63–66.

4. Childs, "Operation 'TORCH'," pp. 5, 9–10, 12–13, Childs Papers; Langer, *Our Vichy Gamble,* pp. 106–7; Memorandum of conversation by James Rives Childs of the Division of Near Eastern Affairs, 25 October

1940, in *FRUS* (1940), 2:602–3; Matthews to Hull, 6 November 1940, in *FRUS* (1940), 2:613.

5. Memorandum of conversation by Assistant Chief of the Division of European Affairs John D. Hickerson, 27 September 1940, in *FRUS* (1940), 2:594–95; Childs memoranda, 25, 29, and 30 October 1940, in *FRUS* (1940), 2:602–4, 606–7; Memorandum by Chief of the Division of Near Eastern Affairs Wallace Murray, 27 November 1940, in *FRUS* (1940), 2:620; Memorandum of conversation by Henry S. Villard of the Division of Near Eastern Affairs, 18 December 1940, in *FRUS* (1940), 2:632–34.

6. Childs, "Operation 'TORCH'," pp. 13–17, Childs Papers.

7. Murphy, *Diplomat Among Warriors*, pp. 66, 68–69, 91; Childs, "Operation 'TORCH'," pp. 17–19, Childs Papers.

8. Childs, "Operation 'TORCH'," pp. 20–24, Childs Papers. Childs took up his post in February 1941.

9. Herbert C. Pell [from Murphy] to Hull [for Welles], 14 January 1941, in *FRUS* (1941), 2:208; Villard memorandum, 15 January 1941, in *FRUS* (1941), 2:211.

10. Morize to Noguès, 2 August 1937 (Noguès Papers).

11. Pell [from Murphy] to Hull [for Welles], 14 January 1941, in *FRUS* (1941), 2:206–11; Murphy, *Diplomat Among Warriors*, pp. 79–80. Although America was to provide North Africa with desperately needed items, nothing was given gratis. All was purchased with French funds that had been blocked in the United States. On the subject of American aid to North Africa, see Dougherty, *The Politics of Wartime Aid*.

12. Marchal was Morocco's director of commerce and industry and had been the top negotiator in 1939 on the capitulations question with America. Robert Marjolin was Mönick's second at Rabat. On Britain's blockade policy toward Morocco in 1940, see Thomas, *Britain and Vichy*, pp. 65–69, 94–96.

13. Pell [from Murphy] to Hull [for Welles], 16 January 1941, in *FRUS* (1941), 2:213; Hull [from Welles] to Pell [for Murphy], 17 January 1941, in *FRUS* (1941), 2:214.

14. "Rapport de Marjolin," n.d., and Marchal to Mönick, 19 January 1941, both in letter from Noguès to the Ministry of Foreign Affairs, 25 January 1941, Noguès Papers. Also see Ambassador of France in Spain to Minister of Foreign Affairs, 11 January 1941, Noguès Papers.

15. Noguès to the Ministry of Foreign Affairs, 25 January 1941, Noguès Papers.

16. "Rapport de Marjolin," n.d.; Marchal to Mönick, 19 January 1941, both in letter from Noguès to the Ministry of Foreign Affairs, 25 January 1941, Noguès Papers; Thomas, *Britain and Vichy*, p. 101.

17. Noguès to Diplomatie, Vichy, 27 January 1941, Noguès Papers.

18. Weygand to Pétain, 1 February 1941, Noguès Papers.

19. "La position du problème du ravitaillement de l'Afrique du nord française," 11 June 1941, Noguès Papers; Memorandum of conversation by the Acting Chief of the Division of European Affairs Ray Atherton, 5 February

1941, in *FRUS* (1941), 2:251–53; the British Embassy to the Department of State, 24 January 1941, in *FRUS* (1941), 2:242–45; Villard memorandum, 11 February 1941, in *FRUS* (1941), 2:255–57. On Britain's secret proposals to Weygand, see Thomas, *Britain and Vichy*, pp. 82–87.

20. Hull memorandum, 10 February 1941, in *FRUS* (1941), 2:255; Villard memorandum, 11 February 1941, in *FRUS* (1941), 2:257; Paxton, *Vichy France*, p. 104.

21. The British Embassy to the Department of State, 24 January and 7 February 1941, in *FRUS* (1941), 2:246, 253–54; Atherton memorandum, 27 January 1941, in *FRUS* (1941), 2:248; Hull memorandum, 10 February 1941, in *FRUS* (1941), 2:255; Memorandum of conversation by Under Secretary of State Sumner Welles, 15 February 1941, in *FRUS* (1941), 2:261–62.

22. Murray memorandum, 13 February 1941, in *FRUS* (1941), 2:260. See Thomas, *Britain and Vichy*, pp. 103–4.

23. Hull to Pell [for Murphy], 8 February 1941, in *FRUS* (1941), 2:220; Villard memorandum, 17 February 1941, in *FRUS* (1941), 2:223; Welles memorandum, 19 February 1941, in *FRUS* (1941), 2:263–64; Childs to Hull, 20 February 1941, in *FRUS* (1941), 2:264–65; Welles memorandum, 20 February 1941, in *FRUS* (1941), 2:265–66; Hull to Leahy, 21 February 1941, and Leahy to Hull, 28 February 1941, in *FRUS* (1941), 2:225, 228; Murphy, *Diplomat Among Warriors*, p. 84.

24. Noguès to Darlan, 22 February 1941, Noguès Papers; Leahy to Hull, 28 February 1941, in *FRUS* (1941), 2:228. For background on the German control commission in Morocco and French protests, see General Paul Doyen to General Vogl, 21 March 1941, in *La Délégation française auprès de la Commission allemande d'armistice* (*29 juin 1940–21 décembre 1941*), 5 vols. (Paris, 1947–59), 4:210–12 (hereafter cited as *DFCAA*). Also see "Dossier: Commission d'armistice allemande au Maroc," Noguès Papers.

25. Leahy to Hull, 28 February and 9 March 1941, in *FRUS* (1941), 2:226–27, 235; Darlan to Leahy, 10 March 1941, in *FRUS* (1941), 2:237–38; Gaston Henry-Haye to Hull, 3 June 1941, in *FRUS* (1941), 2:239–41; Murray memorandum, 20 March 1941, in *FRUS* (1941), 2:273. Also see Murray memorandum, 29 March 1941, in *FRUS* (1941), 2:280; Murphy memorandum, n.d. [17 April 1941], in *FRUS* (1941), 2:287–90.

26. Leahy to Hull, 17 April 1941, in *FRUS* (1941), 2:292; Doyen to Vogl, 21 and 31 March 1941, in *DFCAA*, 4:211, 290; "Procès-verbal de l'entretien du 18 avril [1941] entre le général Doyen et le général Vogl," in *DFCAA*, 4:317.

27. Sûreté Régionale de Casablanca, Police Administrative, Le Commissaire, Chef de la Police Administrative Pierre Ninet, "Note de renseignements," 8 February 1941, Noguès Papers.

28. Lt.-Col. Maurice Herviot, "Note de renseignements," 26 March 1941, Noguès Papers.

29. Edwin F. Stanton to Hull, 22 March 1941, in *FRUS* (1941), 2:275.

30. News from the north also played a part: the ouster of the sultan's

representative from Tangier, the opening of a German consulate and the entry of the khalif into that city, and the clamor of the northern nationalists for the restoration of the former sultan, Moulay Abd el-Aziz; see Noguès to Darlan, 30 April 1941, Noguès Papers.

31. Noguès to Darlan, 30 April 1941, Noguès Papers. Also see Childs to Hull, 20 April 1941, in *FRUS* (1941), 2:298–300; Stanton to Hull, 22 April 1941, in *FRUS* (1941), 2:302–3. On German wartime propaganda in North Africa, see Évariste Levi-Provençal, "Compte rendu de la mission du capitaine Levi-Provençal au Maroc du 23 au 26 septembre 1939," Noguès Papers; Ageron, "Contribution à l'étude de la propagande allemande au Maghreb," pp. 16–32; Ageron, "Les populations du Maghreb face à la propagande allemande," pp. 1–39.

32. Noguès to Weygand, 9 May 1941, Noguès Papers.

33. Hull to Leahy, 18 April 1941, in *FRUS* (1941), 2:292–93; Leahy to Hull, 18 April 1941, in *FRUS* (1941), 2:294–95; Childs to Hull, 24 June 1941, in *FRUS* (1941), 2:383; Felix Cole [from Murphy] to Hull, 30 May 1941, in *FRUS* (1941), 2:354–55.

34. Eccles memorandum, 20 April 1941, in *FRUS* (1941), 2:297–98.

35. Childs to Hull, 20 April 1941, in *FRUS* (1941), 2:300; Cole to Hull, 23 April 1941, in *FRUS* (1941), 2:303–4; Leahy to Hull, 18 April 1941, in *FRUS* (1941), 2:295.

36. Murphy memorandum, 24 April 1941, in *FRUS* (1941), 2:305–6; Murphy, *Diplomat Among Warriors*, p. 88; Hull to Cole, 24 April 1941, in *FRUS* (1941), 2:308; Cole to Hull, 28 April 1941, in *FRUS* (1941), 2:309. For Weygand's account of the economic relations with the United States, see Weygand, *Mémoires*, 3:480–94.

37. Mönick, *Pour mémoire*, pp. 81–107; Leahy to Hull, 30 April 1941, in *FRUS* (1941), 2:321–22; Leahy to Hull, 1 May 1941, in *FRUS* (1941), 2:323–24; Childs, "Operation 'TORCH'," pp. 83–85, Childs Papers; Murphy to Murray, 13 October 1941, in *FRUS* (1941), 2:320; Childs to Hull, 15 May 1941, in *FRUS* (1941), 2:333–34; Cole [from Murphy] to Hull [for Welles], 21 May 1941, in *FRUS* (1941), 2:344–46; "La position du problème du ravitaillement de l'Afrique du nord française," 11 June 1941, Noguès Papers. In his memoirs Weygand implied that he authorized Murphy to be told of North Africa's needs in armaments "for a resumption of hostilities," but there is no contemporary evidence for this; see Weygand, *Mémoires*, 3:492.

38. Mönick, *Pour mémoire*, pp. 75–77; Noguès to Weygand, 19 May 1941, Noguès Papers.

39. Childs to Hull, 20 April 1942, in *FRUS* (1942), 2:287–88.

40. "Communication au Conseil des Ministres du 14 mai 1941," Noguès Papers. On Darlan and collaboration with Germany, see Melka, "Darlan between Britain and Germany," pp. 57–80.

41. Pétain, *Paroles aux français*, p. 117.

42. Weygand, *Mémoires*, 3:423, 429.

43. Noguès to Weygand, 19 May 1941, Noguès Papers.

44. Cole [from Murphy] to Hull [for Welles], 21 May 1941, in *FRUS* (1941), 2:345. The protocols are printed in Langer, *Our Vichy Gamble*, pp. 402–12.

45. Leahy to Hull, 4 June 1941, in *FRUS* (1941), 2:361–62; Weygand, *Mémoires*, 3:431; Cole to Hull, 7 June 1941, in *FRUS* (1941), 2:368–69. For Weygand's account of the meetings on 3, 4, and 6 June, see *Mémoires*, 3:430–37. Also see Weygand's letter to Pétain, 1 June 1941, in *Les événements survenus en France, Témoignages*, 6:1576–78.

46. Leahy to Hull, 4 June 1941, in *FRUS* (1941), 2:362; "Note," 11 July 1941, in letter from Weygand to Noguès, 15 July 1941, Noguès Papers; Weygand, *Mémoires*, 3:432, 434–35. *Ostland* referred to the lands in eastern France (the Ardennes, Aisne, Meuse, Meurthe-et-Moselle, Vosges) to be settled by German, Czech, and Polish farmers.

47. Weygand, *Mémoires*, 3:432, 436–40; Cole [from Murphy] to Hull, 8 June 1941, in *FRUS* (1941), 2:371–72; Leahy to Hull, 7 June 1941, in *FRUS* (1941), 2:370–71; Paxton, *Parades and Politics at Vichy*, pp. 235–39; Warner, *Iraq and Syria*, pp. 143–47.

48. "Note," 11 July 1941, in letter from Weygand to Noguès, 15 July 1941, Noguès Papers.

49. "Note," 11 July 1941, in letter from Weygand to Noguès, 15 July 1941, Noguès Papers.

50. Weygand to Noguès, 15 July 1941, Noguès Papers. Also see Cole [from Murphy] to Hull [for the Acting Secretary], 10 July 1941, in *FRUS* (1941), 2:389; Leahy to Hull, 10 July 1941, in *FRUS* (1941), 2:390. Jacques Benoist-Méchin was Secrétaire Général à la Vice Présidence du Conseil and Darlan's Paris representative to the Germans.

51. Paxton, *Vichy France*, pp. 121–23.

52. Weygand, *Mémoires*, 3:442–46; Paxton, *Parades and Politics at Vichy*, pp. 259–60.

53. Cole [from Murphy] to Hull [for the Acting Secretary], 2 August 1941, in *FRUS* (1941), 2:406–7; Murphy to Welles, 11 September 1941, in *FRUS* (1941), 2:428–29.

54. Marchal to Bernard Hardion, 10 June 1941, Noguès Papers.

55. Childs to Hull, 29 August 1941, in *FRUS* (1941), 2:423–24. Darlan told Mönick that the Germans said that there could be no "collaboration" in Morocco so long as he remained (Leahy to Hull, 26 July 1941, in *FRUS* [1941], 2:402).

56. Leahy [from Murphy] to Hull, 4 October 1941, in *FRUS* (1941), 2:443; Paxton, *Vichy France*, p. 125. On Weygand's ouster, see Leahy to Hull, 21 October 1941, in *FRUS* (1941), 2:447–48; Cole [from Murphy] to Hull, 23 October 1941, in *FRUS* (1941), 2:449; Leahy to Hull, 28 October 1941, in *FRUS* (1941), 2:455; Leahy to Hull, 18 November 1941, in *FRUS* (1941), 2:460–61; Cole [from Murphy] to Hull [for Welles], 19 November 1941, in *FRUS* (1941), 2:466–68. Also see Weygand, *Mémoires*, 3:522–33.

57. Hull to Leahy, 20 November 1941, in *FRUS* (1941), 2:468–69; Leahy to Hull, 11 November 1941, in *FRUS* (1941), 2:457–58; Leahy to Hull, 12 November 1941, in *FRUS* (1941), 2:458.

58. Childs to Hull, 21 and 24 November 1941, in *FRUS* (1941), 2:472–75; Matthews to Hull, 8 November 1940, in *FRUS* (1940), 2:615.

59. Childs to Hull, 25 November 1941, in *FRUS* (1941), 2:476–77.

60. Darlan to Noguès, 23 November 1941, and Noguès, "Extraits Instructions Darlan," n.d., both in Noguès Papers.

61. Cole [from Murphy] to Hull, 25 November 1941, in *FRUS* (1941), 2:479–81; Russell [from Murphy] to Hull, 1 December 1941, in *FRUS* (1941), 2:484–86; Childs to Hull, 1 December 1941, in *FRUS* (1941), 2:488; Noguès to Darlan, 30 April 1941, Noguès Papers.

62. Childs to Hull, 1 December 1941, in *FRUS* (1941), 2:489.

63. Murphy to James Clement Dunn, 9 January 1942, in *FRUS* (1942), 2:227–28; Hooker A. Doolittle to Hull, 7 January 1942, in *FRUS* (1942), 2:226–27; Paul H. Alling to Doolittle, 14 April 1942, in *FRUS* (1942), 2:281.

64. Leahy to Hull, 27 January and 27 April 1942, in *FRUS* (1942), 2:125, 181–82. Also see Cole [from Murphy] to Hull [for Acting Secretary], 18 April 1942, in *FRUS* (1942), 2:285.

65. Cole [from Murphy] to Hull, 15 February 1942, in *FRUS* (1942), 2:248–49; Welles memorandum, 10 February 1942, in *FRUS* (1942), 2:130; Russell [from Murphy] to Hull, 5 February 1942, in *FRUS* (1942), 2:241–43; Leahy to Hull, 14 March 1942, in *FRUS* (1942), 2:148–49.

66. Cole [from Murphy] to Hull [for Acting Secretary], 18 April 1942, in *FRUS* (1942), 2:285–86; Cole [from Murphy] to Hull, 21 April 1942, in *FRUS* (1942), 2:289.

67. Cole [from Murphy] to Hull [for Welles], 29 April 1942, in *FRUS* (1942), 2:293; Childs to Hull, 21 May 1942, in *FRUS* (1942), 2:301; Murray memorandum to Assistant Secretary of State Adolf A. Berle, Jr., 4 May 1942, in *FRUS* (1942), 2:295–97.

68. Cole [from Murphy] to Leahy, 1 April 1942, in *FRUS* (1942), 2:277.

69. Childs to Hull, 8 June 1942, in *FRUS* (1942), 2:308; Cole [from Murphy] to Hull, 22 June 1942, in *FRUS* (1942), 2:319.

70. Blair, "Amateurs in Diplomacy," p. 613; U.S. Office of Strategic Services, *Morocco*, 5 vols. (Washington, D.C., 1942), 2:17–20.

71. De Loustal to Noguès, 17 October 1941, Noguès Papers.

72. De Loustal to Noguès, 17 October 1941, Noguès Papers; Blair, "Amateurs in Diplomacy," pp. 614–15, 617–18.

73. U.S. Office of Strategic Services, *Morocco*, 1:87–88, 92, 96, 98–99. After the American landings, it became clear that the reports had been correct. In a secret meeting with Harry Hopkins, Roosevelt's confidant, el-Mokri and Si Mammeri said that at the war's end the sultan would be ready "to throw himself in the arms of Mr. Roosevelt. Provided Mr. Roosevelt will accept him and his country"; see "Hopkins-El Mokri Conversation, January 23, 1943, Casablanca," in U.S. Department of State, *Foreign Relations of the United States: The Conferences at Washington, 1941–1942, and Casablanca, 1943* (Washington, 1968), p. 702 (hereafter cited as *FRUS: Conferences at Washington and Casablanca*). There was talk by

the sultan, el-Glaoui, and Moulay Larbi of ending the French protectorate and creating some joint protectorate or inter-Allied mandate in which the United States and Britain would share authority with France and Spain; see Hull to Russell, 5 May 1943, in *FRUS* (1943), 4:738–39; Murphy to Hull, 26 June 1943, in *FRUS* (1943), 4:742–43; Memorandum by Chargé at Tangier C. Burke Elbrick, 30 September 1943, in letter from Childs to Hull, 2 October 1943, in *FRUS* (1943), 4:744–45. These anti-French, pro-American appeals continued until the end of the war and the departure of American troops from Morocco; see Hall, *The United States and Morocco*, pp. 1007–11.

74. Cole [from Murphy] to Hull, 22 June 1942, in *FRUS* (1942), 2:320–22.

75. Childs to Hull, 9 June 1942, in *FRUS* (1942), 2:310–11; Warner, *Pierre Laval*, pp. 311–12; S. Pinkney Tuck to Hull, 11 October 1942, in *FRUS* (1942), 2:389.

76. Cole [from Murphy] to Hull, 22 June 1942, in *FRUS* (1942), 2:319–20; Childs to Hull, 8 June 1942, in *FRUS* (1942), 2:309.

77. On Giraud and the French conspiracy with the Americans, see Funk, *The Politics of TORCH*. Also see Béthouart, *Cinq années d'espérance*.

78. Cole [from Murphy] to War Department, 3 November 1942 [received], in *FRUS* (1942), 2:423.

79. Murphy, *Diplomat Among Warriors*, pp. 104–5.

80. Cole [from Murphy] to War Department, n.d., in *FRUS* (1942), 2:392–94; Villard memorandum, 26 October 1942, in *FRUS* (1942), 2:404; Cole [from Murphy] to War Department, 20 October 1942, in *FRUS* (1942), 2:398–400; Funk, *The Politics of TORCH*, pp. 178–79; Cole [from Murphy] to War Department, 5 November 1942 [received], in *FRUS* (1942), 2:425; Murphy, *Diplomat Among Warriors*, p. 112.

EIGHT

1. Noguès, "8 novembre 1942," n.d., p. 2, Noguès Papers.

2. Béthouart to Noguès, 7 November 1942; General Jean Bergeret (Vichy's air minister) to Maître Pierre Courteault, 8 October 1948; Noguès, "8 novembre 1942," n.d., p. 4; Noguès, "Note d'ensemble sur le 8 novembre 1942," n.d.; Béthouart dossier, all in Noguès Papers; Haute Cour de Justice (1956), AN, Noguès testimony, 1:82–86; Haute Cour de Justice (1956), AN, Colonel Guy de Verthamon testimony, 3:84–98.

3. Haute Cour de Justice (1956), AN, Michelier testimony, 3:122–25; Haute Cour de Justice (1956), AN, Béthouart testimony, 2:28.

4. Haute Cour de Justice (1956), AN, Verthamon testimony, 3:88; Noguès, "8 novembre 1942," n.d., p. 5, Noguès Papers; "Plaidoirie de Maître Viénot," pp. 37–38, Noguès Papers; Michelier to Admiralty and Admiralty to Michelier, 8 November 1942, in *Les événements survenus en France, Rapport*, 2:516–17.

5. Noguès reported that the dissidence had been crushed in a telegram to Laval and a public proclamation, both dated 8 November 1942, in Haute Cour de Justice (1956), AN, statement of Procureur Général Pierre Besson, 6:34–35.

6. Noguès, "8 novembre 1942," n.d., p. 7, Noguès Papers; Noguès to Michelier, 8 November 1942, in Haute Cour de Justice (1956), AN, Besson statement, 6:33; Noguès, "Observations sur la lettre de l'Amiral Michelier du 15 juillet 1956," Noguès Papers.

7. Noguès to Darlan, 27 October 1942; Noguès declaration, 28 October 1942; *Le Petit marseillais*, 29 October 1942, all in Direction de la Documentation, Dossier Biographique "Noguès," Secrétariat Général du Gouvernement; Nicolle, *Cinquante mois d'armistice*, diary entries for 26 and 27 October 1942, 2:46–47.

8. Noguès, "8 novembre 1942," n.d., pp. 2–4, Noguès Papers.

9. Darlan to Admiralty, 7 November 1942, and Admiralty to Michelier, 7 November 1942, in *Les événements survenus en France, Rapport*, 2:514–15; Haute Cour de Justice (1956), AN, Michelier testimony, 3:130–31.

10. See Howe, *Northwest Africa*, and Morison, *Operations in North African Waters*.

11. Patton diary, 30 October 1942, in Patton, *The Patton Papers*, 2:97.

12. Howe, *Northwest Africa*, pp. 104–5, 109, 127, 133–34, 155–57, 159–61, 165–68.

13. Noguès to Laval, 8 November 1942, in Haute Cour de Justice (1956), AN, Besson statement, 6:34; Noguès, "8 novembre 1942," n.d., p. 10, Noguès Papers; Howe, *Northwest Africa*, pp. 111–14, 141–42, 160.

14. See Funk, *The Politics of TORCH*, and Mast, *Histoire d'une rébellion*.

15. Darlan to Admiralty, 8 November 1942; Darlan to Pétain, 9 November 1942; Darlan to Estéva and military commanders, 9 November 1942, all in *Les événements survenus en France, Rapport*, 2:517–18, 520; Noguès, "8 novembre 1942," n.d., p. 12, Noguès Papers.

16. Haute Cour de Justice (1956), AN, Noguès testimony, 1:101–2; Noguès, "Note d'ensemble sur le 8 novembre 1942," n.d., Noguès Papers.

17. Noguès, "8 novembre 1942," n.d., pp. 14–15; Noguès to Pétain, 10 November 1942; Captain Gaston Bataille (Noguès's envoy to Pétain) to the President of the Republic, 15 October 1948, all in Noguès Papers; Patton diary, 8 November 1942, in Patton, *The Patton Papers*, 2:106; Howe, *Northwest Africa*, pp. 132–33.

18. Noguès, "8 novembre 1942," n.d., pp. 16–17, Noguès Papers; Haute Cour de Justice (1956), AN, General André Dorange testimony, 4:12–13, and Michelier testimony, 3:148–55. See the telegrams from Michelier to the Admiralty and from the Admiralty to Michelier on 10 and 11 November 1942 and Darlan's cease fire order, in *Les événements survenus en France, Rapport*, 2:522–24, 538–39.

19. "Record of Events and Documents from the date that Lieutenant-

General Mark W. Clark entered into negotiations with Admiral Jean-François Darlan until Darlan was assassinated on Christmas Eve, 1942," 22 February 1943, pp. 4–11, 14, Clark Papers (hereafter cited as "Record of Events"); Admiralty to Michelier, 11 November 1942, in *Les événements survenus en France, Rapport*, 2:539; Kammerer, *Du débarquement africain*, pp. 398, 408.

20. Noguès to Pétain, 11 November 1942, Noguès Papers.

21. Haute Cour de Justice, Ministère Public c/ M. Noguès, Audience du 28 novembre 1947, AN, 1:11–12, 68; Haute Cour de Justice (1956), AN, 7:61–63. On the secret forces, see "L'Effort de résistance du Maroc de juin 1940 à novembre 1942 et la préparation à la reprise de la lutte contre l'Allemagne," Noguès Papers. On the Noguès trial, see Morice, *Du maréchal Ney au général Noguès*.

22. "Plaidoirie de Maître Viénot," pp. 42–43, Noguès Papers; Haute Cour de Justice (1956), AN, Noguès testimony, 1:107, LaHoulle testimony, 4:24–28, General André Dody testimony, 3:103–4, and General Henri Martin testimony, 3:180; Ribbentrop to German Embassy in Paris, 19 November 1942, Noguès Papers; Noguès "8 novembre 1942," n.d., pp. 11–13, Noguès Papers; Noguès to Admiralty, 9 November 1942, in *Les événements survenus en France, Rapport*, 2:529; Noguès to Pétain, 10 November 1942, Noguès Papers; Noguès to Admiralty, 9 November 1942, Noguès Papers. The sultan had in fact been asked to accompany Noguès, but he declined, saying it would cause anxiety among his people; see Noguès, "8 novembre 1942," n.d., p. 12, Noguès Papers. For another version that explains Sidi Mohammed's refusal as an act of resistance to France, see Blair, *Western Window in the Arab World*, pp. 66–68.

23. Haute Cour de Justice (1956), AN, Noguès testimony, 1:86, 101; Childs, *Diplomatic and Literary Quests*, pp. 42–45; Childs, "Operation 'TORCH'," pp. 135, 153–58, Childs Papers.

24. "Plaidoirie de Maître Viénot," p. 46, Noguès Papers; Noguès to Pétain, 11 November 1942, in Kammerer, *Du débarquement africain*, p. 458. Also see Noguès, "8 novembre 1942," n.d., p. 18, Noguès Papers; "Commentaires du général Jean Piatte," 25 October 1973, Dorange Papers; Howe, *Northwest Africa*, pp. 172–74. The meeting is described in Farago, *Patton*, pp. 212–16.

25. Patton to Eisenhower, 14 November 1942, in Patton, *The Patton Papers*, 2:115. Also see diary entries for 11 and 12 November 1942 and letters from Patton to Beatrice Patton, 11 November 1942, and to Henry L. Stimson, 7 December 1942, all in Patton, *The Patton Papers*, 2:110–13. Eisenhower not only endorsed the Patton policy but recommended it to Clark: "It is important also that we do not create any dissension among the tribes or encourage them to break away from existing methods of control"; see Eisenhower to Mark Wayne Clark, 12 November 1942, in Eisenhower, *The Papers of Dwight D. Eisenhower*, 2:699.

26. Farago, *Patton*, p. 215; Patton diary, 21 November 1942, in Patton, *The Patton Papers*, 2:128.

27. Howe, *Northwest Africa*, pp. 57–58, 178.

28. Pendar, *Adventure in Diplomacy*, p. 123; Patton to Beatrice Patton, 11 November 1942, and Patton to Stimson, 7 December 1942, in Patton, *The Patton Papers*, 2:111, 134; Patton, *The Patton Papers*, 2:118.

29. Morison, *Operations in North African Waters*, p. 175; Charles R. Codman to Theo Codman, 13 November and 25 December 1942, in Codman, *Drive*, pp. 50, 65–66.

30. Noguès, "Note d'ensemble sur le 8 novembre 1942," n.d., and untitled memorandum on the "idées maîtresses" that guided Noguès's conduct in 1942, both in Noguès Papers; Noguès to Pétain, 11 November 1942, in Kammerer, *Du débarquement africain*, p. 458. General Piatte said the accord made Morocco an ally rather than a conquered country; see "Commentaires du général Piatte," 25 October 1973, Dorange Papers.

31. Noguès to Pétain, 12 November 1942, Noguès Papers.

32. Patton to Eisenhower, 14 November 1942, in Patton, *The Patton Papers*, 2:115.

33. Clark to Eisenhower, 11 and 12 November 1942, in Clark, "Record of Events," pp. 13, 23–36, Clark Papers; Noguès to Pétain, 12 November 1942, Noguès Papers.

34. Funk, *The Politics of TORCH*, pp. 246–47; Noguès, "8 novembre 1942," n.d., p. 21, Noguès Papers; Noguès to Pétain, 13 November 1942, in *Les événements survenus en France, Rapport*, 2:542–43. Also see Haute Cour de Justice (1956), AN, Juin testimony, 2:55–57. Noguès said the phrase "benevolent neutrality" was only an attempt to "camouflage" the cooperation between the Americans and the French to the Germans; see Haute Cour de Justice (1956), AN, 2:69; Noguès testimony, 1:115–17. Kenneth Pendar, Clark's interpreter at some of these meetings, concluded that Noguès had "no intention" of bringing Morocco into the war on the American side: "He proposed merely to give us 'the right of passage'"; see *Adventure in Diplomacy*, p. 118.

35. Noguès, "8 novembre 1942," n.d., p. 21, Noguès Papers; Noguès to Pétain, 13 November 1942, in Kammerer, *Du débarquement africain*, pp. 673–74.

36. Noguès to Pétain, 13 November 1942, in Kammerer, *Du débarquement africain*, pp. 673–74; Funk, *The Politics of TORCH*, p. 247; Kammerer, *Du débarquement africain*, p. 481. Juin relates that he brought Noguès to his senses on the role that Giraud had to play in the North African command, but in general his recollections are confused; see *Mémoires*, 1:104–8. Noguès said simply that he, Giraud, and Darlan finally decided that the volunteer corps was a "bad idea" since it too would split the army; see "8 novembre 1942," n.d., p. 21, Noguès Papers.

37. Noguès to Pétain, 13 November 1942, in Kammerer, *Du débarquement africain*, pp. 673–74; Darlan to Laval, 13 November 1942, in *Les événements survenus en France, Rapport*, 2:543–44; Clark, "Record of Events," pp. 42–43, Clark Papers. Also see Eisenhower to Walter Bedell Smith, 13 November 1942, and Eisenhower to Combined Chiefs of Staff, 14

November 1942, both in Eisenhower, *The Papers of Dwight D. Eisen-hower*, 2:706–11. Giraud's appointment as commander-in-chief of French armed forces was announced on 15 November. For Noguès's proclamation transferring his powers as Pétain's delegate to Darlan, see Darlan, *L'amiral Darlan parle*, pp. 207–8.

38. Pétain to Darlan, 14 November 1942, in *Les événements survenus en France, Rapport*, 2:544.

39. Darlan, "Circulaire aux postes diplomatiques," 5 December 1942, Noguès Papers.

40. Childs, "Operation 'TORCH'," p. 167, Childs Papers; Clark, "Record of Events," pp. 91–92, Clark Papers; Eisenhower to George C. Marshall, 17 November 1942, and Eisenhower to Clark, 25 December 1942, in Eisenhower, *The Papers of Dwight D. Eisenhower*, 2:729–30, 860–61.

41. Patton to Stimson, 7 December 1942, and Patton to Beatrice Patton, 21 December 1942, in Patton, *The Patton Papers*, 2:134, 142.

42. Henry Marchat, "Note pour Monsieur le Résident Général," 13 January 1943, Noguès Papers.

43. Macmillan, *The Blast of War*, pp. 186, 197–98, 201, 232–33.

44. "Procès-verbal du Comité de Guerre des 8, 9, et 10 mars 1943," Noguès Papers.

45. Patton diary, 20 December 1942, in Patton, *The Patton Papers*, 2:141; Butcher diary, 17 December 1942, in Butcher, *Three Years with Eisen-hower*, p. 192.

46. Childs, "Operation 'TORCH'," pp. 180–88, Childs Papers. For American media criticism of Noguès and the situation in Morocco, see Kaspi, *La Mission de Jean Monnet à Alger*, pp. 50, 112. Childs wrote that "[h]ad Darlan been thrust aside and Noguès confirmed by us in the authority conferred upon him by Pétain, there need never have been any deal with Darlan, any question of expediency to throw confusion among our friends and disunity among the French"; see "Operation 'TORCH'," p. 178, Childs Papers. However, Noguès would have been no more acceptable to the British or the Gaullists than Darlan.

47. On the organizing of civilian lend-lease in North Africa, see Dougherty, *The Politics of Wartime Aid*, pp. 68–122. On American military aid, see Vigneras, *Rearming the French*.

48. Noguès, "8 novembre 1942," n.d., p. 25, Noguès Papers; Rodière, *Législation de l'Afrique du nord en guerre*, pp. 9–10, 12.

49. See Childs, "Operation 'TORCH'," p. 190, Childs Papers, for the American view that after Darlan's death Noguès intended to maintain himself in power as the sole repository of legitimate French authority in North Africa with a view to handing it back at some future time to Pétain or his successors.

50. "Joint Chiefs of Staff minutes of a meeting at the White House," 7 January 1943, in *FRUS: Conferences at Washington and Casablanca*, p. 514. Roosevelt vacillated between considering North Africa occupied territory and free soil allied to the United States. See Murphy, *Diplomat*

Among Warriors, p. 169. Although the Clark-Darlan agreement seemed to render the Murphy-Giraud accords null and void (and was interpreted as such by the partisans of Giraud), it is clear that neither Darlan nor Noguès thought so. See Funk, "The 'Anfa Memorandum'," pp. 246–54; Darlan, "Circulaire aux postes diplomatiques," 5 December 1942, Noguès Papers.

51. Murphy, *Diplomat Among Warriors*, p. 173; Funk, *Charles de Gaulle*, p. 85; Bernard, *The Franco-Moroccan Conflict*, pp. 15–16.

52. See the account of Pierre Bourdan's interview with Noguès (29 December 1942) in which the resident emphasized the need for continuity and prestige in Morocco; see *Carnet des jours d'attente*, pp. 158–62.

53. "Compte rendu d'un entretien entre le général Catroux et M. Lemaigre Dubreuil," 11 February 1943, Lemaigre Dubreuil Papers. Jacques Lemaigre Dubreuil was Giraud's delegate for Inter-Allied Affairs. General Georges Catroux, the former governor general of Indochina, had rallied to de Gaulle in 1940.

54. Noguès to Giraud, 28 April 1943, Noguès Papers; Noguès to Roosevelt, 12 May 1943, cited in Blair, *Western Window in the Arab World*, p. 95.

55. Catroux, *Dans la bataille de la Méditerranée*, pp. 362–63.

56. Giraud to Noguès, 3 June 1943, Noguès Papers. For Noguès's resignation note, see Noguès to Giraud, 4 June 1943, Noguès Papers. Noguès left Morocco for Portugal on 14 June 1943 at the invitation of the Portuguese consuls at Casablanca and Rabat, after his request to retire in Algeria or Tangier had been rejected by Governor General Catroux; see "Conditions dans lesquelles le général Noguès a quitté le Maroc pour se rendre au Portugal le 15 juin 1943," n.d., Noguès Papers.

57. Noguès, "Message du général Noguès aux populations du Maroc," 4 June 1943, Noguès Papers.

58. Secretary of State Edward R. Stettinius, Jr., to Russell, 1 December 1943, in *FRUS* (1943), 4:745–46. See Zingg, "The Cold War in North Africa," pp. 40–61; Blair, "The Impact of Franco-American Military Agreements on Moroccan Nationalism," pp. 61–68; Blair, *Western Window in the Arab World*.

59. Catroux, *Lyautey*, p. 305.

60. Guillaume, *Homme de guerre*, p. 239.

61. Noguès was called on by the French government to advise in this delicate matter for he had remained on good terms with the sultan through it all; see Si Mammeri to Noguès, 22 December 1955 and 24 May 1956, Noguès Papers. For the postwar years and Morocco's independence, see Bernard, *The Franco-Moroccan Conflict*, and Cerych, *Européens et marocains*.

62. Point, "Le général Charles Noguès"; Jean Lacouture in *Le Monde*, 23 April 1971.

NINE

1. Noguès's speech at funeral services for General Bernard Vergez, 1942, Noguès Papers.

2. Ordioni, *Le secret de Darlan*, p. 73.

3. On "colonial humanism" and the Popular Front's colonial policy, see Girardet, *L'Idée coloniale en France*, pp. 175–90; Semidei, "Les socialistes français et le problème colonial," pp. 1115–53; Marseille, "La conférence des gouverneurs généraux des colonies," pp. 61–84; Cohen, "The Colonial Policy of the Popular Front," pp. 368–93.

4. "Message du général Noguès aux populations du Maroc," 4 June 1943, Noguès Papers.

5. Haute Cour de Justice (1956), AN, Besson statement, 6:91–92; Catroux, *Lyautey*, pp. 90–93, 96–97.

Bibliography

INTERVIEWS AND CORRESPONDENCE

Interviews
Jacques Berque, General Antoine Béthouart, Pierre Charpentier, General André Dorange, Robert Roger du Gardier, General Maurice Durosoy, General Augustin Guillaume, Bernard Hardion, Georges Hutin, Charles-André Julien, Henry Marchat, Emmanuel Mönick, Baron Pierre Ordioni, Jean Pasquier, Robert Ricard, Eugène and Françoise Simoneau, Yves Sourisse, General Georges Spillmann, Colonel Guy and Odile de Verthamon, Pierre Voizard

Correspondence
James Rives Childs, Giovani Fornari, Carlo de Franchis, Fabrizio Franco, Marcel Peyrouton, Père René Point

MANUSCRIPT SOURCES

Private Papers
Pierre Charpentier Papers, Paris
James Rives Childs Papers, Richmond, Virginia
Mark W. Clark Papers, The Citadel, Charleston, South Carolina
André Dorange Papers, Paris
Jacques Lemaigre Dubreuil Papers, Paris
Georges Hutin Papers, Paris
Charles-André Julien Papers, Paris
Charles Noguès Papers, Paris

Official Archives
Archives Nationales, Paris (Cited as AN)
 Haute Cour de Justice. Ministère Public c/ M. Noguès, Audience du 28 novembre 1947. (This is a stenographic transcript in one part.)
 ———. Ministère Public c/ Général Noguès, Audiences du 23, 24, 25, 26 octobre 1956. (This is a stenographic transcript in seven parts.)
Centre des Hautes Études sur l'Afrique et l'Asie Modernes, Paris (Cited as CHEAM)

Abadie, Captain Jean. "Les tendances à l'insurrection en pays berbère." CHEAM report, 1939.

Berenguier, Captain Hippolyte. "Le syndicalisme marocain sous le protectorat français." CHEAM report, 1955.

Berque, Jacques. "La question agraire au Maroc: Nouvelle politique rurale de la France au Maroc." CHEAM conference, 8 October 1945.

Bois, Jacques. "La surpopulation rurale des Doukkala: Les problèmes qu'elle pose." CHEAM report, 1938.

Bourgeois. "L'artisanat fassi depuis la guerre." CHEAM conference, 3 November 1941.

Clément, Captain Jean-Henri. "À propos de la revendication de droit syndical pour les musulmans marocains." CHEAM report, 1938.

———. "L'Espagne phalangiste et le Maroc." CHEAM report, 1941.

Debraisne, Captain Jacques. "Dix ans d'expérience coopérative forestière dans la région de Meknès." CHEAM report, 1949.

Dutheil, Jean. "Les juifs au Maroc." CHEAM conference, 16 December 1941.

Estève, Charles. "Contribution à l'enquête sur l'artisanat marocain. Nécessité d'une politique artisanale appliquée à l'industrie rurale du tapis. Essai de rénovation de l'industrie familiale des tapis de Chichaoua." CHEAM report, 1938.

Flye-Sainte-Marie, Captain Laurent. "L'évolution du nationalisme à Meknès jusqu'en 1937." CHEAM conference, 9 June 1938.

———. "L'exploitation forestière et les coopératives de bûcherons en pays Ait Yahia et Beni Mguild." CHEAM report, 1939.

———. "Le nationalisme en pays berbère." CHEAM report, 1938.

———. "Tendances à l'insurrection chez les transhumants berbères du Moyen-Atlas." CHEAM conference, 9 May 1938.

Granges, Claude. "Le mouvement coopératif en milieu artisanal au Maroc de 1936 à 1956." CHEAM report, 1956.

Haut Comité Méditerranéen. Session de [8–12] mars 1938 (procès-verbaux des séances).

Ladriet de Lacharrière, Jacques. "La politique de l'Allemagne au Maroc." CHEAM conference, 26 June 1937.

Le Tourneau, Roger. "L'artisanat en Tunisie et au Maroc." CHEAM conference, [1945].

———. "Les corporations au Maroc." CHEAM conference, 7 June 1938.

———. "Les émeutes de Fès." CHEAM conference, 1939.

———. "La jeunesse marocaine." CHEAM conference, 30 June 1938.

[———]. "Le mouvement nationaliste dans la zone française du protectorat marocain d'avril 1936 à octobre 1937." CHEAM report, [1938].

———. "Le mouvement nationaliste marocain de 1930 à 1937." CHEAM report, 1937.

———. "Le nationalisme marocain." CHEAM conference, 1 December 1945.

Matte, Marcel. "Éléments d'une politique berbère au Maroc." CHEAM conference, 20 February 1937.

Montagne, Robert. "Les berbères en Afrique du nord," in "Six conférences d'initiation à la politique musulmane de la France en Afrique du nord." CHEAM conferences, March–May 1943.

———. "La crise nationaliste au Maroc." CHEAM conference, 18 December 1941.

———. "Les tendances du Jeune Maroc." CHEAM report, 15 July 1929.

———. "Un essai de régionalisme au Maroc." CHEAM conference, 5 August 1941.

Moussard, Paul. "De la coopération dans l'économie indigène au Maroc." CHEAM report, 1937.

———. "Les corporations au Maroc." CHEAM conference, 2 March 1937.

Pagès, André. "L'impôt agricole et les musulmans." CHEAM conference, 21 April 1947.

———. "Les impôts directs urbains du protectorat marocain." CHEAM report, 1947.

Paye, Lucien. "L'agriculture dans la Région de Fès." CHEAM conference, 2 June 1937.

———. "Déchéance des corporations marocaines." CHEAM conference, 19 May 1937.

———. "La politique marocaine de la République espagnole, 1931–1936." CHEAM report, [1936].

Protectorat de la République française au Maroc, Gouvernement Chérifien. "Compte rendu des opérations organismes de crédit et de coopération en milieu marocain au cours des exercices 1938–1939 à 1945–1946." n.d. (Cited as Protectorat, "Compte rendu des opérations organismes de crédit," CHEAM)

Résidence Générale de la République française au Maroc, Direction de l'Intérieur, Division des Affaires Rurales. "Rapport général sur le mouvement coopératif au Maroc en milieu autochtone (1934–1950)." 30 April 1950. (Cited as Résidence Générale, "Rapport général sur le mouvement coopératif au Maroc," CHEAM)

Ricard, Prosper. "L'artisanat marocain." CHEAM report, 1937.

Roux, Captain Jacques. "Essai monographique sur le bidonville de la Cité Yacoub el Mansour (Douar Debbagh)." CHEAM report, 1949.

Saulay, Captain Jean. "Les coopératives oléicoles au Maroc." CHEAM conference, 11 June 1949.

Tallec, Corentin. "L'équipement hydraulique de la plaine des Beni Amir et ses incidences politiques." CHEAM report, 1941.

Ministère des Affaires Étrangères, Paris
Archives Diplomatiques, Maroc, 1917–38. (Cited as MAE, Maroc)
Le Sultan et les Personnages Marocains:
413: Le Sultan, 1928–37.
422: Personnages Marocains, 1923–37.

423: El Glaoui, 1931–37.
Résidence Générale:
  426: Le Résident Général, 1927–36.
  427: Bureau Diplomatique, 1917–36.
  428: Affaires Diverses, 1917–36.
Politique Générale Marocaine:
  490: Situation Politique et Économique, August 1937–July 1938.
  491: Situation Politique et Économique, August 1938–March 1939.
Le Rif:
  498: Opérations Militaires, 1 January 1925–15 August 1925.
  499: Opérations Militaires, 16 August 1925–31 October 1926.
Suppression des Capitulations:
  563: Dossier Général, 1918–39.
  564: Belgique–États-Unis, 1918–39.
  564 bis: États-Unis, 1939.
  566: Grande Bretagne, 1918–37.
  567: Grande Bretagne, 1–31 July 1937.
  568: Grande Bretagne. Traité de Commerce Anglo-Marocain, 1 November 1937–31 March 1938.
  569: Grande Bretagne. Traité de Commerce Anglo-Marocain, 1937.
  570: Grande Bretagne. Négotiations Commerciales. Traité Anglo-Marocain, March–August 1938.
  571: Grande Bretagne. Négotiations Commerciales. Traité Anglo-Marocain, 1 September 1938–31 March 1939.
Zone Espagnole du Maroc:
  604: Sédition au Maroc Espagnol, July–August 1936.
  605: Sédition au Maroc Espagnol, July–August 1936.
Personnel du Protectorat:
  722: Dossier Général, 5 April 1934–18 January 1937.
  723: Dossier Général, 12 February 1937–30 December 1938.
  726: Personnel Administratif, 1930–38.
Administration Générale:
  769–770: Dossier Général, July 1936–December 1937.
  773: Notes pour les Parlementaires, January 1929–September 1937.
Finances:
  796: Affaires Financières Diverses, 1932–36.
  797: Affaires Financières Diverses, 1938–39.
Secrétariat Général du Gouvernement, Paris
  Direction de la Documentation. Dossier Biographique "Noguès."
Service Historique de l'Armée de Terre, Vincennes
  Extrait de l'état des services du Général d'Armée Noguès, Auguste, Paul, Charles, Albert (dossier N° 463 / Généraux / 5ème série), années 1920 à 1943.

GOVERNMENT DOCUMENTS
AND OFFICIAL PUBLICATIONS

France

Assemblée Nationale. *Les événements survenus en France de 1933 à 1945: Rapport fait au nom de la Commission chargée d'enquêter sur les événements survenus en France de 1933 à 1945 par M. Charles Serre, rapporteur général.* 2 vols. Paris, [1952]. (Cited as *Les événements survenus en France, Rapport*)

———. *Les événements survenus en France de 1933 à 1945: Témoignages et documents recueillis par la Commission d'enquête parlementaire.* 9 vols. Paris, [1951–52]. (Cited as *Les événements survenus en France, Témoignages*)

La Délégation française auprès de la Commission allemande d'armistice (29 juin 1940–21 décembre 1941). Recueil de documents publié par le Gouvernement français. 5 vols. Paris, 1947–59. (Cited as *DFCAA*)

État-Major de l'Armée. *Les Opérations militaires au Maroc.* Collection "Les Armées françaises d'outre-mer" éditée à l'occasion de l'Exposition Coloniale Internationale de Paris de 1931. Paris, 1931.

Ministère des Affaires Étrangères, Commission de publication des documents relatifs aux origines de la guerre, 1939–45. *Documents diplomatiques français, 1932–1939.* Series 2 (1936–39), 15 vols. to date. Paris, 1963–. (Cited as *DDF*)

Théâtre d'Opérations de l'Afrique du Nord, État-Major, Bureau Politique. *Bulletin d'information,* Algiers, 1939–40. (Cited as TOAFN, *Bulletin d'information*)

Germany

Documents on German Foreign Policy, 1918–1945. Series D (1937–45), 13 vols. London and Washington, D.C., 1949–64. (Cited as *DGFP*)

Great Britain

Documents on British Foreign Policy, 1919–1939. Edited by E. L. Woodward and Rohan Butler. Series 2 (1930–38), 9 vols. to date; Series 3 (1938–39), 10 vols. London, 1946–.

Morocco

Bulletin Officiel du Protectorat de la République française au Maroc. Rabat, 1936–43. (Cited as *Bulletin Officiel*)

Protectorat de la République française au Maroc, Gouvernement Chérifien, Direction des Affaires Économiques. *Annuaire de statistique générale de la Zone française du Maroc.* Vol. 12. Rabat, 1937. (Cited as *Annuaire de statistique générale du Maroc*)

Résidence Générale de France au Maroc, Direction du Cabinet. *Bulletin d'informations et de documentation du Maroc.* Rabat, 1937–43.

United States

Department of State. *Foreign Relations of the United States: Diplomatic Papers.* 1937–43. Washington, D.C., 1955–64. (Cited as *FRUS*)

———. *Foreign Relations of the United States: The Conferences at Washington, 1941–1942, and Casablanca, 1943.* Washington, D.C., 1968. (Cited as *FRUS: Conferences at Washington and Casablanca*)

———. *The Spanish Government and the Axis: Documents.* Washington, D.C., 1946.

Office of Strategic Services, Research and Analysis Branch. *Morocco.* 5 vols. Washington, D.C., 1942.

BOOKS

Abu-Lughod, Janet L. *Rabat: Urban Apartheid in Morocco.* Princeton, 1980.

Adam, André. *Casablanca: Essai sur la transformation de la société marocaine au contact de l'Occident.* 2 vols. Paris, 1968.

Adamthwaite, Anthony. *France and the Coming of the Second World War.* Totowa, N.J., 1977.

Ageron, Charles-Robert. *Politiques coloniales au Maghreb.* Paris, 1972.

Allain, Jean-Claude. *Agadir, 1911.* Paris, 1976.

Anderson, Eugene N. *The First Moroccan Crisis, 1904–1906.* Chicago, 1930.

Andrew, Christopher M. *Théophile Delcassé and the Making of the Entente Cordiale.* London, 1968.

Auffray, Bernard. *Pierre de Margerie (1861–1942) et la vie diplomatique de son temps.* Paris, 1976.

Auphan, Paul. *L'Honneur de servir: Mémoires.* Paris, 1978.

———. *La lutte pour la vie (1940–1942): La marine au service des français.* Paris, 1947.

Ayache, Albert. *Le Maroc: Bilan d'une colonisation.* Paris, 1956.

Bankwitz, Philip C. F. *Maxime Weygand and Civil-Military Relations in Modern France.* Cambridge, Mass., 1967.

Barlow, Ima Christina. *The Agadir Crisis.* Chapel Hill, 1940.

Baudouin, Paul. *Neuf mois au gouvernement (avril–décembre 1940).* Paris, 1948.

Belal, Abdel Aziz. *L'Investissement au Maroc (1912–1964) et ses enseignements en matière de développement économique.* Paris, 1968.

Bell, Philip M. H. *A Certain Eventuality: Britain and the Fall of France.* London, 1974.

Bernard, Stéphane. *The Franco-Moroccan Conflict, 1943–1956.* New Haven, 1968. Published in the unabridged French edition as *Le conflit franco-marocain, 1943–1956,* 3 vols. (Brussels, 1963).

Berque, Jacques. *French North Africa: The Maghrib Between Two World*

Wars. Translated by Jean Stewart. New York, 1967. Originally published as *Le Maghreb entre deux guerres* (Paris, 1962).

Berteil, Louis. *L'Armée de Weygand: La chance de la France, 1940–1942*. Paris, 1975.

Béthouart, Antoine. *Cinq années d'espérance: Mémoires de guerre, 1939–1945*. Paris, 1968.

Betts, Raymond F. *Assimilation and Association in French Colonial Theory, 1890–1914*. New York, 1961.

Bidwell, Robin. *Morocco Under Colonial Rule: French Administration of Tribal Areas, 1912–1956*. London, 1973.

Blair, Leon Borden. *Western Window in the Arab World*. Austin, 1970.

Blum, Léon. *L'Oeuvre de Léon Blum*. 6 vols. Paris, 1954–72.

Bond, Brian. *France and Belgium, 1939–1940*. London, 1975.

Bonnefous, Édouard. *Histoire politique de la troisième république*. Vol. 7, *La course vers l'abime: La fin de la IIIe république (1938–1940)*. Paris, 1967.

Bourdan, Pierre [Pierre Maillaud]. *Carnet des jours d'attente (juin 40–juin 44)*. Paris, 1945.

Brémard, Frédéric. *Les droits publics et politiques des français au Maroc*. Paris, 1950.

———. *L'Organisation régionale du Maroc*. Paris, 1949.

Brown, Kenneth. *People of Salé: Tradition and Change in a Moroccan City, 1830–1930*. Cambridge, Mass., 1976.

Burdick, Charles B. *Germany's Military Strategy and Spain in World War II*. Syracuse, 1968.

Burke, Edmund III. *Prelude to Protectorate in Morocco: Precolonial Protest and Resistance, 1860–1912*. Chicago, 1977.

Butcher, Harry C. *Three Years with Eisenhower: The Personal Diary of Captain Harry C. Butcher, USNR, Naval Aide to General Eisenhower, 1942 to 1945*. London, 1946.

Carr, Raymond, *Spain, 1808–1939*. Oxford, 1966.

Catroux Georges. *Dans la bataille de Méditerranée: Egypte-Levant-Afrique du nord, 1940–1944*. Paris, 1949.

———. *Lyautey, le marocain*. Paris, 1952.

Cerych, Ladislav. *Européens et marocains, 1930–1956: Sociologie d'une décolonisation*. Bruges, 1964.

Chambre de Commerce de Marseille. *Le traité anglo-chérifien du 18 juillet 1938: Rapport présenté par M. Jacques-J. Dailloux et adopté par cette compagnie dans sa séance du 4 octobre 1938*. Marseilles, 1938.

Chapman, Guy. *Why France Fell: The Defeat of the French Army in 1940*. New York, 1969.

Charles-Roux, François. *Cinq mois tragiques aux affaires étrangères (21 mai–1 novembre 1940)*. Paris, 1949.

Childs, James Rives. *Diplomatic and Literary Quests*. Richmond, 1963.

Clark, Mark W. *Calculated Risk*. New York, 1950.

Codman, Charles R. *Drive.* Boston, 1957.

Colton, Joel. *Léon Blum: Humanist in Politics.* New York, 1966.

Cordero Torres, José María. *Organización del protectorado español en Marruecos.* 2 vols. Madrid, 1942–43.

Coverdale, John F. *Italian Intervention in the Spanish Civil War.* Princeton, 1975.

Darlan, Alain. *L'amiral Darlan parle.* Paris, 1953.

De Gaulle, Charles. *The Complete War Memoirs of Charles de Gaulle.* Translated by Jonathan Griffin and Richard Howard. New York, 1972. Originally published as *Mémoires de guerre,* 3 vols. (Paris, 1954–59).

———. *Discours et messages.* 5 vols. Paris, 1970.

Detwiler, Donald S. *Hitler, Franco und Gibraltar: Die Frage des spanischen Eintritts in den Zweiten Weltkrieg.* Wiesbaden, 1962.

Dillon, Eric. *Memories of Three Wars.* London, 1951.

Dougherty, James J. *The Politics of Wartime Aid: American Economic Assistance to France and French Northwest Africa, 1940–1946.* Westport, Conn., 1978.

Dreifort, John E. *Yvon Delbos at the Quai d'Orsay: French Foreign Policy during the Popular Front, 1936–1938.* Lawrence, Kans., 1973.

Duff Cooper, Sir Alfred. *Old Men Forget: The Autobiography of Duff Cooper (Viscount Norwich).* London, 1954.

Dunn, Ross E. *Resistance in the Desert: Moroccan Responses to French Imperialism, 1881–1912.* Madison, 1977.

Durosoy, Maurice. *Avec Lyautey: Homme de guerre, homme de paix.* Paris, 1976.

Eisenhower, Dwight D. *The Papers of Dwight David Eisenhower: The War Years.* Edited by Alfred D. Chandler, Jr. 5 vols. Baltimore, 1970.

Famchon, Yves. *Le Maroc, d'Algéciras à la souveraineté économique.* Paris, 1957.

Farago, Ladislas. *Patton: Ordeal and Triumph.* New York, 1964.

al-Fāsī, Alāl [el-Fassi, Allal]. *The Independence Movements in Arab North Africa.* Translated by Hazem Zaki Nuseibeh. Washington, D.C., 1954.

Funk, Arthur Layton. *Charles de Gaulle: The Crucial Years, 1943–1944.* Norman, Okla., 1959.

———. *The Politics of TORCH: The Allied Landings and the Algiers Putsch, 1942.* Lawrence, Kans., 1974.

Gallissot, René. *Le patronat européen au Maroc—action sociale, action politique (1931–1942).* Rabat, 1964.

Gann, Lewis H., and Duignan, Peter, eds. *African Proconsuls: European Governors in Africa.* New York, 1978.

Garcia Figueras, Tomás. *España y su protectorado en Marruecos, 1912–1956.* Madrid, 1957.

Garcin, Pierre. *La politique des contingents dans les relations franco-marocaines.* Paris, 1937.

Gates, Eleanor M. *End of the Affair: The Collapse of the Anglo-French Alliance, 1939–40.* Berkeley, 1981.

Geschke, Günter. *Die deutsche Frankreichpolitik 1940 von Compiègne bis Montoire: Das Problem einer deutsch-französischen Annäherung nach dem Frankreichfeldzug.* Frankfurt-am-Main, 1960.

Girardet, Raoul. *L'Idée coloniale en France de 1871 à 1962.* Paris, 1972.

Gómez-Jordana Souza, Francisco. *La tramoya de nuestra actuación en Marruecos.* Madrid, 1976.

Goulven, Joseph. *La France au Maroc: Vingt-cinq ans de protectorat (1912–1937).* Paris, 1937.

Griffiths, Richard. *Pétain: A Biography of Marshal Philippe Pétain of Vichy.* Garden City, 1972.

Guernier, Eugène L. *Pour une politique d'empire: Doctrine et action.* Paris, 1938.

Guillan, Pierre. *L'Allemagne et le Maroc, de 1870 à 1905.* Paris, 1967.

Guillaume, Albert. *L'évolution économique de la société rurale marocaine.* Paris, 1955.

Guillaume, Augustin. *Homme de guerre.* Paris, 1977.

Hall, Luella J. *The United States and Morocco, 1776–1956.* Metuchen, N.J., 1971.

Halstead, John P. *Rebirth of a Nation: The Origins and Rise of Moroccan Nationalism, 1912–1944.* Cambridge, Mass., 1967.

Harper, Glenn T. *German Economic Policy in Spain during the Spanish Civil War, 1936–1939.* The Hague, 1967.

Harris, Walter Burton. *France, Spain, and the Rif.* London, 1927.

Haute Cour de Justice. *Le procès du maréchal Pétain,* compte rendu sténographique. Collection des grands procès contemporains publiée sous la direction de Maurice Garçon. 2 vols. Paris, 1945.

Hayes, Carlton J. H. *Wartime Mission in Spain, 1942–1945.* New York, 1945.

Hoare, Sir Samuel. *Complacent Dictator.* New York, 1947.

Howe, George F. *Northwest Africa: Seizing the Initiative in the West.* United States Army in World War II, The Mediterranean Theater of Operations, vol. 11, pt. 1. Washington, 1957.

Huré, Antoine. *La pacification du Maroc: Dernière étape, 1931–1934.* Paris, 1952.

Hytier, Adrienne Doris. *Two Years of French Foreign Policy: Vichy, 1940–1942.* Geneva, 1958.

Jäckel, Eberhard. *La France dans l'Europe d'Hitler.* Paris, 1968.

Jacques, Hubert. *L'Aventure riffaine et ses dessous politiques.* Paris, 1927.

Jeanneney, Jules. *Journal politique, septembre 1939–juillet 1942.* Edited by Jean-Noël Jeanneney. Paris, 1972.

Juin, Alphonse. *Mémoires (1941–1958).* 2 vols. Paris, 1959–60.

Julien, Charles-André. *L'Afrique du nord en marche: Nationalismes musulmans et souveraineté française.* Paris, 1952.

———. *Le Maroc face aux impérialismes, 1415–1956.* Paris, 1978.

Kammerer, Albert. *Du débarquement africain au meurtre de Darlan.* Paris, 1949.

———. *La tragédie de Mers-el-Kébir: L'Angleterre et la flotte française.*
Paris, 1945.

Kaspi, André. *La mission de Jean Monnet à Alger, mars–octobre 1943.*
Paris, 1971.

Knight, Melvin M. *Morocco as a French Economic Venture: A Study of
Open Door Imperialism.* New York, 1937.

Lacouture, Jean. *Cinq hommes et la France.* Paris, 1961.

Landau, Rom. *Moroccan Drama, 1900–1955.* San Francisco, 1956.

Langer, William L. *Our Vichy Gamble.* New York, 1947.

Leahy, William D. *I Was There.* New York, 1950.

Le Révérend, André. *Lyautey écrivain: 1854–1934.* Gap, 1976.

Le Tourneau, Roger. *Évolution politique de l'Afrique du nord musulmane,
1920–1961.* Paris, 1962.

Lévy, Roger. *Les conséquences du développement économique du Japon
pour l'empire français.* Paris, 1936.

Lipschits, Isaac. *La politique de la France au Levant, 1939–1941.* Paris,
1963.

Loustaunau-Lacau, Georges. *Mémoires d'un français rebelle.* Paris, 1948.

Lyautey, Louis-Hubert. *Choix de lettres, 1882–1919.* Edited by Paul de Pon-
ton d'Amécourt. Paris, 1947.

———. *Lettres du Tonkin et de Madagascar (1894–1899).* 2 vols. Paris,
1920–21.

———. *Lyautey l'Africain: Textes et lettres du maréchal Lyautey.* Edited
by Pierre Lyautey. 4 vols. Paris, 1953–57.

———. *Paroles d'action—Madagascar, Sud-Oranais, Oran, Maroc
(1900–1926).* Paris, 1927.

Lyet, Commandant Pierre. *La Bataille de France (mai–juin 1940).* Paris,
1947.

Macmillan, Harold. *The Blast of War, 1939–1945.* London, 1967.

Marchal, Léon. *Vichy: Two Years of Deception.* Translated by Jean David-
son and Don Schwind. New York, 1943. Originally published as *De Pétain à Laval* (Montreal, 1943).

Marrus, Michael R., and Paxton, Robert O. *Vichy France and the Jews.*
New York, 1981.

Martin du Gard, Maurice. *La chronique de Vichy, 1940–1944.* Paris, 1948.

Mast, Charles. *Histoire d'une rébellion: Alger, 8 novembre 1942.* Paris,
1969.

Medlicott, William N. *The Economic Blockade: History of the Second
World War.* Edited by W. K. Hancock. 2 vols. London, 1952–59.

Michel, Henri. *Vichy: Année quarante.* Paris, 1966.

Mönick, Emmanuel. *Pour mémoire.* Paris, 1970.

Montagne, Robert. *Révolution au Maroc.* Paris, 1953.

Morice, Bernard. *Du maréchal Ney au général Noguès: Les procès de
haute justice au palais du Luxembourg.* Paris, 1972.

Morison, Samuel Eliot. *Operations in North African Waters, October*

1942–June 1943. Vol. 2 of *History of United States Naval Operations in World War II.* Boston, 1962.

Murphy, Robert D. *Diplomat Among Warriors.* Garden City, 1964.

Nicolle, Pierre. *Cinquante mois d'armistice: Vichy, 2 juillet 1940–26 août 1944, journal d'un témoin.* 2 vols. Paris, 1947.

Ordioni, Pierre. *Le secret de Darlan, 1940–1942: Le vrai rival de De Gaulle.* Paris, 1974.

Patton, George S., Jr. *The Patton Papers.* Edited by Martin Blumenson. 2 vols. Boston, 1972–74.

Paxton, Robert O. *Parades and Politics at Vichy: The French Officer Corps Under Marshal Pétain.* Princeton, 1966.

———. *Vichy France: Old Guard and New Order, 1940–1944.* New York, 1972.

Pendar, Kenneth. *Adventure in Diplomacy: The Emergence of General De Gaulle in North Africa.* London, 1966.

Pétain, Philippe. *Paroles aux français: Messages et écrits, 1939–1941.* Lyon, 1941.

Peyrouton, Marcel. *Du service public à la prison commune; Souvenirs: Tunis, Rabat, Buenos-Aires, Vichy, Alger, Fresnes.* Paris, 1950.

Piétri, François. *Mes années d'Espagne, 1940–1948.* Paris, 1954.

Porch, Douglas. *The Conquest of Morocco.* New York, 1983.

Pratt, Lawrence R. *East of Malta, West of Suez: Britain's Mediterranean Crisis, 1936–1939.* Cambridge, 1975.

Puzzo, Dante A. *Spain and the Great Powers, 1936–1941.* New York, 1962.

Rézette, Robert. *Les partis politiques marocains.* Paris, 1955.

Rodière, René. *Législation de l'Afrique du nord en guerre, 8 novembre 1942–8 novembre 1943.* Algiers, [1946].

Sainsbury, Keith. *The North African Landings, 1942: A Strategic Decision.* London, 1976.

Scham, Alan. *Lyautey in Morocco: Protectorate Administration, 1912–1925.* Berkeley, 1970.

Schmokel, Wolfe W. *Dream of Empire: German Colonialism, 1919–1945.* New Haven, 1964.

Serrano Suñer, Ramón. *Entre Hendaya y Gibraltar.* Madrid, 1947.

Sherwood, John M. *Georges Mandel and the Third Republic.* Stanford, 1970.

Spears, Sir Edward L. *Assignment to Catastrophe.* 2 vols. New York, 1954–55.

Spillmann, Georges. *Du protectorat à l'indépendance: Maroc, 1912–1955.* Paris, 1967.

———. *Souvenirs d'un colonialiste.* Paris, 1968.

Steele, Richard W. *The First Offensive, 1942: Roosevelt, Marshall, and the Making of American Strategy.* Bloomington, 1973.

Stewart, Charles F. *The Economy of Morocco, 1912–1962.* Cambridge, Mass., 1964.

Stuart, Graham H. *The International City of Tangier*. 2d ed. Stanford, 1955.

Thomas, R. T. *Britain and Vichy: The Dilemma of Anglo-French Relations, 1940–1942*. New York, 1979.

Tony-Révillon, Marie-Michel. *Mes carnets (juin–octobre 1940)*. Paris, 1945.

Trout, Frank E. *Morocco's Saharan Frontiers*. Geneva, 1969.

Truchet, André. *L'armistice de 1940 et l'Afrique du nord*. Paris, 1955.

Vigneras, Marcel. *Rearming the French*. United States Army in World War II, Special Studies, vol. 8, pt. 3. Washington, 1957.

Villelume, Paul. *Journal d'une défaite (23 août 1939–16 juin 1940)*. Paris, 1976.

Voinot, Louis. *Sur les traces glorieuses des pacificateurs du Maroc*. Paris, 1939.

Warner, Geoffrey. *Iraq and Syria, 1941*. London, 1974.

———. *Pierre Laval and the Eclipse of France, 1931–1945*. New York, 1969.

Weygand, Maxime. *En lisant les mémoires de guerre du général de Gaulle*. Paris, 1959.

———. *Mémoires*. 3 vols. Paris, 1950–57.

Woodward, Sir Llewellyn. *British Foreign Policy in the Second World War*. 4 vols. London, 1970–75.

Woolman, David S. *Rebels in the Rif: Abd el Krim and the Rif Rebellion*. Stanford, 1968.

Young, Robert J. *In Command of France: French Foreign Policy and Military Planning, 1933–1940*. Cambridge, Mass., 1978.

ARTICLES

Ageron, Charles-Robert. "Contribution à l'étude de la propagande allemande au Maghreb pendant la deuxième guerre mondiale." *Revue d'histoire maghrébine*, nos. 7–8 (January 1977): 16–32.

———. "La politique berbère du protectorat marocain de 1913 à 1934." *Revue d'histoire moderne et contemporaine* 18, no. 1 (January–March 1971): 50–90.

———. "Les populations du Maghreb face à la propagande allemande." *Revue d'histoire de la deuxième guerre mondiale* 29 (April 1979): 1–39.

Andrew, Christopher M., and Kanya-Forstner, A. S. "The French 'Colonial Party': Its Composition, Aims, and Influence, 1885–1914." *Historical Journal* 14, no. 1 (March 1971): 99–128.

Berque, Jacques. "Deux ans d'action artisanale à Fès." *Questions nord-africaines*, 25 June 1939. Reprinted as brochure. Paris, 1940.

Béthouart, Antoine. "Le débarquement allié au Maroc." *Revue des deux mondes* (April 1977): 39–74.

Blair, Leon Borden. "Amateurs in Diplomacy: The American Vice Consuls in North Africa, 1941–1943." *The Historian* 35, no. 4 (August 1973): 607–20.

———. "The Impact of Franco-American Military Agreements on Moroccan Nationalism, 1940–1956." *Rocky Mountain Social Science Journal* 9, no. 1 (January 1972): 61–68.

Burke, Edmund III. "A Comparative View of French Native Policy in Morocco and Syria, 1912–1925." *Middle Eastern Studies* 9, no. 2 (May 1973): 175–86.

Catroux, Georges. "La position stratégique de l'Italie en Afrique du nord." *Politique étrangère* 4, no. 3 (June 1939): 271–81.

Cohen, William B. "The Colonial Policy of the Popular Front." *French Historical Studies* 7, no. 3 (Spring 1972): 368–93.

Coudry, Commandant. "L'Effort de guerre du Maroc." *Revue historique de l'Armée* 8 (June 1952): 85–96.

Damis, John. "Developments in Morocco under the French Protectorate, 1925–1943." *The Middle East Journal* 24, no. 1 (Winter 1970): 74–86.

De la Baume, Robert Renom. "L'Espagne 'non bélligérante' (1940)." *Revue d'histoire diplomatique* 69 (April–June 1955): 126–29.

Fleming, Shannon E. "North Africa and the Middle East." In *Spain in the Twentieth-Century World: Essays on Spanish Diplomacy, 1898–1978*, edited by James W. Cortada, pp. 121–54. Westport, Conn., 1980.

———. "Spanish Morocco and the *Alzamiento Nacional*, 1936–1939: The Military, Economic and Political Mobilization of a Protectorate." *Journal of Contemporary History* 18 (1983): 27–42.

Fleming, Shannon E. and Ann K. "Primo de Rivera and Spain's Moroccan Problem, 1923–1927." *Journal of Contemporary History* 12, no. 1 (January 1977): 85–99.

Fogg, Walter. "The Economic Revolution in the Countryside of French Morocco." *Journal of the Royal African Society* 35 (April 1936): 123–29.

Funk, Arthur L. "The 'Anfa Memorandum': An Incident of the Casablanca Conference." *Journal of Modern History* 26, no. 3 (September 1954): 246–54.

Gadille, Jacques. "L'Agriculture européenne au Maroc: Étude humaine et économique." *Annales de Géographie*, no. 354 (March–April 1957): 144–58.

Gallissot, René. "Le Maroc et la crise." *Revue française d'histoire d'outre-mer* 63 (1976): 477–91.

Goutard, Adolphe. "La réalité de la 'menace' allemande sur l'Afrique du nord en 1940." *Revue d'histoire de la deuxième guerre mondiale* 11 (1961): 1–20.

Halstead, Charles R. "Un africain méconnu: le colonel Juan Beigbeder." *Revue d'histoire de la deuxième guerre mondiale* 21 (July 1971): 31–60.

———. "A 'Somewhat Machiavellian' Face: Colonel Juan Beigbeder as High Commissioner in Spanish Morocco, 1937–1939." *The Historian* 37, no. 1 (November 1974): 46–66.

Halstead, Charles R. and Carolyn J. "Aborted Imperialism: Spain's Occupation of Tangier, 1940–1945." *Iberian Studies* 7, no. 2 (Autumn 1978): 53–71.

Hoffherr, René. "Comment organiser une économie française d'empire." *Politique étrangère* 3, no. 2 (April 1938): 183–96.

Hoisington, William A., Jr. "Cities in Revolt: The Berber Dahir (1930) and France's Urban Strategy in Morocco." *Journal of Contemporary History* 13, no. 3 (July 1978): 433–48.

Jouin, Yves. "Le 'camouflage' des goums marocains pendant la période d'armistice (juin 1940–novembre 1942)." *Revue historique de l'Armée* 28, no. 2 (1972): 100–117.

Julien, Charles-André. "Léon Blum et les pays d'outre-mer." In *Léon Blum: Chef de gouvernement, 1936–1937*, by the Foundation Nationale des Sciences Politiques, pp. 377–90. Paris, 1967.

Kaspi, André. "Les États-Unis et le problème français de novembre 1942 à juillet 1943." *Revue d'histoire moderne et contemporaine* 18, no. 2 (April–June 1971): 203–36.

La Bruyère, René. "L'Espagne et les routes navales de la France en Afrique." *Politique étrangère* 2, no. 6 (December 1937): 520–34.

Ladreit de Lacharrière, Jacques. "La zone espagnole du Maroc et la guerre civile." *Politique étrangère* 1, no. 1 (February 1937): 28–44.

Marchat, Henry. "La France et l'Espagne au Maroc pendant la période du protectorat (1912–1956)." *Revue de l'Occident musulman et de la Méditerranée* 10, no. 2 (1971): 81–109.

———. "Les origines diplomatiques du 'Maroc espagnol' (1880–1912)." *Revue de l'Occident musulman et de la Méditerranée* 7, no. 1 (1970): 101–70.

———. "Le régime économique de l'Acte d'Algéciras." *Revue juridique et politique de l'Union française* 1 (January–March 1958): 18–30.

Marseille, Jacques. "La conférence des gouverneurs généraux des colonies (novembre 1936)." *Mouvement social* (October–December 1977): 61–84.

Melka, Robert L. "Darlan between Britain and Germany, 1940–1941." *Journal of Contemporary History* 8, no. 2 (April 1973): 57–80.

Montagne, Robert. "Comment organiser politiquement l'empire français." *Politique étrangère* 3, no. 2 (April 1938): 156–82.

———. "La crise nationaliste au Maroc." *Politique étrangère* 2, no. 6 (December 1937): 535–62.

———. "La politique africaine de l'Espagne." *Politique étrangère* 4, no. 4 (August 1939): 417–48.

Müller, Klaus-Jürgen. "Französisch-Nordafrika und der deutsch-französische Waffenstillstand von 1940." *Wehrwissenschaftliche Rundschau* 7 (December 1957): 687–700.

Munholland, Kim. "Rival Approaches to Morocco: Delcassé, Lyautey, and the Algerian-Moroccan Border, 1903–1905." *French Historical Studies* 5, no. 3 (Spring 1968): 328–43.

Oved, Georges. "Contribution à l'étude de l'endettement de la colonisation agricole au Maroc." *Revue française d'histoire d'outre-mer* 63, nos. 232–33 (1976): 492–505.

Philibert, J. "Les forces françaises d'Afrique du nord, septembre 1939–juin 1940." *Revue historique de l'Armée* 9 (December 1953): 105–10.

Point, Père René. "Le général Charles Noguès (1876–1971)." *Bulletin de Garaison*, no. 141 (July 1971).

Pröbster, Edgar. "Die nordafrikanische Krise, 1934–1938." *Die Welt des Islams* 20 (1938): 74–109.

Queuille, Pierre. "Le décisif armistice franco-italien, 23–24 juin 1940." *Revue d'histoire diplomatique* 90 (1976): 100–11.

Rivet, Daniel. "Le commandement français et ses réactions vis-à-vis du mouvement rifain (1924–1926)." In *Abd el-Krim et la république du Rif* [Actes du Colloque International d'Études Historiques et Sociologiques, 18–20 January 1973], pp. 101–36. Paris, 1976.

Semidei, Manuela. "Les socialistes français et le problème colonial entre les deux guerres (1919–1939)." *Revue française de science politique* 18, no. 6 (December 1968): 1115–53.

[Simoneau, Eugène]. "De Lyautey à Noguès." *La Revue hebdomadaire*, 12 November 1938, 150–72.

Truchet, André. "L'armistice de juin 1940 et l'Afrique du nord." *Revue d'histoire de la deuxième guerre mondiale* 1, no. 3 (June 1951): 27–50.

Wendel, Hugo C. M. "The *Protégé* System in Morocco." *Journal of Modern History* 2, no. 1 (March 1930): 48–60.

Zingg, Paul J. "The Cold War in North Africa: American Foreign Policy and Postwar Muslim Nationalism, 1945–1962." *The Historian* 39, no. 1 (November 1976): 40–61.

NEWSPAPERS AND PERIODICALS

L'Afrique française. 1936–40.
La Bougie de Fès. 1936.
Bulletin de la Chambre d'Agriculture de Casablanca. 1937–43.
Bulletin de la Chambre de Commerce et d'Industrie de Rabat. 1936–43.
Bulletin du Comité Central des Industriels du Maroc. 1939.
L'Information marocaine. 1936.
Le Journal de Casablanca. 1936.
Maroc-Matin. 1936.
Le Petit marocain. 1936.
La Presse marocaine. 1936.
Le Soir marocain. 1936.
La Vigie marocaine. 1936–43.

Index

Abda-Doukkala Plain, 91
Abd el-Aziz, Sultan Moulay, 281 (n. 30)
Abdeljalil, Omar, 42–43, 68, 72
Abd el-Krim, Mohamed, 18–19, 21, 23–24, 111
Abetz, Ambassador Otto, 209, 213
Achir, Allal ben, 68
Acquaviva, Marcel, 278 (n. 75)
Afrika Korps, 214
Agadir, 14, 133, 136–37, 141, 144, 192, 202–3, 217, 228
Agriculture, European, 78, 109, 112–14, 117–18, 135
Aïn Aïcha, 20, 23
Aïn Maatouf, 23
Algeciras, Act of (1906), 26, 110–11, 113, 118, 123–36 passim, 150, 194, 246
Algeria, 8–11, 13, 19, 21, 35, 94, 104, 106–8, 117, 131–32, 151, 166, 170, 172–73, 192, 200, 214, 229, 269 (n. 18), 290 (n. 56)
Algero-Libyan border, 173
Algero-Moroccan border, 83, 153; border regions, 13, 24–25
Algiers, 25, 152, 162, 166–70, 172, 175, 177, 179–82, 184, 186–88, 194, 207, 210, 213, 216, 219, 224–39 passim
Allies. See Great Britain; United States
Alsace-Lorraine, 15
Amin, 95
Anglo-French declaration on Egypt and Morocco (1904), 124
Anglo-Italian "gentleman's agreement" (1937), 139, 144
Anglo-Moroccan commercial treaty (1938), 125–30
Anglo-Moroccan Treaty of Commerce and Navigation (1856), 126, 265 (n. 45)
Annoual, 18

ANTON (German occupation of France), 224
Arabs, 30–31, 35, 39–40, 149, 221, 234, 239
Araquistain, Luis, 270 (n. 33)
Army of Africa, 237
Army of the Levant, 168
Arslan, Chekib, 35
Artisans, Moroccan, 41, 49, 52–54, 75, 79, 98, 245; artisan corporations, 8, 44, 76–77, 93–98, 100, 103
Assimilationism, 5, 109
Association des Anciens Élèves du Collège Musulman de Fès, 52
Association des Étudiants Musulmans Nord-Africains en France, 32, 65
Associationism, 5
Atlantic Charter, 243
Atlas mountains, 24–25, 60, 89, 133, 202, 220, 222
Axis. See Germany; Italy

el-Baghdadi, Pasha Mohammed, 32, 34, 37
Balearic Islands, 53, 126, 139
Banque d'État du Maroc, 80
Banques populaires, 81
Bargach, Pasha Abderrahman, 37, 220
Bataille, Captain Gaston, 286 (n. 17)
Baudouin, Paul, 155–56, 169, 172–74, 182–84, 275 (n. 37)
Baufine-Ducrocq, Colonel Raymond, 275 (n. 37)
Beigbeder, Colonel Juan, 142, 146–56, 271 (n. 53)
Belgium, 129, 136; empire, 166
Ben M'Sik (Casablanca), 102
Beni Amir perimeter, 92–93, 192
Beni M'guild, 6
Beni Ouarain, 60

Beni Ouriaghel, 220
Beni Snassen, 14, 152–53
Beni Yazrha, 60
Beni Zeroual, 18, 20, 23, 152–55
Bennani, Ahmed, 220
Benoist-Méchin, Jacques, 212
Berber *dahir*, 11, 25, 43, 54–55, 60–61, 65, 67, 75, 110, 124, 243, 245, 251 (n. 1), 253 (n. 24); and urban unrest, 29–39
Berber policy, 30–31, 37, 39, 43
Berbers, 29–31, 33, 35–36, 39, 60, 73, 148, 203, 220, 234
Bergeret, General Jean, 285 (n. 2)
Berque, Jacques, 92–96
Berrada, Abdelkadar, 52
Berriau, Colonel Henri, 107
Berthelot, Jean, 191
Berthelot, Philippe, 20
Bertrand, Colonel René, 277 (n. 72)
Besson, Pierre, 286 (n. 5)
Béthouart, General Antoine, 225–27, 240
Bibane, 20
Billotte, General Gaston, 21
Bizerte, 164, 180, 209–14, 218, 221, 229
Bizerte-Gabès railroad, 209, 212
Blanc, General Amédée, 61, 69, 71–72, 94, 97
Blanc, Urbain, 29–30, 32–34, 36
Bled, 39, 58
Blum, Léon, 3, 42, 99, 115, 256 (n. 78); and Noguès, 27–28, 75, 80, 189; fear of war in Mediterranean, 83, 141; and colonial reform, 116, 246; and Spanish civil war, 126. *See also* Popular Front government
Boichut, General Edmond, 24
Bonnet, Georges, 128
Bordeaux: government at, 152, 165, 168–69, 173, 176–78, 209
Borotra, Jean, 191
Bouayed, Ahmed, 52
Bouayed, Hassan, 52
Boufekrane River, 61–62, 64–65
Bouquet, Henri, 278 (n. 75)
Bourdan, Pierre, 290 (n. 52)
Bou Regreg River, 177
Bourgeoisie, Moroccan, 31, 36, 66, 73,

78, 85, 94, 100, 103, 245. *See also* Nationalists, Moroccan
Bouyssi, Raymond, 65
Branes, 21
Briand, Aristide, 15, 20
Broustra, Vincent, 277 (n. 72)
Brunel, René, 65
Bullitt, Ambassador William C., 130, 196
Buot de l'Épine, General Étienne, 271 (n. 53)
Bureau de Recherches et de Participations Minières, 101
Businessmen, European (*patronat*), 26, 100–102, 118–20, 122–23, 265 (n. 39)

Cadet, Roland, 279 (n. 93)
Caillault, General Henri, 63
Caisse Centrale de Crédit Agricole et de Prévoyance Indigènes, 259 (n. 21)
Caisse de Prévoyance des Fonctionnaires, 102
Caisse des Prêts Immobiliers, 265 (n. 35)
Caisse Fédérale de la Mutualité et de la Coopération Agricole, 118
Caisse Nationale de Crédit Agricole, 84
Caisse Régionale d'Épargne et de Crédit Indigènes: at Fez-Taza, 94; at Casablanca, Meknès, and Marrakesh, 98
Cambay, General Albert, 20
Cambon, Ambassador Jules, 137, 150
Canary Islands, 53, 126
Capitulations: France, 123–31; Great Britain, 123–27; United States, 124, 129–31, 267 (n. 61)
Carnot, Lazare, 114
Casablanca, 14, 26, 77, 96, 98, 109, 114, 140, 168, 176–78, 184, 192, 204, 232; and Berber *dahir*, 33–34; November 1936 events, 44–45, 48–50, 53–54, 65, 67, 79, 116; June 1936 strikes, 99; urban renewal projects, 101–2; pro-German sentiment at, 202; French concern over maintenance of order, 220; Allied attack and capture of, 227–28, 230; in 1942, 240
Casablanca Chamber of Agriculture, 85, 112, 117
Casablanca Chamber of Commerce, 113

Casablanca Conference (1943), 241
Casablanca International Fair, 120
Casablanca Municipal Council, 49
Casablanca region, 178
Catroux, General Georges, 290 (nn. 53, 56)
Centre des Hautes Études d'Administration Musulmane, 252 (n. 7)
Ceuta, 140–41, 151
Chambers of agriculture, commerce, and industry: European, 108, 111, 120; Moroccan, 8, 263 (n. 9)
Chambrun, General Aldebert de, 17, 19–21
Chaouïa region, 50
Chapon, Marcel, 113
Charles-Roux, François, 152–53, 155, 182
Chemao, Mohamed, 32, 44
Chemin de Fer du Maroc, 101–2
Cheraya, 21, 60
Chiappe, Jean, 115
Childs, James Rives, 196, 204–5, 217–19, 221, 240–41; on Noguès, 214–15, 232, 289 (n. 46)
Chorfa, 38, 60
Churchill, Winston S., 157, 173, 180–81, 194, 200, 239, 276 (n. 55)
Ciano, Count Galeazzo, 139, 156
Cité Yacoub el-Mansour (Rabat), 101–2
Clark, General Mark W., 230, 235–36, 239–40
Clark-Darlan agreement (22 November 1942), 241, 289 (n. 50)
Codman, Charles R., 288 (n. 29)
Collaboration: Franco-German, 157, 207–18 passim, 231
Collège Moulay Idriss (Fez), 252 (n. 7)
Collège Moulay Youssef (Rabat), 117
Colombat, General Paul, 20
Colonial party, 104
Colonists: political power and pretensions, 10–11, 108–9, 111, 116, 119, 135; economic difficulties of, 26, 76–78, 110–19 passim; and Peyrouton, 26, 76, 112, 114–16, 118, 120; and Ponsot, 26, 109–13, 118, 122–23; and Popular Front, 28, 56, 80, 115, 118, 132–33; and Noguès, 43, 49,

56, 76, 78–80, 100–102, 115–27 passim, 134–35, 245–46; and Beni Amir lands, 92–93; and Lyautey, 104–8, 112, 135; and Steeg, 108–9; and Saint, 109; and Vichy, 120, 183–84, 190; and France's defeat, 166; resistance to armistice, 176; and Germany, 211, 217
Colons. See Colonists
Comité Central Économique, 120
Comité de Guerre (Algiers), 240
Comité de la Foire (Fez), 94
Comité de l'Habitat Indigène, 101
Comité Français de la Libération Nationale, 242
Comité Permanent de Défense Économique, 112, 120
Comité Supérieur d'Action Sociale et du Travail, 112, 120
Comités d'Études Économiques, 108
Comptoir Artisanal Marocain, 96
Confédération Générale du Patronat Français, 131
Conférence Impériale, 26
Conseil Central de la Famille et de l'Assistance, 192
Conseil Central de la Jeunesse et des Sports, 192
Conseil des Vizirs, 8–9
Conseil du Gouvernement, 75–76, 78, 83, 86–87, 89, 125, 128, 132, 134, 190, 263 (n. 11), 265 (n. 39); described, 9, 108; established, 108; colonists and right to vote, 111, 119; suspended, 120; abolished, 120, 191
Conseil Économique, 192
Constantine (Algeria), 168, 229
Contard, Louis, 277 (n. 63), 278 (n. 75)
Contrôleurs civils, 74, 191
Convention for the Abolition of Capitulations in Morocco and Zanzibar (1937), 104
Cooperatives, agricultural, 82, 85–86
Coopératives Indigènes Agricoles, 86
Coopératives Indigènes de Blés, 85–86
Corbin, Ambassador Charles, 127, 140–43
Cordier, Marcellin, 278 (n. 75)
Corporations. *See* Artisans
Corsica, 208

Council of Ministers (Vichy), 208, 211
Courteault, Pierre, 271 (n. 53)
Courtin, Jean, 48
Cyrenaica, 171, 203

Dadès, 25
Dakar, 184, 204, 209, 226, 231; attack on, 156, 194, 240
Daladier, Édouard, 27–28
Damascus, 69, 211, 240
Darlan, Admiral François, 188–89, 218, 220; and North Africa in 1940, 166–68, 170; and Franco-German armistice, 174; and Franco-German collaboration, 208–14, 216; and United States, 208, 214, 217; and Allied invasion of North Africa, 222–23, 226–31, 233, 235–37, 288 (nn. 36, 37), 289 (n. 46); assassinated, 238. *See also* Clark-Darlan agreement
Daugan, General Albert, 21
Debeney, General Eugène, 20
De Gaulle, General Charles, 169, 192, 246; on the sultan, 160, 162; and Noguès, 162, 242, 274 (n. 21); London broadcasts of, 167, 172, 274 (n. 21)
De la Baume, Robert Renom, 152, 154
Delbos, Yvon, 41, 57, 60, 66, 68, 98; and colonial reform, 75, 133; and Anglo-Moroccan commercial treaty, 128; on quotas and government subsidies, 133; and Germany in Morocco, 140–42
Delcassé, Théophile, 16
Delcassé-Noguès, Suzanne, 16–17
De Loustal, General Jacques, 176, 220
De Tessan, François, 64
Dillon, General Eric, 173
Diouri, Mohamed, 253 (n. 35)
Direction des Affaires Chérifiennes, 9
Direction des Affaires Indigènes, 253 (n. 36)
Direction des Affaires Politiques, 79, 191, 253 (n. 36)
Direction des Habous, 101
Direct rule, 5, 8–9
Djebabra, 61–62
Djemaa Chleuh Mosque (Casablanca), 48
Dody, General André, 287 (n. 22)

Doolittle, Hooker A., 284 (n. 63)
Dorange, General André, 286 (n. 18)
Douar Debbagh (Rabat), 101
Doukkala, 86
Doyen, General Paul, 202
Doynel de Saint-Quentin, René, 267 (n. 59)
Dra, 25, 83
Duff Cooper, Alfred, 177–79, 276 (n. 55)
Dunkirk, 151

Eccles, David, 198–99, 204
École d'Application de l'Artillerie (Fontainebleau), 13, 24, 29
École des Sciences Politiques, 32
École Polytechnique, 13
Economic conditions, 26, 36, 41, 54, 61, 74–103, 109–35, 138, 148, 150, 159, 184, 192–221 passim, 241, 245–47
Eden, Anthony, 127, 139, 142, 173
Egypt, 35, 68, 124–25
Eisenhower, General Dwight D., 230, 233–35; Allied commander of North African invasion, 222; and French North African command, 237; on Noguès, 238–39; and Vichy control in North Africa, 287 (n. 25)
Entente Cordiale, 16, 173
Estéva, Admiral Pierre, 229
État français, 180
Exchange Stabilization Fund, 81

el-Fassi, Allal: on French reforms, 40; and Moroccan nationalist movement, 41, 44, 58–61, 67; and 1936 Casablanca march, 44; arrest and exile, 68, 72
Fedala, 195, 202; Allied attack on, 227–28; armistice meeting at, 231
Fez, 77, 85, 117, 153–54, 197, 202, 226; municipal council (Medjlis), 8, 22, 52; artisan corporations, 8, 94–98; and Rif war, 18–19, 21–24; 1912 riots at, 25; and Berber *dahir*, 29, 31–37; delegations to the sultan, 33–34, 37, 53; nationalists at, 43, 49–54, 59, 67–72, 96–97, 116; French leadership at, 61; reforms at, 78–79, 94–98; and Allied invasion, 227–28, 232
Fez Chamber of Agriculture, 52

Fez Chamber of Commerce, 34, 52, 94
Fez region, 17, 69
Fez territory, 17–18
Fez, Treaty of (30 March 1912), xiii–xiv, 14, 18, 33, 50–51, 74, 243
Foch, Marshal Ferdinand, 13, 23, 164, 244
Four Freedoms, 243
Franco, General Francisco, 41, 150, 198; and foreign troops in Spanish Morocco, 142; and Germany, 145; and Beigbeder, 146–47, 149; and Serrano Suñer, 151
Franco-American armistice in Morocco (11 November 1942), 224, 233, 288 (n. 30)
Franco-American economic agreement in North Africa. *See* Murphy-Weygand agreement
Franco-German accords (1911), 14
Franco-German armistice (22 June 1940), 172–76, 180, 182, 187, 193, 207, 209, 216, 233, 246; request for terms, 152, 165, 167–69
Franco-German protocols. *See* Protocols of Paris
Franco-Italian armistice (24 June 1940), 152, 172–73, 246
Franco-Spanish boundary accord (1925), 153–56
Franco-Spanish treaty on Morocco (27 November 1912), 140
François, General Jules, 170, 188
François-Poncet, Ambassador André, 143, 270 (n. 33)
Freemasons, 179, 186, 192, 277 (n. 72), 278 (n. 74)
French Equatorial Africa, 155
Freydenberg, General Henri, 20

Gabès (Tunisia), 212
Gallieni, Marshal Joseph, 100
Gallissot, René, 100, 118, 262 (n. 61)
Gamelin, General Maurice, 28, 163–64
Gaullists, 186, 218; anti-Gaullist legislation, 192; and Noguès, 239–40, 242; prison sentences of, 279 (n. 91)
Gayet, Georges, 277 (n. 72)
Georges, General Alphonse, 189, 242
Germany, 151; and Agadir (1911), 14, 136, 141, 144, 217; and Moroccan population, 52, 140–41, 197, 201–4; in Spanish zone, 55, 138, 140–41, 144–45; threat to France, 55, 83, 141; and Tangier (1905), 136, 141, 144, 217; 1937 war scare, 141–46; Franco-German armistice, 152, 167, 169, 172; Franco-German collaboration, 157, 207–18 passim; 1940 threat to North Africa, 170, 275 (n. 32); air bases in Morocco, 181; control commissions, 201–2, 204–5, 210, 216; invasion of Greece, 203; invasion of Soviet Union, 211; and Allied invasion of North Africa, 224–25, 229, 231–32; invasion of Tunisia, 231; invasion of unoccupied France, 237
Ghazi, Mohamed, 253 (n. 35)
Gherouaou Basin, 155
Gibraltar, 126, 144, 177, 227, 235; Spanish claim to, 151, 156; air strike on, 181
Giraud, General Henri, 21, 234–36; Allied invasion of North Africa, 221–22, 225, 227–28, 230; commander of French forces in North Africa, 237, 288 (nn. 36, 37); high commissioner in French Africa, 239–42. *See also* Murphy-Giraud accords
el-Glaoui, Hadj Thami, 220, 284 (n. 73)
Gort, General John Viscount, 177
Goumiers, 60, 71
Great Britain: *protégés*, 34–35, 52, 124–25; negotiations on capitulations and commercial treaty, 123–29; post offices, 125, 266 (n. 47); Anglo-French relations, 126, 141, 144–46, 173, 181, 194, 197; and establishment of French protectorate, 136; 1937 war scare, 141–46; attack on Mers-el-Kebir, 156, 178, 180, 190, 240; attack on Dakar, 156, 194, 240; encouragement of North African resistance, 166, 168, 173, 177–79; Franco-German armistice, 173; and Vichy regime in North Africa, 181, 194–95, 197–200, 204, 239–40; blockade, 195, 197–200; 1940 Anglo-French trade negotiations, 195, 198–200; and American aid to North Africa, 195, 199–201, 204; attack on Syria, 211

Groupements Économiques, 120
Guedj, Félix, 192
Guillaume, General Augustin, 12, 243
Guizol, Major Marius, 165, 167–69

Hadjoui, Omar, 35, 52
Hajjaoua, 260 (n. 42)
el-Halou, Mohammed ben Abdesselem, 34
Halstead, John, 58, 103
Hardion, Bernard, 283 (n. 54)
Harris, Walter Burton, 6
Hassan, Sultan Moulay (Hassan I), 204
Hassan II, 244
Haut Comité Méditerranéen, 186
Haut Commissariat de France en Afrique Française, 237, 241
Haut Tribunal Chérifien, 53–54
Haute Cour de Justice, 231
Hayaina, 21, 60
Hellu, Jean, 264 (n. 14)
Henry, Jules, 267 (n. 58)
Herviot, Lieutenant-Colonel Maurice, 281 (n. 28)
Hitler, Adolf, 55, 134, 143, 145, 150, 170, 181, 195, 208, 213, 224, 240; and Morocco, 156–57
Hopkins, Harry, 284 (n. 73)
Huber, Gustave, 278 (n. 75)
Hull, Cordell, 129–30, 200–201, 204, 206
Huré, General Antoine, 251 (n. 54)
Hurst, Leonard H., 177–78
Hutin, Georges, 12, 179, 277 (n. 72)

Ifni, 154–55
Ifrane, 178
Indirect rule, 5, 8–9, 37
Infout, 192
Institut des Hautes Études Marocaines, 148, 252 (n. 7)
International Court of Justice, 267 (n. 62)
Iraq, 208
Islam, 29–31, 33, 35, 40, 44, 56, 107
Italy, 34–35, 52, 129, 138, 142, 151, 167, 171, 175, 191, 197, 207, 269 (n. 18); and security of French North Africa, 126, 139–40; armistice with France,
152, 172–74, 246; threat to Tunisia, 163–64; declaration of war on France, 164

Japan, 36, 127
Jaurès, Jean, 135
Jewish statute, 192
Jews, 40, 179, 184, 186, 192, 278 (n. 74)
Juin, General Alphonse, 189, 222–23, 225–26, 229, 235, 237, 241, 243, 278 (n. 82), 288 (n. 36)
Julien, Charles-André, 9

Karaouiyne Mosque (Fez), 32, 34, 49–50, 69
Karaouiyne University (Fez), 41, 68–69
Kelaa-des-Sless, 23
Khémisset, 68, 228
Koeltz, General Louis, 170–72

Ladreit de Lacharrière, Jacques, 270 (n. 35)
LaHoulle, General Augustin, 231
Larache, 140–41
Larbi, Moulay, 220, 284 (n. 73)
Latif, 31–35, 69, 71
Laure, General Émile, 186, 212
Lauzanne, General André, 255 (n. 62)
Laval, Pierre, 157, 207, 212, 217–18, 221–23
Leahy, Admiral William D., 201, 204–6, 218, 220
Lebanon, 11, 35, 243
Le Beau, Georges, 132
Lebrun, Albert, 251 (n. 58)
Left, in European politics, 28, 80, 112, 246. *See also* Socialists
Le Fur, Pierre, 150
Légion Française des Anciens Combattants de l'Afrique du Nord, 187–88
Lemaigre Dubreuil, Jacques, 290 (n. 53)
Léris, Pierre, 278 (n. 75)
Le Tourneau, Roger, 31, 38, 71, 97, 252 (n. 7)
el-Leujd, Abdelkadar, 52
Levant, 20, 173
Libya, 136, 163–64, 171, 209, 227
Libyan-Tunisian border, 223
Lidon, Hippolyte, 278 (n. 75)

Lorraine, 3
Louis-Gentil phosphate mines, 100
Lyautey, Marshal Hubert, 28, 37, 51, 73, 81–82, 89, 124, 131, 154, 170, 184, 190, 197, 221; and French imperialism, xiii, 3, 16, 104–5, 132, 135; colonial policy, xiii, 4–15 passim, 19, 22–25, 30–31, 37, 52–53, 74–75, 78, 94, 104–7, 109, 135, 159, 195; accomplishments, xiii, 7, 74–75, 114; and Noguès, 3–4, 13–24 passim, 135, 244; and protectorate, 4–11, 14–16, 26, 31, 106, 108, 135, 186, 241; Moroccan "team," 6, 105; and Millerand, 15–16; minister of war, 15, 105; and Rif war, 17–23, 72, 105; and Pétain, 22–23, 187; and Weygand, 23, 187; tomb, 77, 244; and colonists, 104–8, 112, 135; Beigbeder and, 148–49; and Giraud, 222
Lyazidi, Mohamed, 44, 68, 72
Lyon Chamber of Commerce, 107

Macmillan, Harold, 239
Maghreb. *See* North Africa
Majorca, 139
Makhzen, xiv, 31, 52, 100, 154, 189; and Lyautey, 7–9; and Berber *dahir*, 32–34, 37–39, 110; and French reform plans, 43, 48; and nationalists, 59–60, 68; and Vichy, 188; and Germany, 203; and United States, 220
Mammeri, Si Mohammed, 53, 110, 159, 255 (n. 54), 284 (n. 73)
Mandel, Georges, 176–80, 246
Marchal, Léon, 198–99, 213, 243, 280 (n. 12)
Mareth Line, 163
Marjolin, Robert, 198, 280 (n. 12)
Marmoucha, 60
Marrakesh, 8, 32, 34, 59, 68, 77, 85, 96, 98, 119, 202, 220, 225, 228; Ramadier visit, 65–66
Marrakesh region, 21, 25, 83
Marseilles, 104, 139, 168, 238
Marseilles Chamber of Commerce, 131
Martin, General Henri, 287 (n. 22)
Martin, Ivan, 277 (nn. 59, 72)
Martin du Gard, Maurice, 190

Massilia, 176–79
Massonnaud, Adrien, 100–101
Mazagan, 91, 119
Mazagan territory, 86
Medersa Ben Youssef (Marrakesh), 65
Medjlis (Fez), 8, 22, 52
Mehdia-Port Lyautey, 227–28
Meknès, 21, 68, 76–77, 98, 117; city fighting at, 61–67, 149; and Allied invasion, 225–28
Meknès territory, 65
Mekouar, Ahmed, 52, 54, 68, 72
Melilla, 140, 143, 151
Mellier, Colonel Albert, 61
Mers-el-Kebir: British attack on, 156, 178, 180, 190, 240
Meyrier, Jacques, 184
Michelier, Admiral François, 224–27, 230
Millerand, Alexandre, 15–17
Missour, 34
Mittelhauser, General Eugène, 168, 174
el-Mokri, Grand Vizier Mohammed, 8–9, 32, 53, 110, 159, 176, 203, 220, 239, 255 (n. 54), 284 (n. 73)
Mönick, Emmanuel, 184, 194–96, 205, 210, 213, 283 (n. 55); on Noguès, 206–7
Montagne, Robert, 31, 83, 252 (n. 7)
Montoire, 157, 209
Morison, Samuel Eliot, 234
Morize, Jean, 82, 85, 125, 152, 162, 173, 176, 184; and Moroccan nationalists, 57, 59–61, 63–64, 96–98; and protectorate finances, 81, 132–34; and *Massilia*, 177–79; Noguès on, 273 (n. 4)
Moulay Idriss Mosque (Fez), 69
Moulay Youssef Mosque (Casablanca), 44
Moulouya River, 14, 21, 91, 137
Municipal commissions, 108, 120, 263 (n. 9), 265 (n. 39)
Murphy, Robert D., 196–97, 210, 213; and Anglo-French trade talks, 198–99; Murphy-Weygand agreement and American aid to North Africa, 201, 206, 216, 218–19; and Franco-German collaboration, 209, 216–17; and pro-American sentiment in Mo-

rocco, 221, 239; and Allied invasion
plans, 221–22; Murphy-Giraud accords, 225, 241, 289 (n. 50)
Murphy-Giraud accords (2 November
1942), 225, 241, 289 (n. 50)
Murphy-Weygand agreement (26 February 1941), 202, 208
Murray, Wallace, 130, 195–96, 218
Mussolini, Benito, 139–40, 156

National Action bloc (Comité d'Action
Marocaine), 40, 42, 51–52, 54, 56–57,
59. *See also* Nationalists, Moroccan
National Action party, 56–57. *See also*
Nationalists, Moroccan
National Party for the Realization of the
Plan of Reforms, 58–59, 68. *See also*
Nationalists, Moroccan
National revolution, 188–89
National Socialist party (Germany), 55,
233
Nationalism, Moroccan, 29, 40, 94, 112.
See also Nationalists, Moroccan
Nationalists, Moroccan: and Berber
dahir, 29–39, 43; and city disturbances, 31–34, 44–45, 48–51, 54,
61–73, 116; and the sultan, 33–34,
37, 44–45, 53, 55, 59, 62, 66–67, 73,
110, 162, 243; and foreign funds and
protection, 34–35, 52–53, 124–25; in
Spanish zone, 35, 41, 125, 147–48,
281 (n. 30); and city merchants, 36,
54; and rural population, 39, 54,
57–58, 60–61, 68, 73, 93; Plan of Reforms, 40, 42, 47, 110; and Popular
Front, 40, 42–43; National Action
bloc, 40, 42–44, 51–52, 54, 56–57,
59; in schools, 40–41; and artisans,
41, 44, 54, 94, 96–98; and working
class, 41, 99–100; and Noguès,
42–43, 45, 76; and Germany, 52, 203;
National Action party, 56–57, 59; and
National Party for the Realization of
the Plan of Reforms, 58–59, 68; and
Makhzen, 59–60, 67–68; nationalist
press, 59, 64–65, 67–68
Nemours (Algeria), 119
Netherlands: empire, 166
Neurath, Constantin von, 143

New Mosque. *See* Moulay Youssef
Mosque
Nivelle, General Robert, 15
Noguès, General Charles: and Lyautey,
xiii, 3–4, 12–24 passim, 75–77, 88,
107, 115, 135, 189–90, 214, 231,
244–45, 247; and Rif war, 18–24, 72,
75; and Pétain, 23, 166, 171, 182, 187,
189–91, 215, 229–31, 235–36; and
Berber *dahir*, 25, 30, 36–39, 43, 54,
75; and Anglo-Moroccan commercial
treaty, 26–29; and Popular Front,
27–28, 56, 75, 99, 115; and Blum,
27–28, 80; and Moroccan nationalists, 39–43, 45, 51–78 passim, 94, 98,
125, 183, 203, 245; and colonists, 43,
49, 56, 76, 78–80, 101–2, 115–27
passim, 134–35, 245–46; and the sultan, 45, 47, 50–51, 53–54, 78,
158–59, 162, 183, 189, 203–4, 231,
243–45, 287 (n. 22), 290 (n. 61); economic and social program, 51–52,
75–103 passim; political reform, 56,
78; and capitulations, 123–31; and
1937 war scare, 141, 144–46 passim;
and Tangier negotiations, 150–51;
fear of native insurrection, 152–53,
166–67, 219–21, 233, 247; and 1940
Franco-Spanish negotiations, 152–55,
182; commander-in-chief of North African Theater of Operations, 159,
162–65; desire to fight on in North
Africa, 165–72, 274 (n. 25); and
Weygand, 165–75, 180, 185–89, 204,
215–16; and Darlan, 166–68,
188–89, 213, 221, 235–37; and
Franco-German armistice, 172–75,
209; decision to stop fighting, 174,
275 (n. 37); *Massilia*, 176–80, 246;
Vichy regime in Morocco, 176,
189–93; and German activity in Morocco, 181, 201–4, 215; and Murphy,
197, 201, 216, 219; and 1941 Anglo-
French trade negotiations, 198–99;
and Franco-German collaboration,
207–9, 216–18, 246; and American
economic aid, 207, 213, 215–16, 218;
and Morocco's defense, 217, 219, 223,
226, 232; and American influence in

Morocco, 219–21, 239; and Laval, 221; and Giraud, 222, 235–37, 242, 288 (n. 36); and Allied invasion of North Africa, 224–31, 237; "benevolent neutrality," 224, 236–37, 288 (n. 34); Pétain's representative, 230–31, 235; and Patton, 230, 233–34, 239–41; and secret military forces, 231; and Haute Cour de Justice, 231–32; and Franco-American armistice, 231, 233; exile, 231, 290 (n. 56); and American occupation, 234–42; resignation, 242; and de Gaulle, 242, 246, 274 (n. 21)
North Africa, 3, 16, 30, 40, 137–38, 178; and Popular Front, 28, 139, 141; and French security, 53, 55, 126, 131, 139, 141; and European war, 155, 157, 159, 163–75, 275 (n. 37); and Franco-German collaboration, 157, 207–18 passim; and Franco-German armistice, 172–76; and Vichy regime, 176, 180–85, 188–90, 199, 204, 207–14, 216–18, 221, 228–37, 241–42; and Allied invasion, 222, 224–34; and American occupation, 233–43

Office Chérifien d'Exportation, 94, 96, 191
Office Chérifien des Phosphates, 81, 99, 101
Office Chérifien du Tourisme, 191
Office Chérifien Interprofessionel du Blé, 85, 191
Office de la Famille Française, 192
Office of Strategic Services, 221
Officiers des affaires indigènes, 74, 82, 191
Operation Menace, 204
Oran, 180, 224, 226–28
Oranais, 153
Oran region, 229
Orgaz, General Luis, 157
Orthlieb, Émile, 50
Ostland, 210, 283 (n. 46)
el-Ouazzani, Mohammed Hassan, 32–33, 41–44, 58, 61, 72
Ouergha River, 19–20, 23, 154–55, 171, 222

Ouezzane, 68
Oujda, 14, 54, 72, 91, 119, 140, 192, 202
Oujda region, 83
Oulema, 32, 38, 45, 52
Oum er Rebia River, 91

Painlevé, Paul, 20
Palestine, 40, 68
Pantelleria, 139, 269 (n. 14)
Patronat. See Businessmen, European
Patton, General George S., Jr., 227, 230; and Noguès, 233–35, 239–41
Paxton, Robert O., 212
Paye, Lucien, 117–18
Pendar, Kenneth, 288 (n. 34)
Pennès, General Roger, 275 (n. 37)
Pétain, Marshal Philippe, 157, 189, 194, 201, 204, 206, 214; and Lyautey, 22–23, 187; and Rif war, 22–24; and Noguès, 28, 230; ambassador to Spain, 150, 271 (n. 43); and North Africa, 165–67, 169, 217–18; and Franco-German armistice, 169, 171; head of French state, 180, 182, 226; cult of Pétain in Morocco, 189–90; and Franco-German collaboration, 207–11; and Allied invasion of North Africa, 221, 229–31, 235–37; and Giraud, 222; and Darlan, 230, 237
Petitjean, 228
Peyrouton, Marcel, 11–12, 26–28, 76, 112, 114–16, 118–20, 137–38
Phipps, Sir Eric, 128
Piatte, General Jean, 287 (n. 24)
Pisani, Rosario, 52
Place Djemaa el-Fna (Marrakesh), 65
Place el-Hédime (Meknès), 63
Plan of Reforms (1934), 40, 42, 47, 110, 140
Poincaré, Raymond, 16
Ponsot, Henri, 11–12, 26, 47, 109–13, 118, 122–23, 255 (n. 54)
Popular Front government, 46, 83, 135; and Peyrouton, 26–28, 112, 115; and Noguès, 27–28, 43, 182; and colonists, 28, 56, 80, 85, 115, 118–19, 133; and Moroccan nationalists, 40, 42–43, 47–48, 50–51, 53, 56, 75; and the sultan, 47–48, 50–51; Moroccan

policy, 47–48, 50–51, 55–56, 64, 75, 79–80, 116; and North African security, 53, 55–56, 139, 141; and Germany, 55–56, 140–46; and protectorate finances, 79–81, 131–33; and labor unions, 99; imperial vigilance, 115; Anglo-French relations, 124–26, 139, 141–46; and relations with Italy, 139–40. *See also* Blum; Delbos; Noguès; Viénot

Port Lyautey, 68–69, 72, 119, 227–228, 232

Portugal, 231, 273 (n. 11), 290 (n. 56)

Primo de Rivera, General Miguel, 18, 137

Protégés, 34–35, 38, 52, 54, 124–25

Protocols of Paris (27 May 1941), 209

Puaux, Gabriel, 243

Quotas: of goods into France, 26, 113, 117, 132–33; of goods into Morocco, 127–29

Rabat: and Berber *dahir*, 29, 31–33, 37; city demonstrations, 49–50, 72; Allied invasion of North Africa, 226, 228, 232

Racism, 9, 106–7, 246

Radical Socialist party, 11, 17, 83, 109

Ramadier, Paul, 65–66

Rethondes, 181

Reynaud, Paul, 165

Rhir River, 87

Ribbentrop, Joachim von, 139, 231

Richert, General Augustin, 253 (n. 36)

Rif war, 17–24, 42, 72–73, 75, 77, 105, 115, 137, 153, 170, 202, 220, 222

Roches Noires (Casablanca), 101–2, 120

Romanones, Álvaro Figueroa y Torres, Conde de, 137

Rommel, General Erwin, 214

Roosevelt, Franklin D., 130, 196, 213, 226, 241–42, 289 (n. 50)

Rsif Mosque (Fez), 69

Safi, 91, 119, 220; Allied attack on, 226–28, 232

Saint, Lucien, 11, 29–31, 38, 109; on Noguès, 24–25

Saint-Jean-d'Acre, 211

Saint-Jean-de-Luz, 198

Salé, 29, 31–32, 36, 43, 49, 54, 96

Sanjurjo, General José, 146

Sarraut, Albert, 17

Sarraut, Maurice, 17

Sbihi, Abdellatif, 32

Sebou River, 137, 146, 171

Serrano Suñer, Ramón, 151, 155–56

Serres, Jean-Claude, 142

Service des Affaires Indigènes, 25. *See also* Direction des Affaires Indigènes

Service des Habous, 62. *See also* Direction des Habous

Service des Travaux Publics, 62

Sétif (Algeria), 25

Settat, 50

Sicot, Louis, 277 (n. 63)

Sidi Slimane, 260 (n. 42)

Simon, General Henri, 30

Socialists, 26, 28, 46, 256 (n. 78), 260 (n. 42)

Sociétés Indigènes de Prévoyance (SIP), 75, 81–82, 89, 95, 259 (n. 21)

Sociétés Indigènes de Prévoyance Urbaines (SIPU), 261 (n. 48)

Souss region, 77, 133, 202

Soviet Union, 157, 211

Spain, 207, 246, 269 (n. 5); and Rif war, 18–19, 22–24, 202, 220; and France, 18, 35, 136–38, 140–42, 150–58, 164, 166, 170–71, 182, 198–99, 270 (n. 33), 271 (n. 53); Spanish civil war, 28, 40, 55, 83, 115, 118, 126, 137, 147, 158; and Italy, 138–39, 142, 152, 155–56, 269 (n. 18); and Germany, 138, 140–45, 151–58; and Tangier, 150–52, 166, 271 (n. 46); and Great Britain, 198–99, 270 (n. 33); and Allied invasion of North Africa, 233. *See also* Beigbeder; Spanish zone

Spanish Morocco. *See* Spanish zone in Morocco

Spanish zone in Morroco, 14, 18, 35, 40, 42, 53, 55, 115, 118, 126, 136–53 passim, 164, 170, 198–99, 269 (nn. 2, 18), 270 (n. 33). *See also* Beigbeder; Spain

Steeg, Théodore, 10–12, 22, 24, 74, 83–84, 108–9, 124

Strikes, 99–100, 118, 135

Supreme War Council (Conseil Supé-

rieur de la Guerre), 22–23, 27, 159
Sûreté Nationale, 179
Syria, 11, 35, 42, 68, 195, 208–9, 211–12, 243, 253 (n. 31)
Syro-Palestino-Maghreb Committee, 35

Tadla, 24, 92
Tadla territory, 25
Tafilalet, 25, 60, 176, 203–4
Tafilalet territory, 83, 87
Tangier, 18, 34–35, 130, 136, 140–41, 150–52, 154–55, 158, 168, 196, 199, 204, 217, 241, 281 (n. 30), 290 (n. 56); Spanish occupation of, 152, 166
Tangier statute (1923), 150
Tariffs, 26, 110–11, 113, 126
Taxes, 52, 60, 78–80, 82, 134, 147
Taza, 19, 21–22, 76, 227–28
Taza territory, 60
Territoire de Fès-Nord, 24
Tertib, 82
Tetouan, 18, 35, 41, 52, 141–42, 146, 198–99
Thierry, René, 44–45, 47–50, 57, 255 (n. 51)
Third Republic, 13, 189, 241
Thorez, Maurice, 28
Todra, 25
Toulon, 238
Tounfit, 25
Trade, Moroccan, 109, 112, 133–34, 241; with France, 113–14, 117, 127, 131–33, 268 (n. 64); with Algeria, 119; with Great Britain, 124–30, 195, 198–200; with United States, 124, 129–31, 194–219 passim, 241; with Japan, 127; with Belgium, 129; with Italy, 129; with Spanish zone, 138, 198–99. *See also* Algeciras, Act of
Triffas Plain, 91
Tripoli, 163
Truchet, André, 260 (n. 43)
Tsoul, 21, 23, 60
Tunisia, 11, 13, 35, 107, 112, 131, 163–64, 166, 170–71, 173, 183, 200, 208–9, 214, 222, 224, 229, 235, 269 (n. 18)

Union des Syndicats Confédérés du Maroc, 99

United States: and capitulations, 124, 129–31, 267 (n. 61); economic aid to North Africa, 194–219 passim, 241, 280 (n. 11); and German activity in North Africa, 195, 201–2, 204–5, 209, 214, 216–18; impact on Moroccan population, 220–21, 239, 241–42, 284 (n. 73); invasion of North Africa, 222, 224–32; occupation of North Africa, 233–43

Van der Straten-Ponthoz, Count Robert, 267 (n. 56)
Vergez, General Bernard, 291 (n. 1)
Vichy government: Vichy regime in Morocco, 120, 182–93; negotiations with Spain on North Africa, 152–58; and French empire, 156–57, 176; and Franco-German collaboration, 157, 207–18 passim; and Mandel, 179; and Noguès, 181–82; and American aid to North Africa, 194, 202, 219; and 1941 Anglo-French trade negotiations, 195, 198–200; and relations with United States, 207, 214, 217–18; and North African defense, 217–18, 221, 223; and Allied invasion of North Africa, 224, 230, 237. *See also* Darlan, Laval, Noguès, Pétain, Weygand
Vielle, Henri Monsignor, 36
Viénot, André, 232, 277 (n. 60)
Viénot, Pierre, 42–43, 47–48, 50–56, 64, 75, 80, 83, 124, 130, 141
Vogl, General Oskar, 202

Welles, Sumner, 130, 196, 201, 218
Western Task Force, 227
Weygand, General Maxime, 23, 28, 204, 215, 217, 220, 230; and North Africa in 1940, 165–75, 180–81; and Franco-German armistice, 165, 167, 171–72, 174, 197; and Germany, 181, 197, 204, 207, 224; government delegate in French Africa, 184–89, 194, 196–97, 199, 201–2, 204–16 passim; and American aid, 196, 201–2, 205–7, 211, 215, 223; and Franco-German collaboration, 207–14, 218
Wiesbaden, 198, 202
Wilson, Woodrow, 243

Working class, Moroccan, 41, 98–102, 119–20
World War I, 3, 14, 16, 105, 136
World War II, xiii, 72, 86, 194, 246

Young, Arthur, 117
Youssef, Sultan Moulay, 7–8, 159
Youssef, Sultan Sidi Mohammed ben, 52, 152; and France, 26, 29–30, 32–34, 36–37, 44–48, 50–51, 53–55, 59, 67–68, 73, 75, 78, 110, 138, 158–62, 182–83, 203–4, 226, 231–32, 243–45, 287 (n. 22); and Ber-

ber *dahir*, 29–39 passim, 110; and Moroccan nationalists, 32–34, 37, 44–48, 50–51, 53–56, 59, 68, 110, 162, 243; and Germany, 203–4; and United States, 220, 226, 239, 241, 284 (n. 73); exile and restoration, 243–44

Zaër, 60
Zaian, 6
Za River, 14
Zemmour, 60, 68
Ziz River, 87